THE ODD 1s OUT

ART AND COMICS COLLECTION

THE ODD 1s OUT

ART AND COMICS COLLECTION

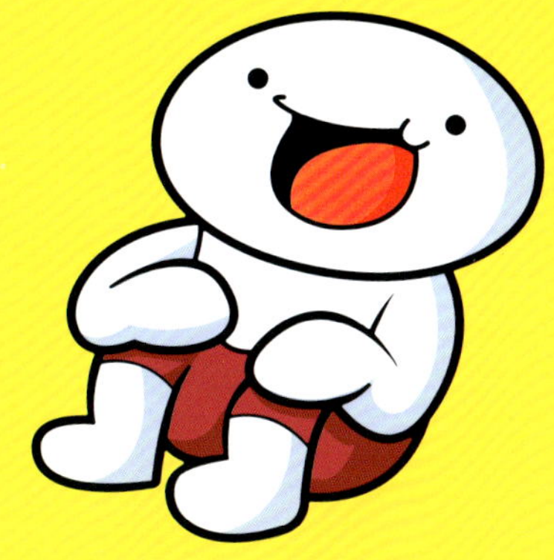

James Rallison

TARCHER
An Imprint of Penguin Random House
New York

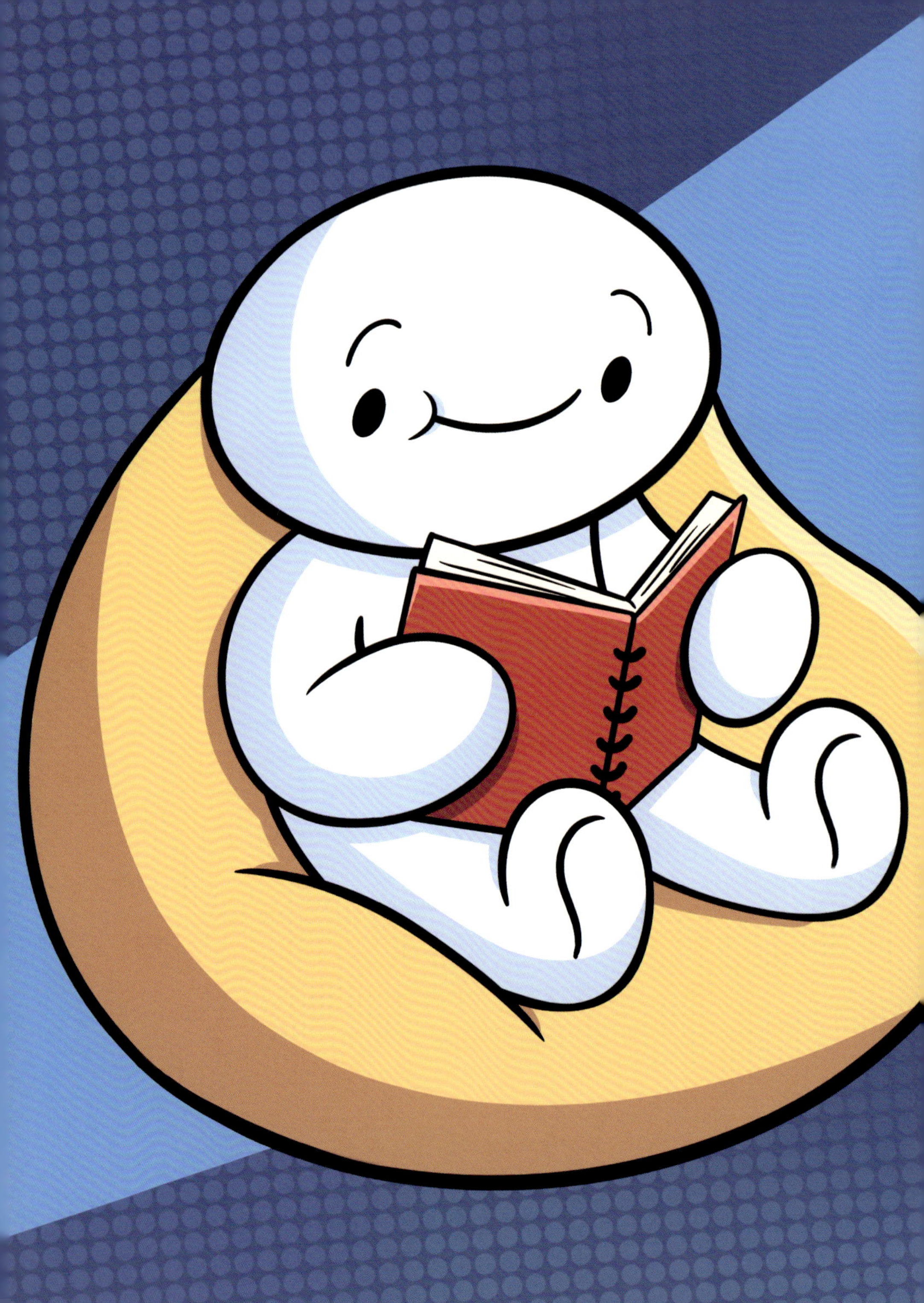

CONTENTS

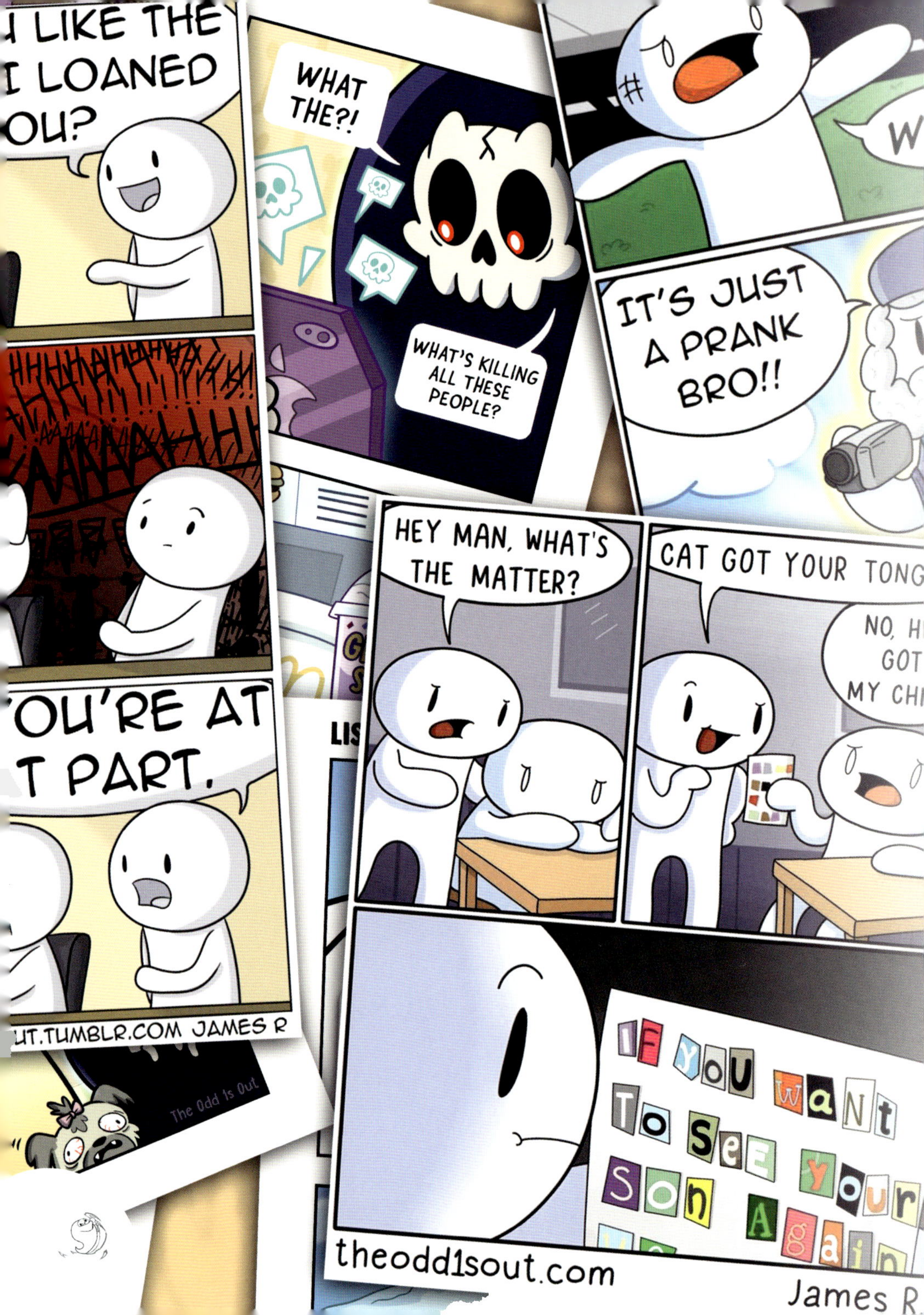

I LIKE THE
I LOANED
OU?
WHAT THE?!
WHAT'S KILLING ALL THESE PEOPLE?
IT'S JUST A PRANK BRO!!
OU'RE AT
T PART.
UT.TUMBLR.COM JAMES R
The Odd 1s Out
HEY MAN, WHAT'S THE MATTER?
CAT GOT YOUR TONG
IF YOU WANT TO SEE YOUR SON AGAIN
theodd1sout.com
James R

WEBCOMICS

AND HOW IT ALL STARTED

I started reading webcomics at a young age—though back then, we just called them comics. They were the only "books" I enjoyed, and despite my teachers' best efforts, I couldn't stop doodling on my homework. (Thankfully, those weren't graded.)

Then I discovered people making comics on the internet, and naturally, I wanted in. I went from sharing stick figure comics with friends to posting them online. I started on Tumblr (yes, I was a Tumblr kid—#I_like_your_shoelaces). I wanted the username The Odd Ones Out, but it was taken, so I came up with The Odd 1s Out about five seconds later.

Not long after, I launched a YouTube channel to entertain people with my art. I juggled both for a while, but people weren't asking, "When's the next comic?" They wanted the next video. So, comics took a back seat.

Now, after a brief five-year break, I'm excited to make comics again. If I can brighten your day—even just enough for a slight nose exhale—then it's all been worth it.

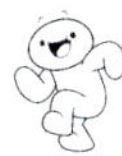

THE PROCESS

The most important part of the process is a good idea. I'll roughly sketch it out, not worrying too much about style yet. From there, I'll do a refined sketch, add the line art and text, and then finally color and shade it (you'll notice James' design jumped around a bit too—all part of the process).

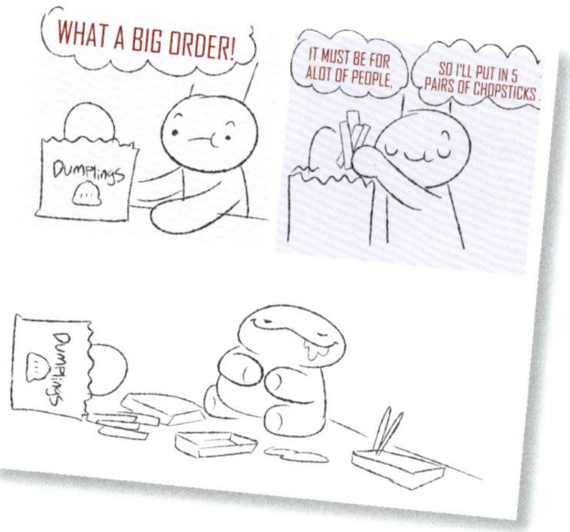

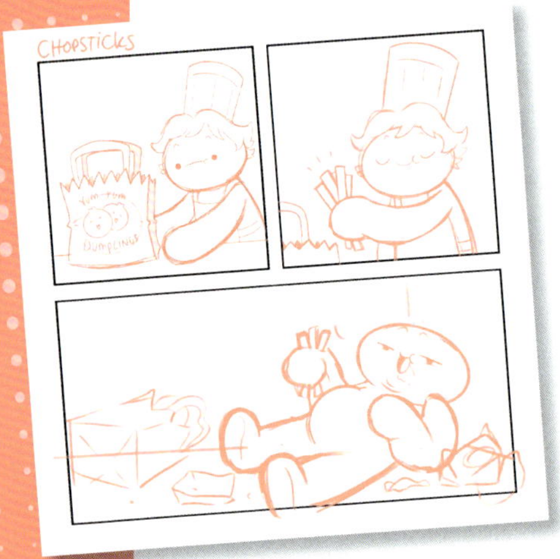

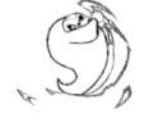

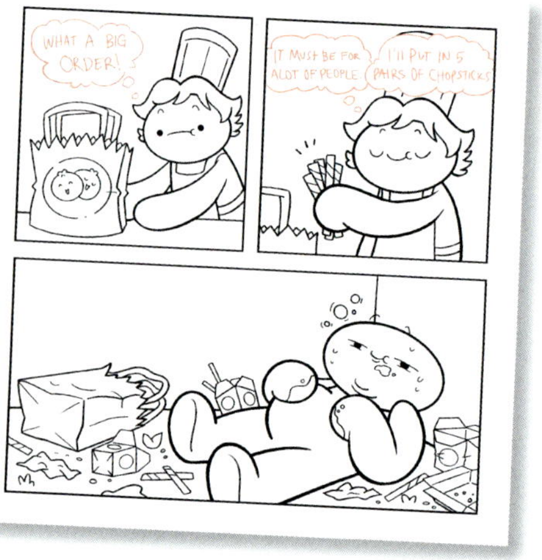

CHOPSTICKS

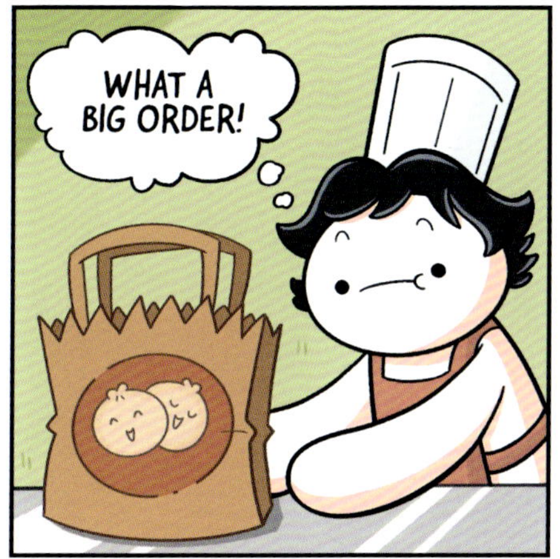

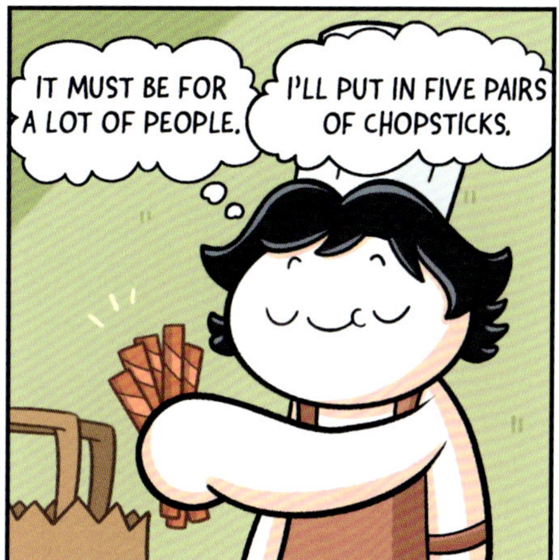

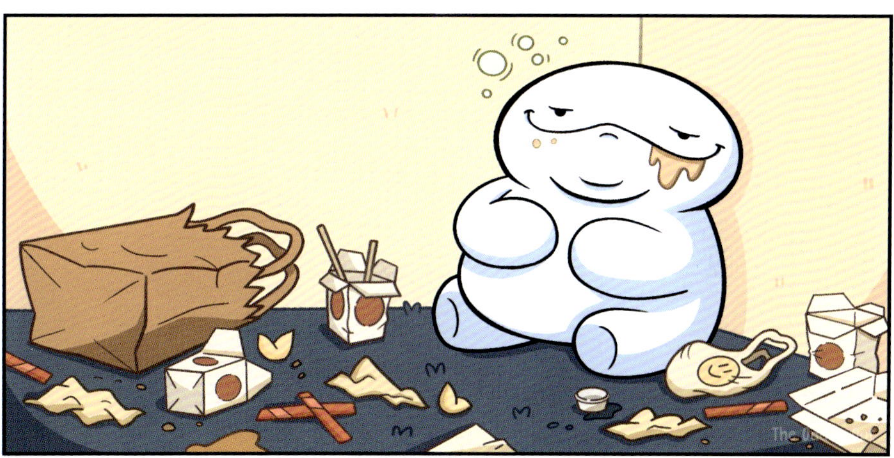

In comics, it's important that everything is clear to the reader, and that includes making sure they're reading the speech bubbles in the right order (it's the small details you have to think about when making comics!).

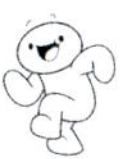

THE "OLDIES"

This is where it all started! Here are some of my oldest comics. Some of them went viral, and others did not. But it's important to remember that I had no idea what I was doing at the time. I was figuring things out as I went, like all people just starting out on something new. Looking back, I can fully appreciate the journey. Even for the ones that make me cringe just a little.

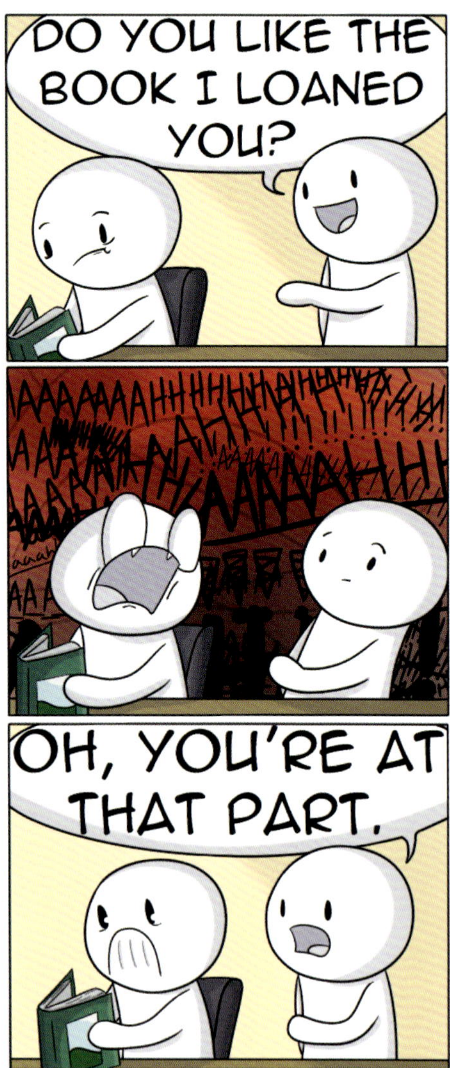

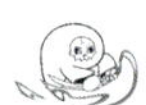

911

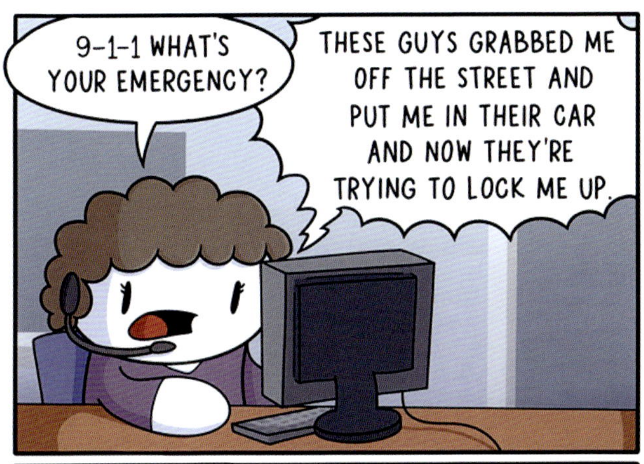
9-1-1 WHAT'S YOUR EMERGENCY?
THESE GUYS GRABBED ME OFF THE STREET AND PUT ME IN THEIR CAR AND NOW THEY'RE TRYING TO LOCK ME UP.

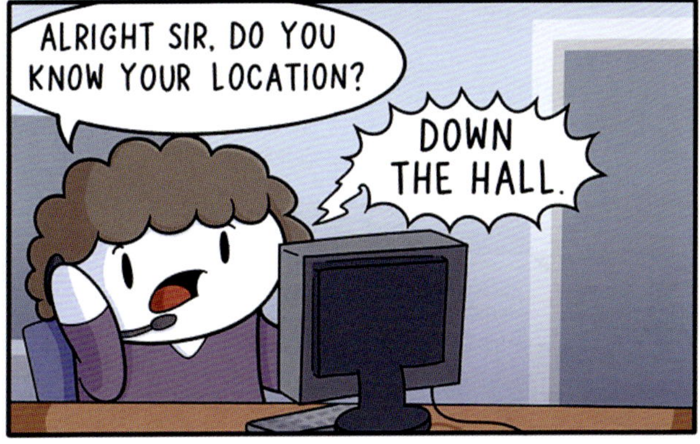
ALRIGHT SIR, DO YOU KNOW YOUR LOCATION?
DOWN THE HALL.

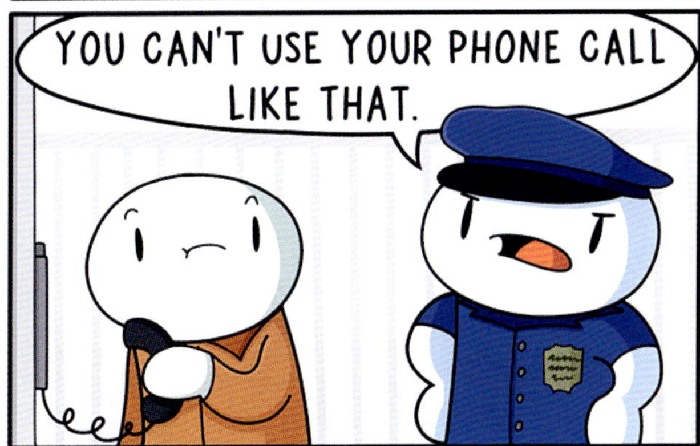
YOU CAN'T USE YOUR PHONE CALL LIKE THAT.

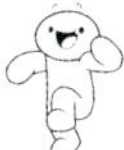

HOW TO EXERCISE

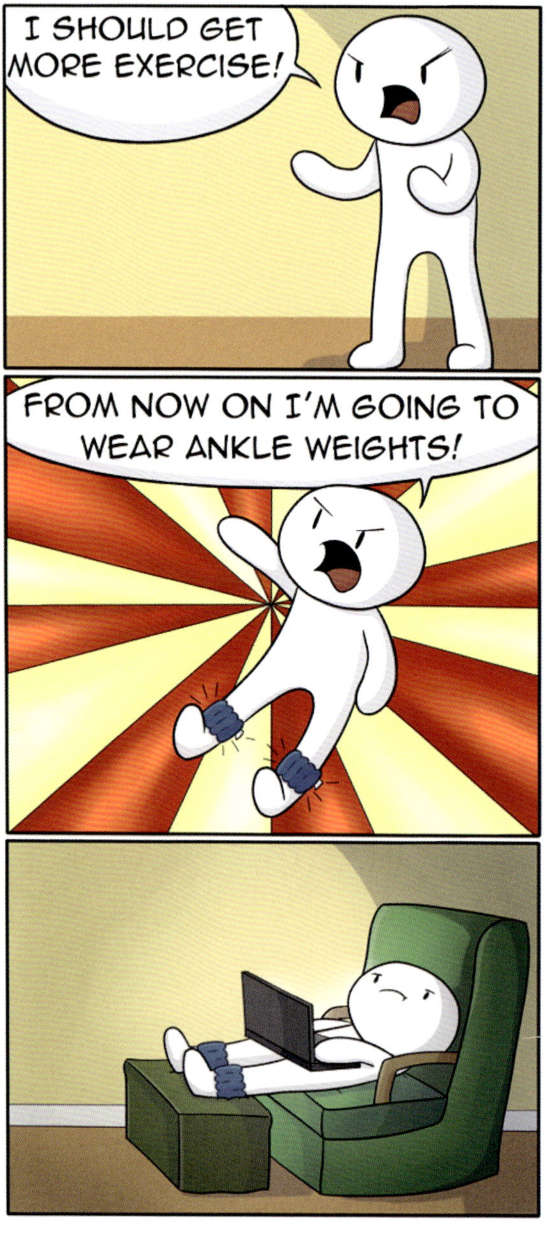

I SHOULD GET MORE EXERCISE!

FROM NOW ON I'M GOING TO WEAR ANKLE WEIGHTS!

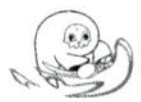

APPLE

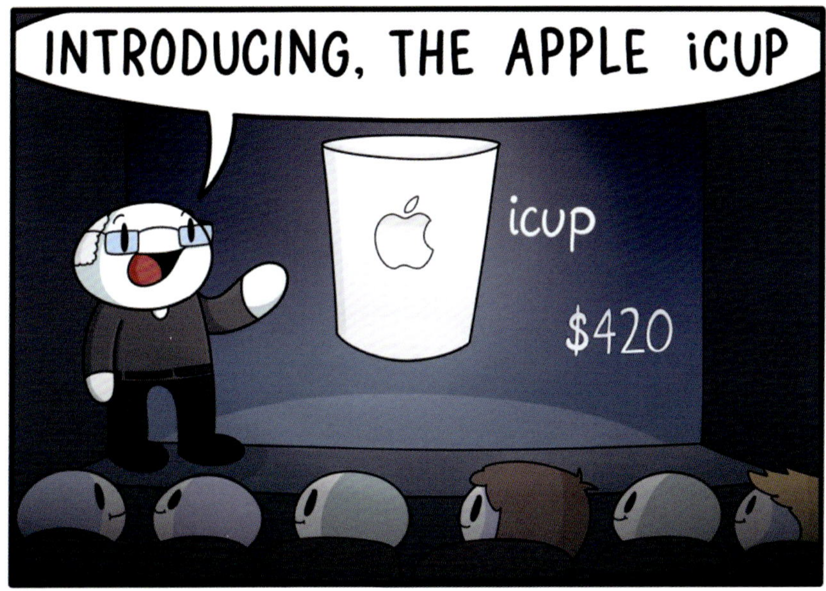

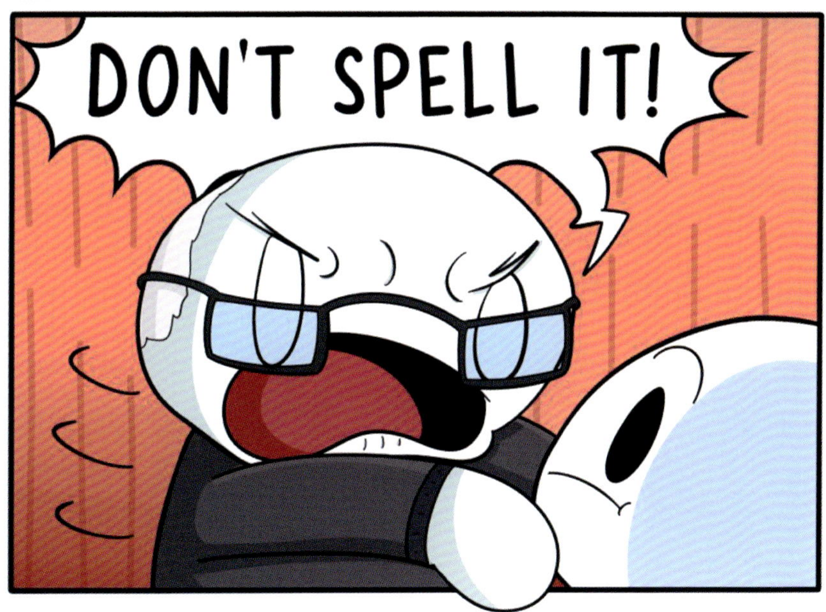

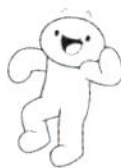

A CAT'S SCHEDULE

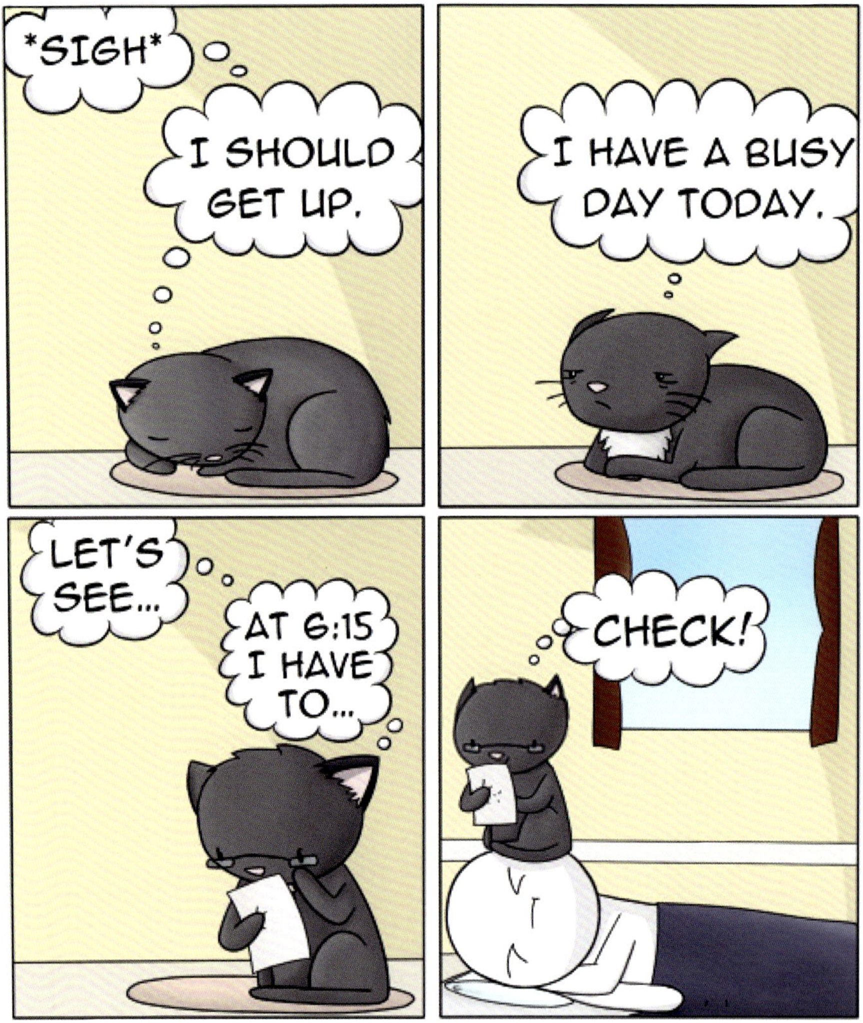

SIGH

I SHOULD GET UP.

I HAVE A BUSY DAY TODAY.

LET'S SEE...

AT 6:15 I HAVE TO...

CHECK!

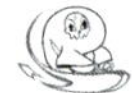

CANNONBALL

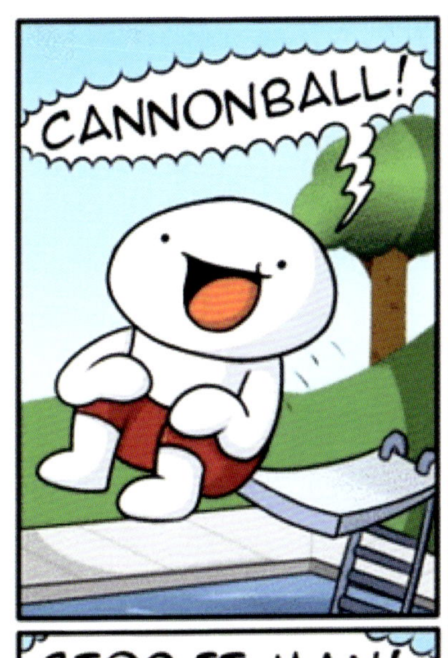
CANNONBALL!

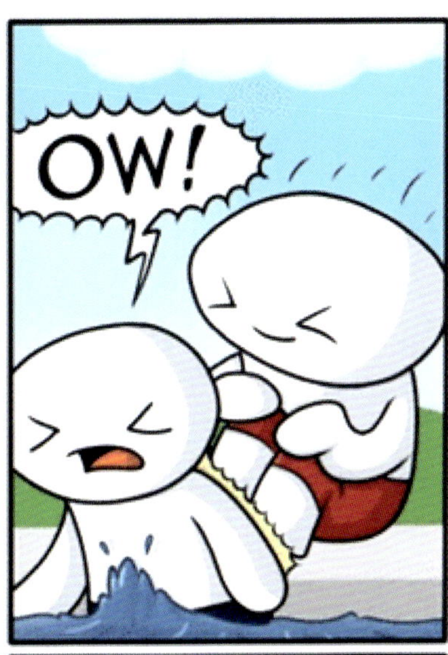
OW!

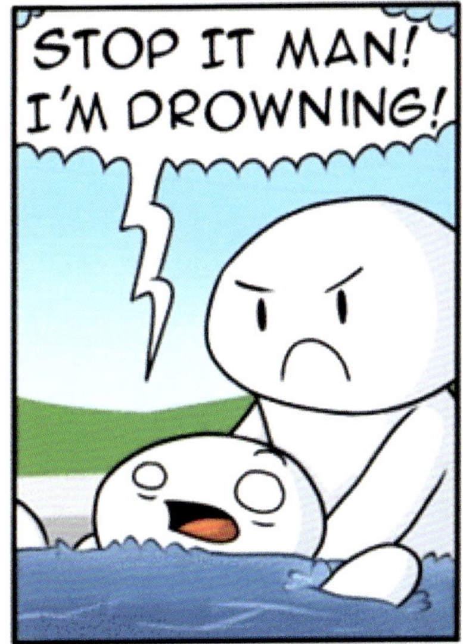
STOP IT MAN!
I'M DROWNING!

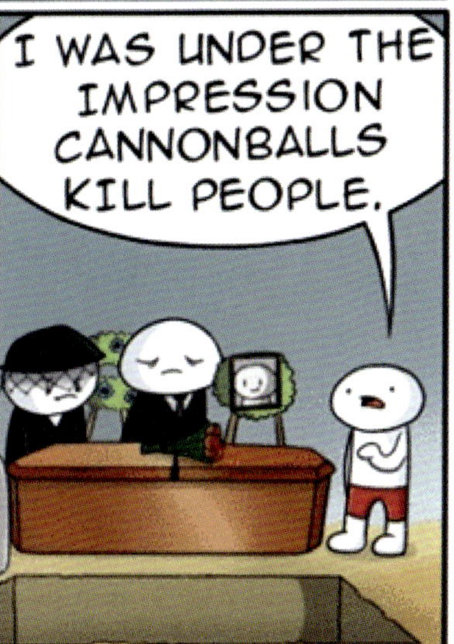
I WAS UNDER THE IMPRESSION CANNONBALLS KILL PEOPLE.

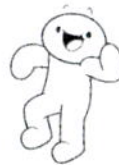

WELCOME TO HELL*

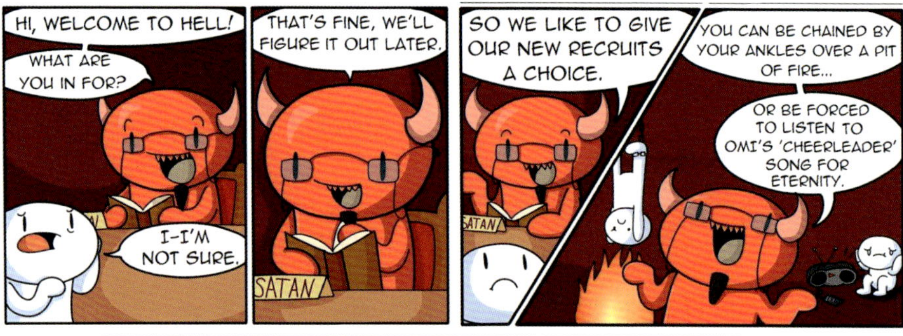

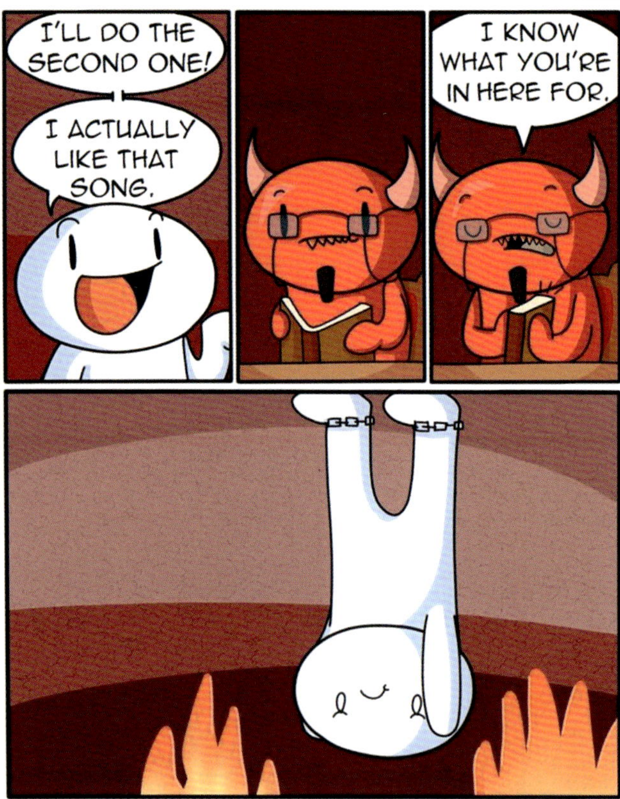

*Author's note: "Cheerleader" was a really annoying song at the time.

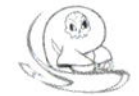

WHO YOU LIKE

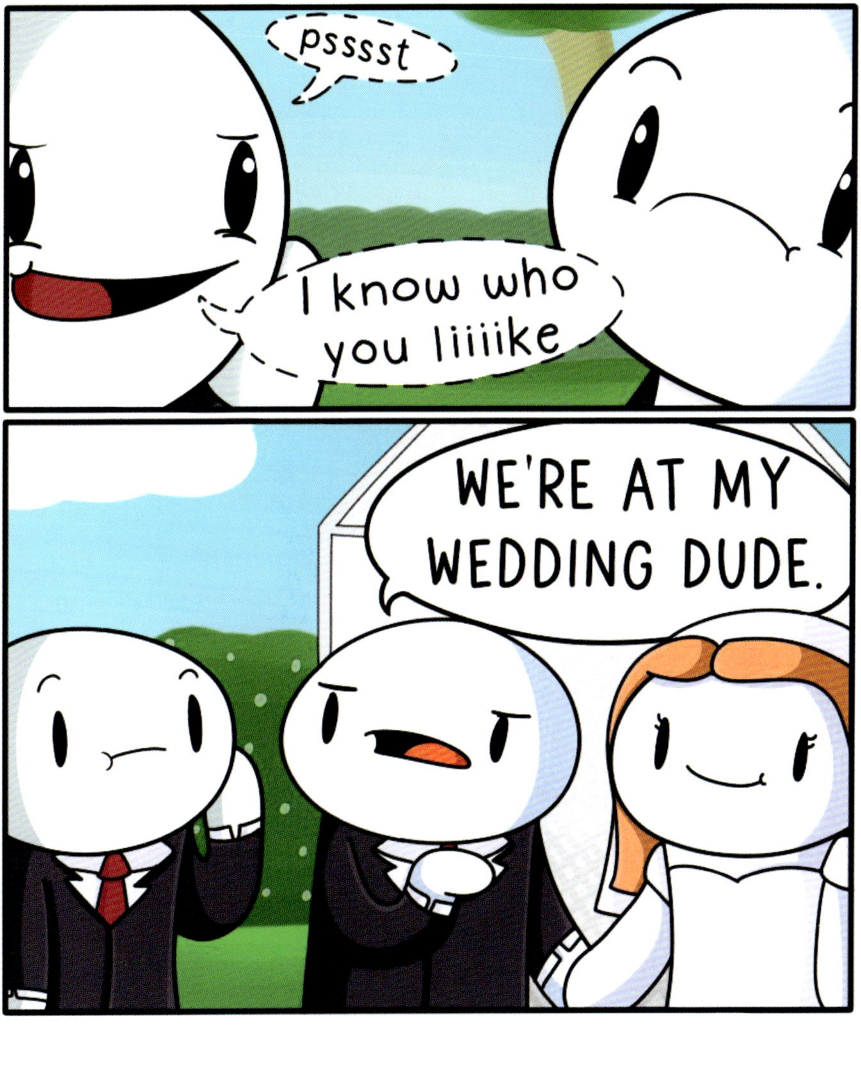

psssst

I know who you liiiike

WE'RE AT MY WEDDING DUDE.

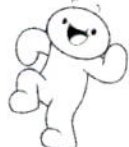

CUPID

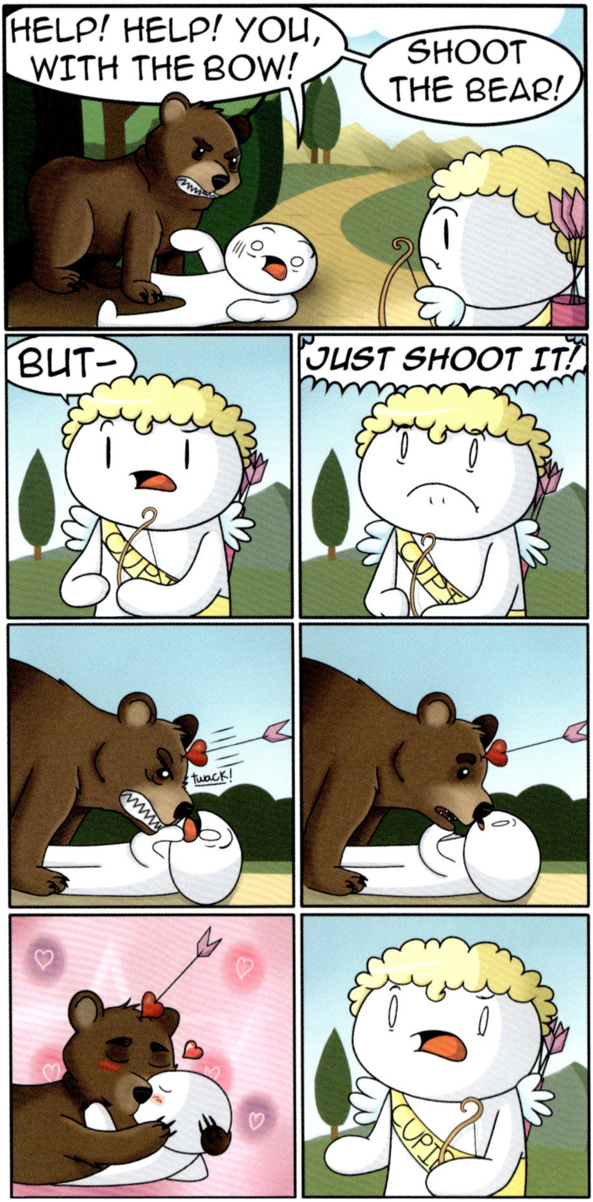

HELP! HELP! YOU, WITH THE BOW!

SHOOT THE BEAR!

BUT-

JUST SHOOT IT!

twack!

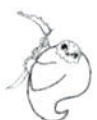

I DON'T CELEBRATE HALLOWEEN

I DON'T CELEBRATE HALLOWEEN

IT'S THE DEVIL'S BIRTHDAY

WELL YOU'RE NOT INVITED!

SNIFF

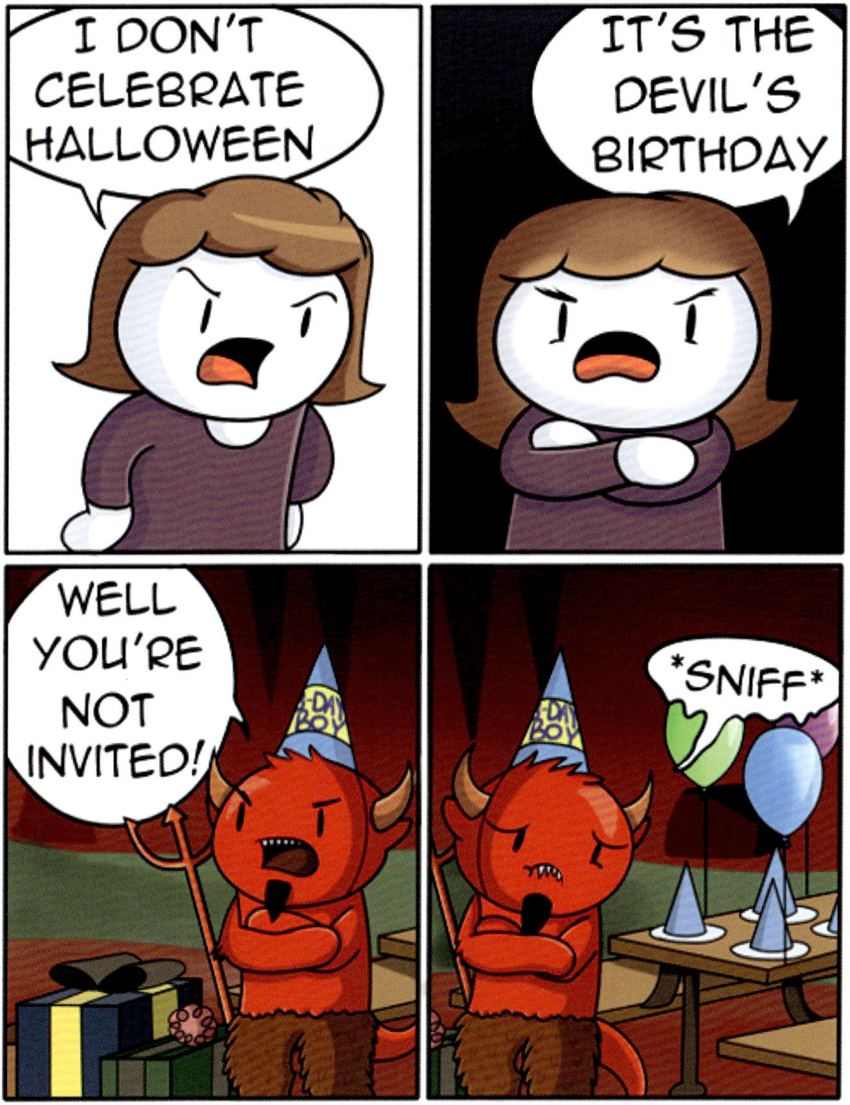

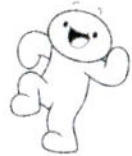

EXCUSES

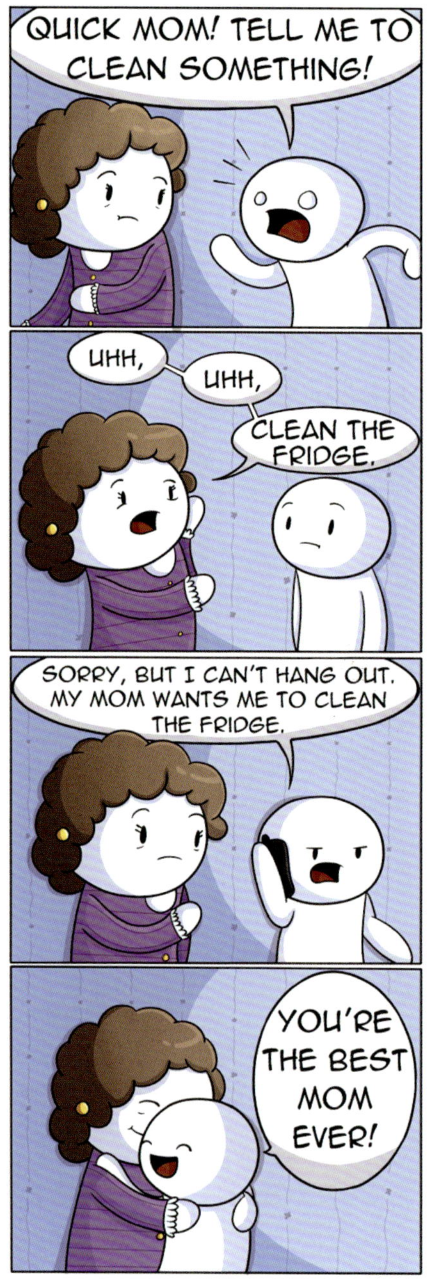

QUICK MOM! TELL ME TO CLEAN SOMETHING!
UHH,
UHH,
CLEAN THE FRIDGE.
SORRY, BUT I CAN'T HANG OUT. MY MOM WANTS ME TO CLEAN THE FRIDGE.
YOU'RE THE BEST MOM EVER!

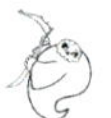

JUST A PRANK

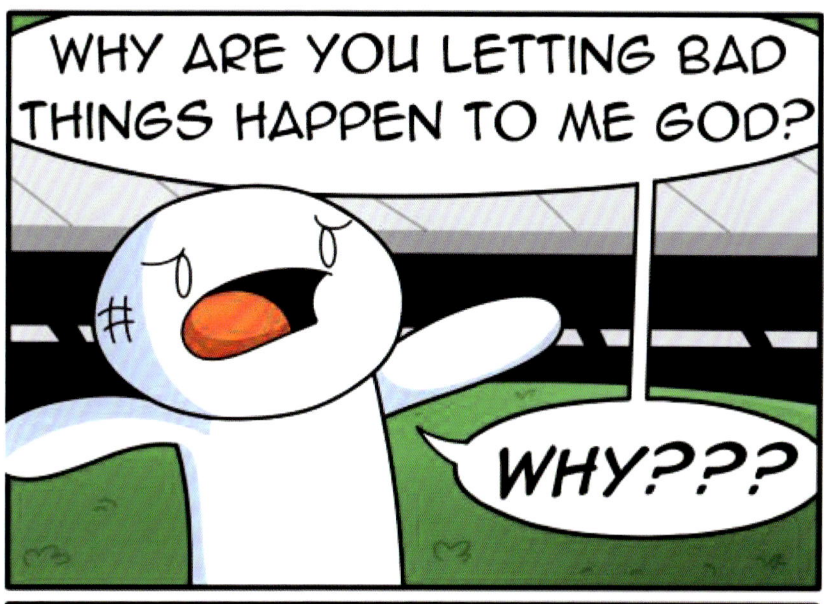
WHY ARE YOU LETTING BAD THINGS HAPPEN TO ME GOD?
WHY???

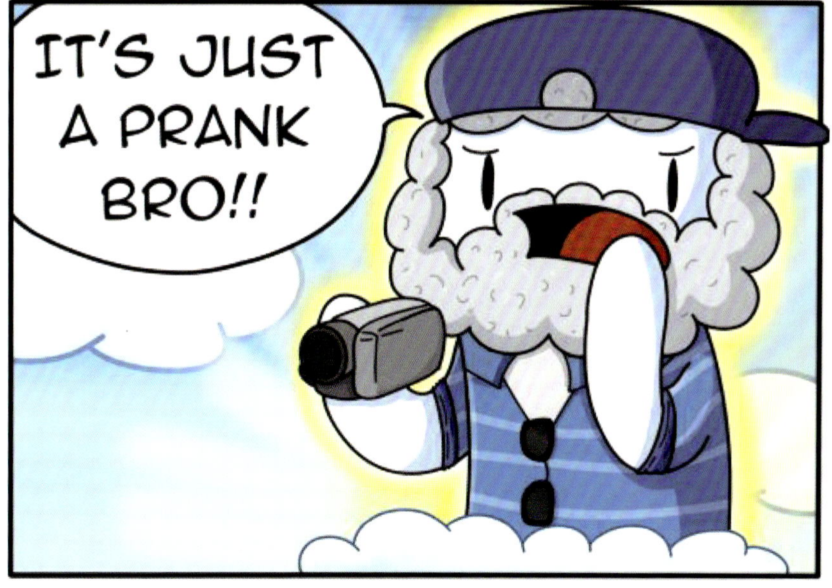
IT'S JUST A PRANK BRO!!

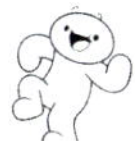

SAME DAY DELIVERY

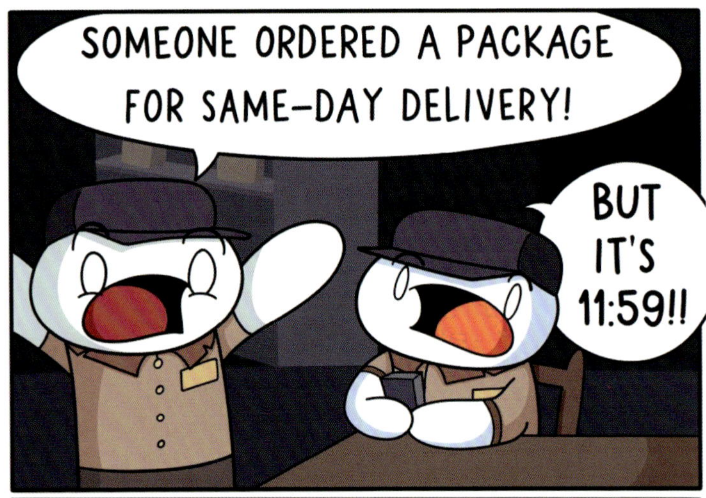

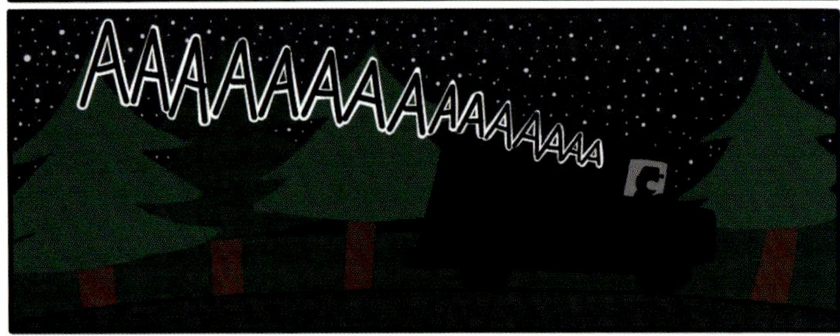

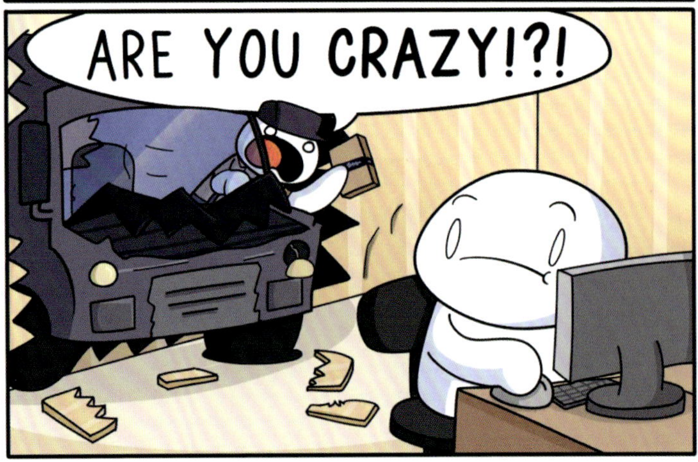

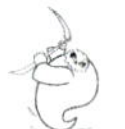

STARLIGHT

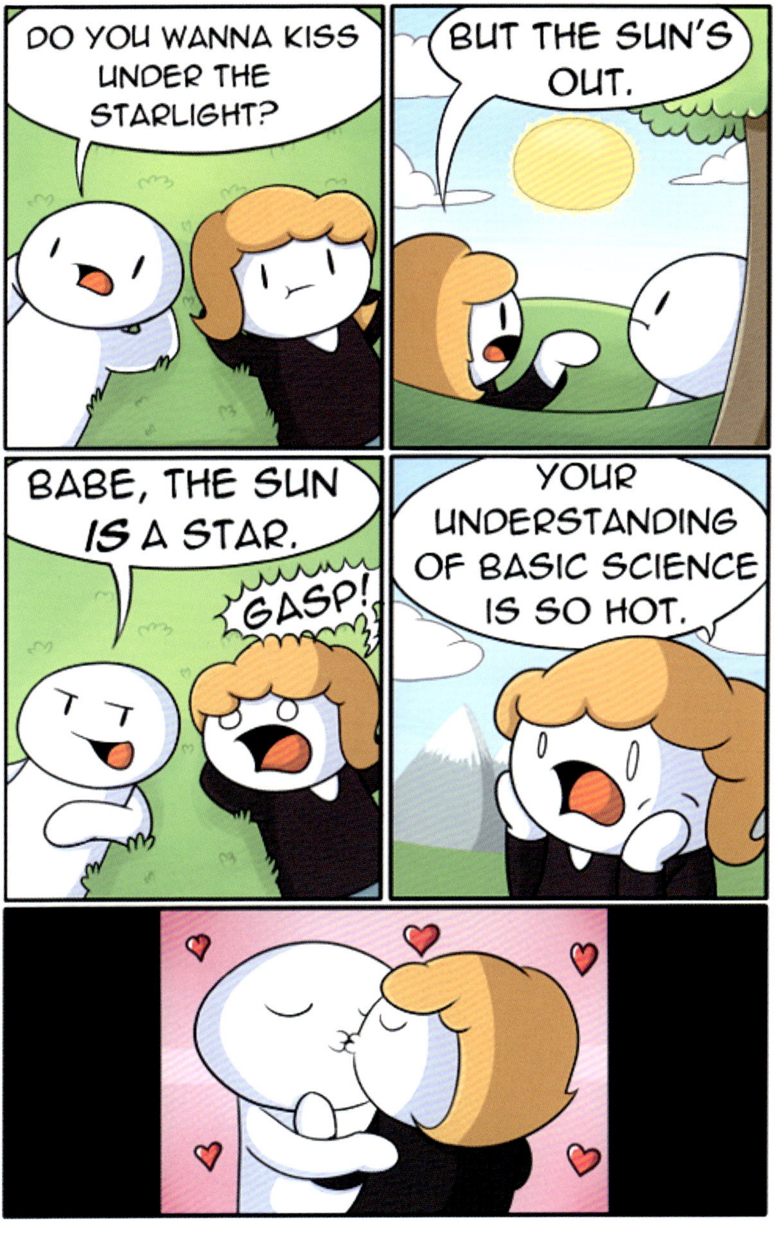

DO YOU WANNA KISS UNDER THE STARLIGHT?

BUT THE SUN'S OUT.

BABE, THE SUN *IS* A STAR.

GASP!

YOUR UNDERSTANDING OF BASIC SCIENCE IS SO HOT.

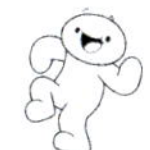

CRASH LANDING

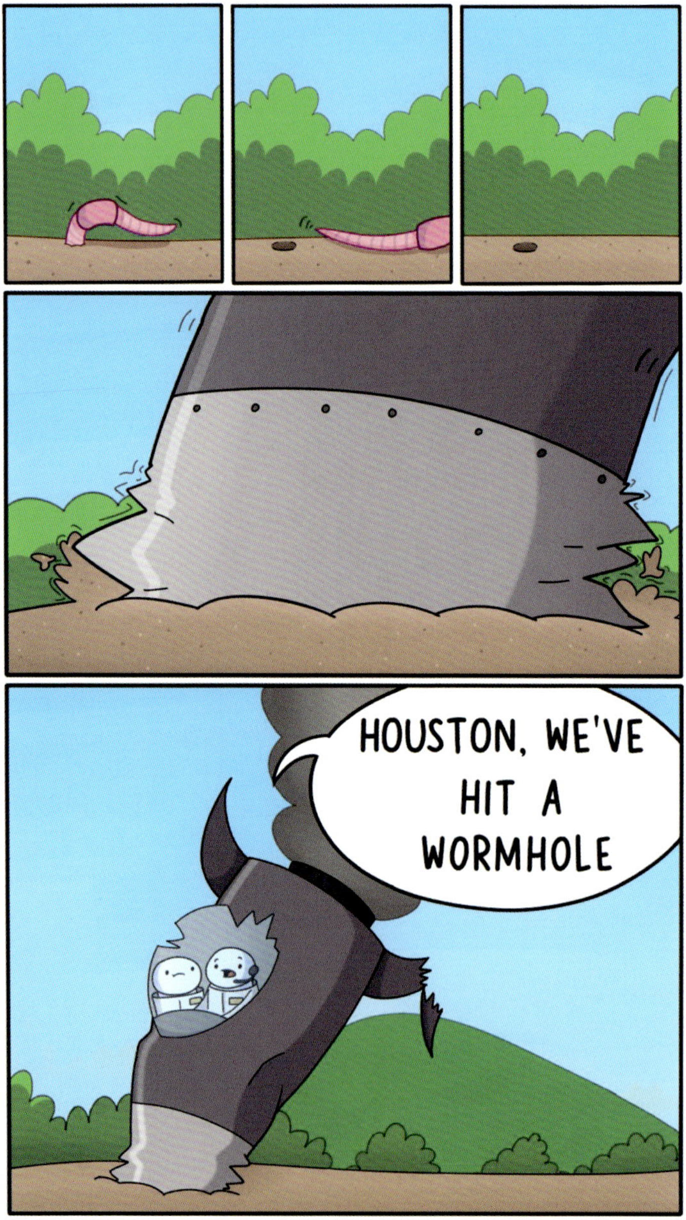

HOUSTON, WE'VE HIT A WORMHOLE

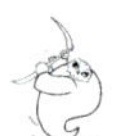

YOUR NEXT

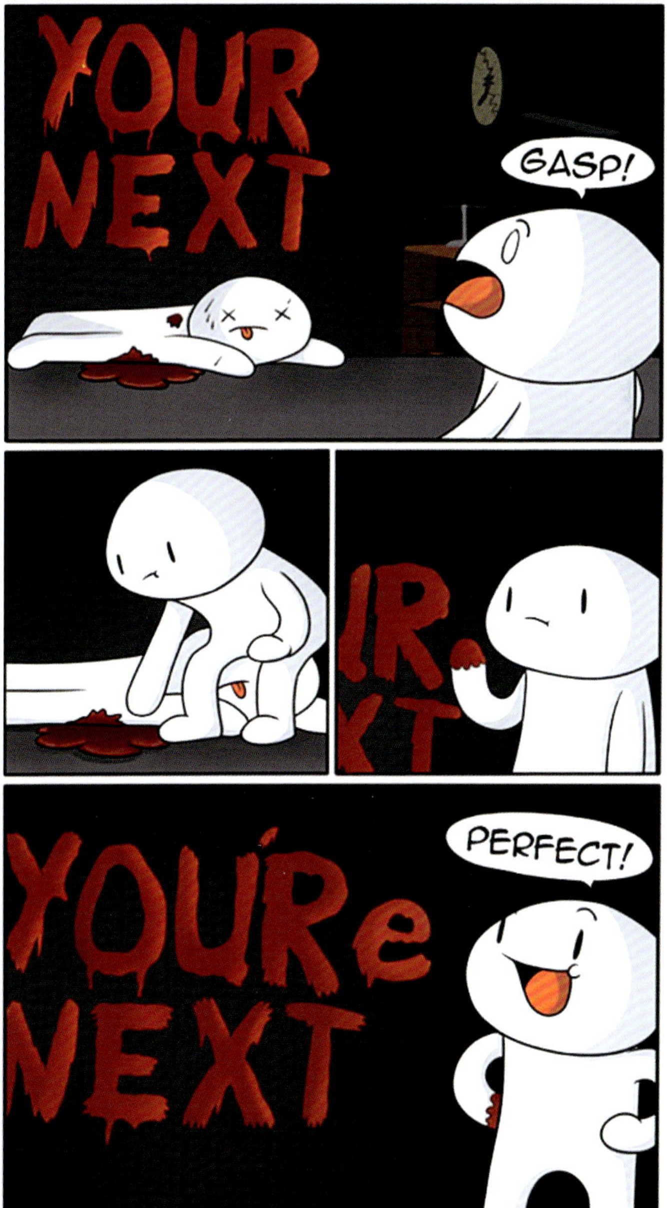

YOUR NEXT

GASP!

YOU'Re NEXT

PERFECT!

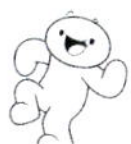

CAT GOT YOUR TONGUE

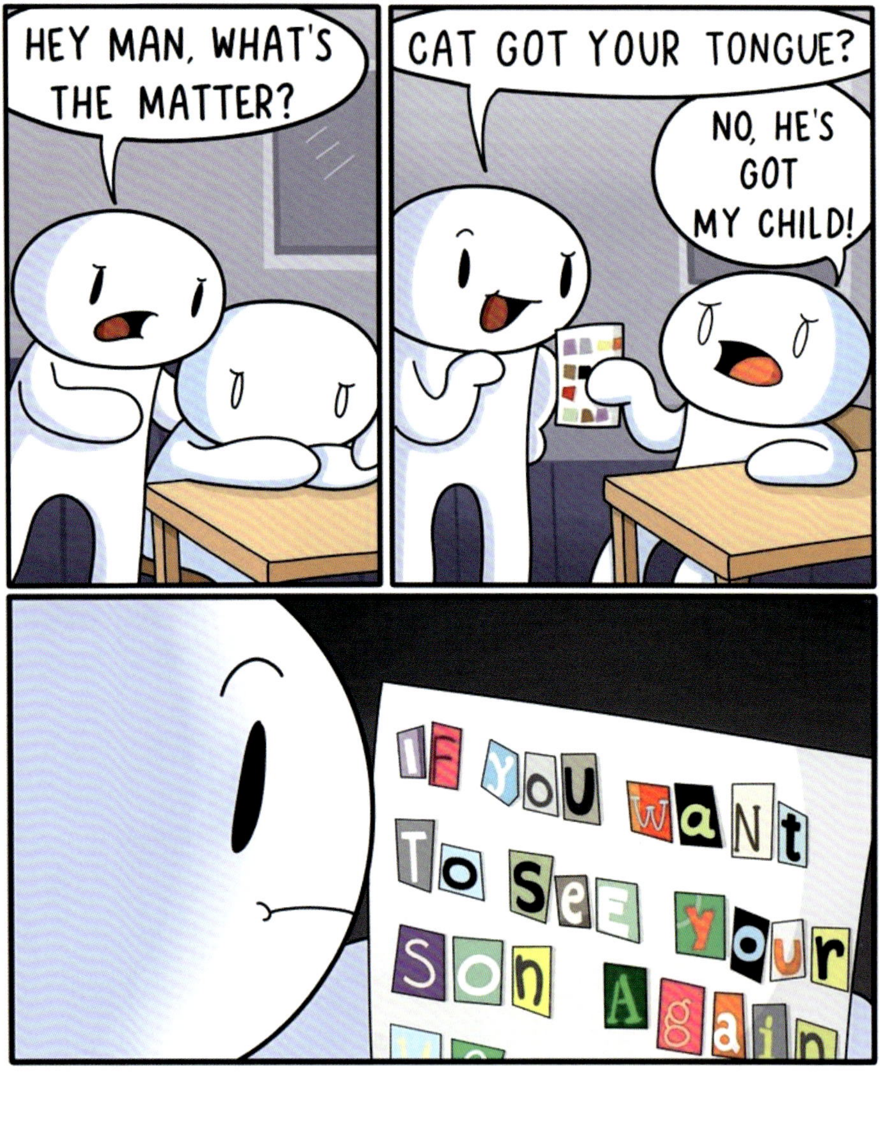

HEY MAN, WHAT'S THE MATTER?

CAT GOT YOUR TONGUE?

NO, HE'S GOT MY CHILD!

IF YOU WANT TO SEE YOUR SON AGAIN

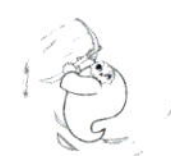

NSA

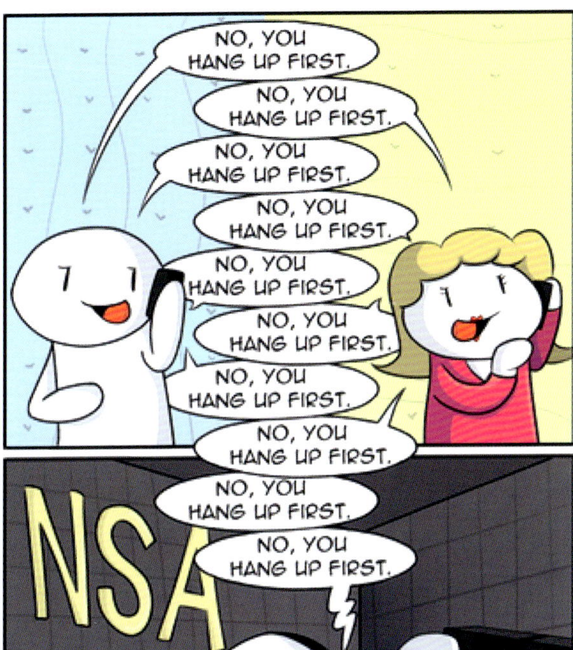

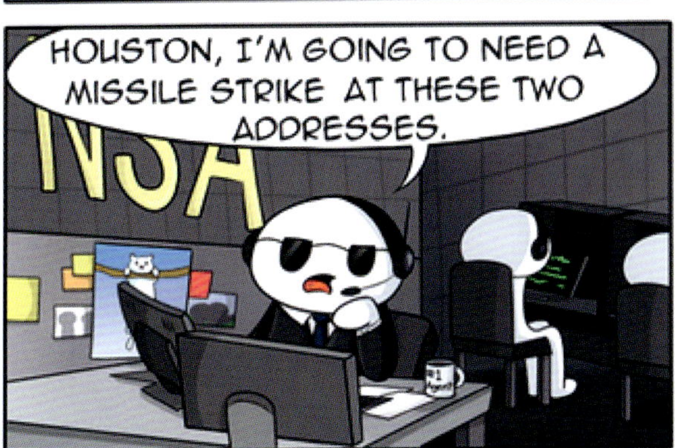

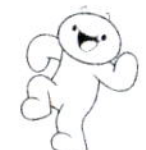

NUMBSKULL

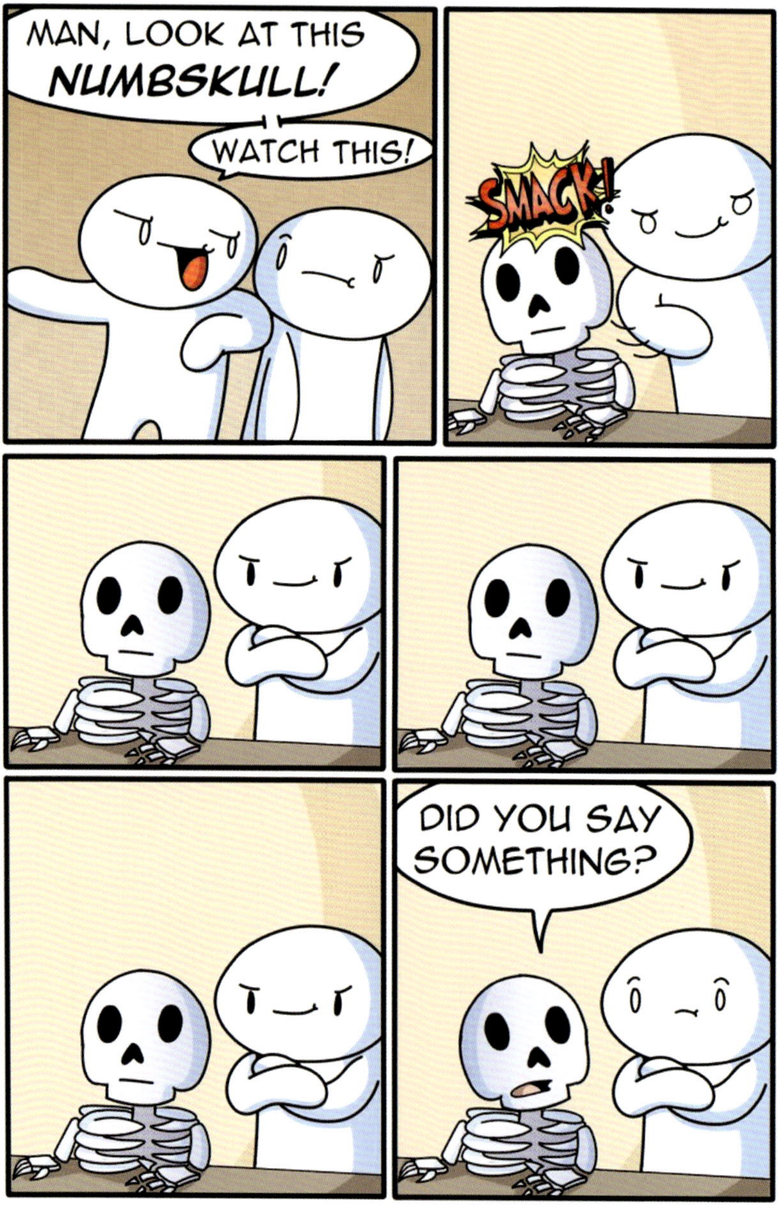

MAN, LOOK AT THIS *NUMBSKULL!*

WATCH THIS!

SMACK!

DID YOU SAY SOMETHING?

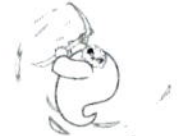

OUIJA BOARD

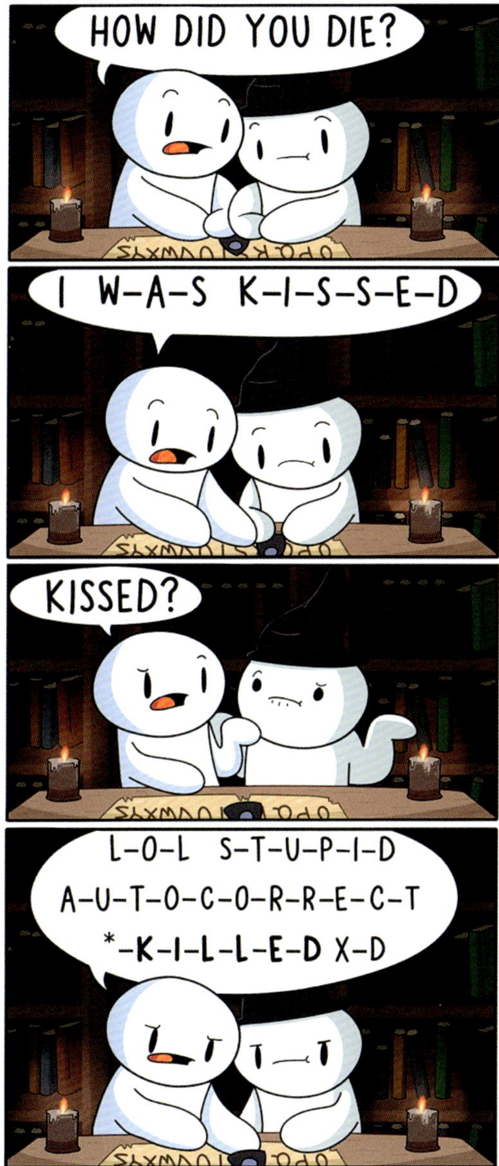
HOW DID YOU DIE?
I W-A-S K-I-S-S-E-D
KISSED?
L-O-L S-T-U-P-I-D
A-U-T-O-C-O-R-R-E-C-T
*-K-I-L-L-E-D X-D

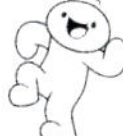

NEW COMICS

As I've been making more comics, I've also gone back and redone a few of my favorites that I thought could use a refresh (for example, this garlic bread comic from years ago)!

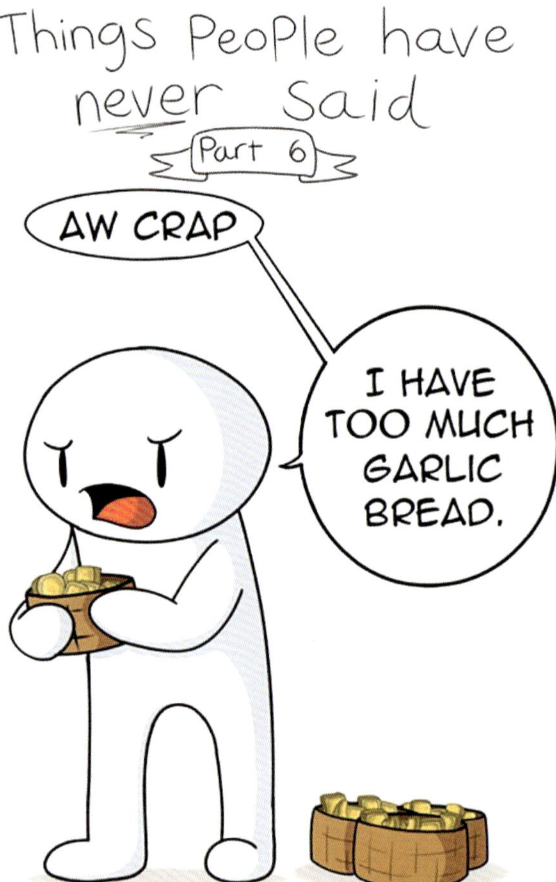

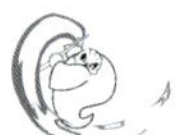

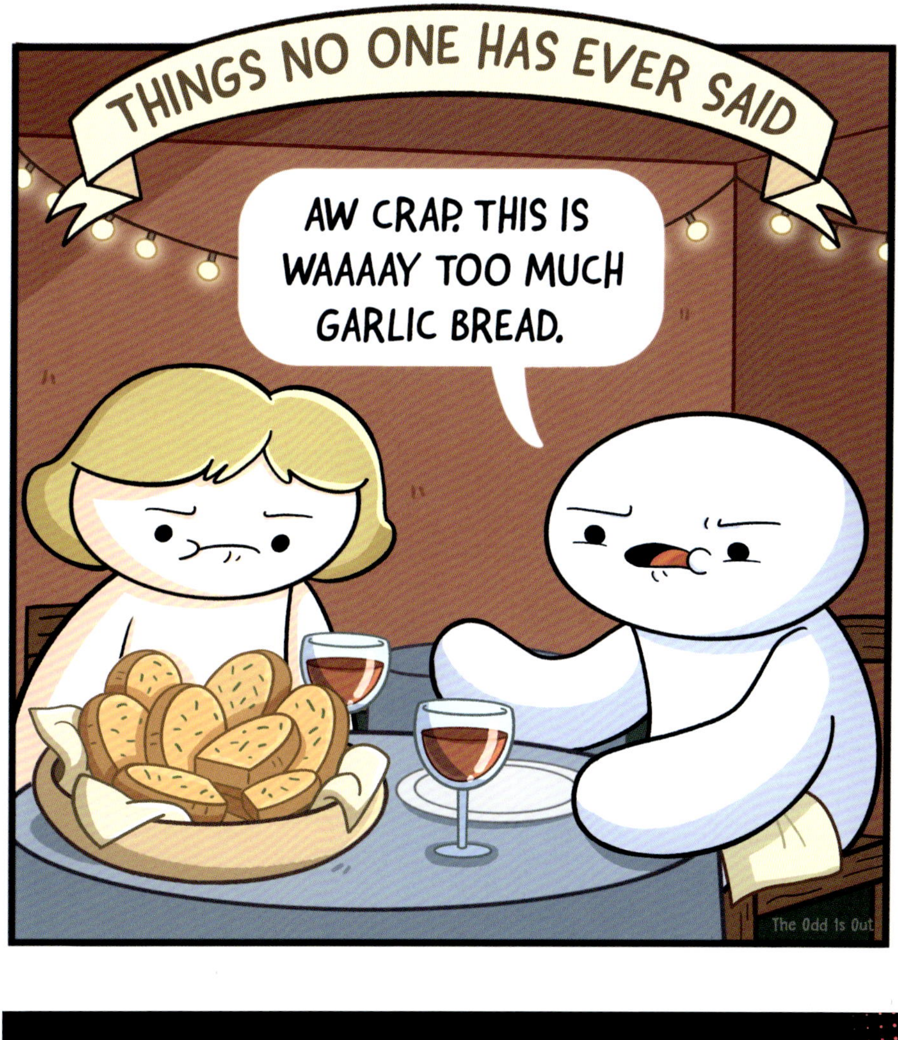

THINGS NO ONE HAS EVER SAID

AW CRAP. THIS IS WAAAAY TOO MUCH GARLIC BREAD.

The Odd 1s Out

AND THUS, A NEW ERA BEGINS...

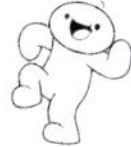

PLAY DEAD

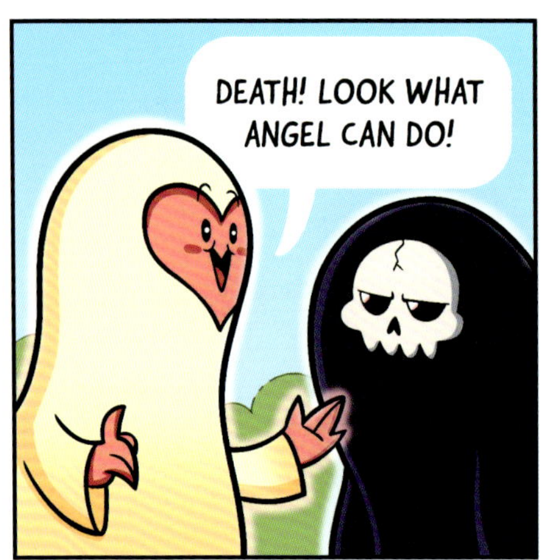
DEATH! LOOK WHAT ANGEL CAN DO!

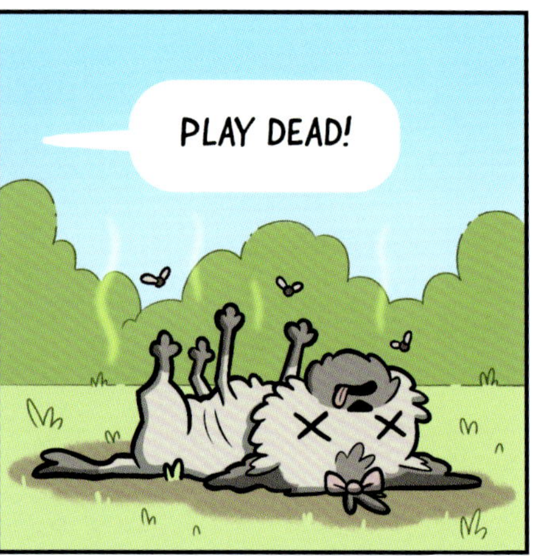
PLAY DEAD!

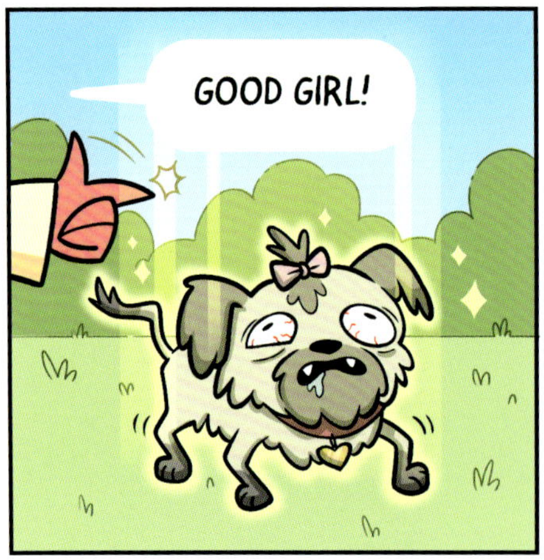
GOOD GIRL!

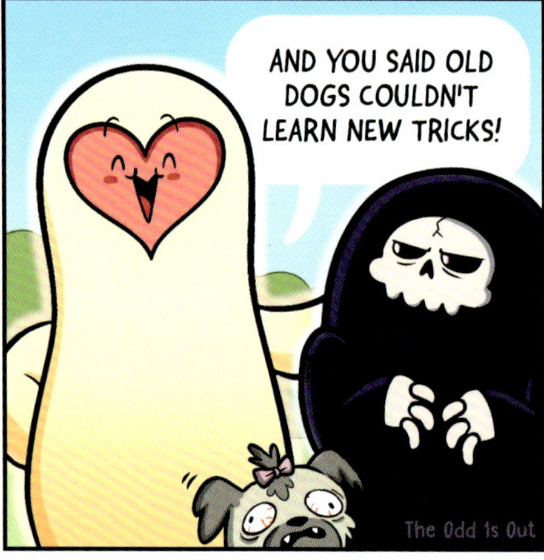
AND YOU SAID OLD DOGS COULDN'T LEARN NEW TRICKS!
The Odd 1s Out

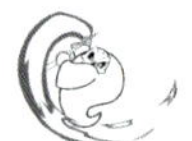

CONCERTS

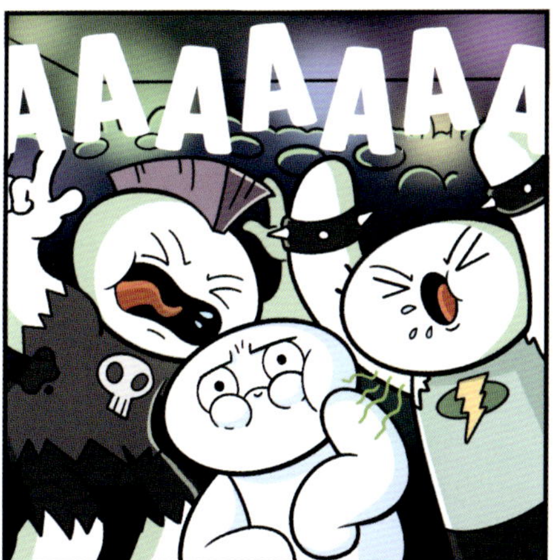

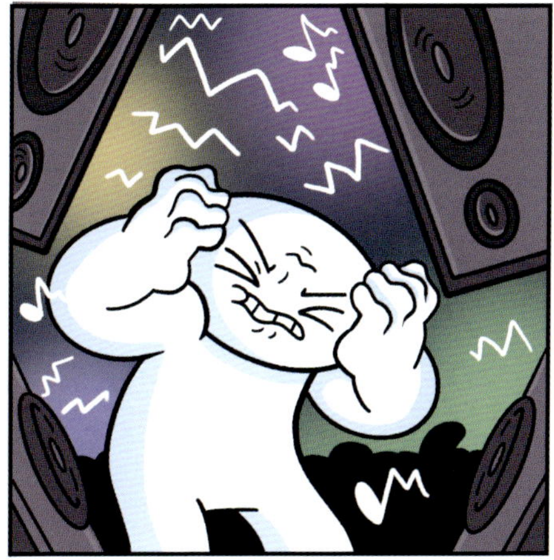

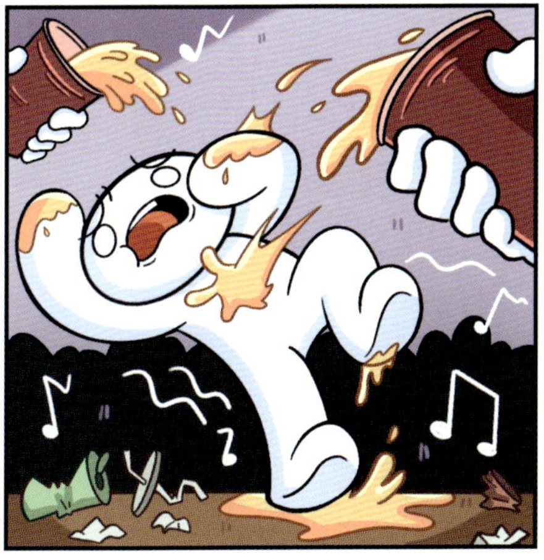

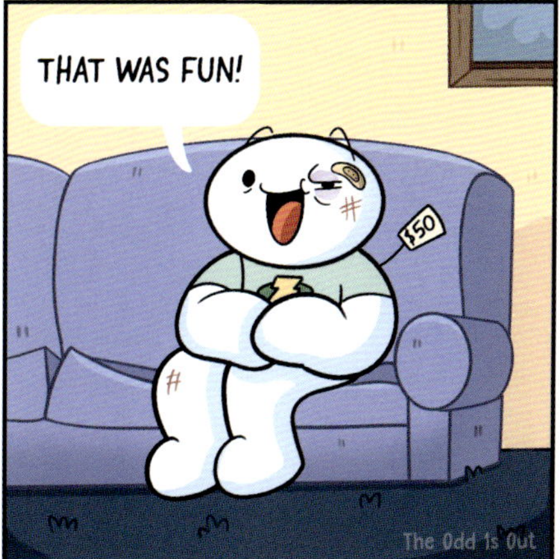

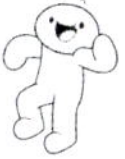

BE REAL

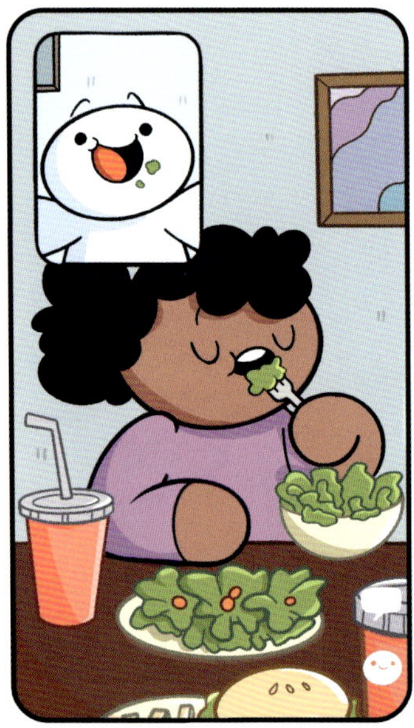

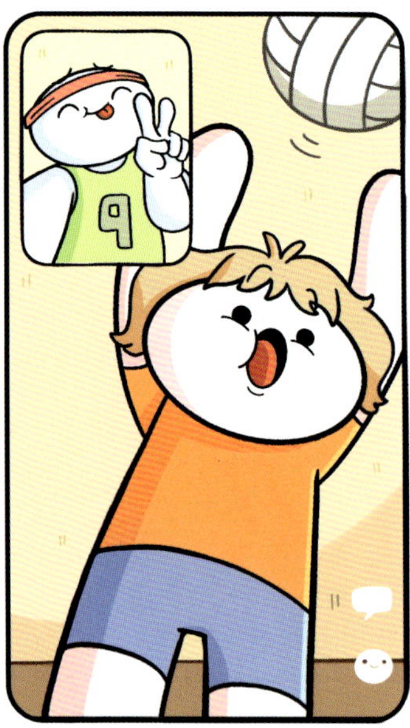

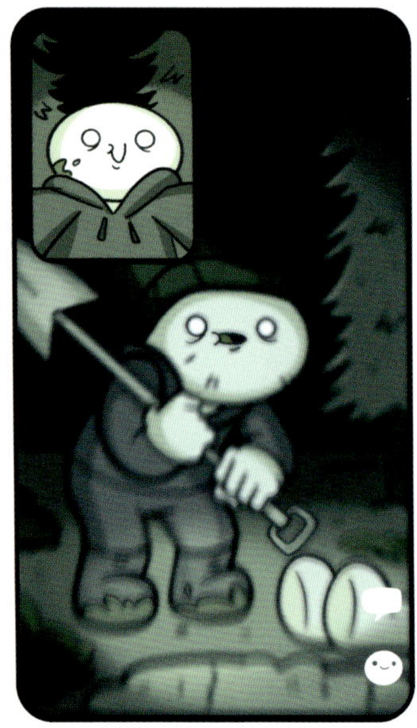

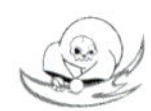

WORST GUY YOU KNOW

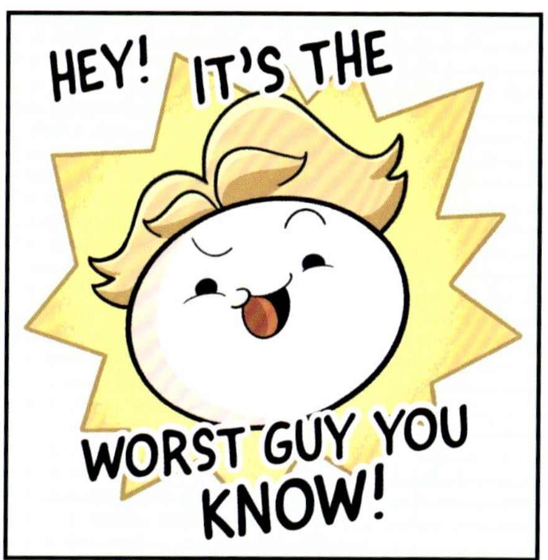

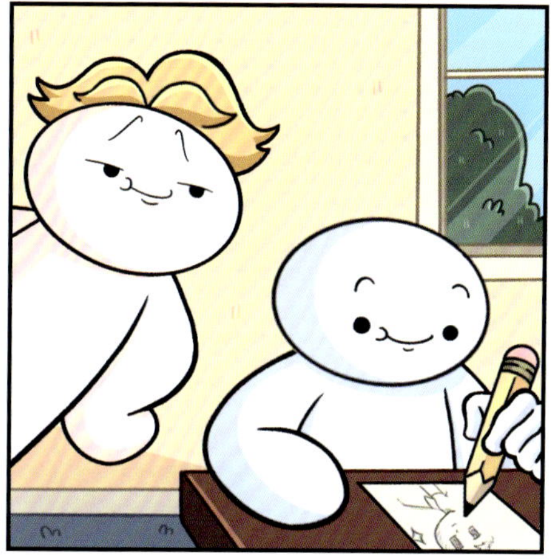

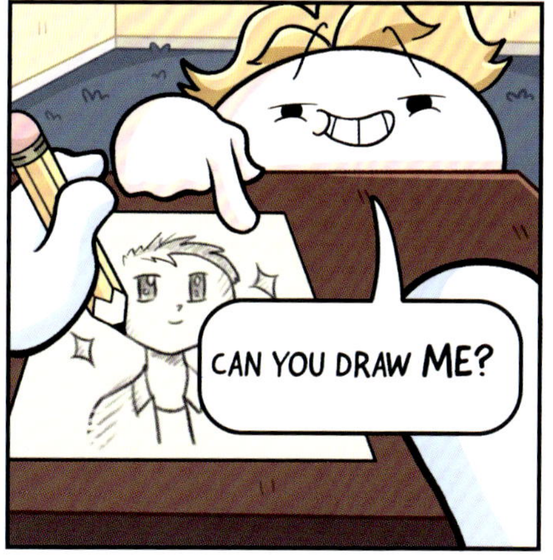

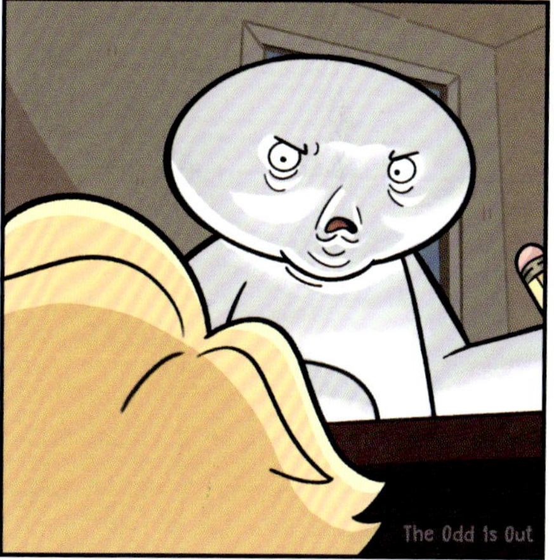

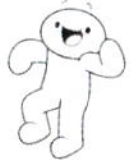

DEVILISH SHOULDER

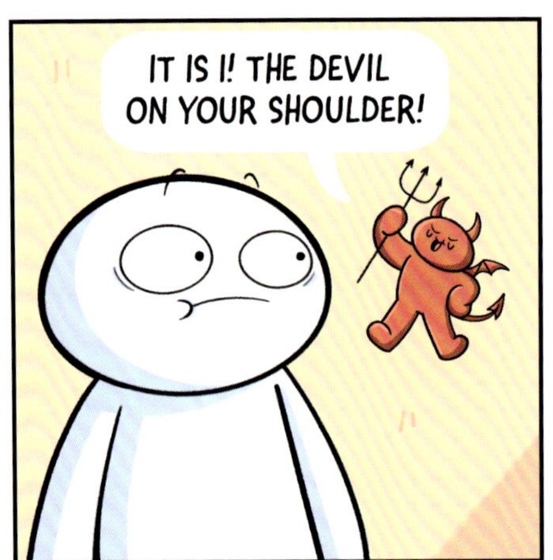

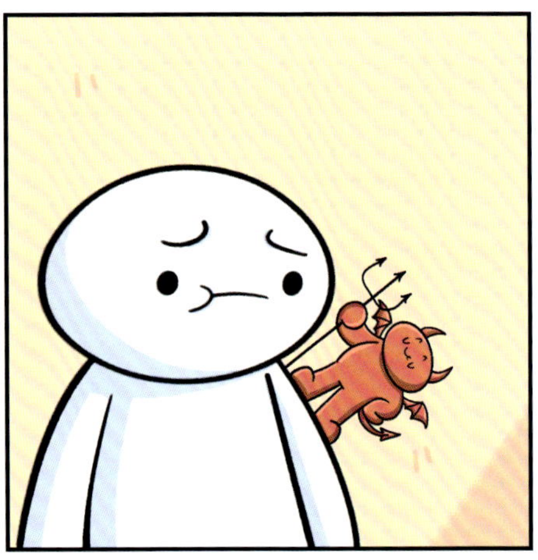

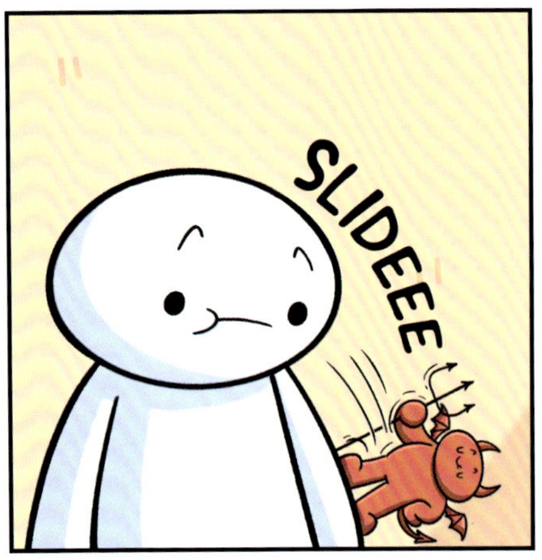

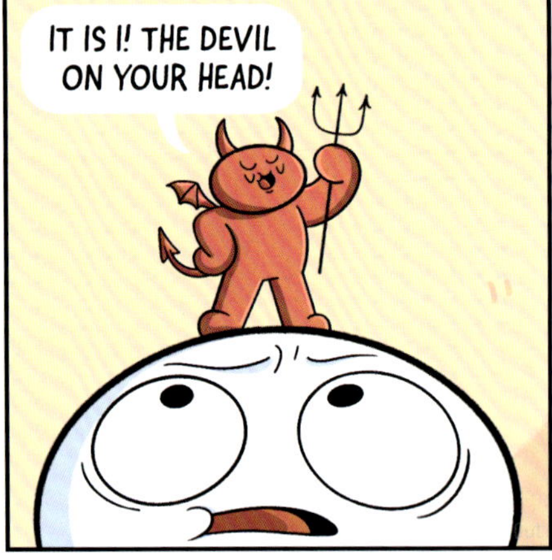

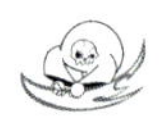

EGG-SPENSIVE

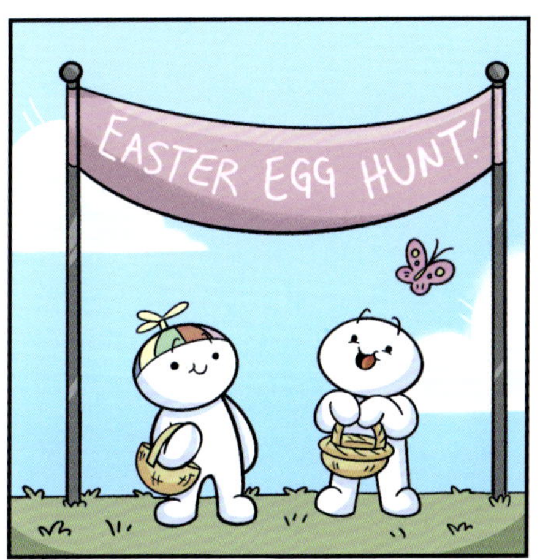

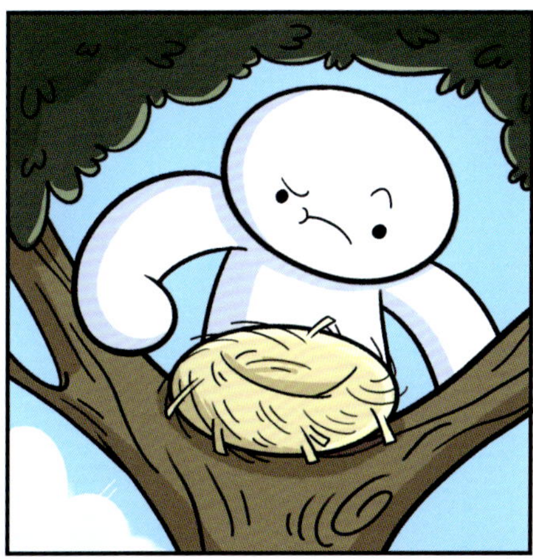

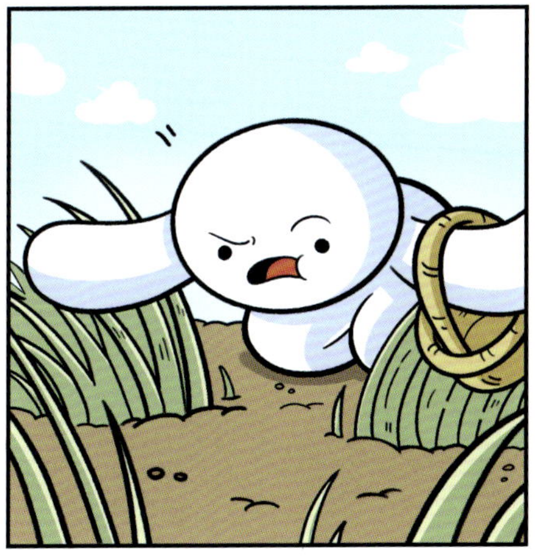

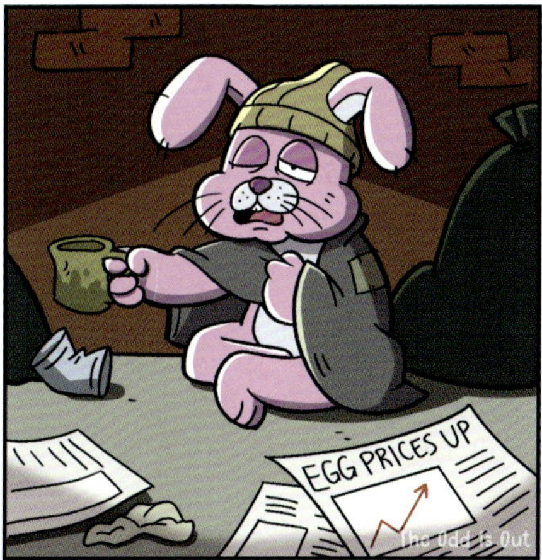

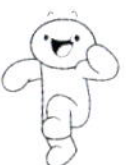

YOUR FLY

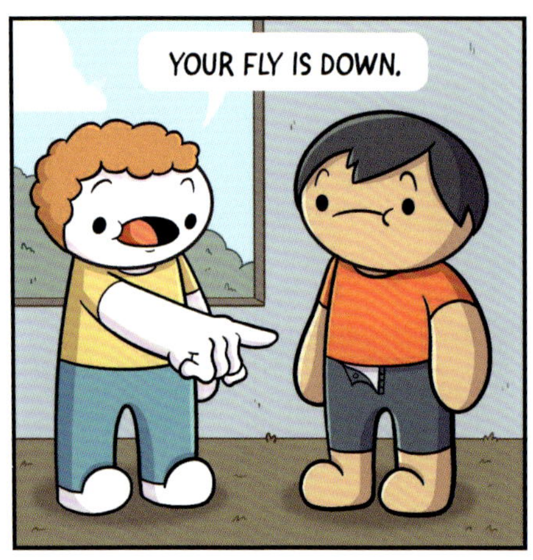

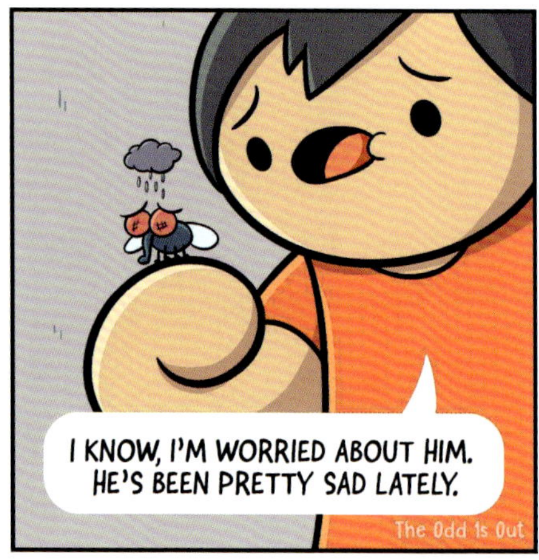

ROOM FOR PIE

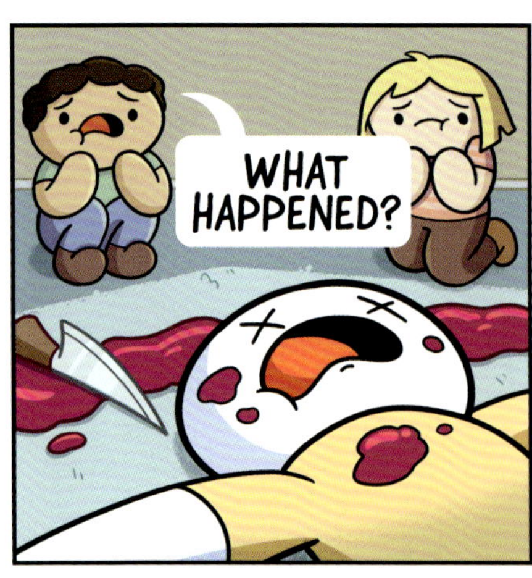

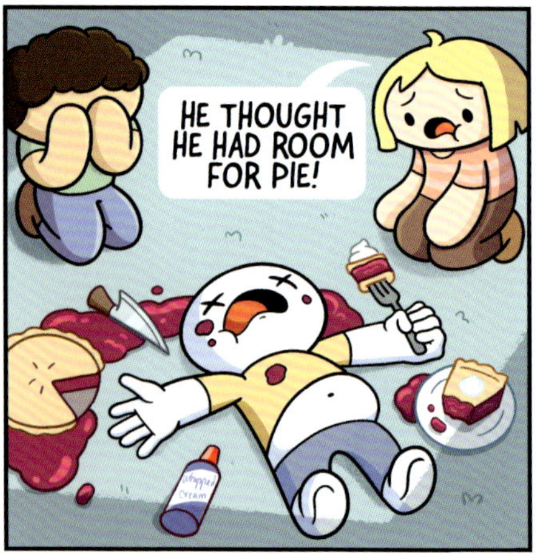

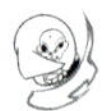

CAT PEOPLE

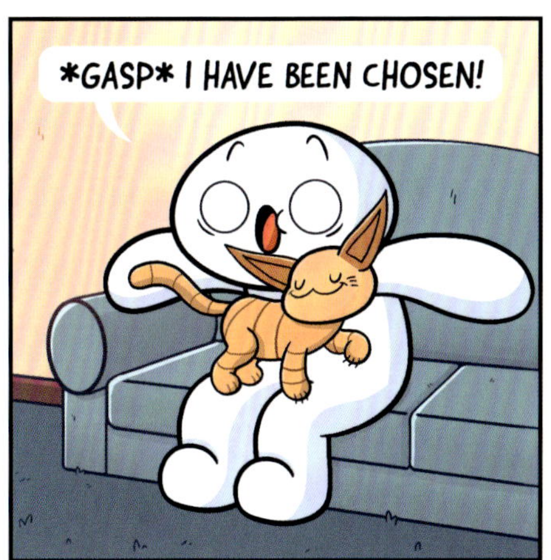

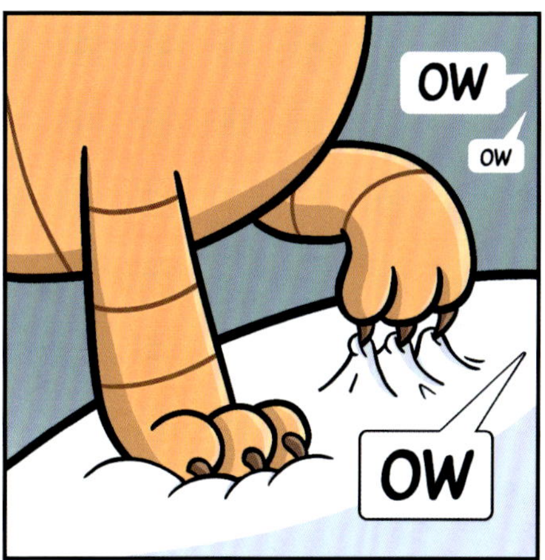

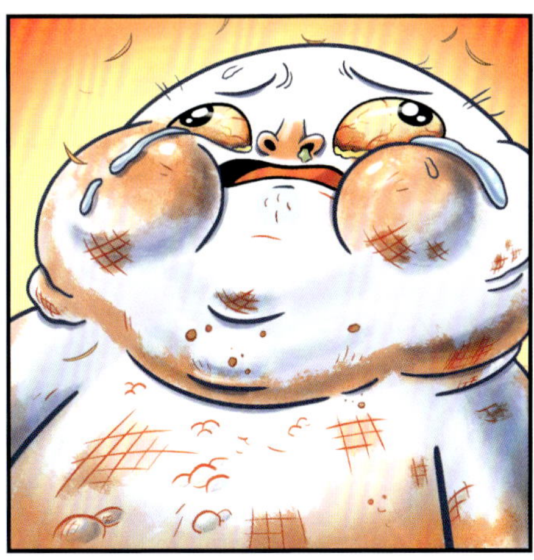

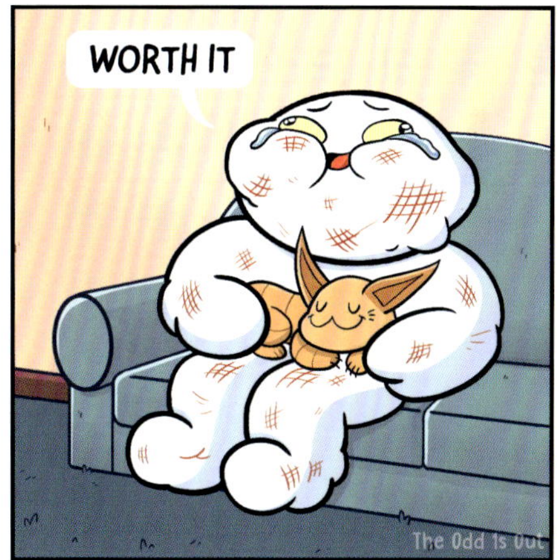

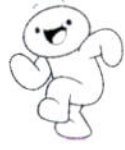

TYRRD JONES

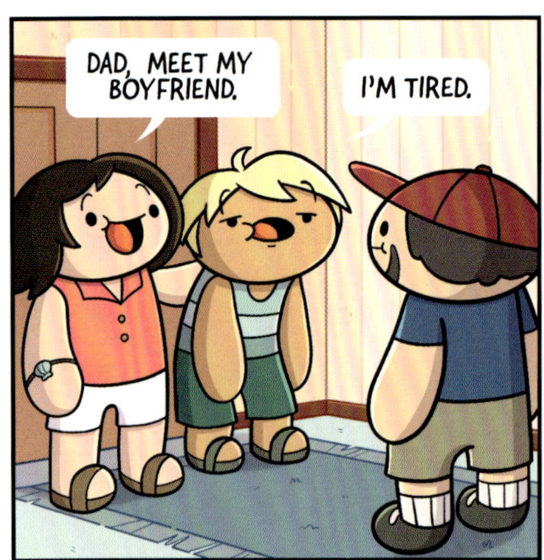
DAD, MEET MY BOYFRIEND.
I'M TIRED.

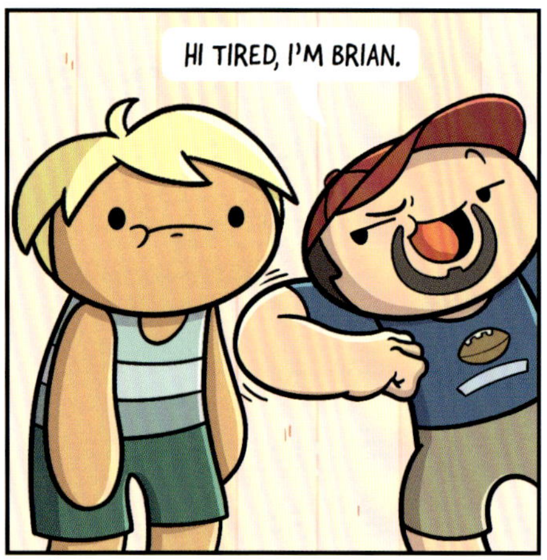
HI TIRED, I'M BRIAN.

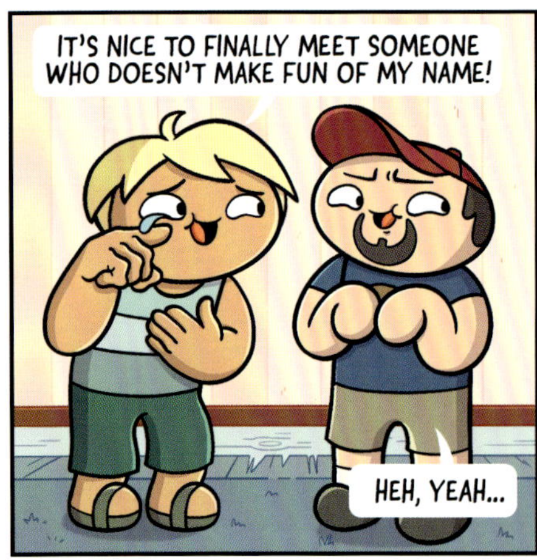
IT'S NICE TO FINALLY MEET SOMEONE WHO DOESN'T MAKE FUN OF MY NAME!
HEH, YEAH...

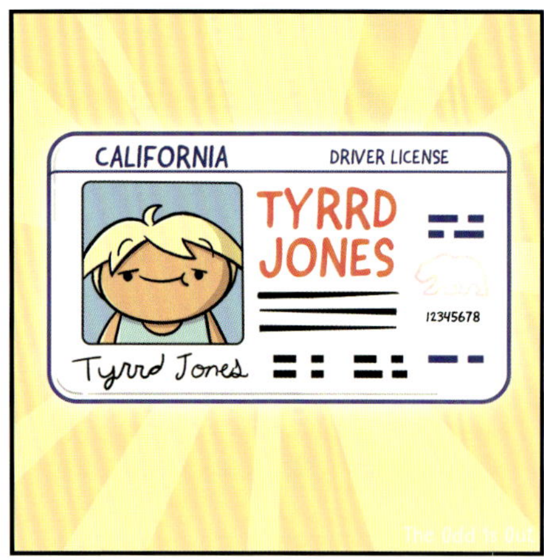
CALIFORNIA
DRIVER LICENSE
TYRRD JONES
12345678
Tyrrd Jones

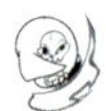

TIMMY TANGENT

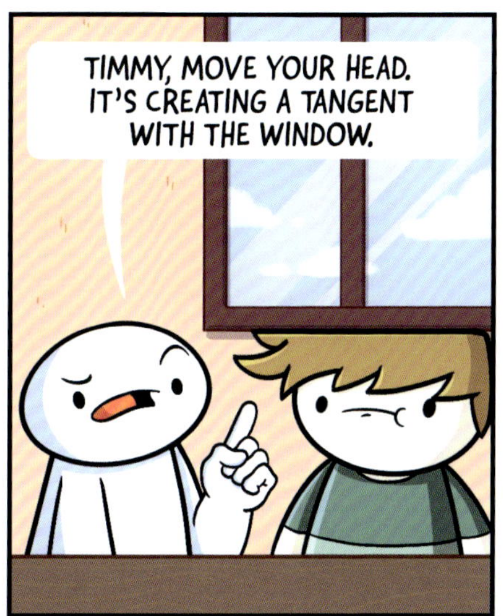

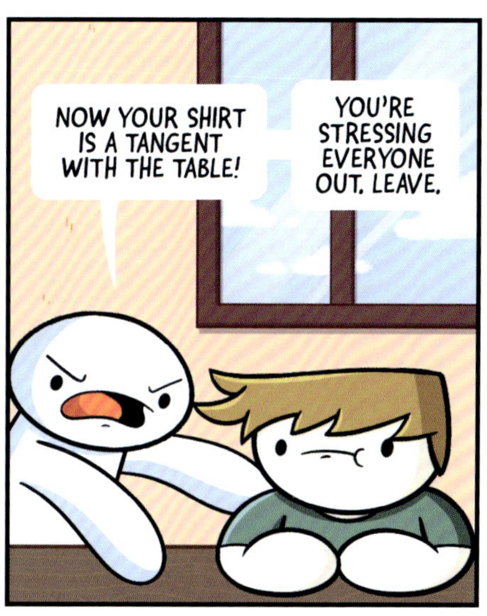

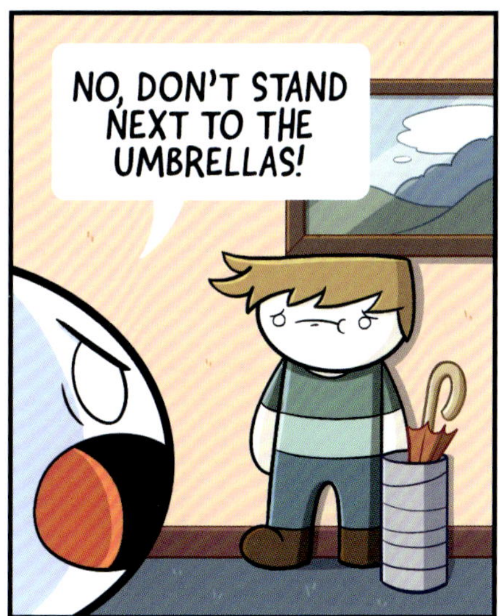

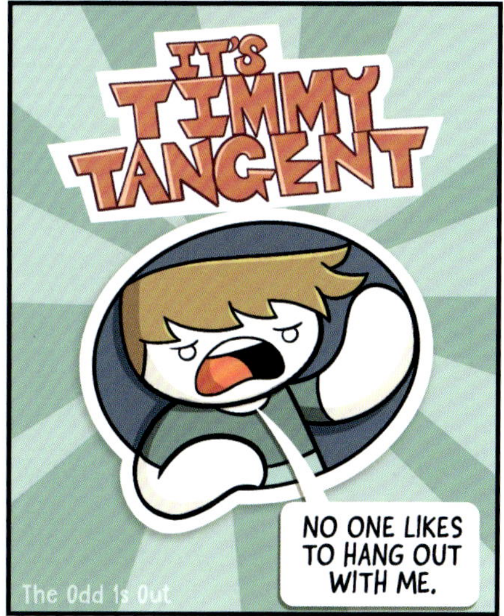

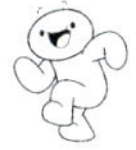

EGG BEATER

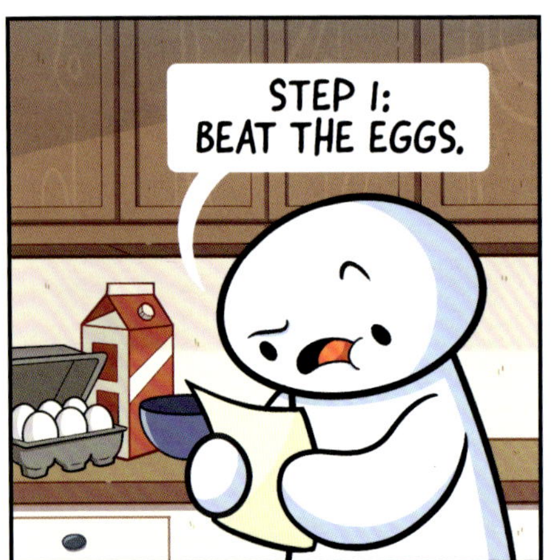

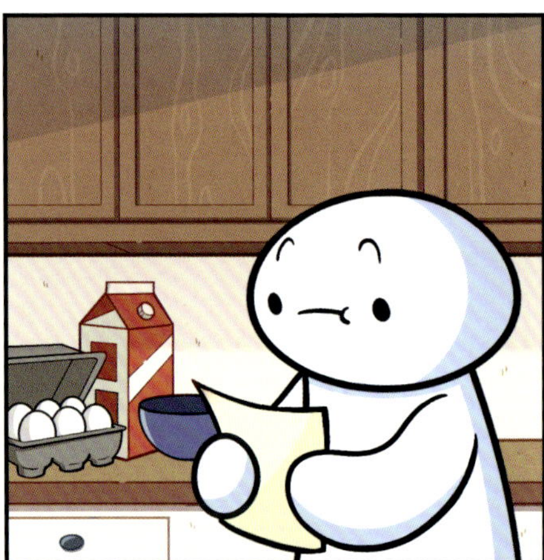

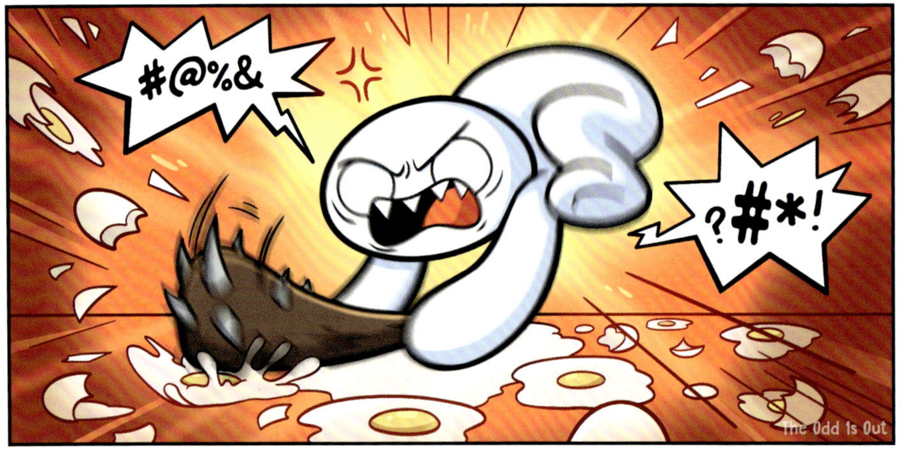

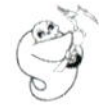

EGG ROLLS

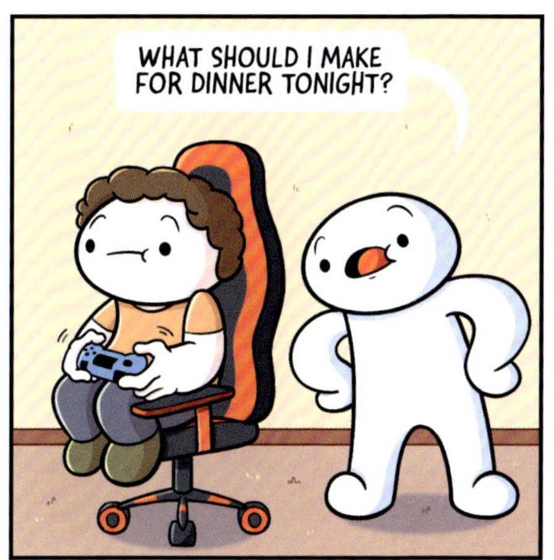
WHAT SHOULD I MAKE FOR DINNER TONIGHT?

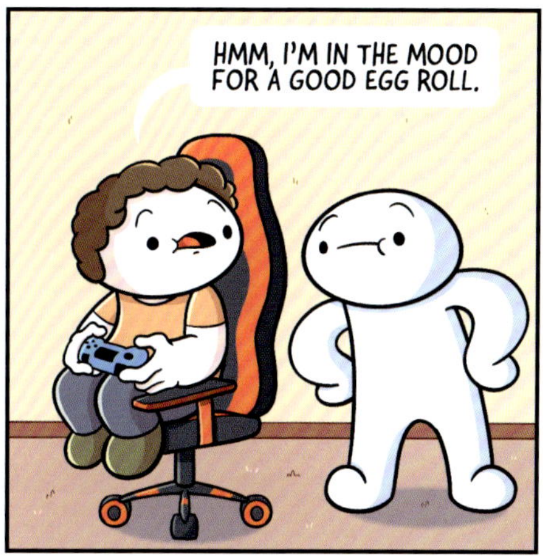
HMM, I'M IN THE MOOD FOR A GOOD EGG ROLL.

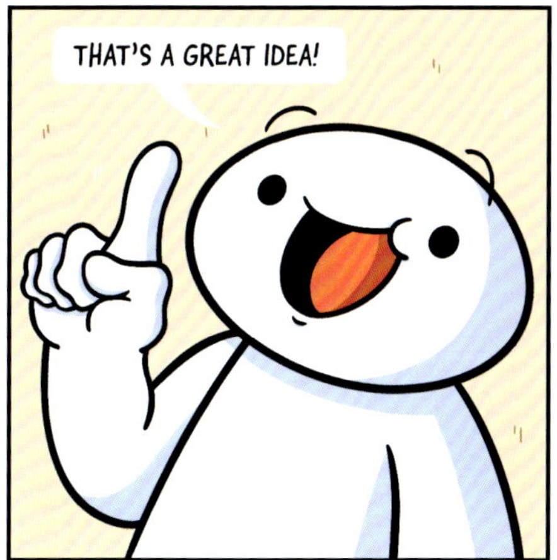
THAT'S A GREAT IDEA!

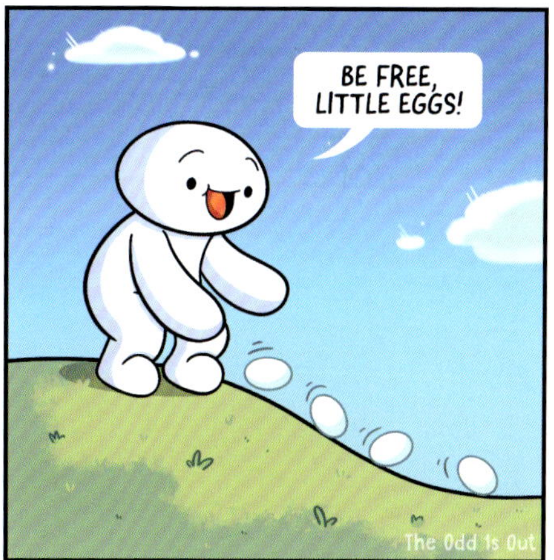
BE FREE, LITTLE EGGS!
The Odd 1s Out

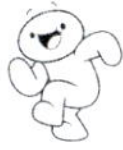

SUPERMAN

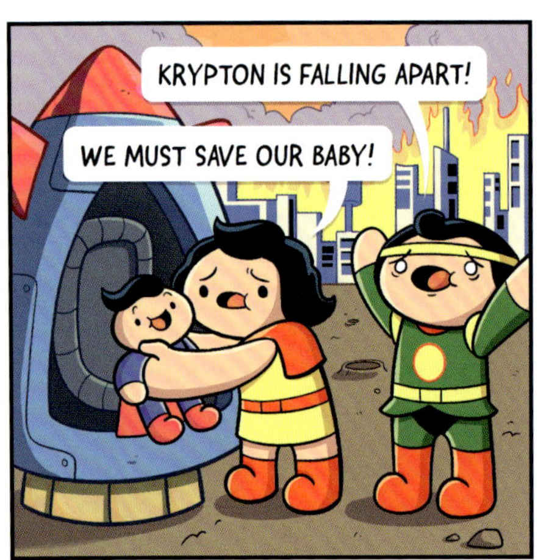
KRYPTON IS FALLING APART!
WE MUST SAVE OUR BABY!

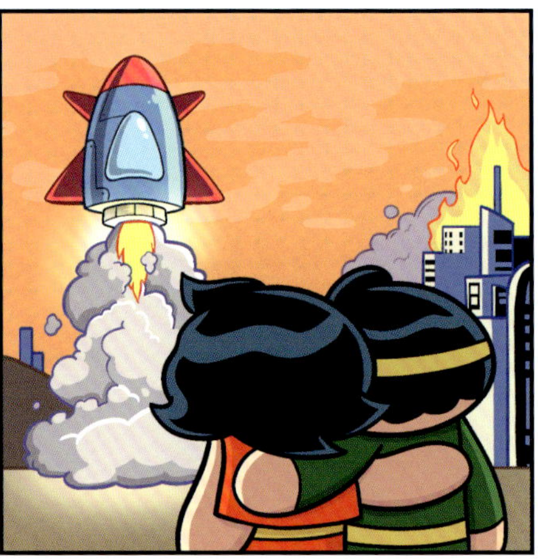

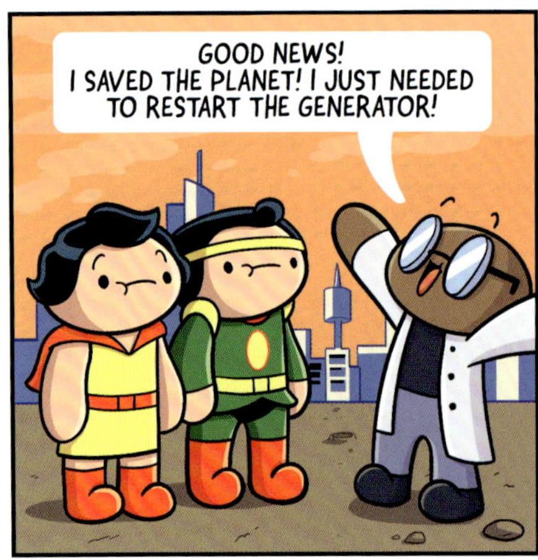
GOOD NEWS!
I SAVED THE PLANET! I JUST NEEDED TO RESTART THE GENERATOR!

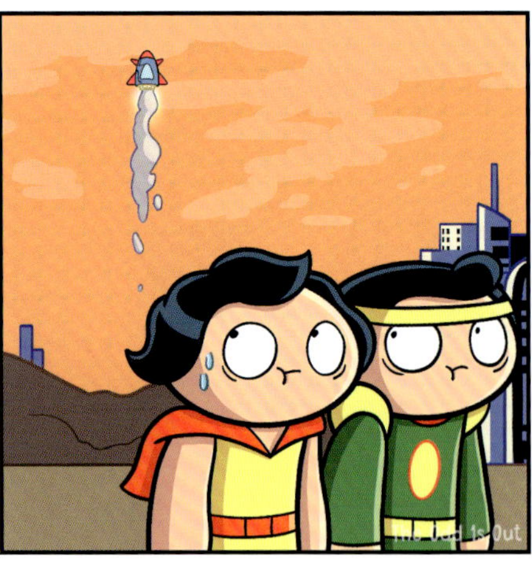

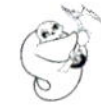

MAILMAN

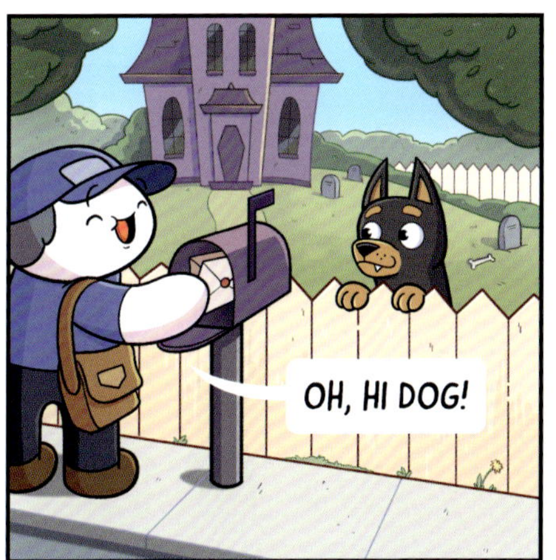

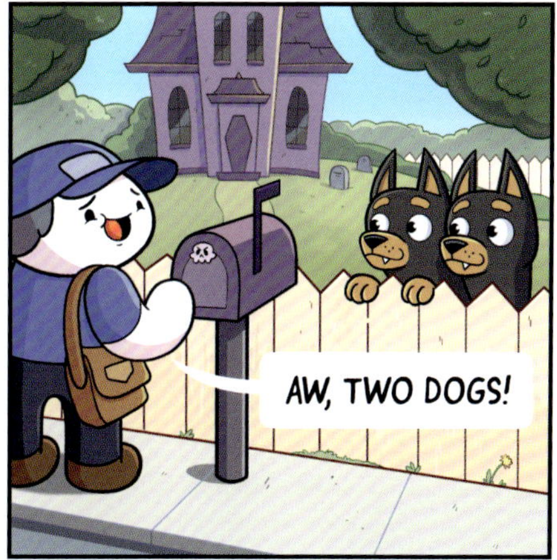

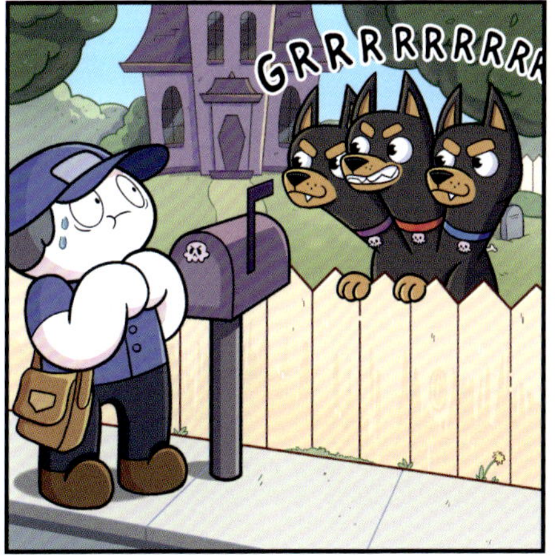

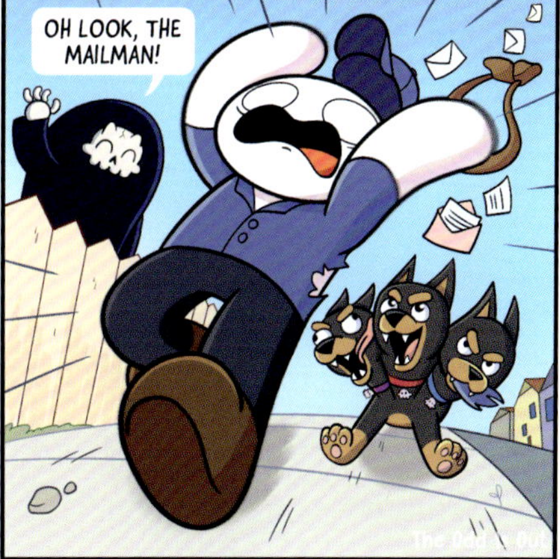

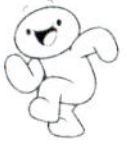

SENIOR DISCOUNT

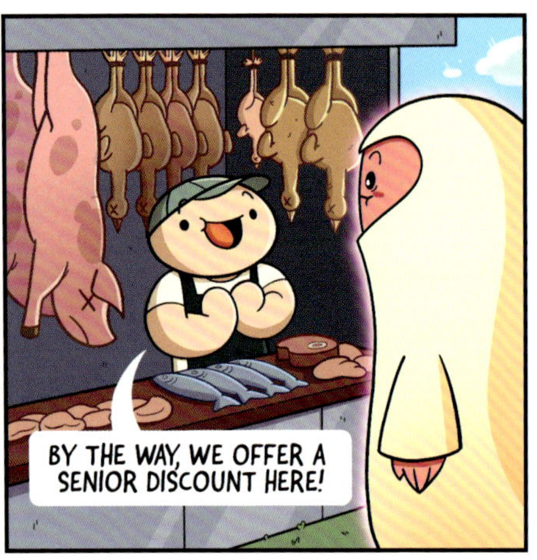

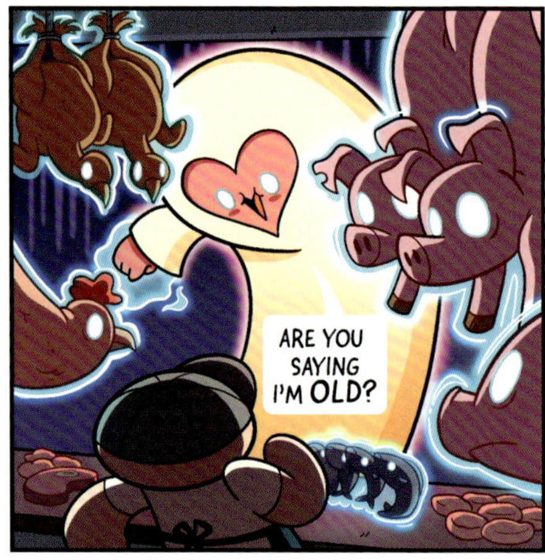

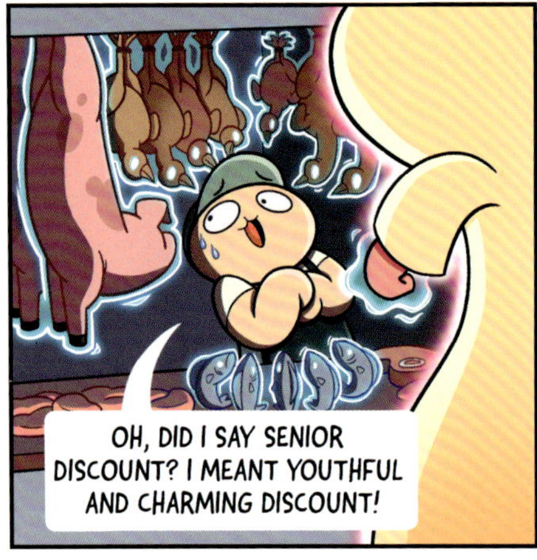

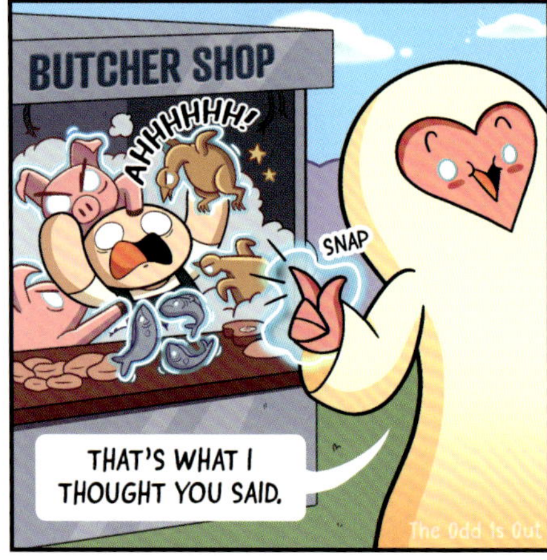

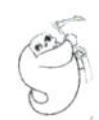

REMOTE DEATH

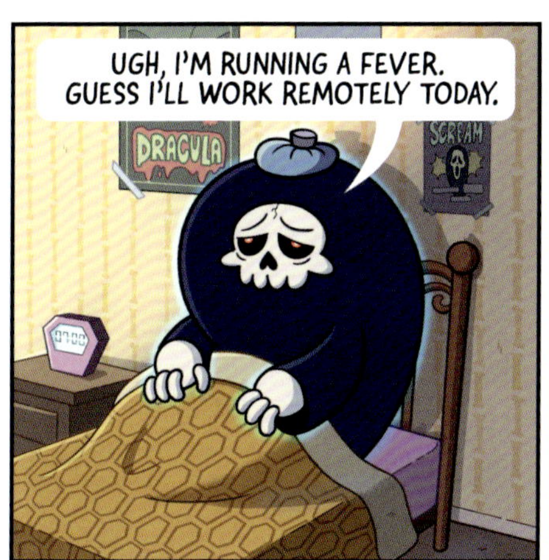

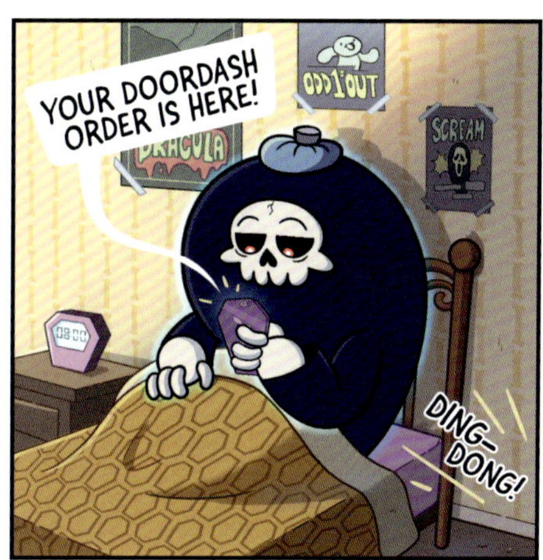

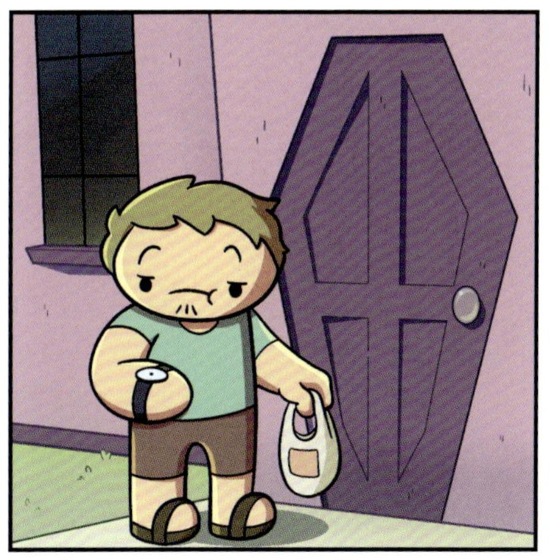

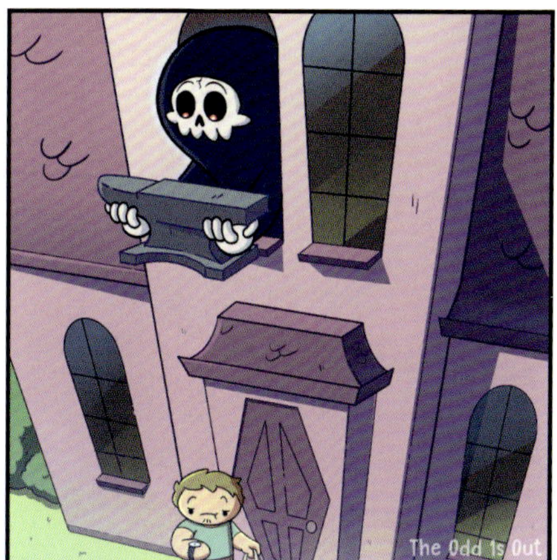

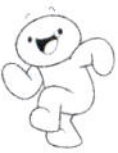

GO FETCH

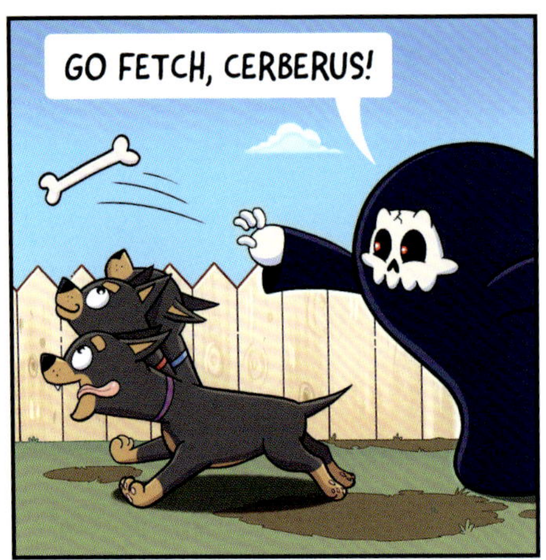

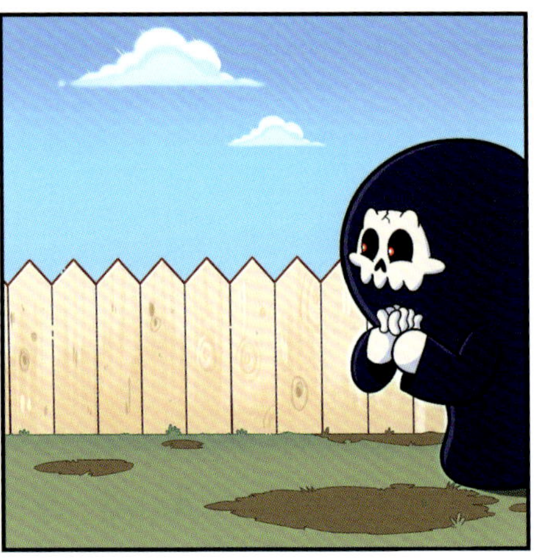

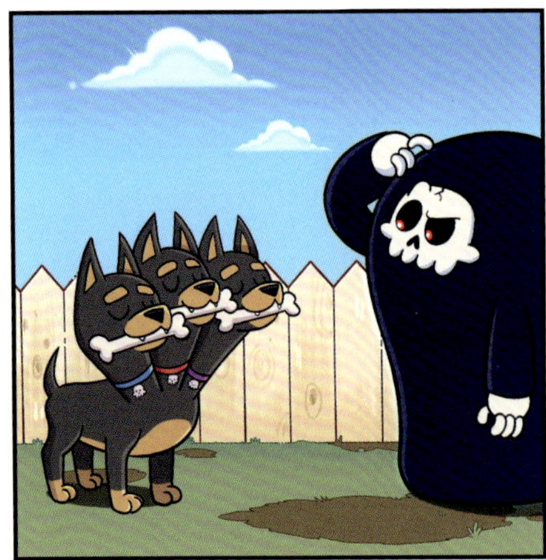

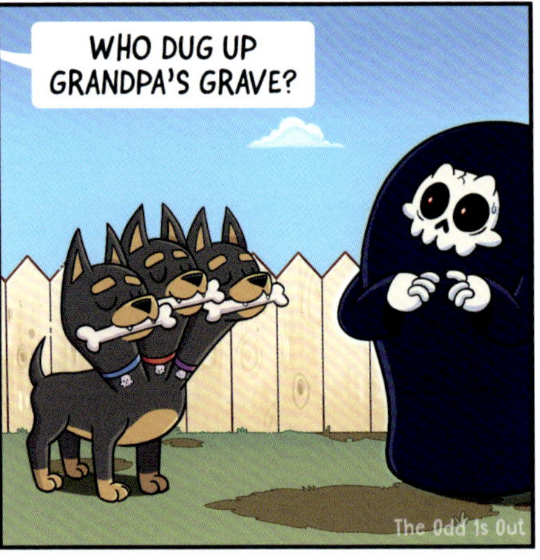

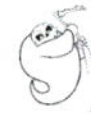

LISTENING SHELL

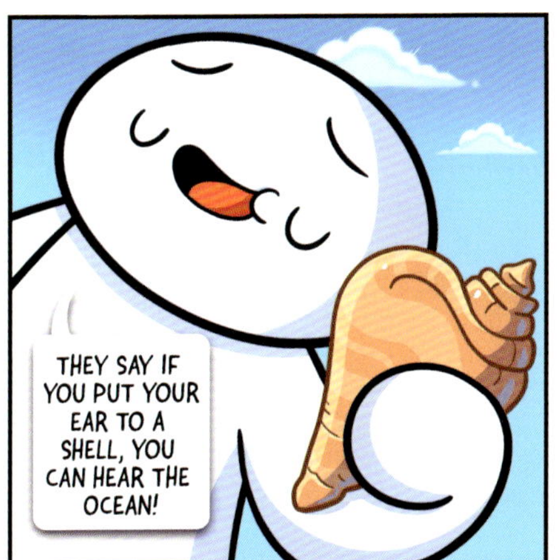

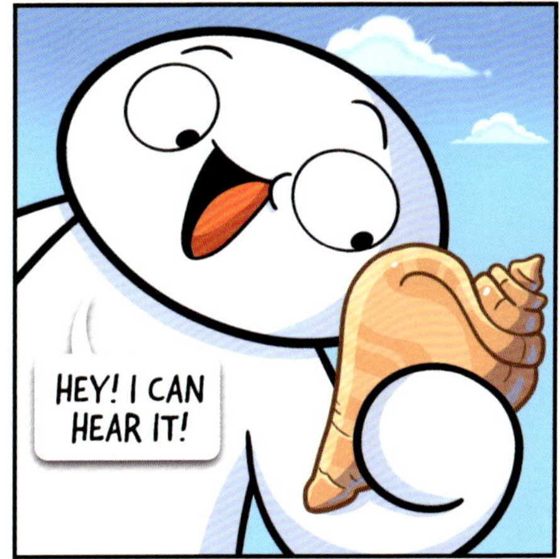

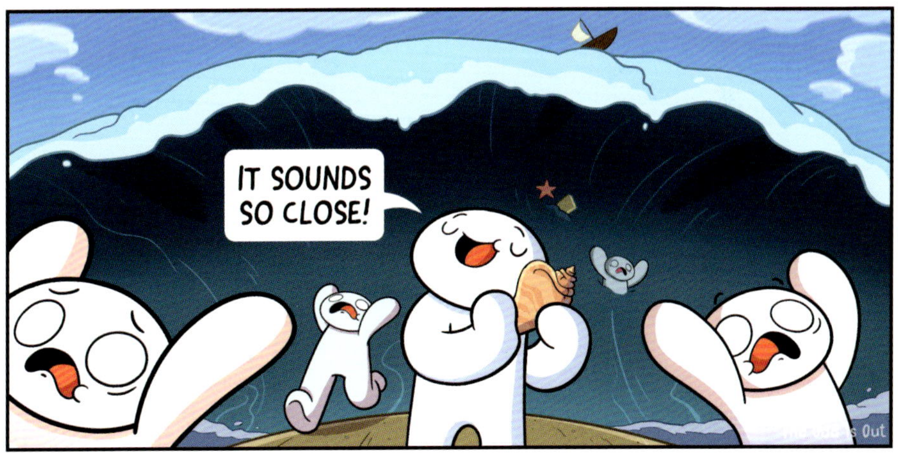

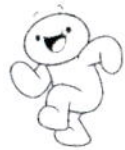

ZOOMIES

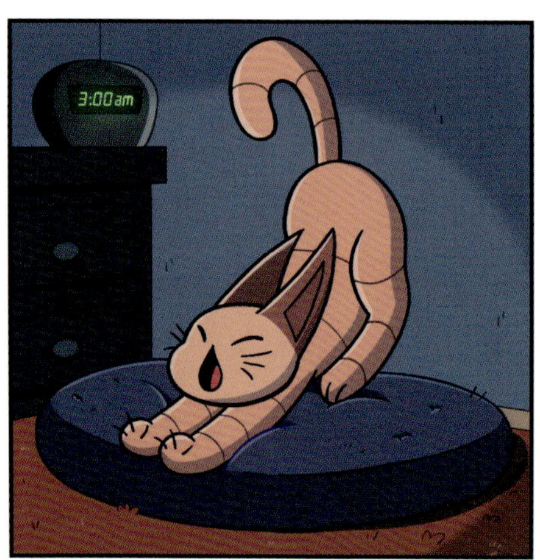

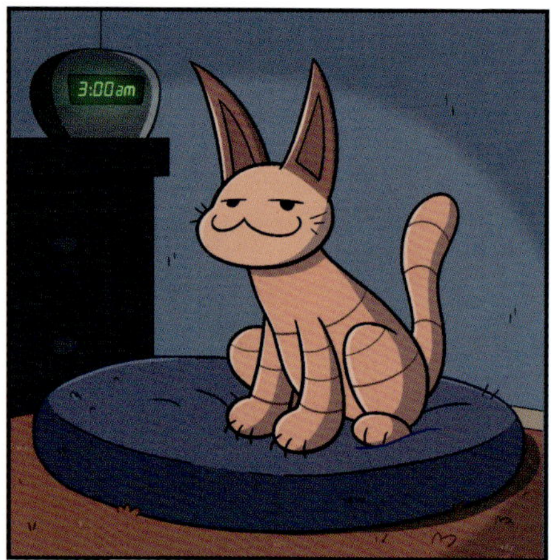

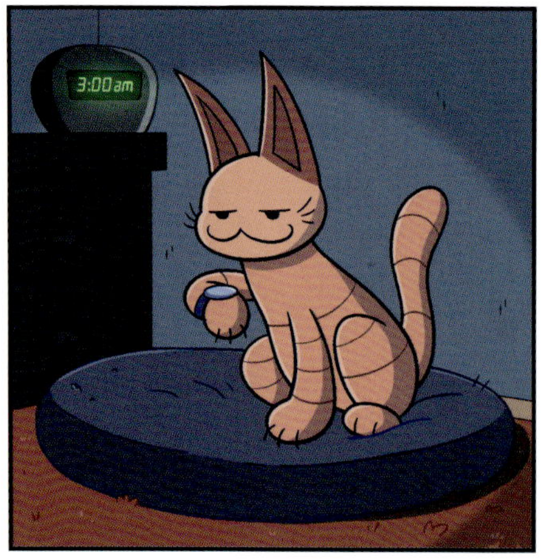

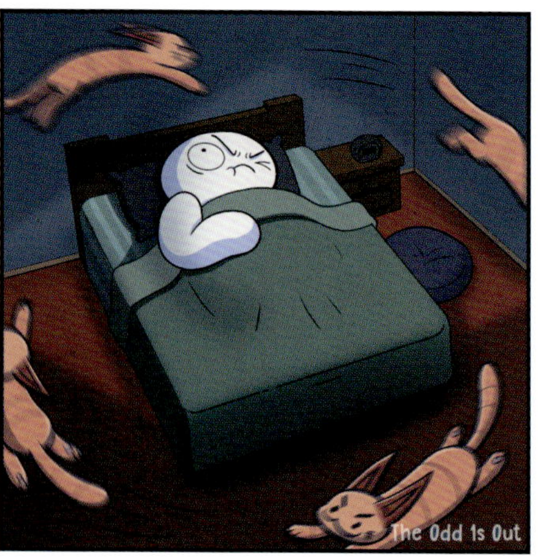

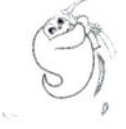

BIGFOOT

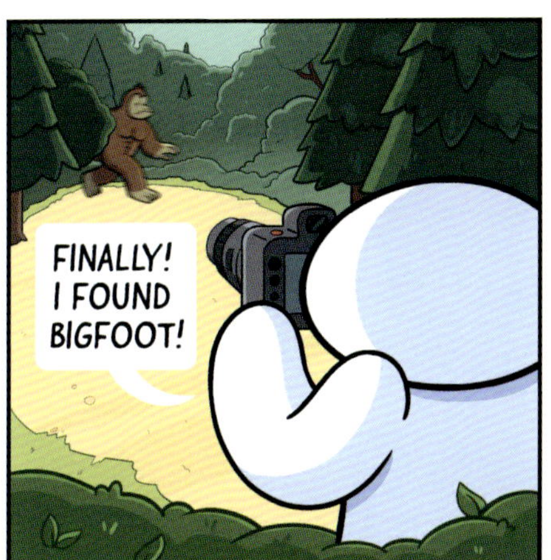
FINALLY!
I FOUND
BIGFOOT!

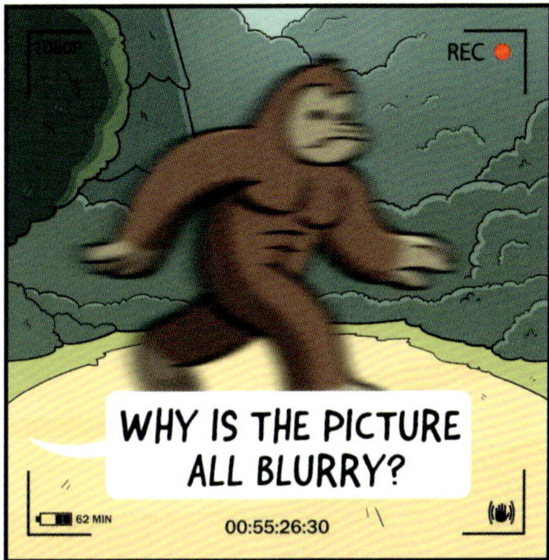
REC
WHY IS THE PICTURE
ALL BLURRY?
62 MIN
00:55:26:30

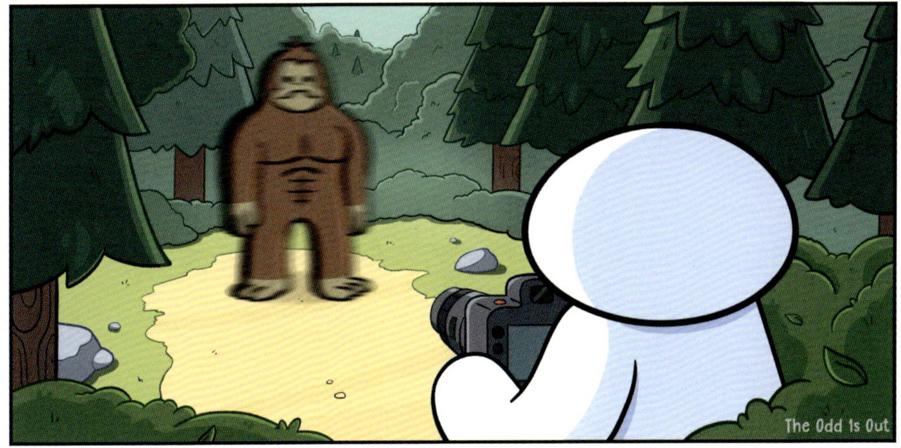
The Odd 1s Out

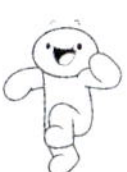

CHECKMATE

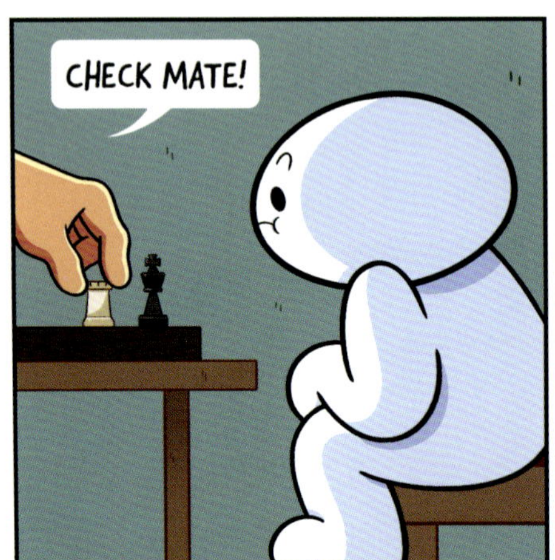
CHECK MATE!

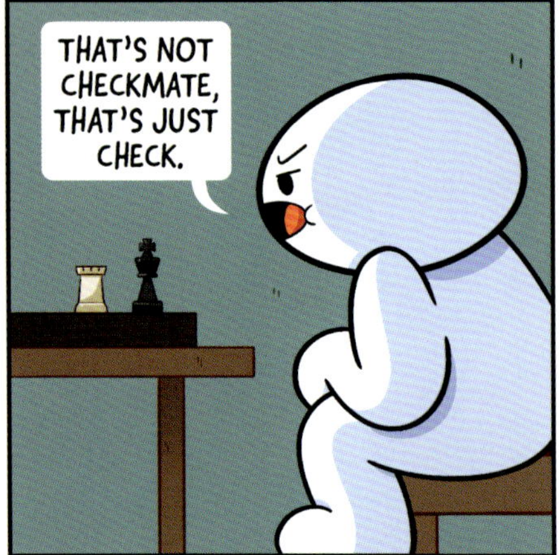
THAT'S NOT CHECKMATE, THAT'S JUST CHECK.

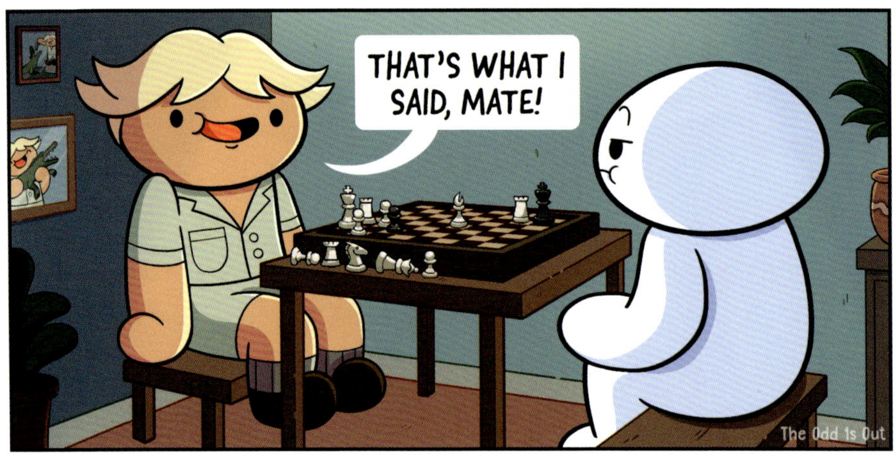
THAT'S WHAT I SAID, MATE!
The Odd 1s Out

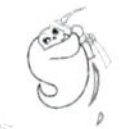

MULTIPLAYER GAME

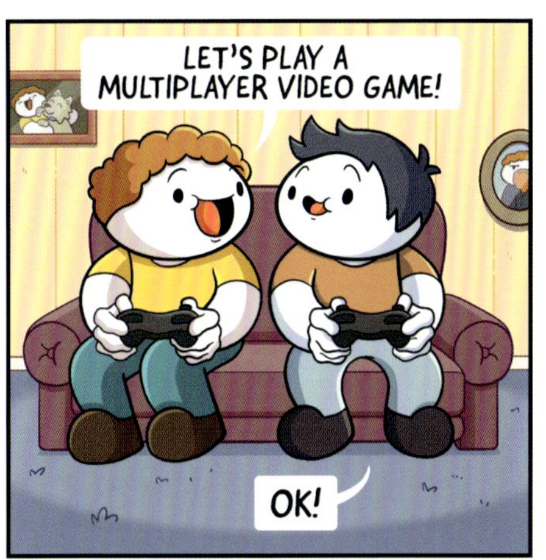

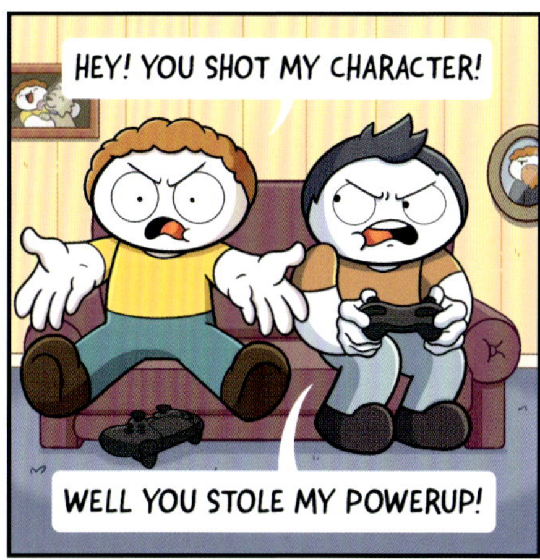

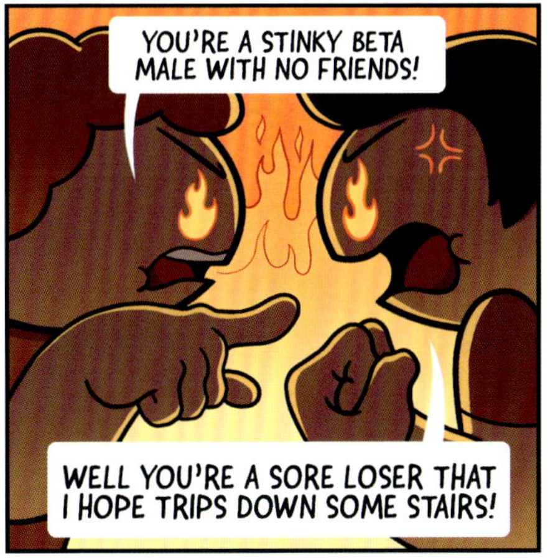

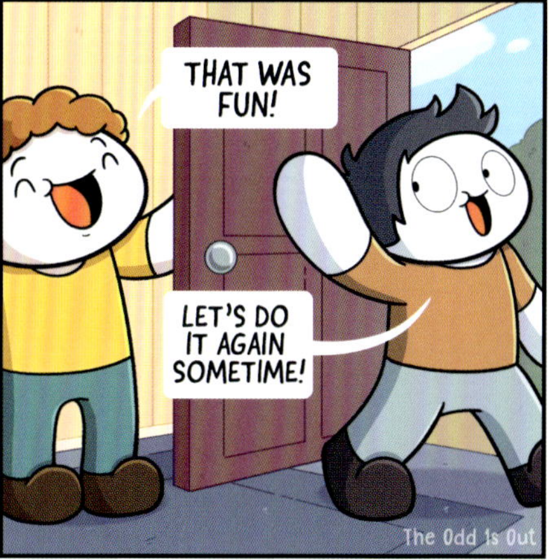

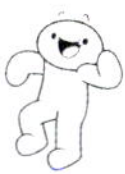

MUSIC

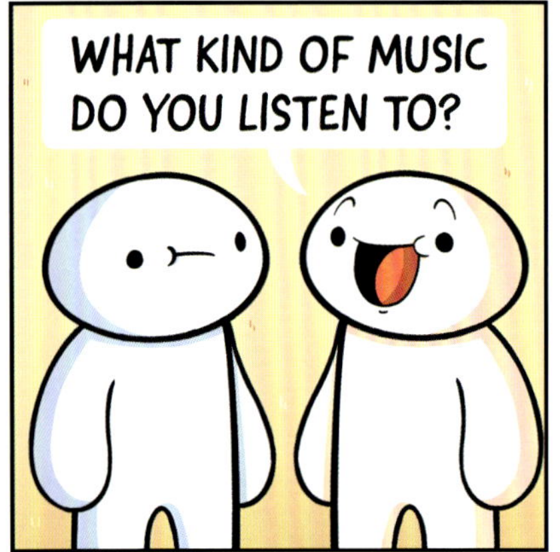

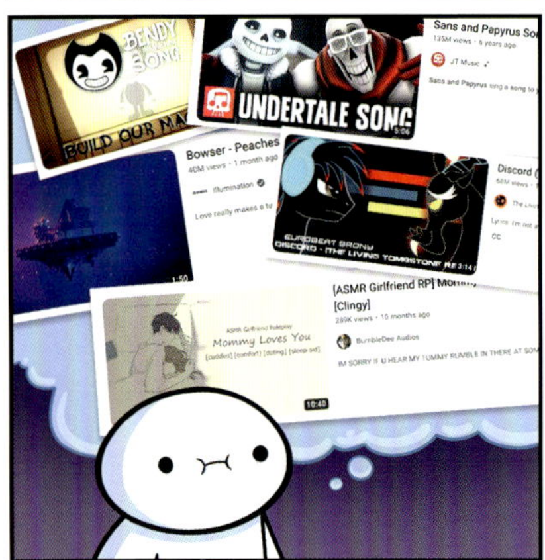

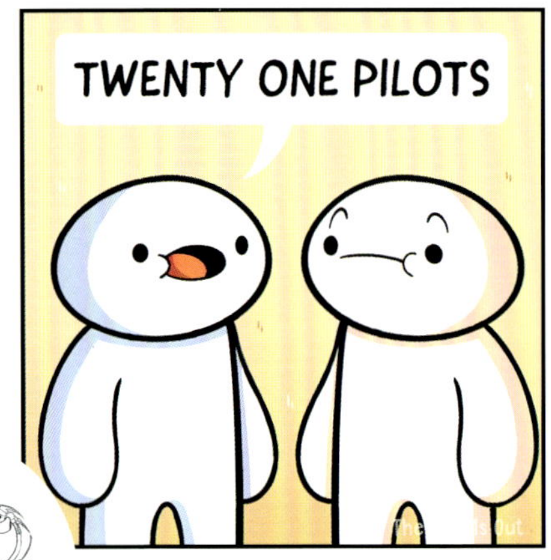

TEXTING WITHOUT EXCLAMATION POINTS

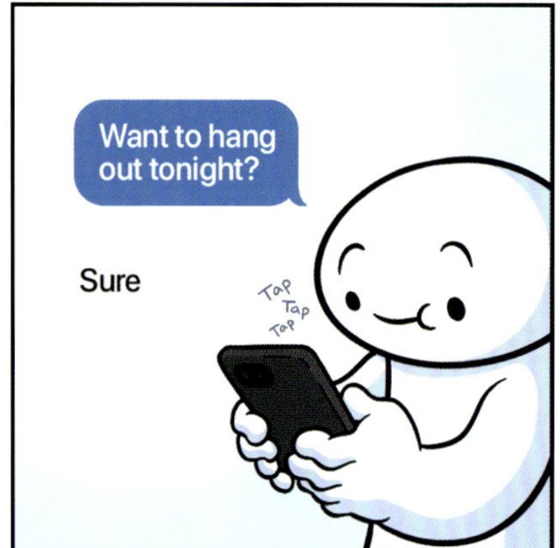

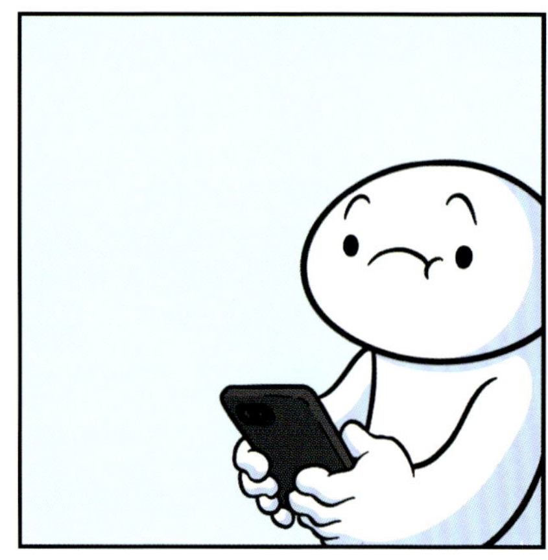

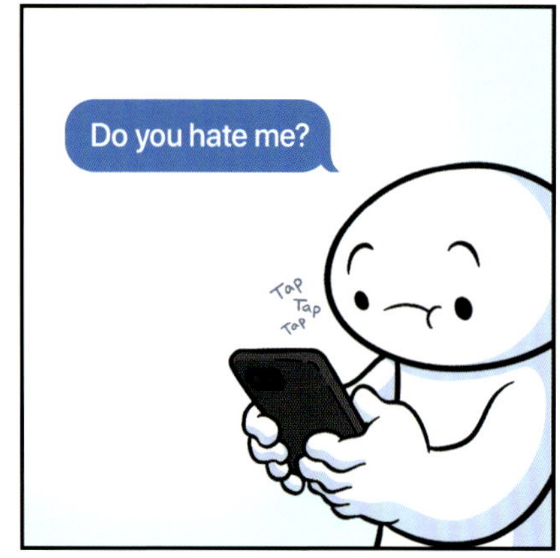

MONSTER UNDER THE BED

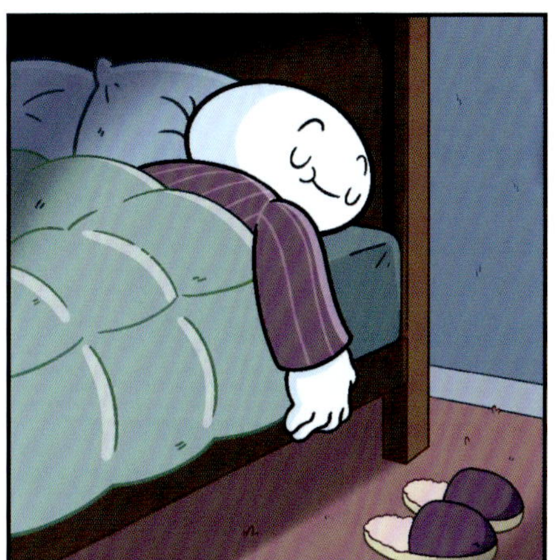

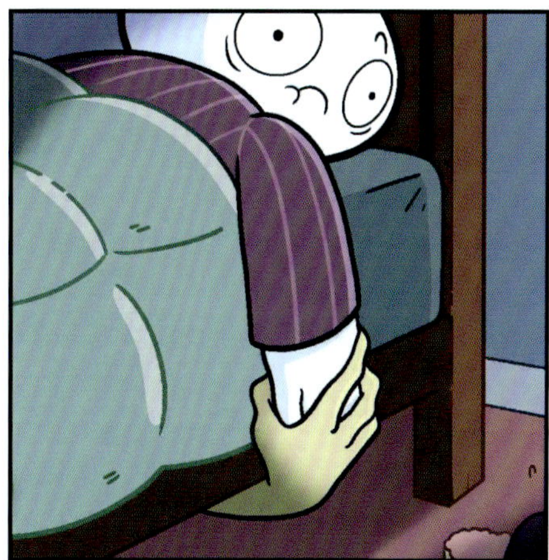

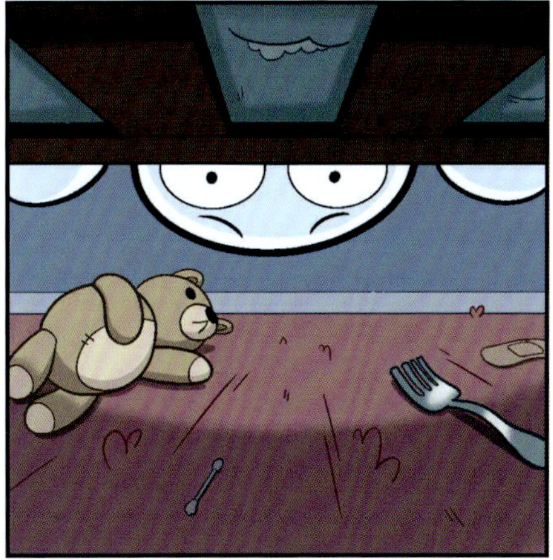

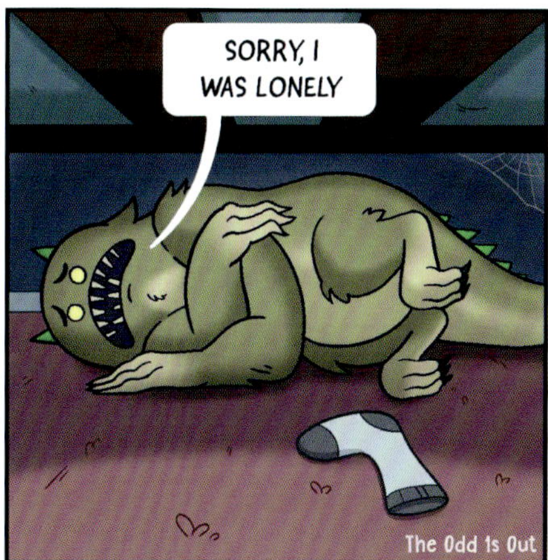

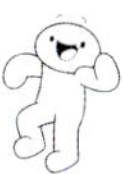

TOUGH GUY

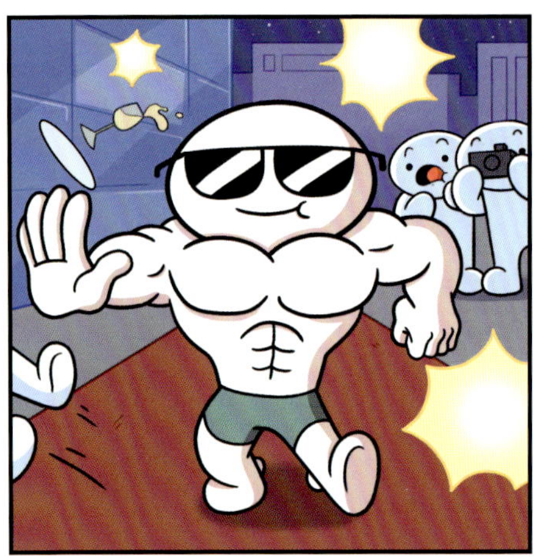

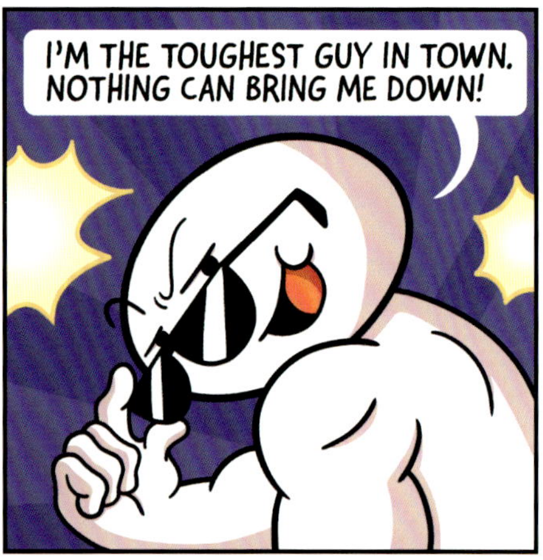
I'M THE TOUGHEST GUY IN TOWN. NOTHING CAN BRING ME DOWN!

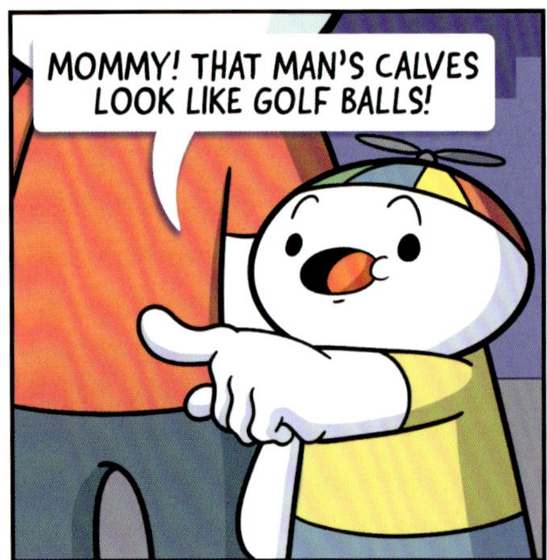
MOMMY! THAT MAN'S CALVES LOOK LIKE GOLF BALLS!

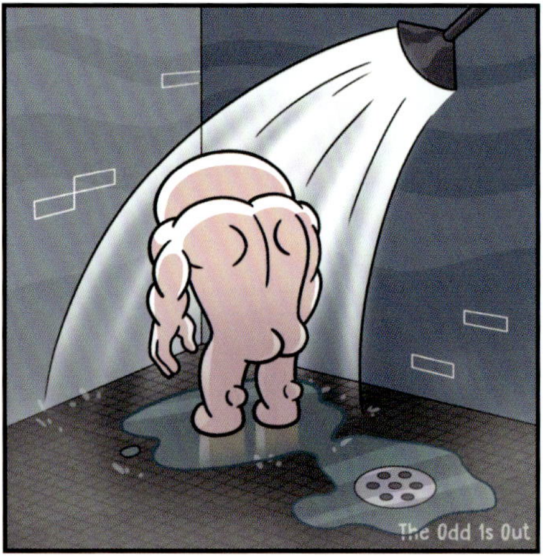
The Odd 1s Out

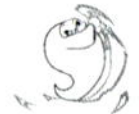

CHOKE

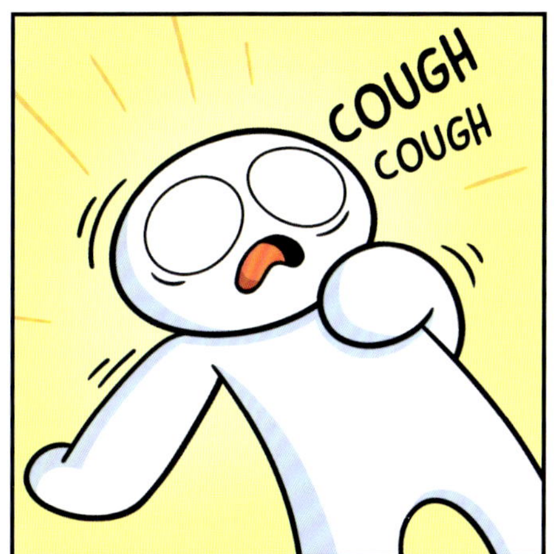
COUGH
COUGH

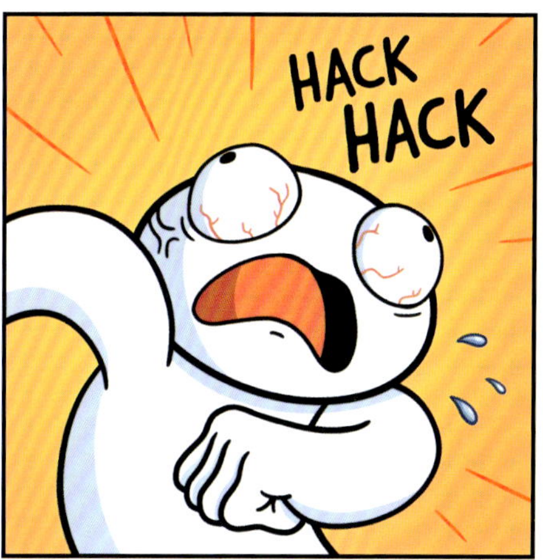
HACK
HACK

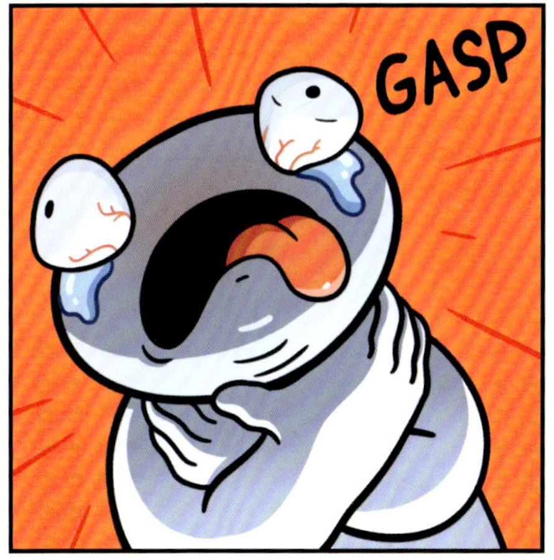
GASP

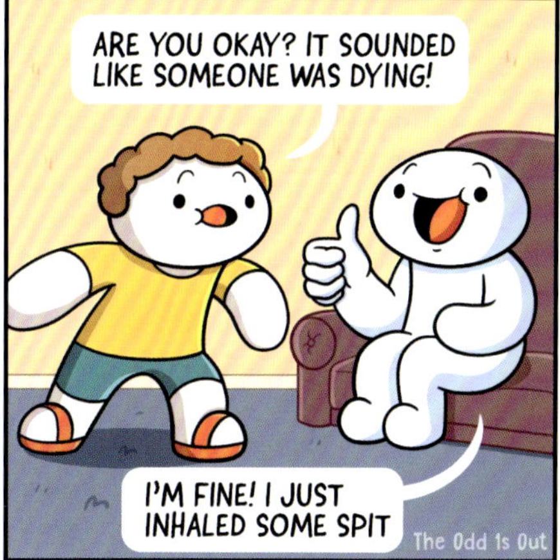
ARE YOU OKAY? IT SOUNDED LIKE SOMEONE WAS DYING!
I'M FINE! I JUST INHALED SOME SPIT
The Odd 1s Out

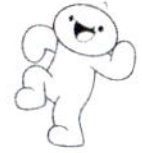

CHIPS

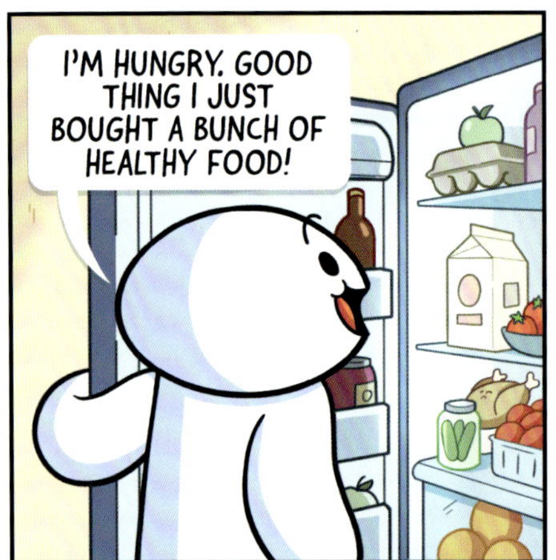
I'M HUNGRY. GOOD THING I JUST BOUGHT A BUNCH OF HEALTHY FOOD!

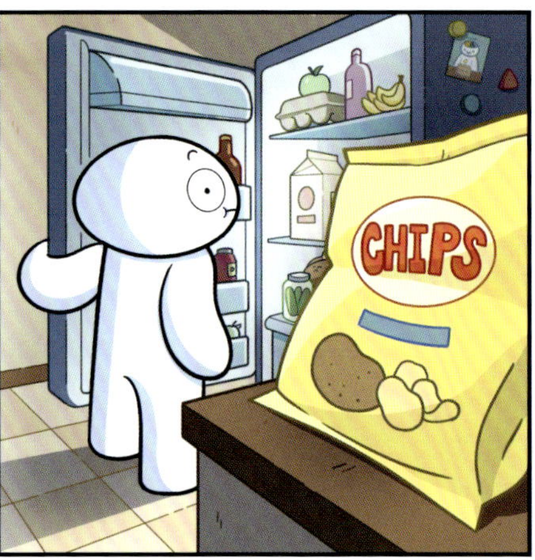
CHIPS

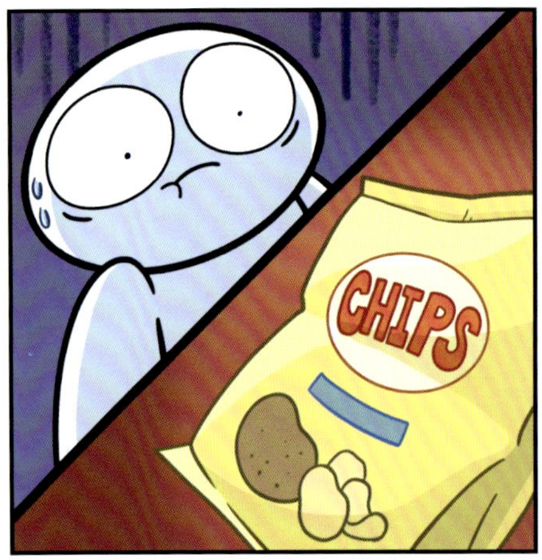
CHIPS

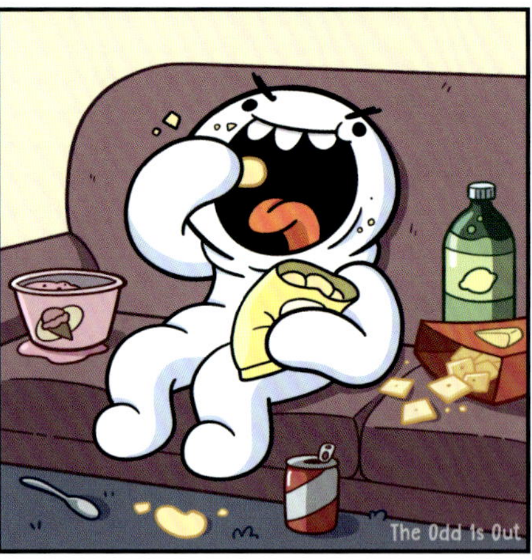
The Odd 1s Out

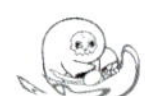

HAVE A BITE

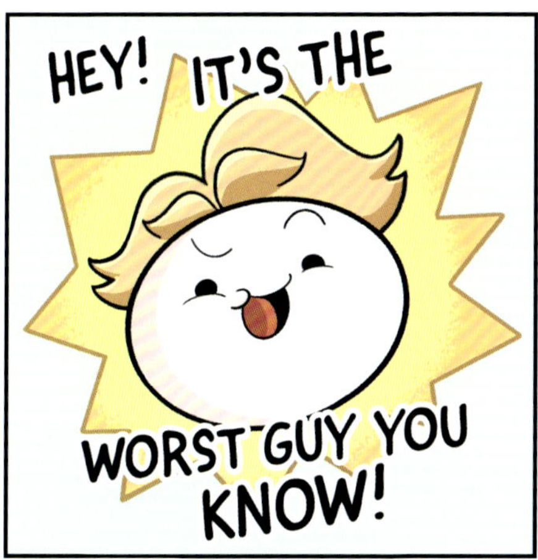

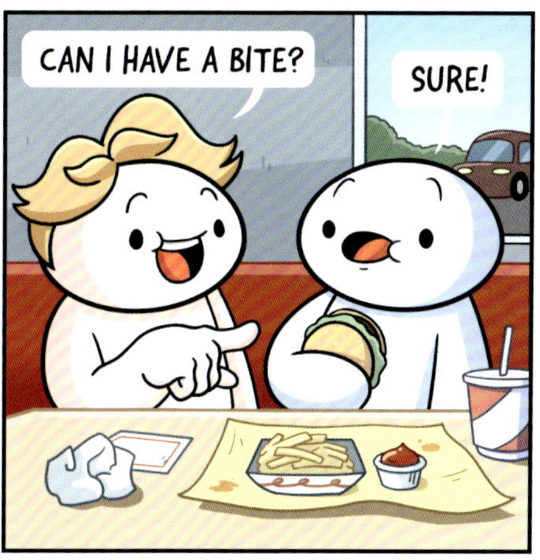

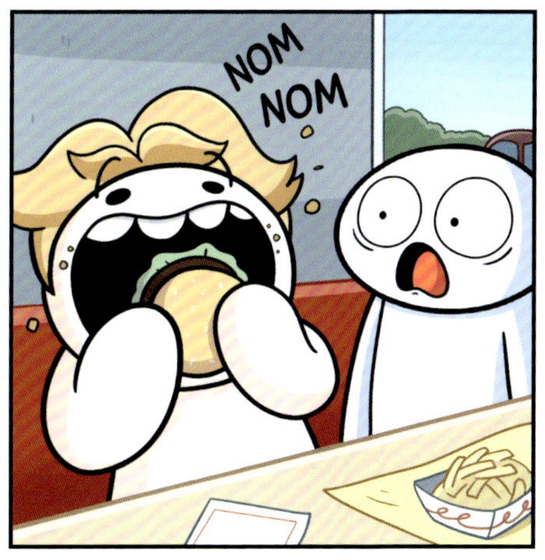

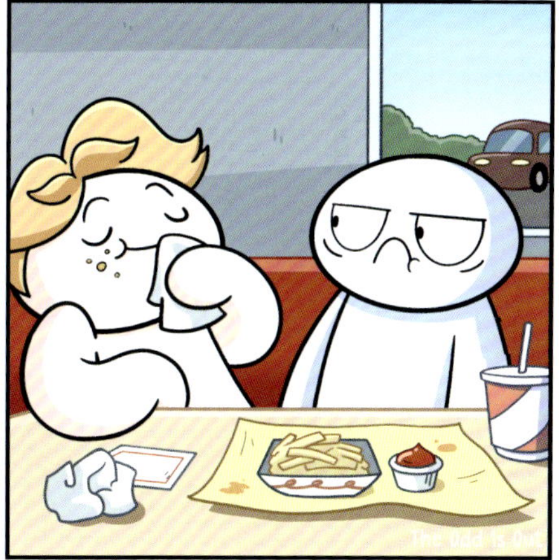

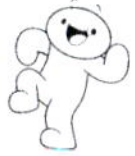

GRIMACE

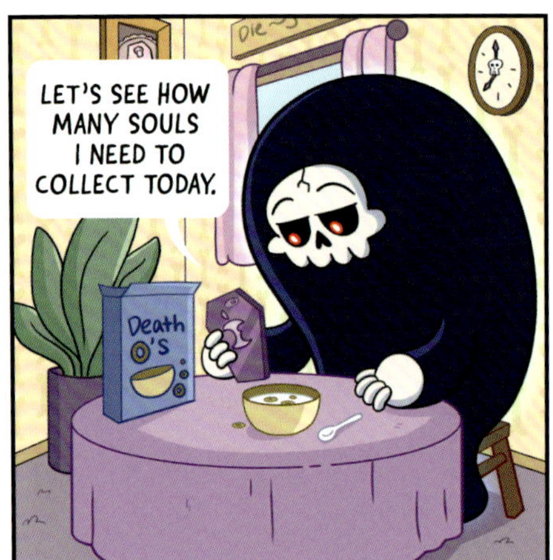
LET'S SEE HOW MANY SOULS I NEED TO COLLECT TODAY.
Death O's

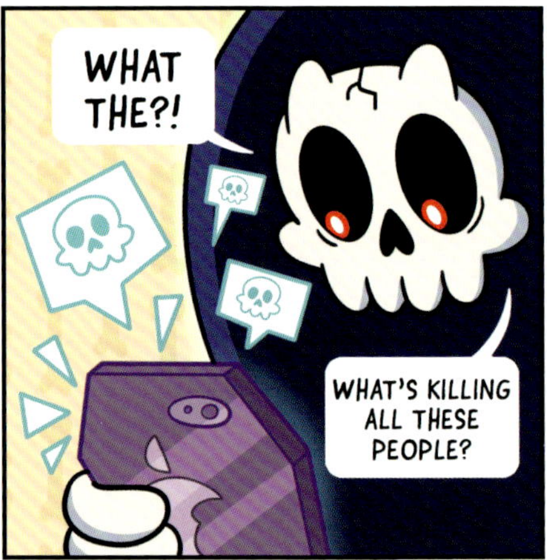
WHAT THE?!
WHAT'S KILLING ALL THESE PEOPLE?

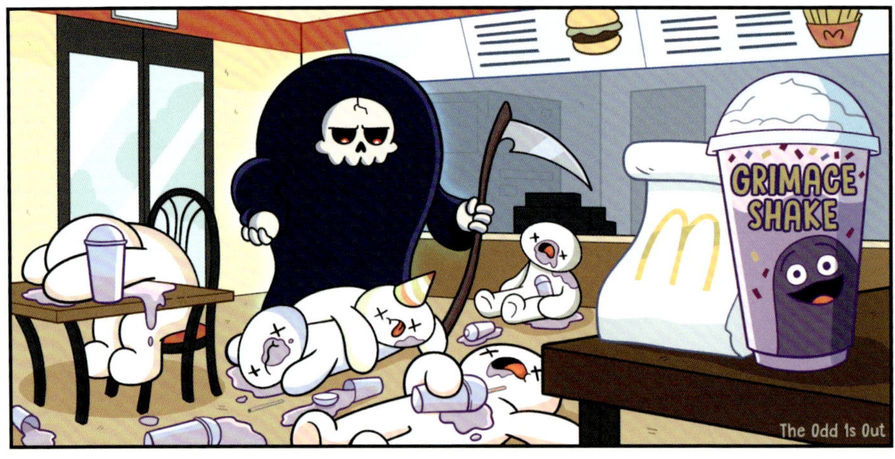
GRIMACE SHAKE
The Odd 1s Out

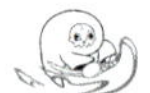

RETIRE

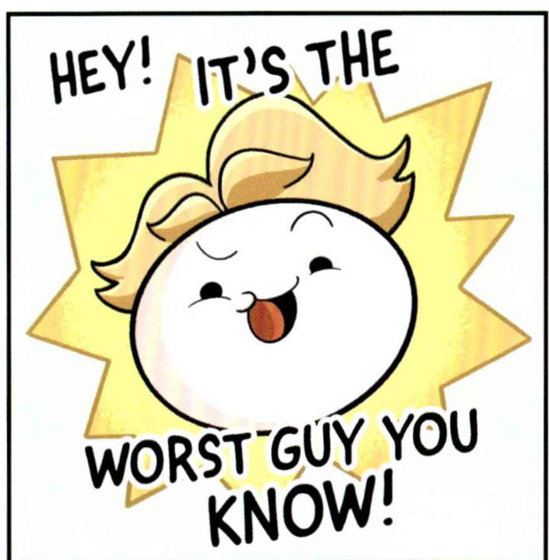
HEY! IT'S THE
WORST GUY YOU KNOW!

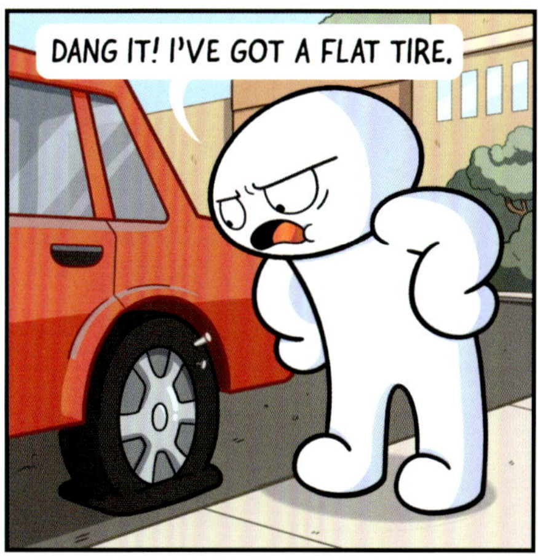
DANG IT! I'VE GOT A FLAT TIRE.

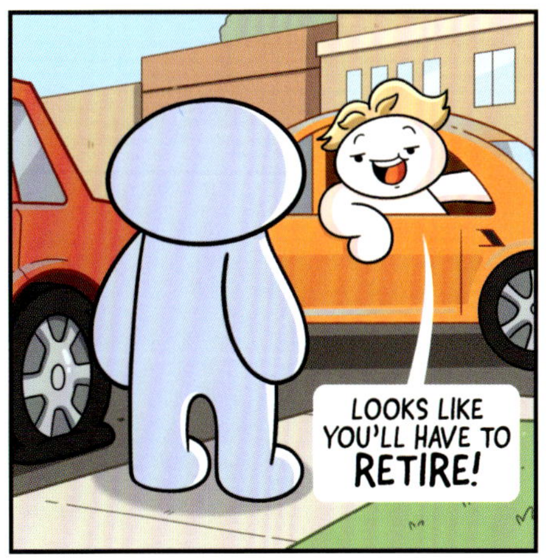
LOOKS LIKE YOU'LL HAVE TO RETIRE!

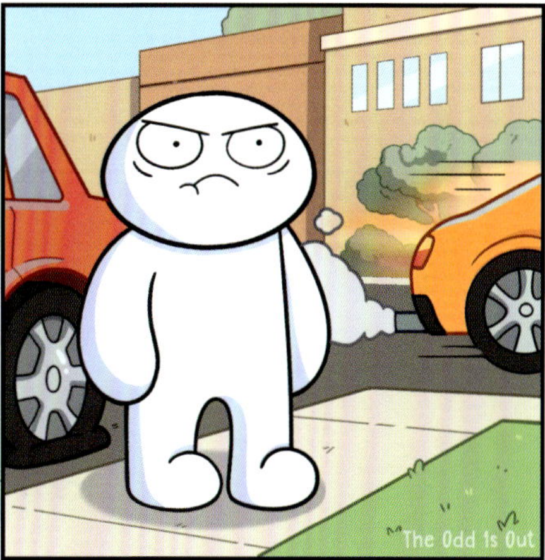
The Odd 1s Out

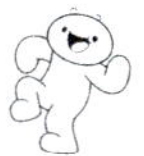

SPIDER

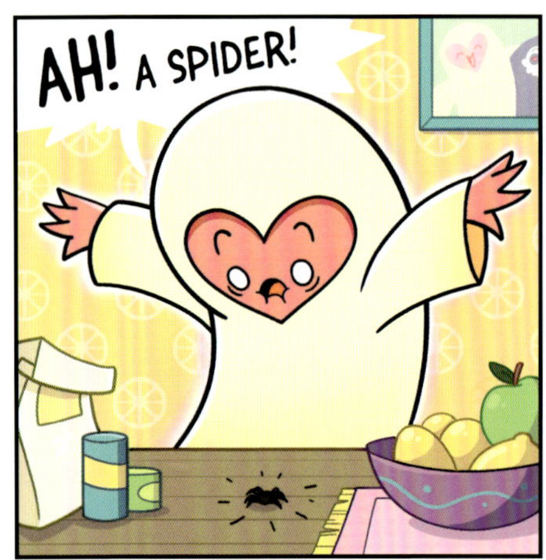

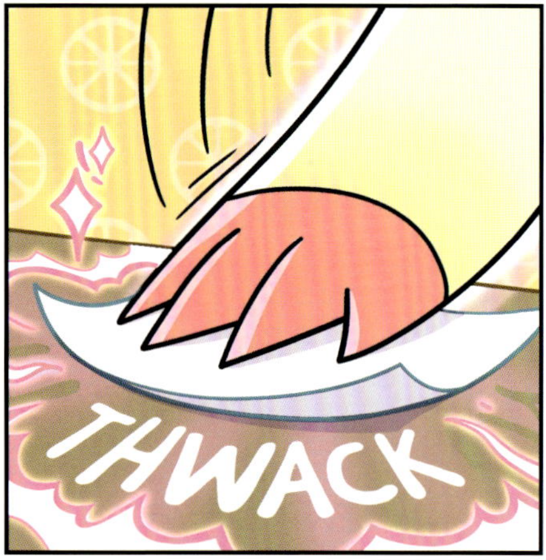

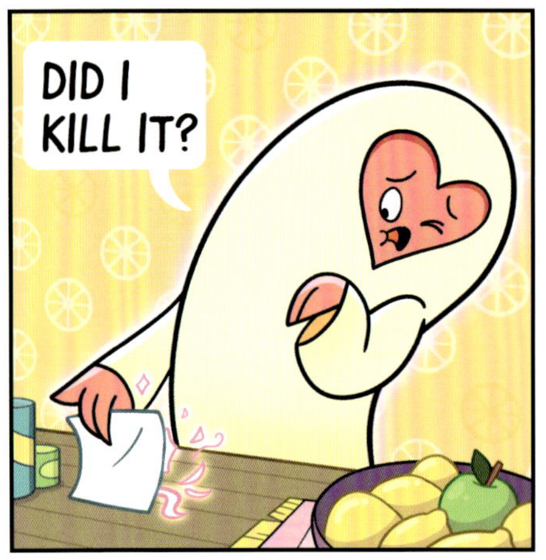

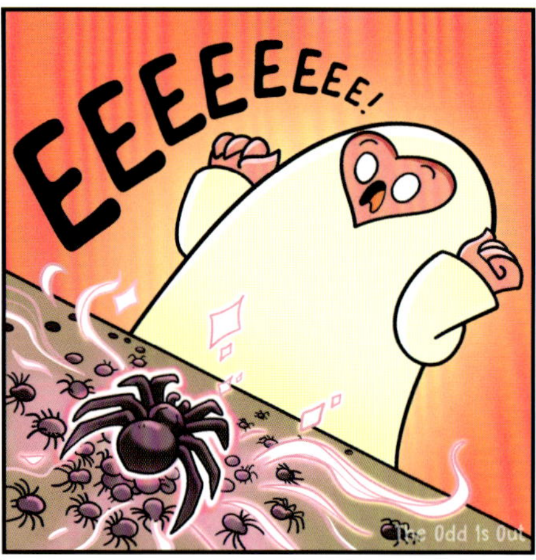

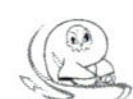

MEETING "NEW" PEOPLE

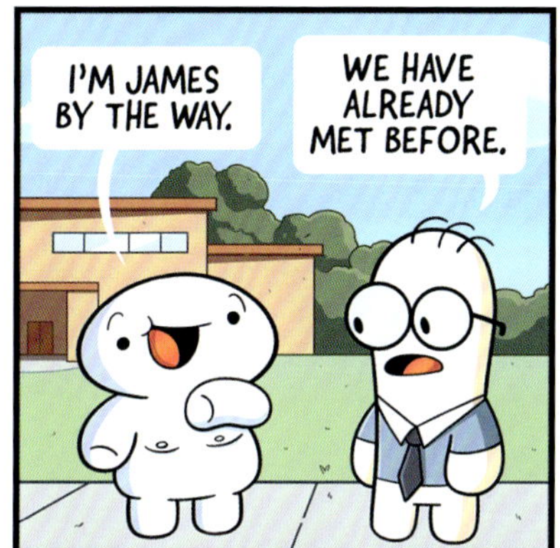

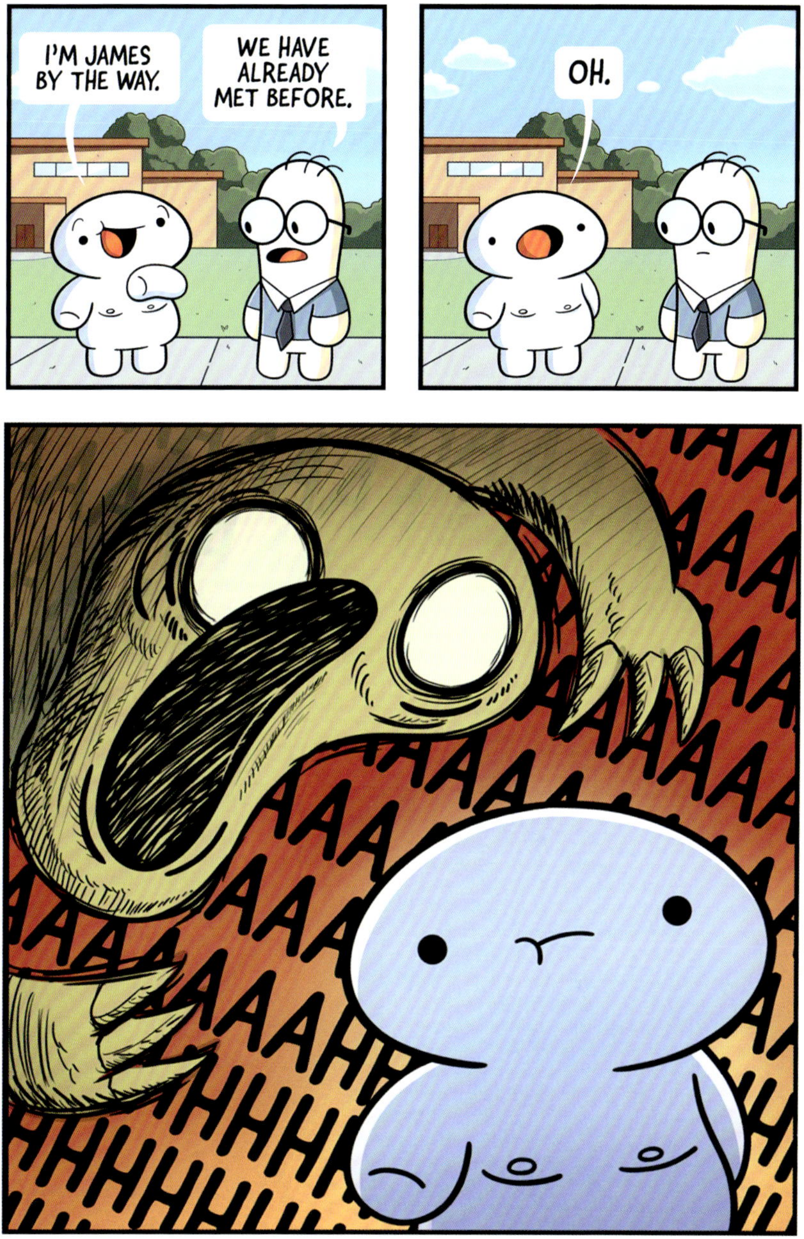

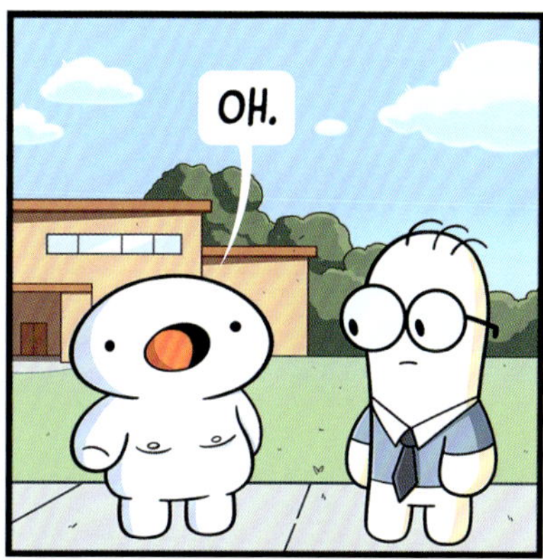

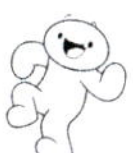

LEAF

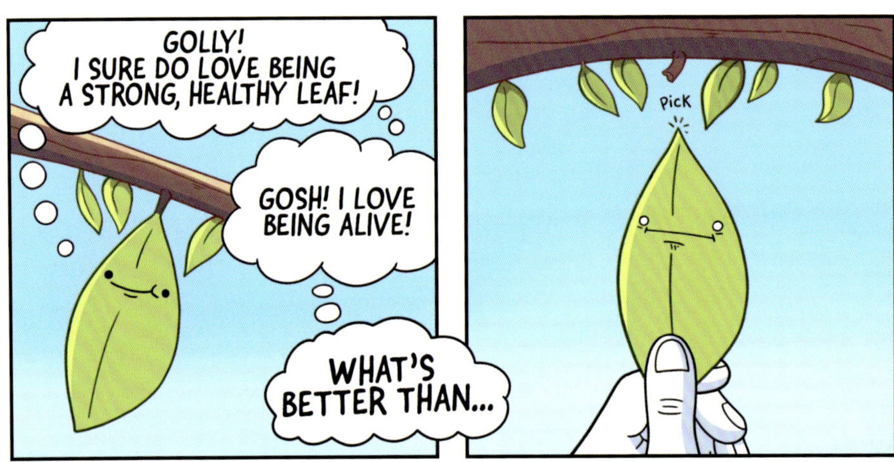
GOLLY!
I SURE DO LOVE BEING
A STRONG, HEALTHY LEAF!
GOSH! I LOVE
BEING ALIVE!
WHAT'S
BETTER THAN...
PICK

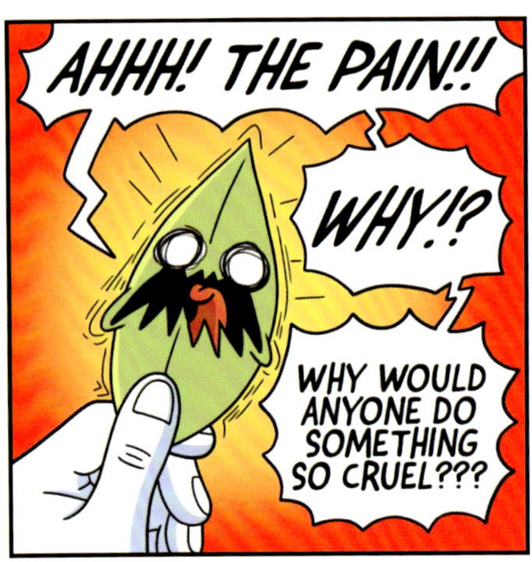
AHHH! THE PAIN!!
WHY!?
WHY WOULD
ANYONE DO
SOMETHING
SO CRUEL???

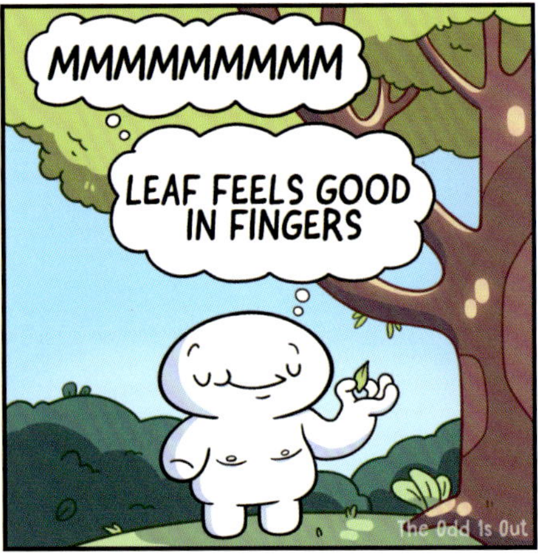
MMMMMMMMM
LEAF FEELS GOOD
IN FINGERS
The Odd 1s Out

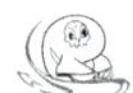

DECORATIONS

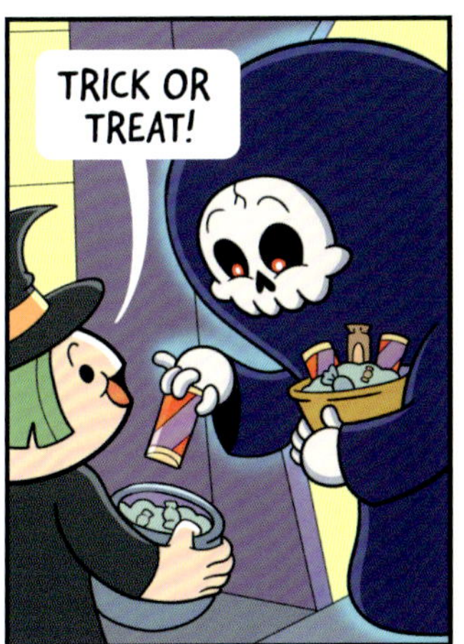

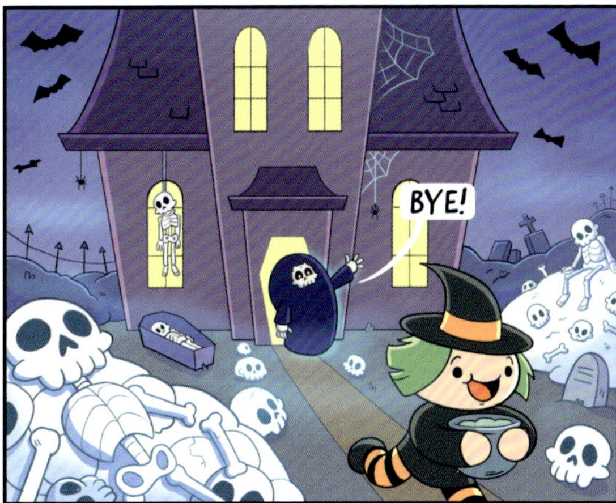

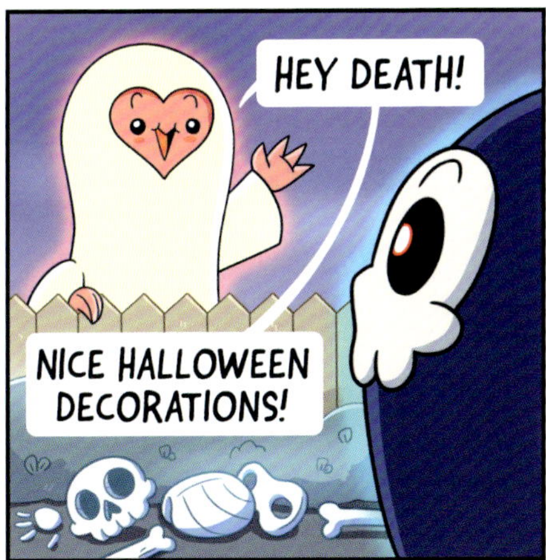

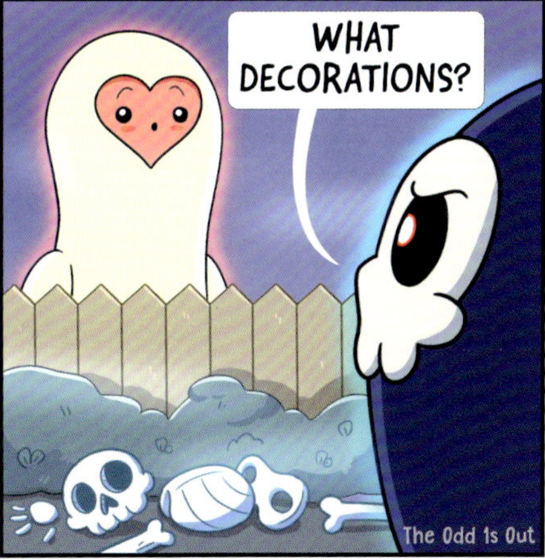

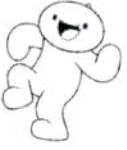

EAVESDROPPING

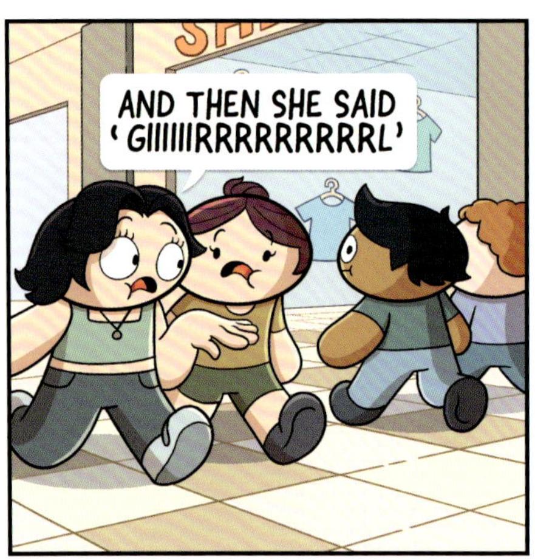

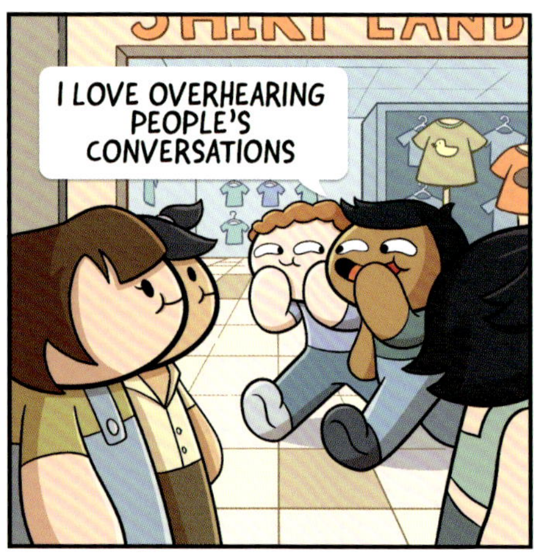

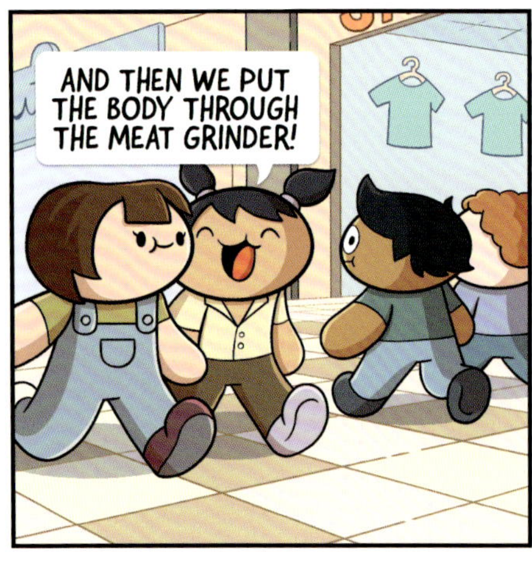

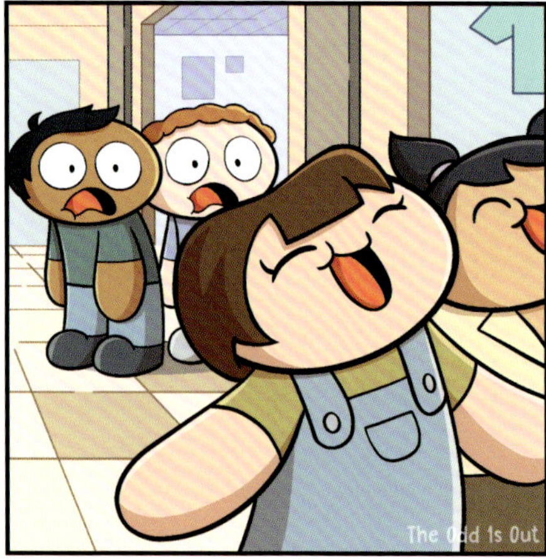

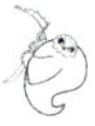

HEADLESS

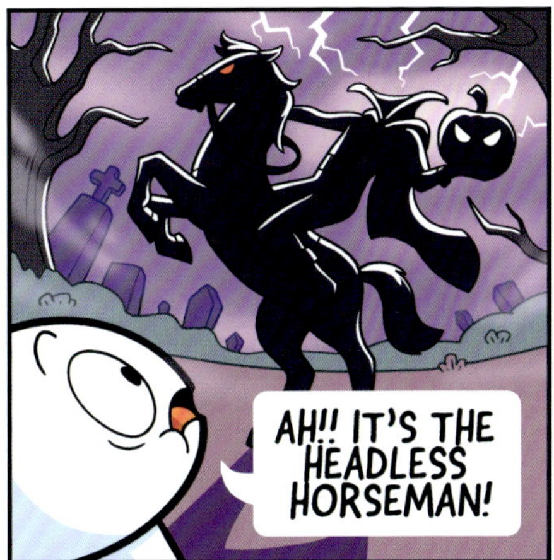
AH!! IT'S THE HEADLESS HORSEMAN!

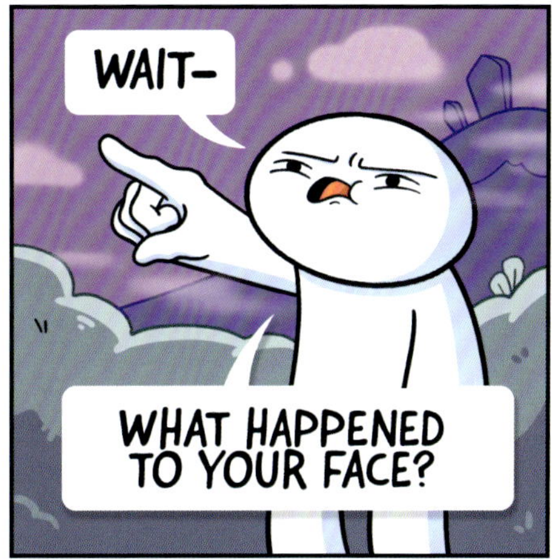
WAIT-
WHAT HAPPENED TO YOUR FACE?

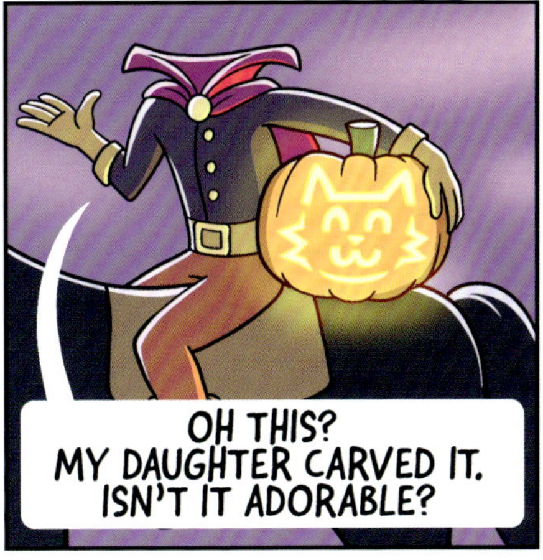
OH THIS? MY DAUGHTER CARVED IT. ISN'T IT ADORABLE?

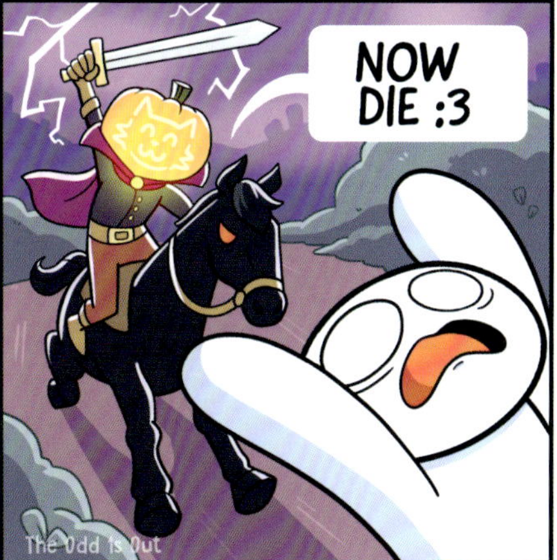
NOW DIE :3
The Odd 1s Out

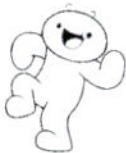

BUSY

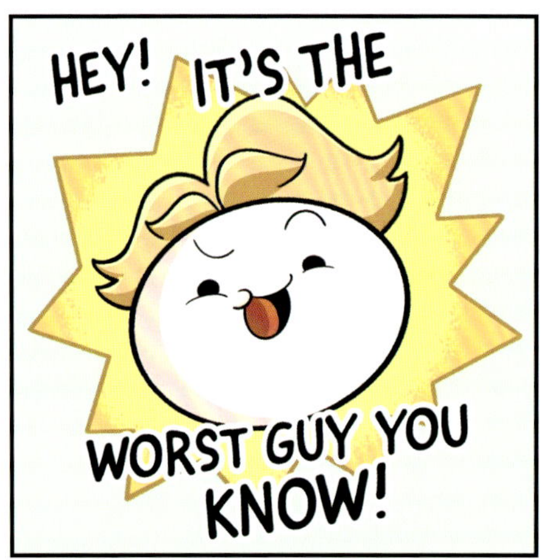
HEY! IT'S THE
WORST GUY YOU KNOW!

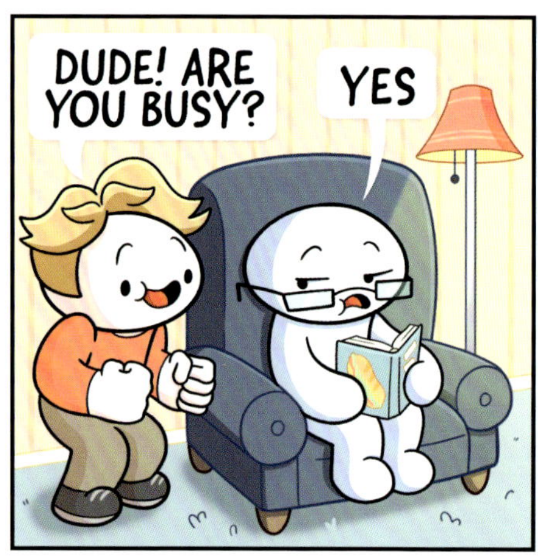
DUDE! ARE YOU BUSY?
YES

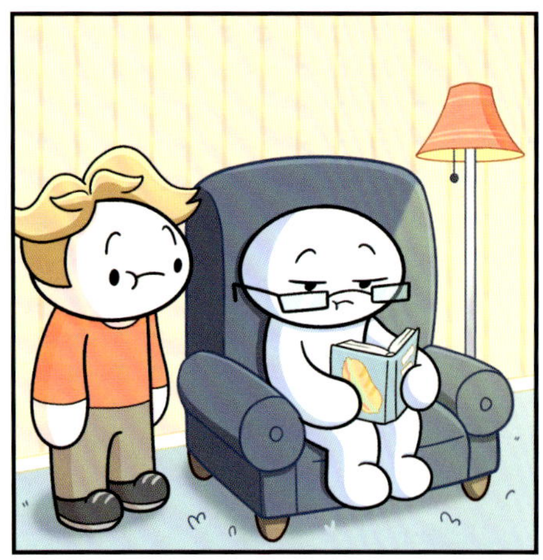

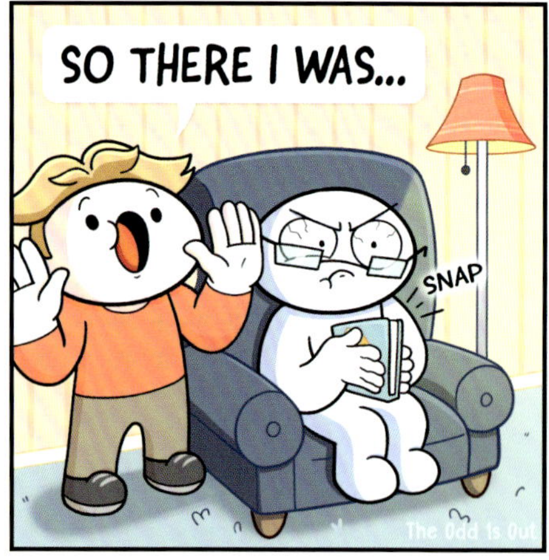
SO THERE I WAS...
SNAP
The Odd 1s Out

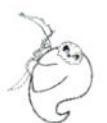

CARAMEL

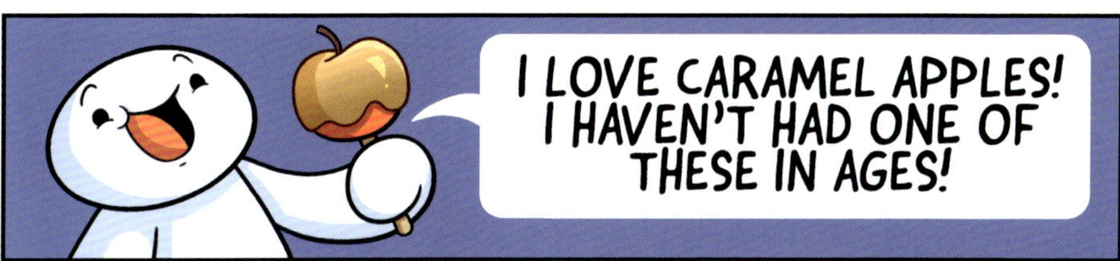
I LOVE CARAMEL APPLES! I HAVEN'T HAD ONE OF THESE IN AGES!

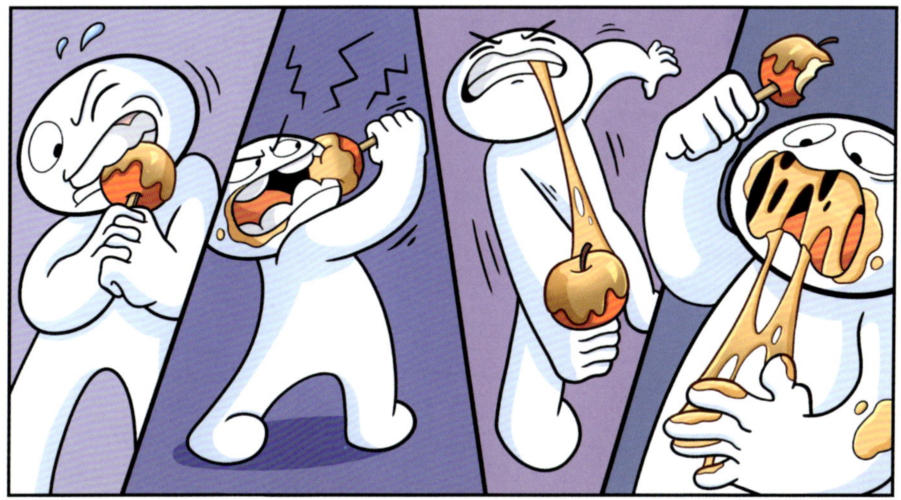

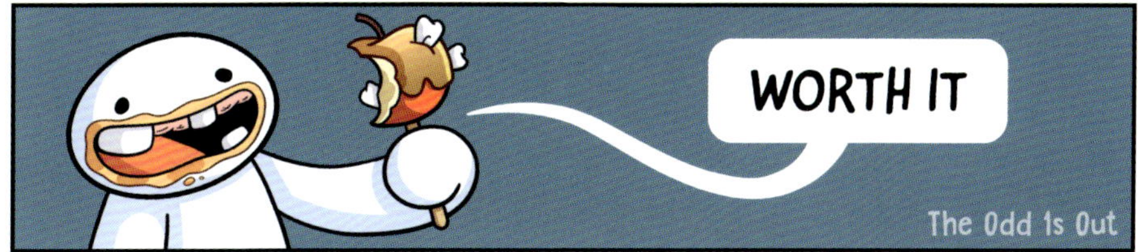
WORTH IT
The Odd 1s Out

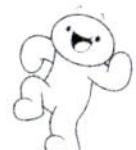

NOVEMBER 1ST

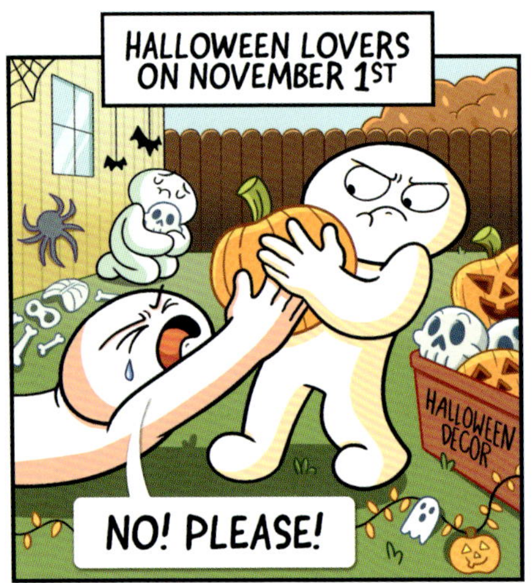

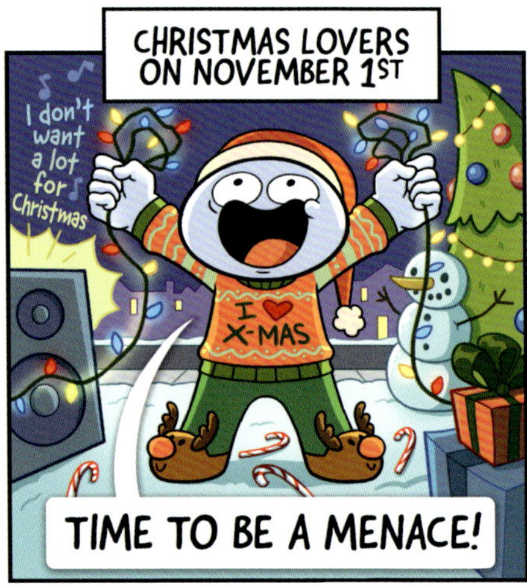

HAND TURKEY

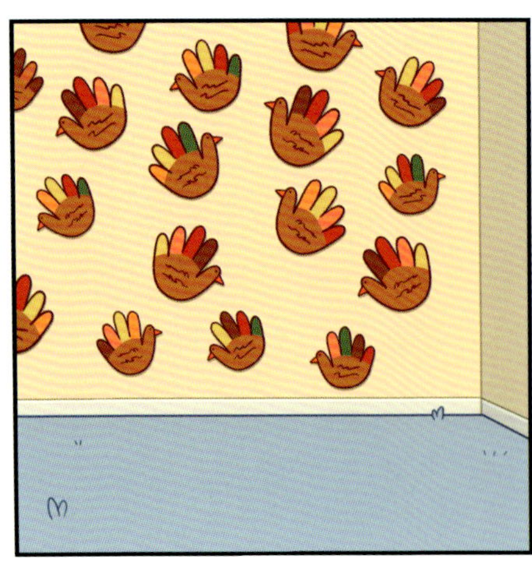

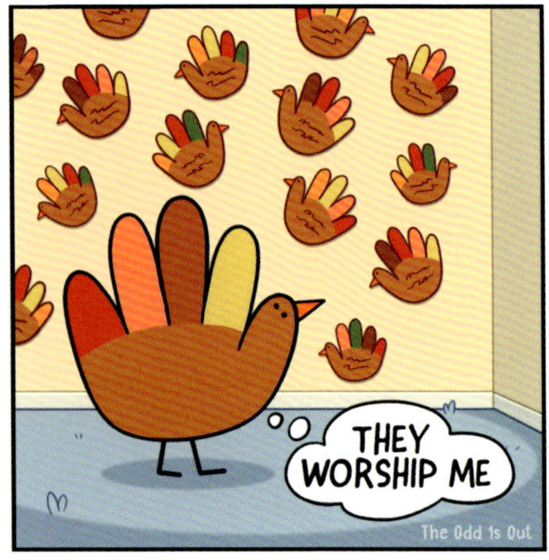

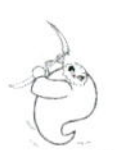

BUNDLED UP

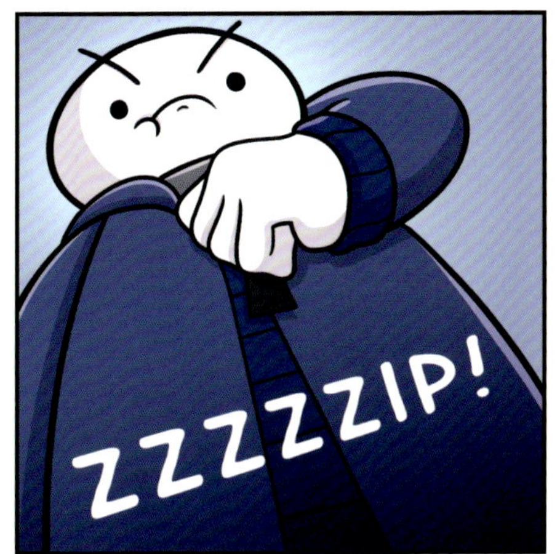
ZZZZZZIP!

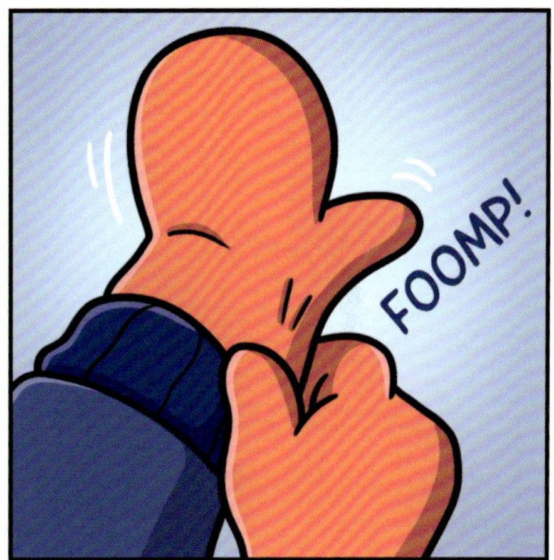
FOOMP!

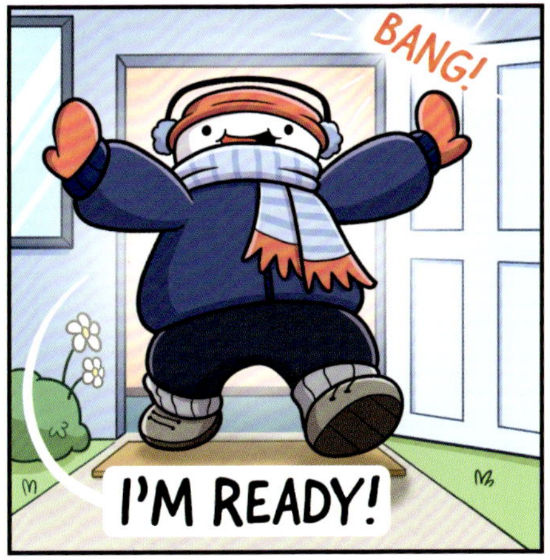
BANG!
I'M READY!

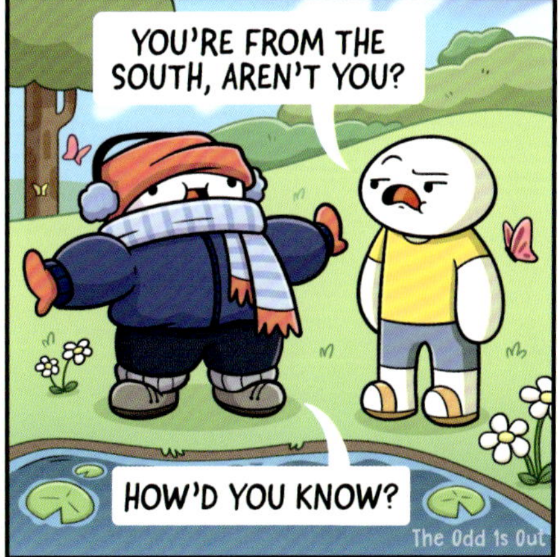
YOU'RE FROM THE SOUTH, AREN'T YOU?
HOW'D YOU KNOW?
The Odd 1s Out

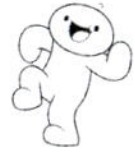

POLAR EXPRESS

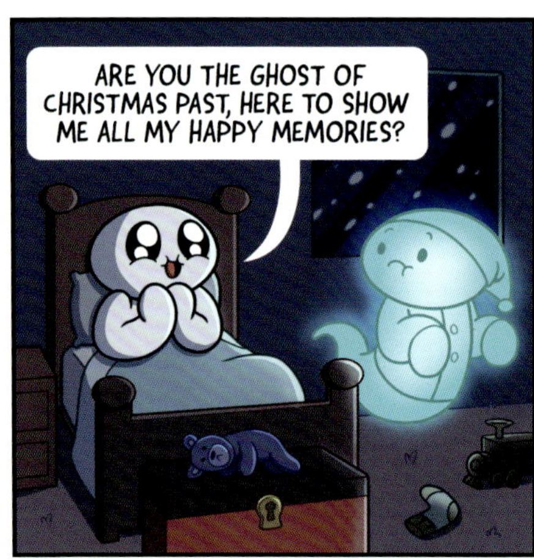

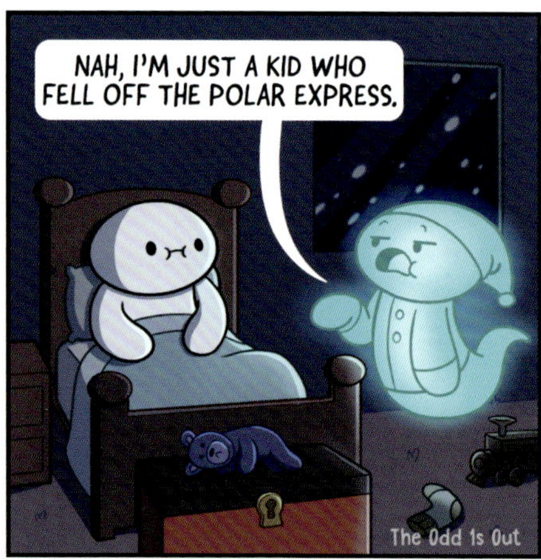

JOBS

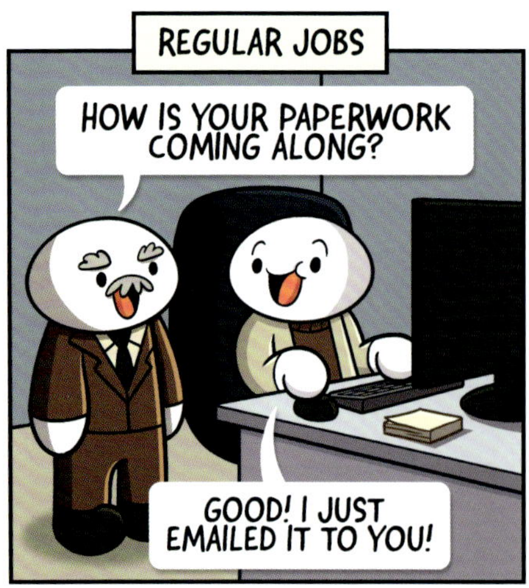

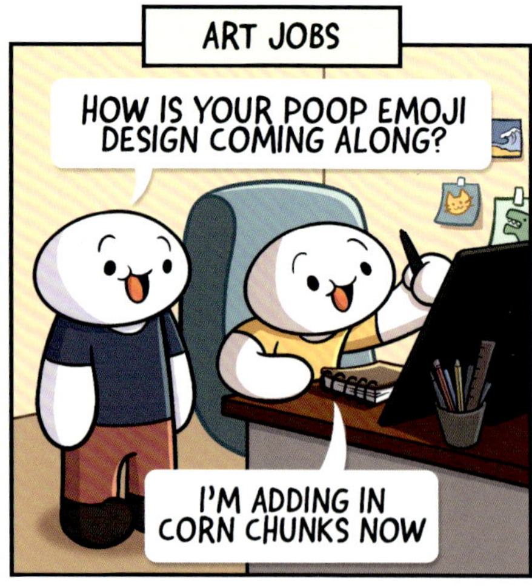

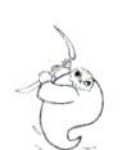

SANTA?

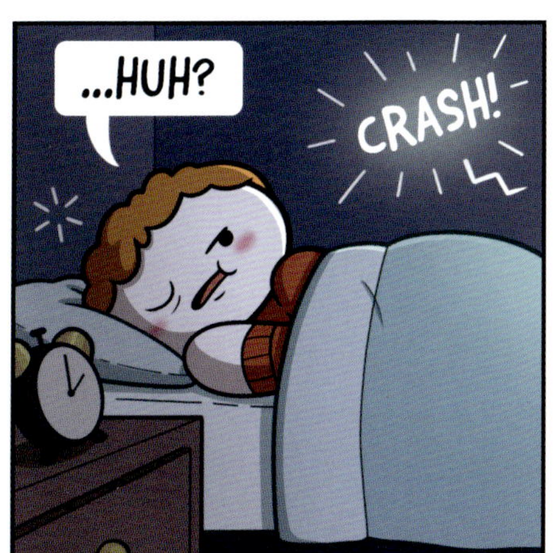

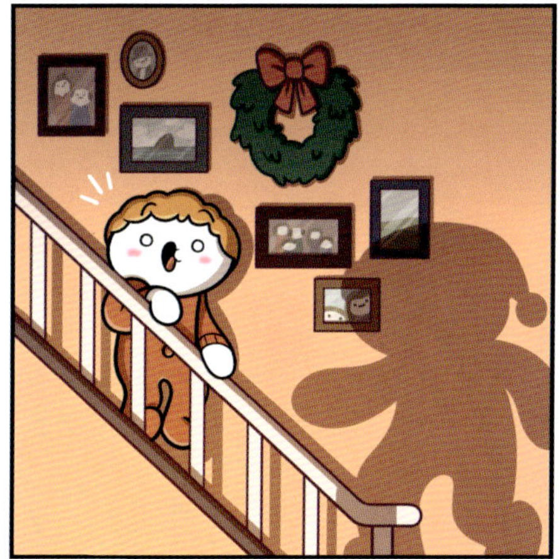

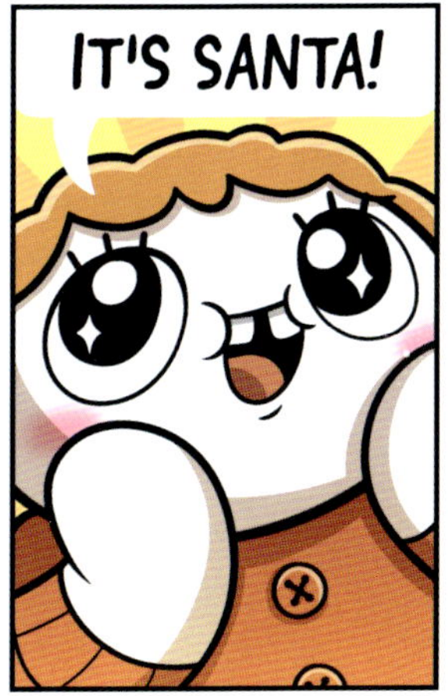

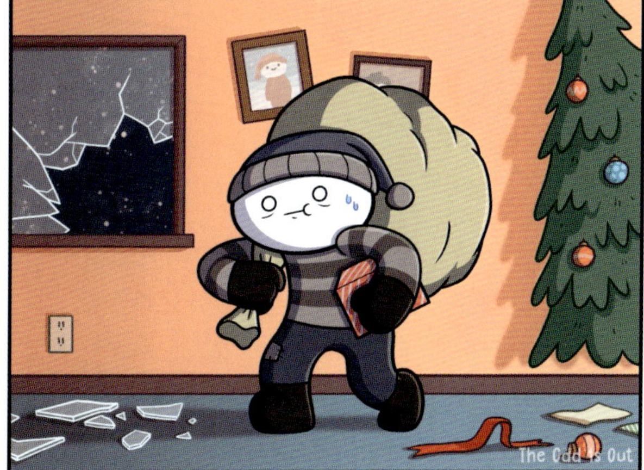

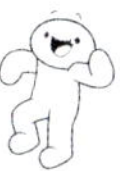

KRISPY KRINGLE

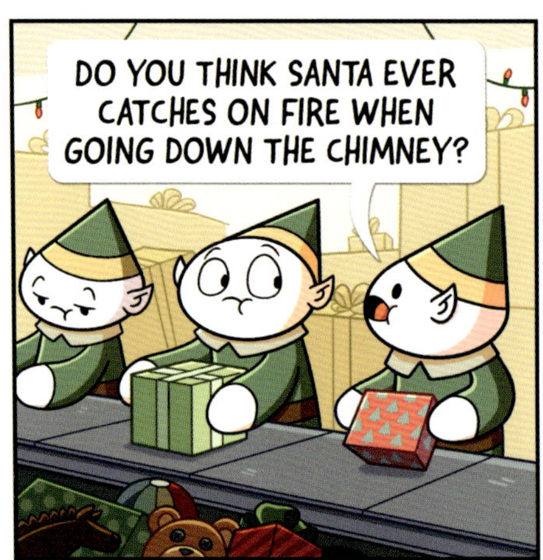

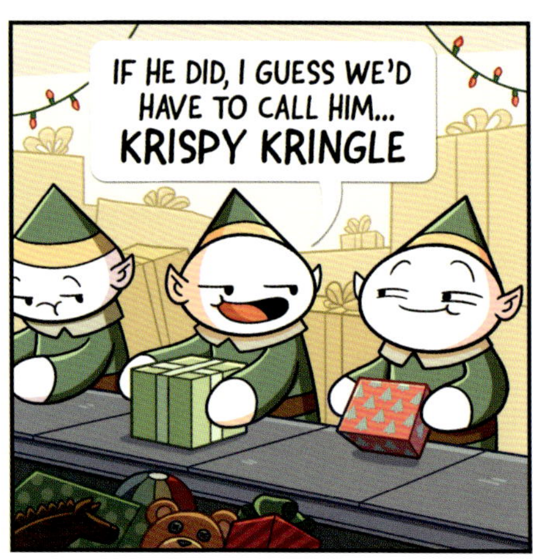

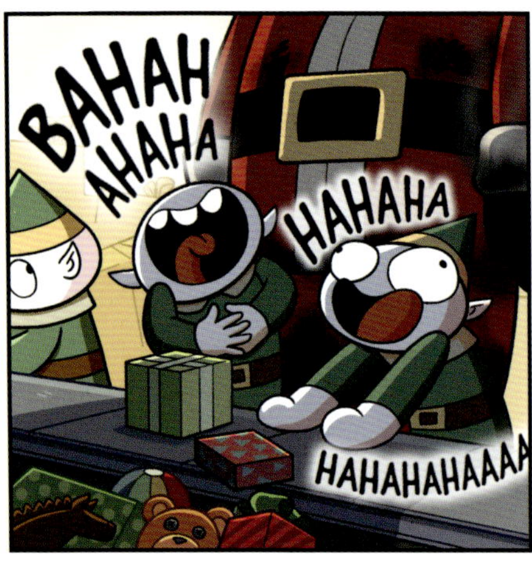

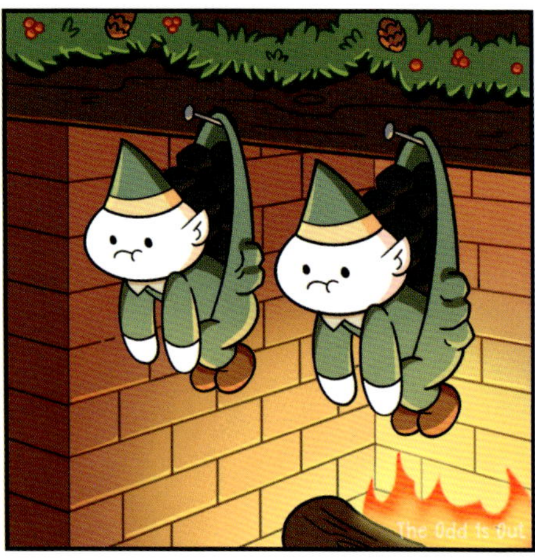

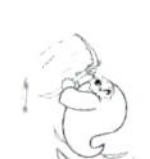

WORK OF ART

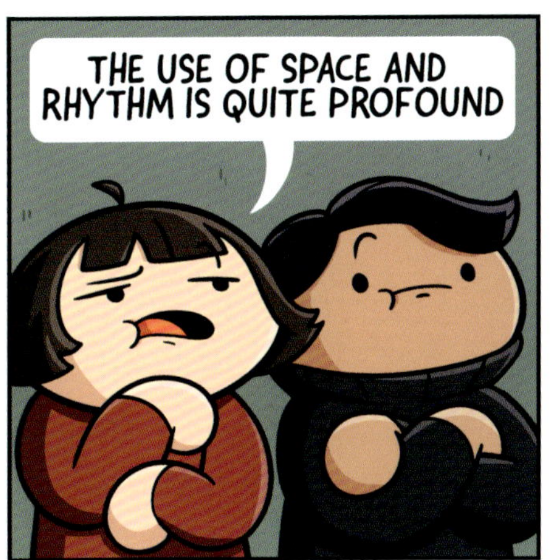
THE USE OF SPACE AND RHYTHM IS QUITE PROFOUND

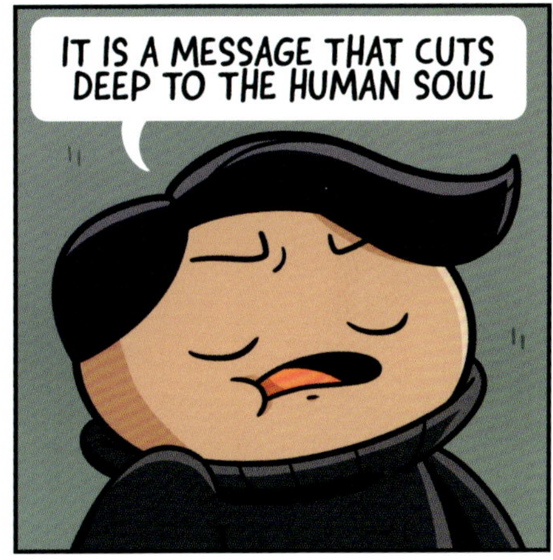
IT IS A MESSAGE THAT CUTS DEEP TO THE HUMAN SOUL

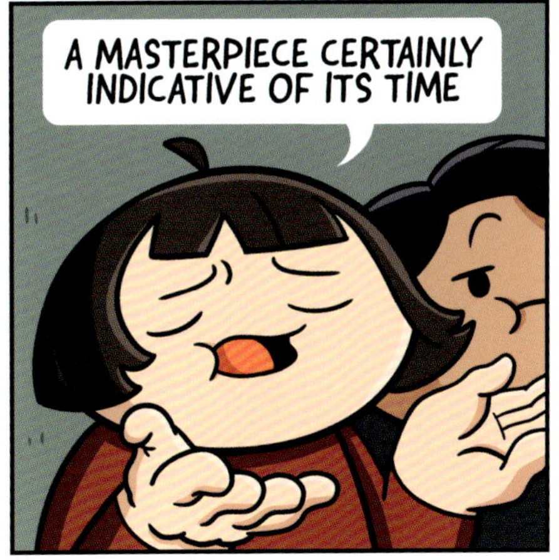
A MASTERPIECE CERTAINLY INDICATIVE OF ITS TIME

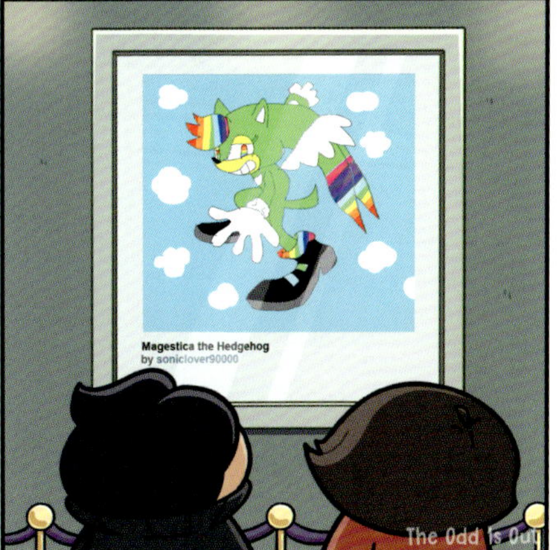
Magestica the Hedgehog
by soniclover90000
The Odd 1s Out

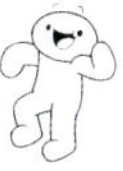

WEREWOLF

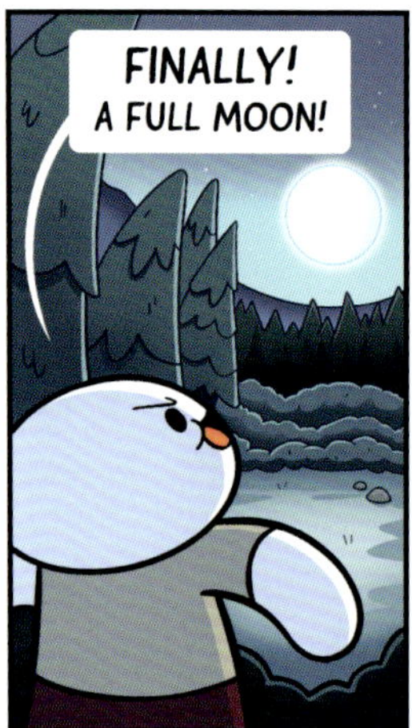
FINALLY!
A FULL MOON!

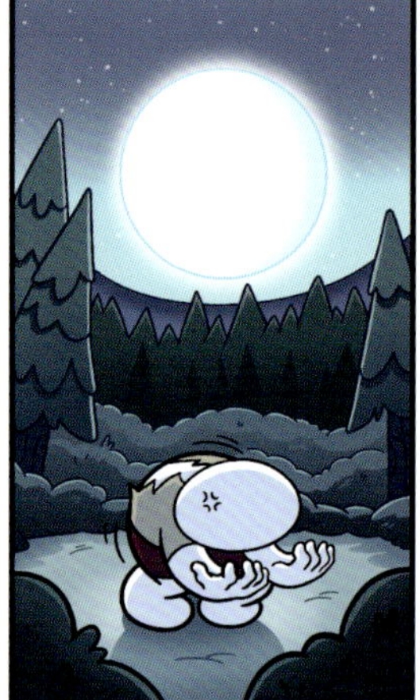

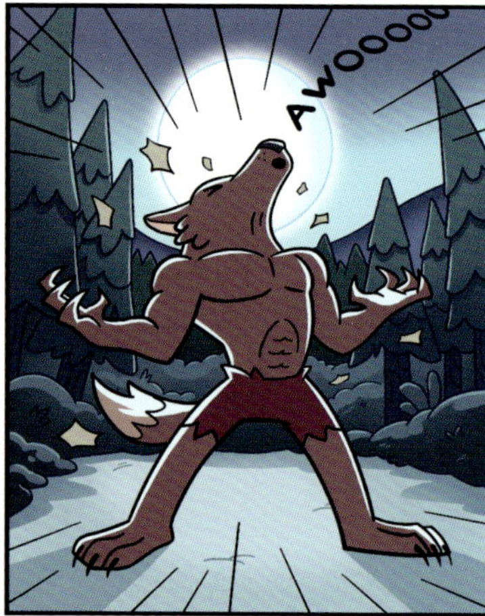
AWOOOOO

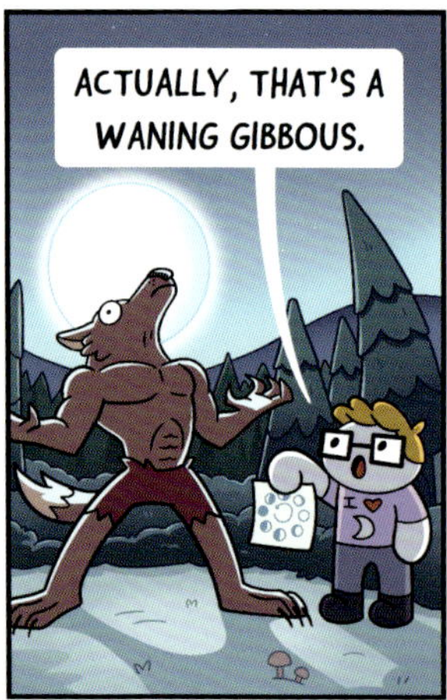
ACTUALLY, THAT'S A WANING GIBBOUS.

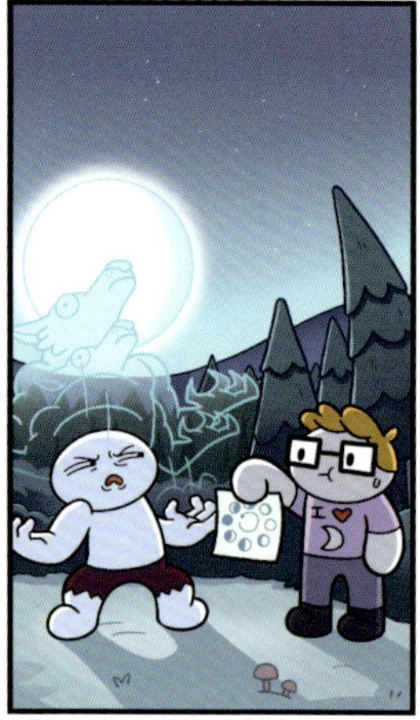

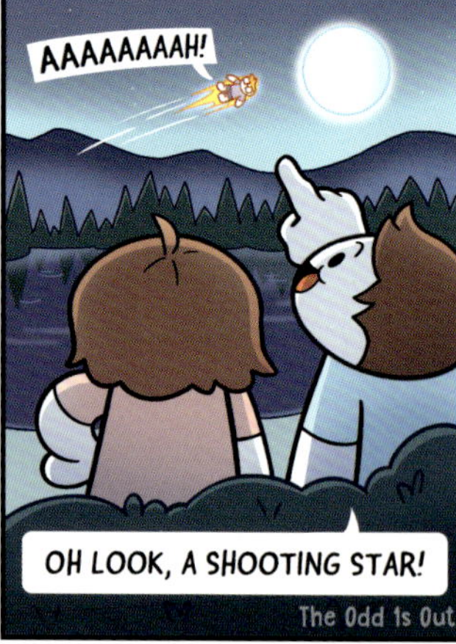
AAAAAAAAH!
OH LOOK, A SHOOTING STAR!
The Odd 1s Out

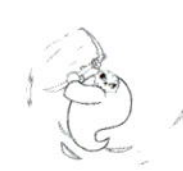

HOW WAS THE MOVIE?

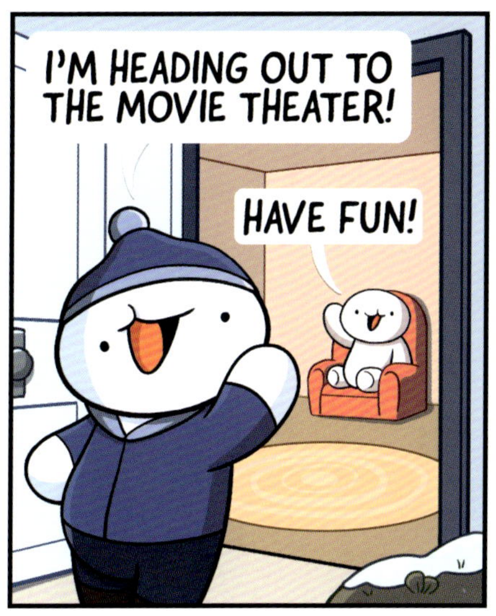

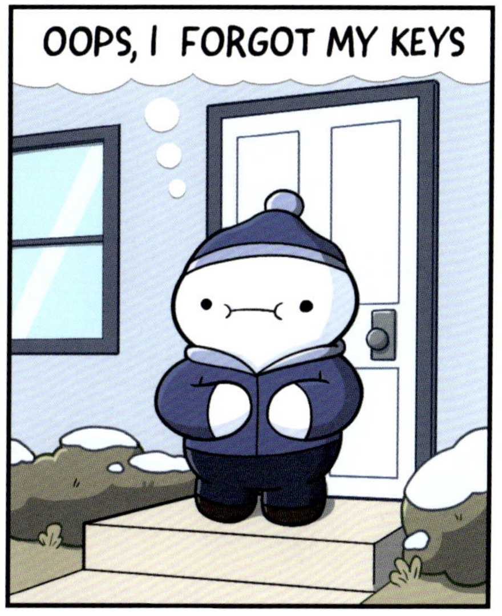

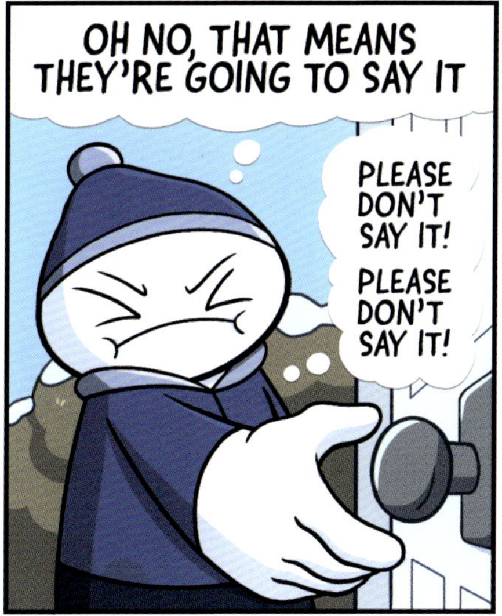

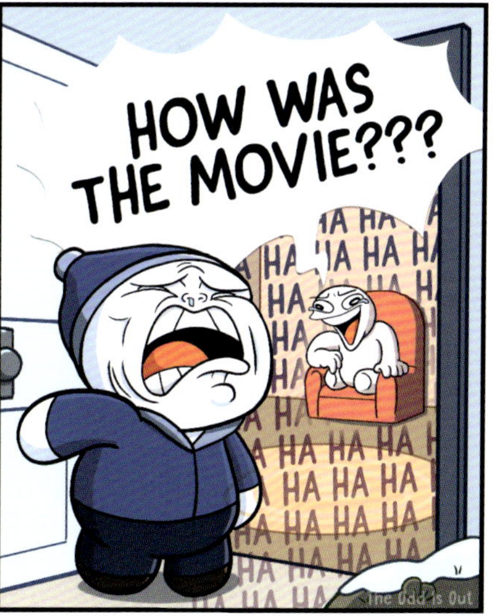

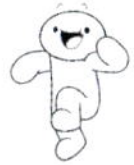

SEE YOU NEXT YEAR

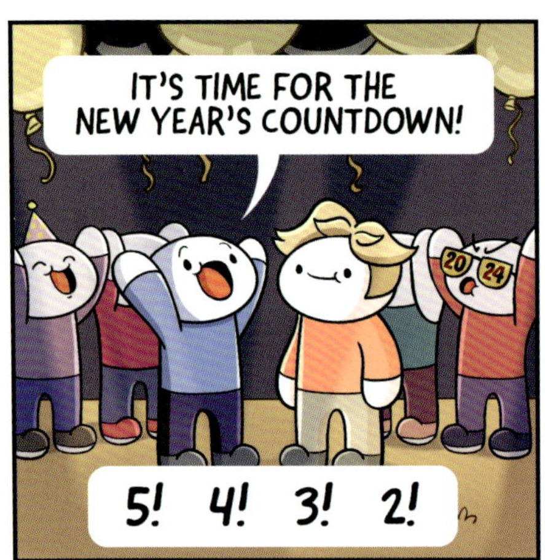

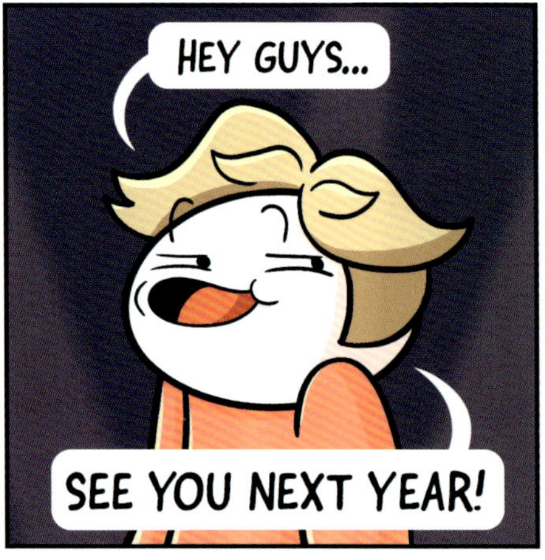

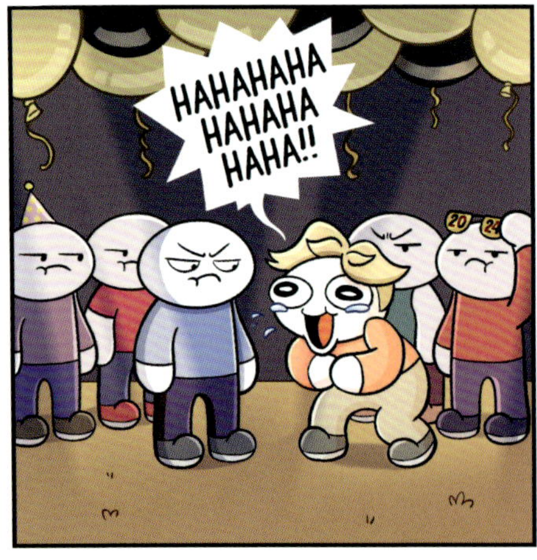

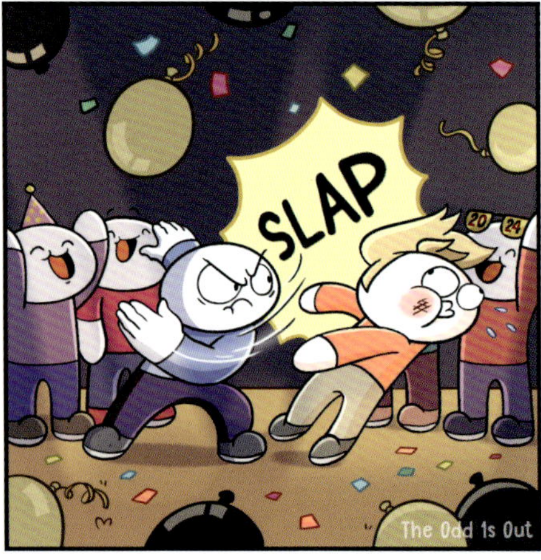

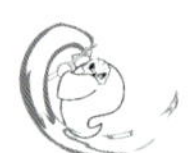

SCYTHE

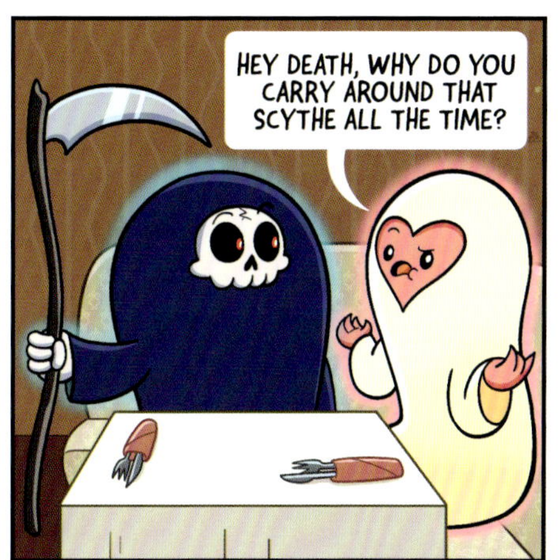
HEY DEATH, WHY DO YOU CARRY AROUND THAT SCYTHE ALL THE TIME?

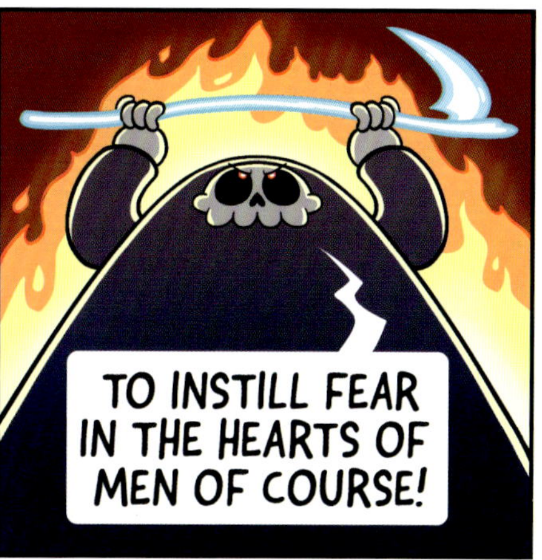
TO INSTILL FEAR IN THE HEARTS OF MEN OF COURSE!

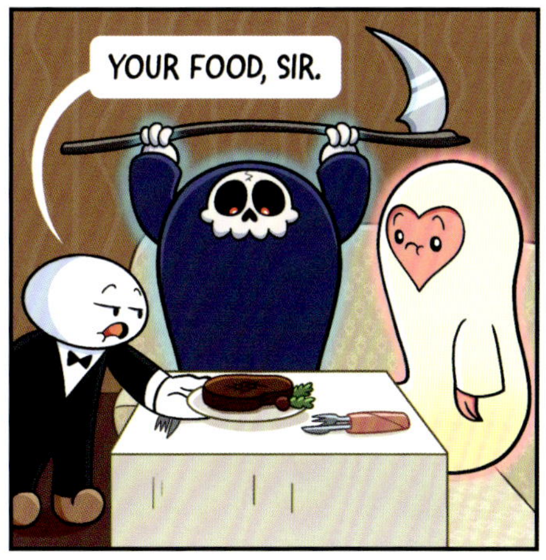
YOUR FOOD, SIR.

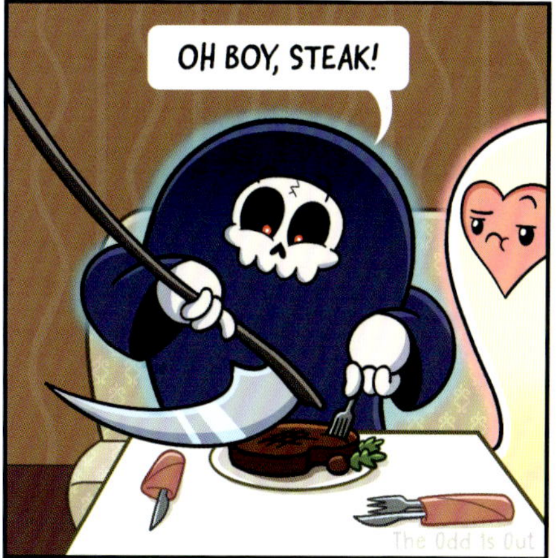
OH BOY, STEAK!
The Odd 1s Out

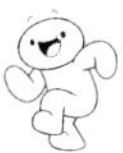

BITTEN

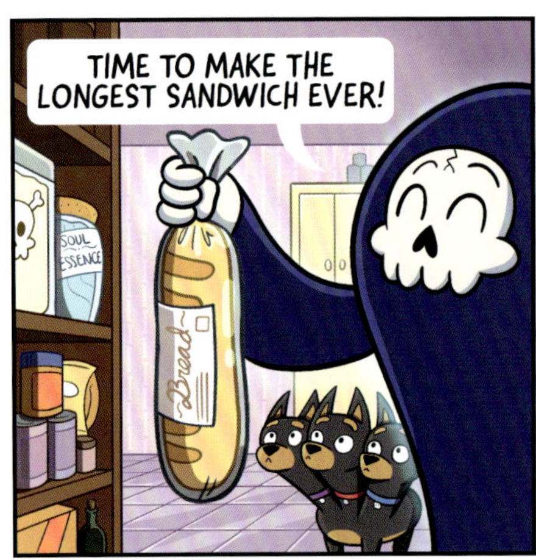
TIME TO MAKE THE LONGEST SANDWICH EVER!
SOUL ESSENCE
Bread

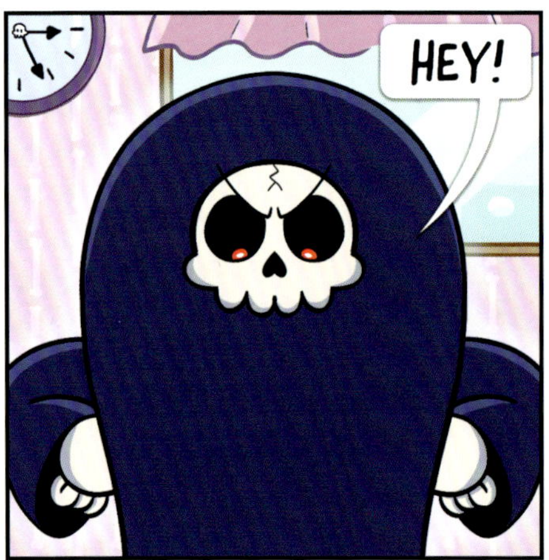
HEY!

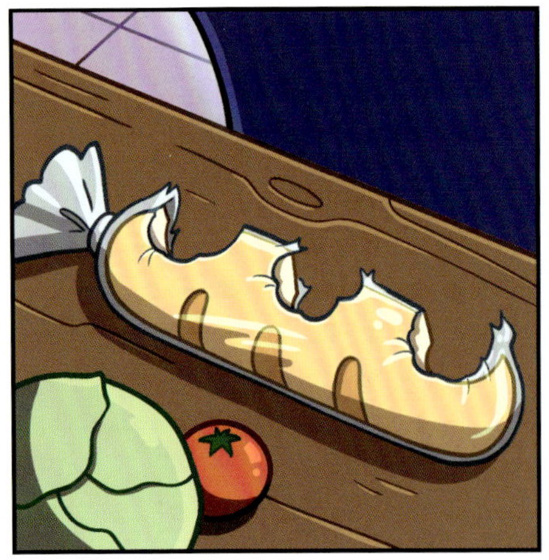

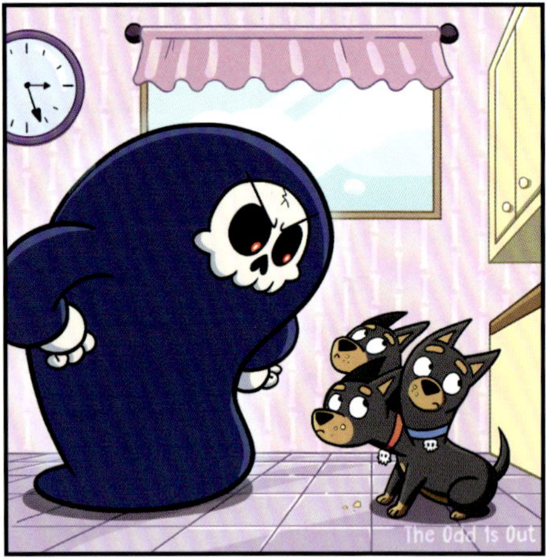
The Odd 1s Out

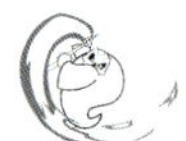

TRANSCEND

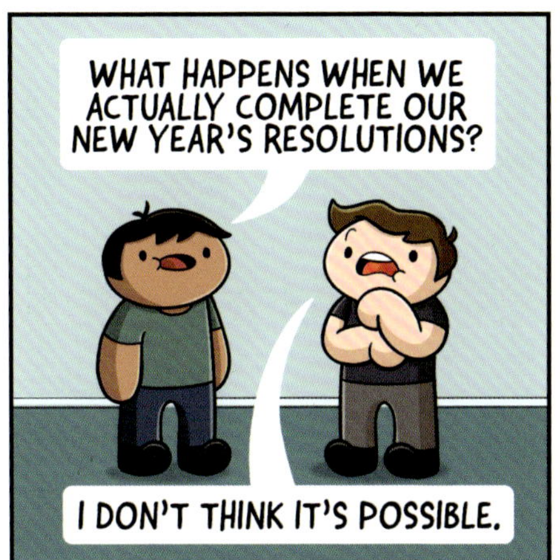
WHAT HAPPENS WHEN WE ACTUALLY COMPLETE OUR NEW YEAR'S RESOLUTIONS?
I DON'T THINK IT'S POSSIBLE.

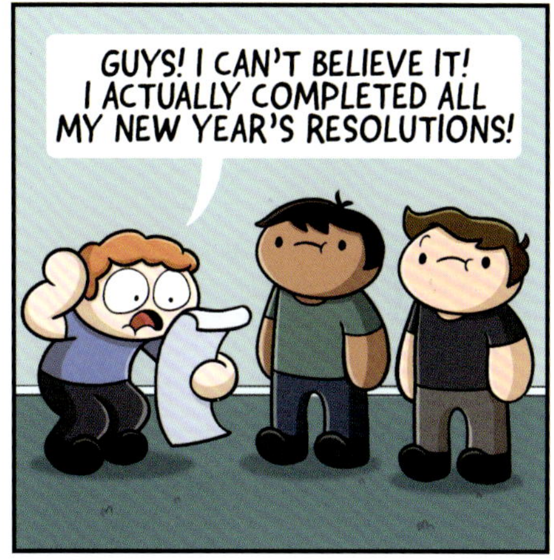
GUYS! I CAN'T BELIEVE IT! I ACTUALLY COMPLETED ALL MY NEW YEAR'S RESOLUTIONS!

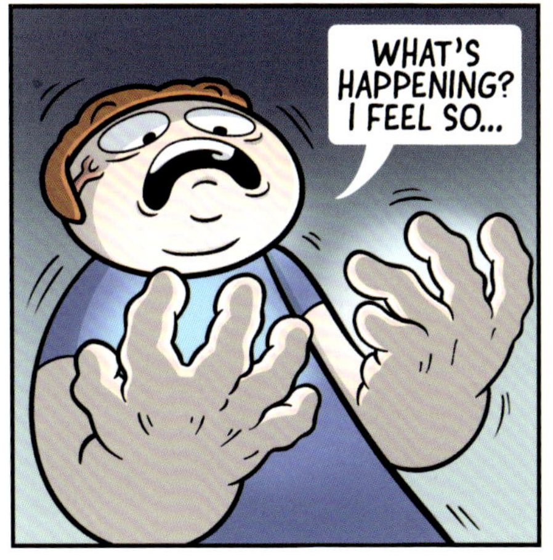
WHAT'S HAPPENING? I FEEL SO...

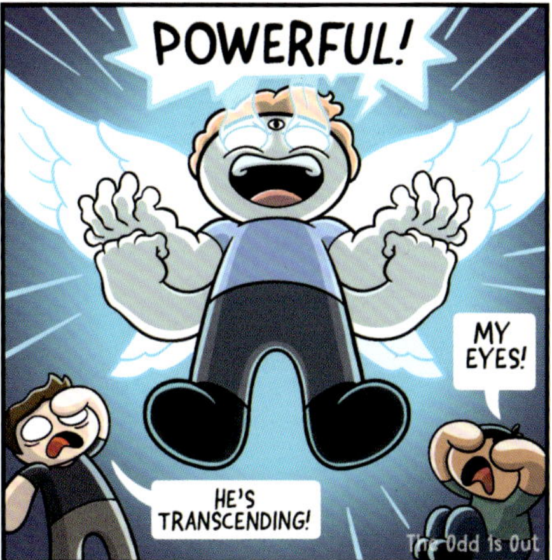
POWERFUL!
MY EYES!
HE'S TRANSCENDING!
The Odd 1s Out

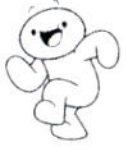

HE DIES

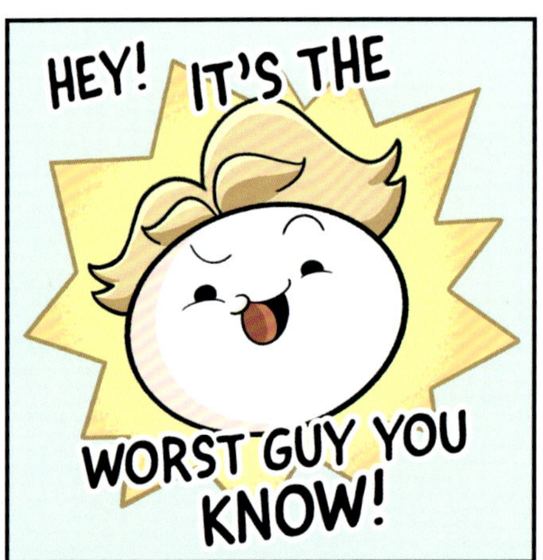
HEY! IT'S THE
WORST GUY YOU KNOW!

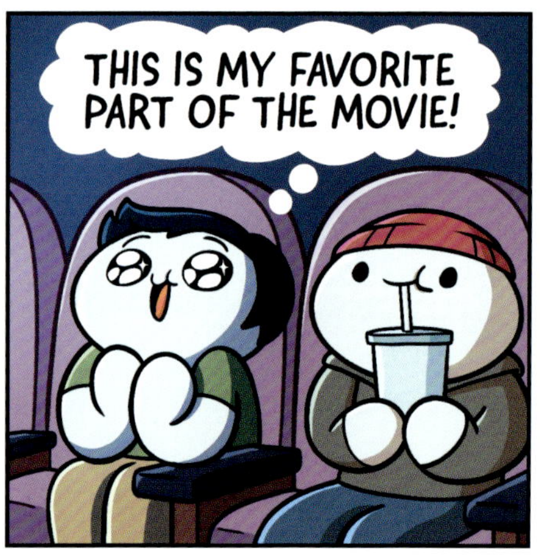
THIS IS MY FAVORITE PART OF THE MOVIE!

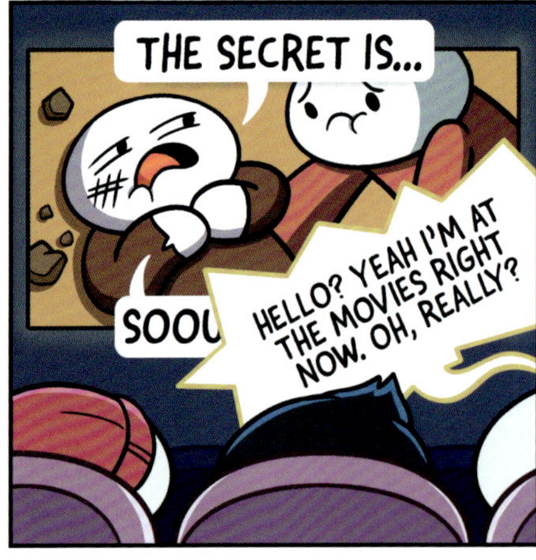
THE SECRET IS...
SOOU
HELLO? YEAH I'M AT THE MOVIES RIGHT NOW. OH, REALLY?

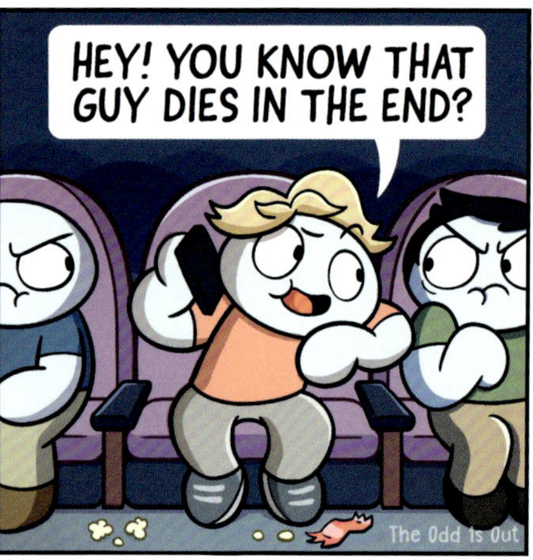
HEY! YOU KNOW THAT GUY DIES IN THE END?
The Odd 1s Out

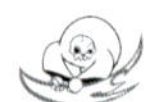

ROMEO AND JULIET

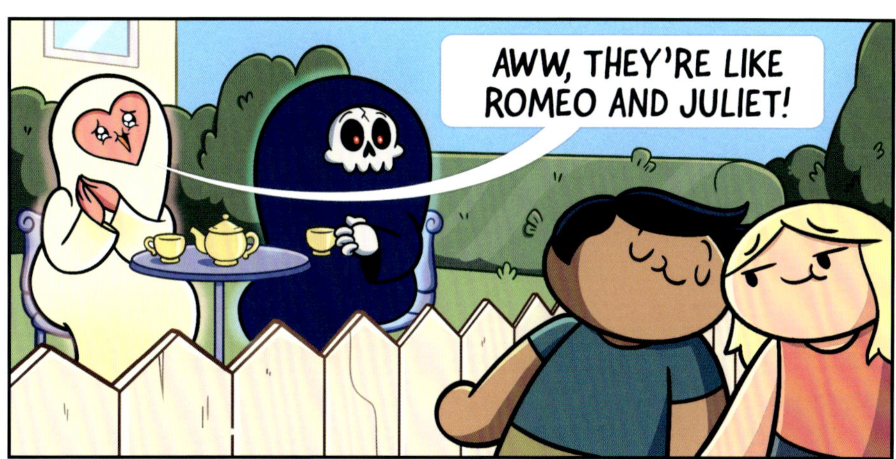

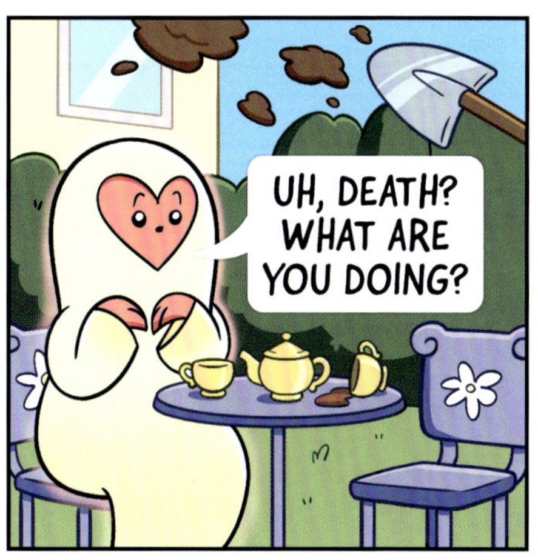

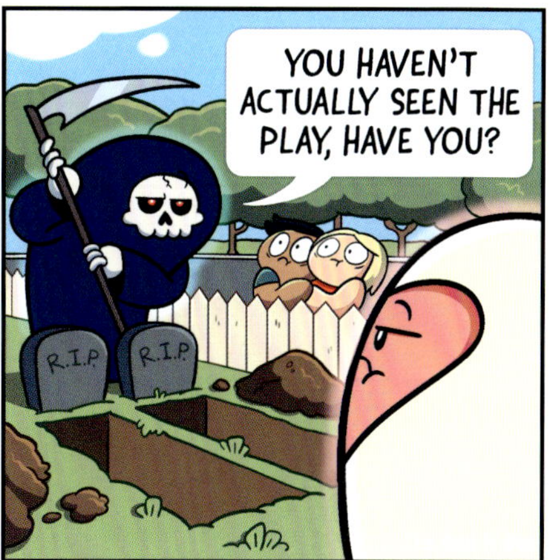

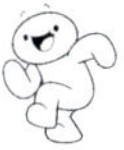

BACK PROBLEMS

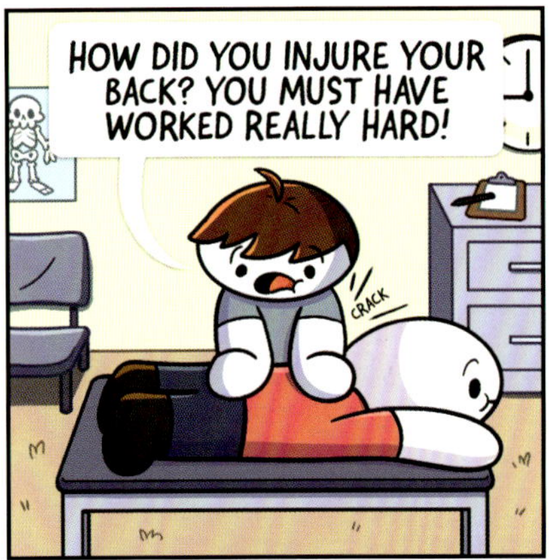

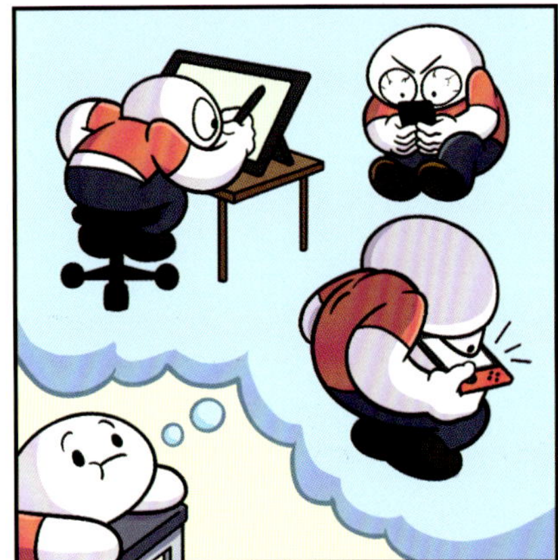

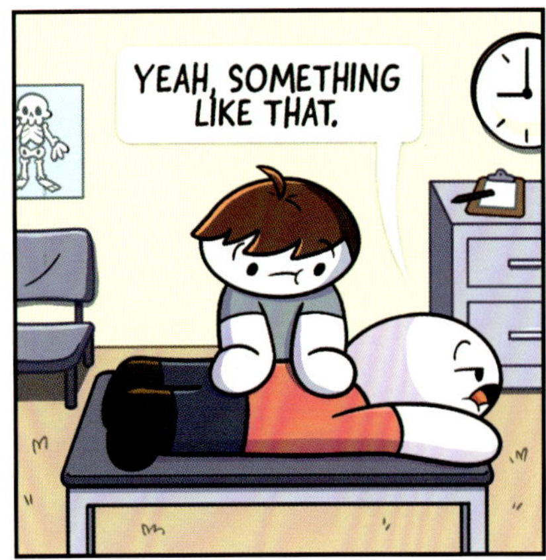

HOW ARE YOU

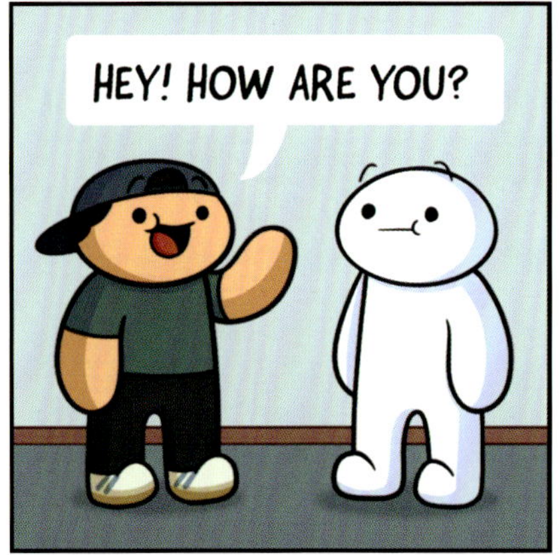

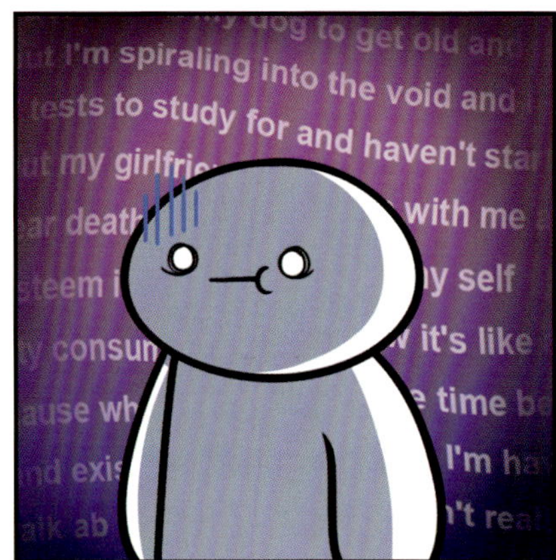

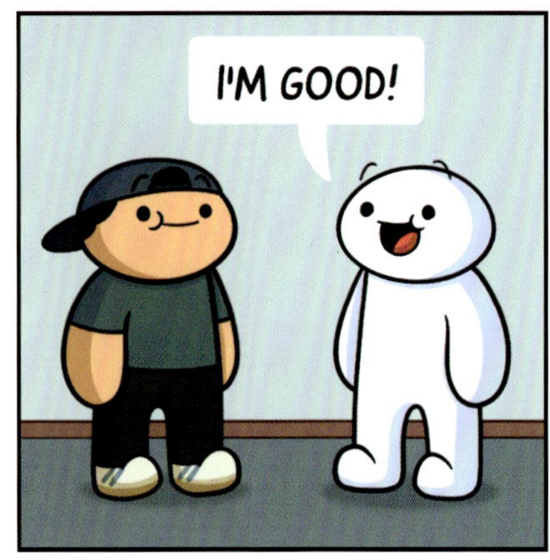

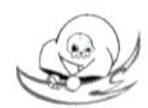

CUPID'S ARROW

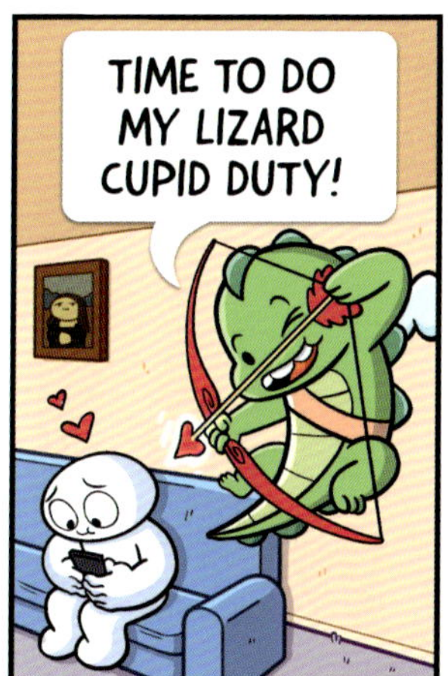

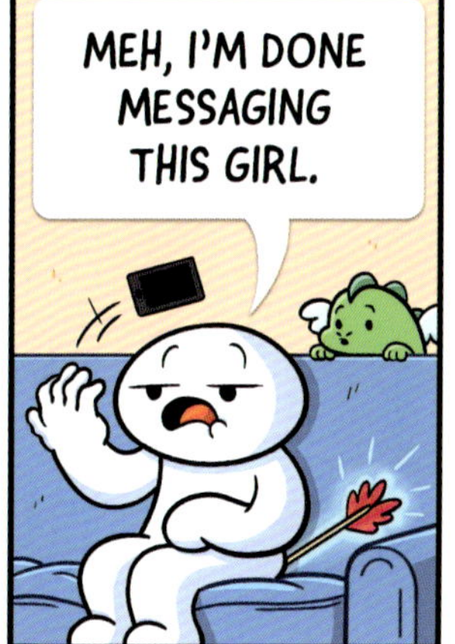

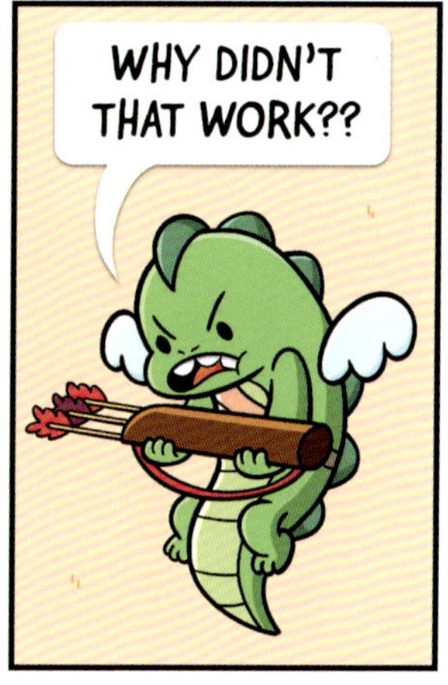

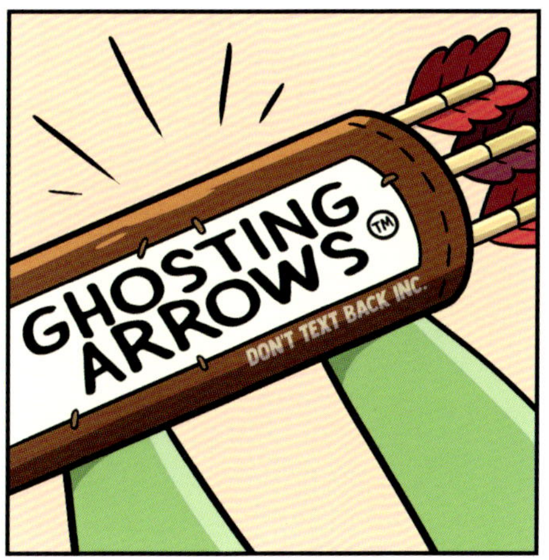

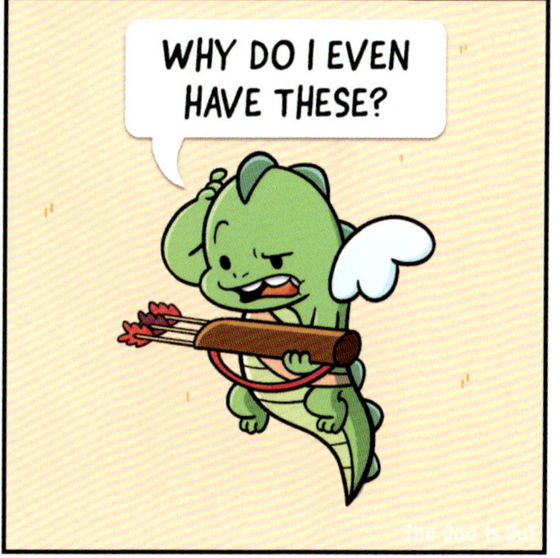

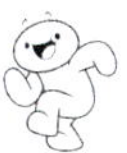

TEXT THEM

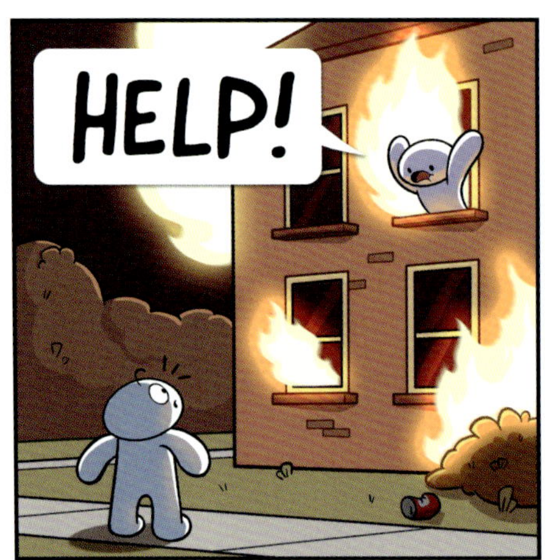
HELP!

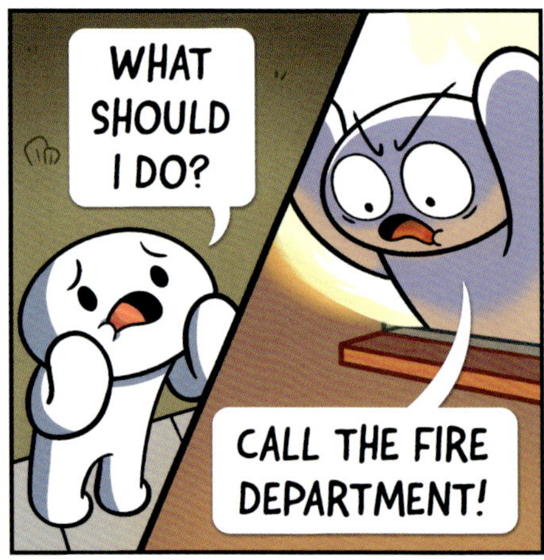
WHAT SHOULD I DO?
CALL THE FIRE DEPARTMENT!

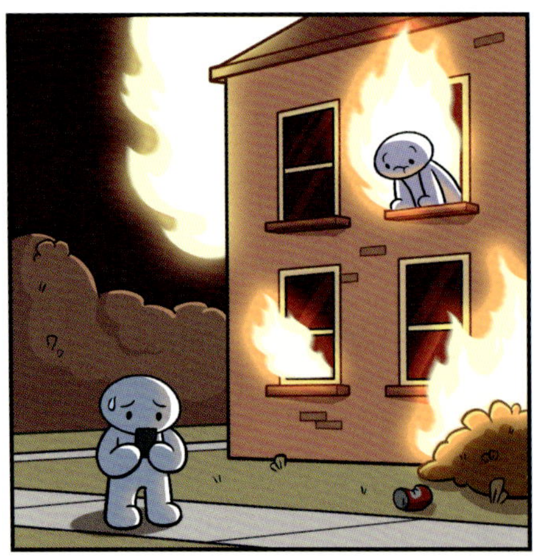

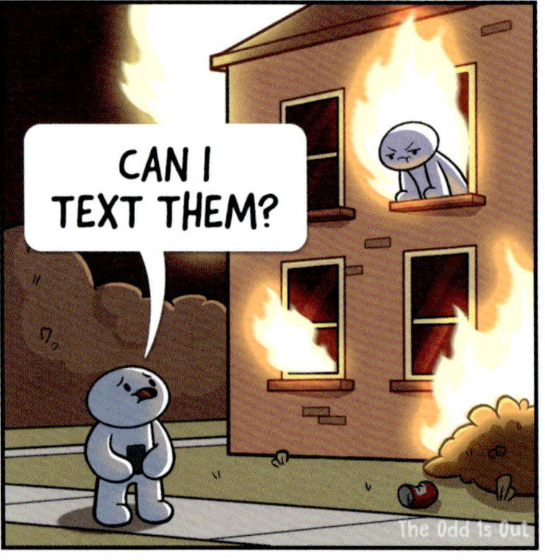
CAN I TEXT THEM?
The Odd Is Out

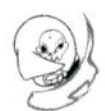

PICKUP LINES

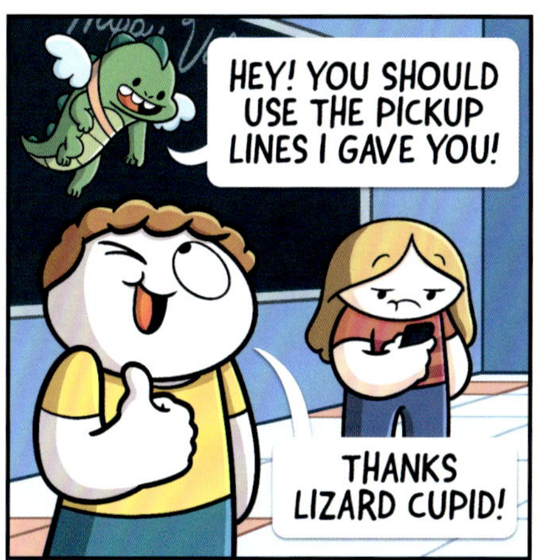

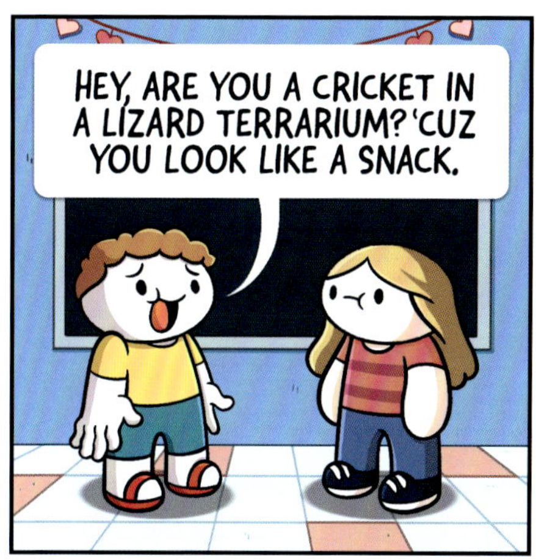

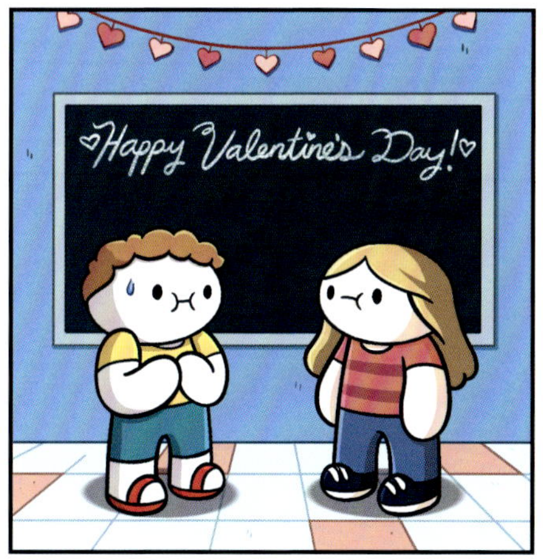

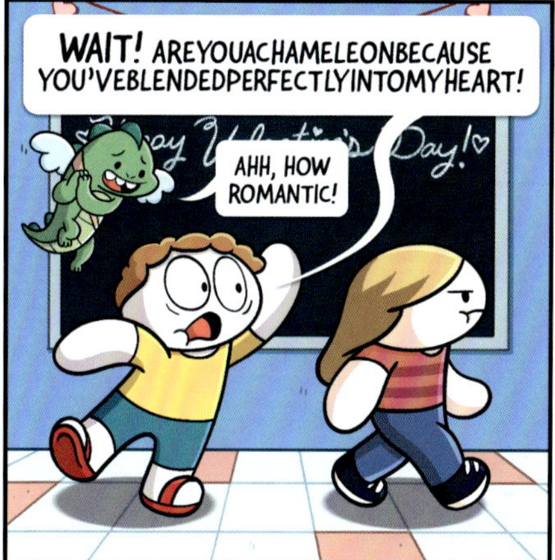

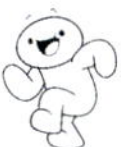

FALSE HAIRBALL

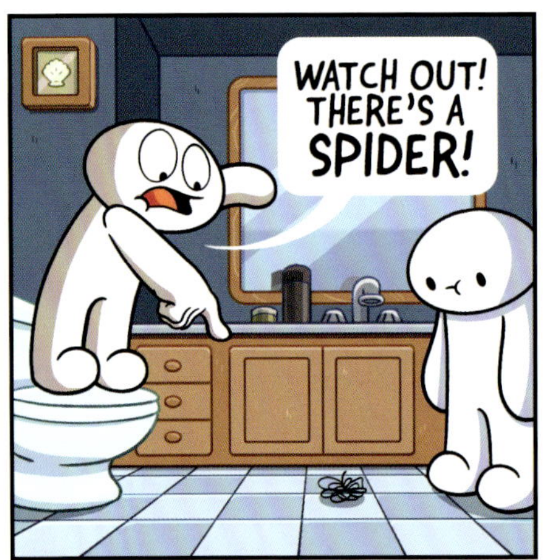

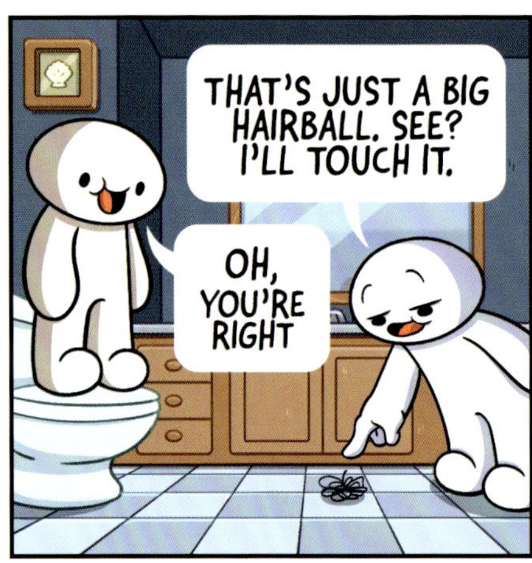

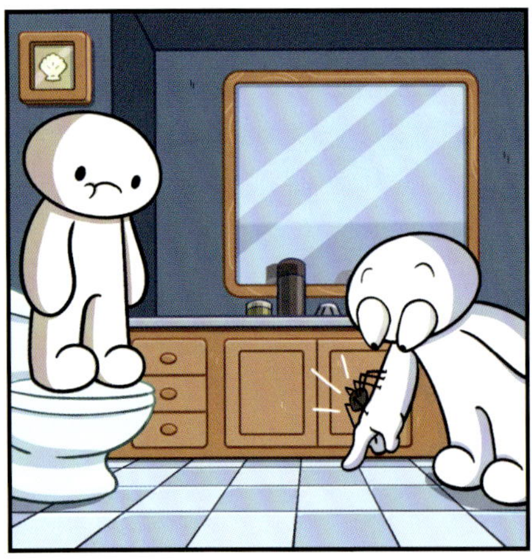

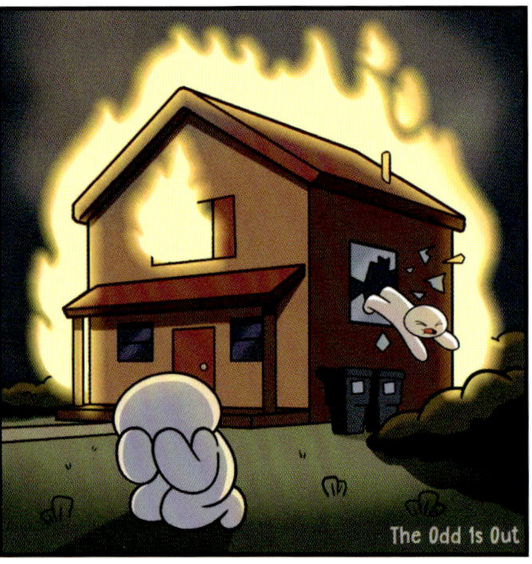

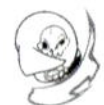

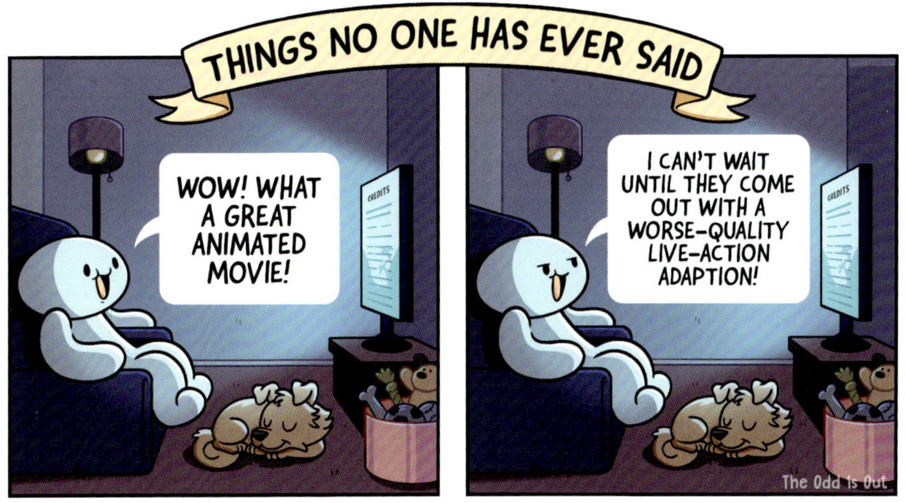
THINGS NO ONE HAS EVER SAID
WOW! WHAT A GREAT ANIMATED MOVIE!
CREDITS
I CAN'T WAIT UNTIL THEY COME OUT WITH A WORSE-QUALITY LIVE-ACTION ADAPTION!
CREDITS
The Odd is Out

DAREDEVIL

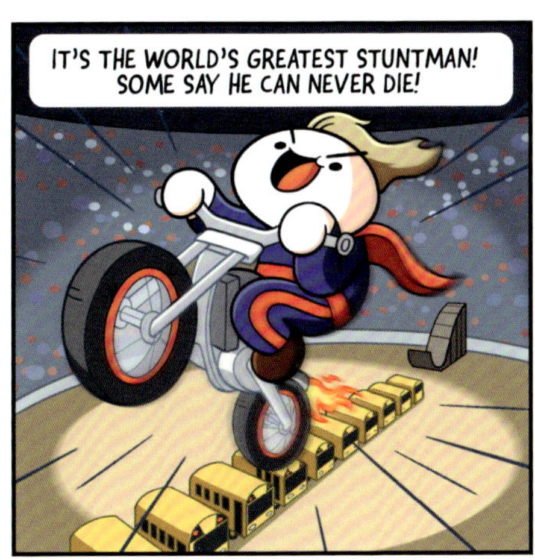
IT'S THE WORLD'S GREATEST STUNTMAN! SOME SAY HE CAN NEVER DIE!

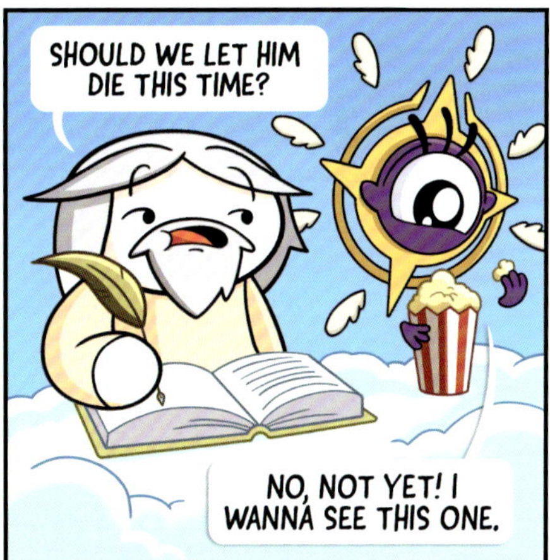
SHOULD WE LET HIM DIE THIS TIME?
NO, NOT YET! I WANNA SEE THIS ONE.

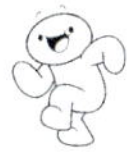

LOVE THIS GAME

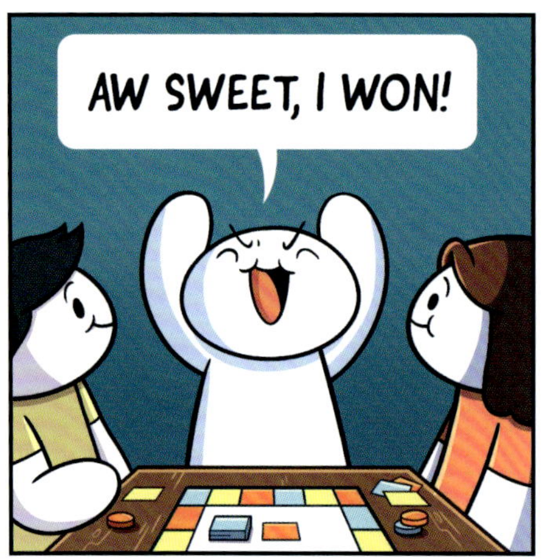

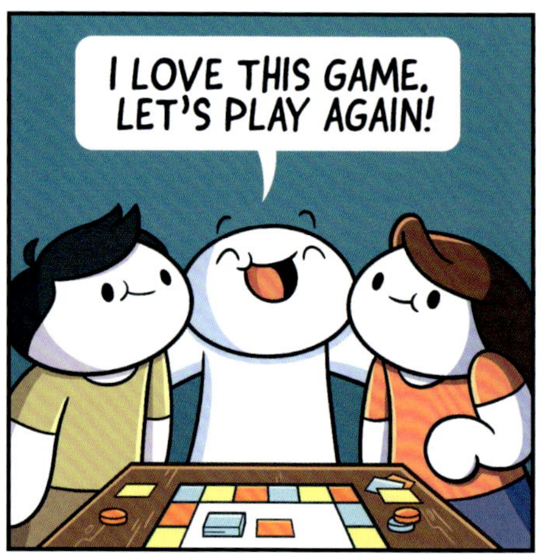

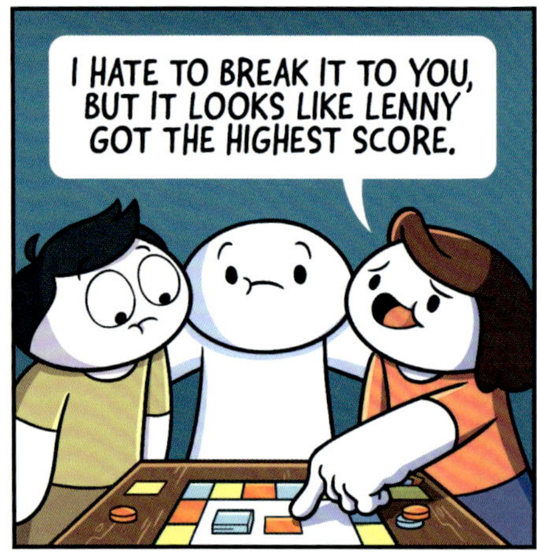

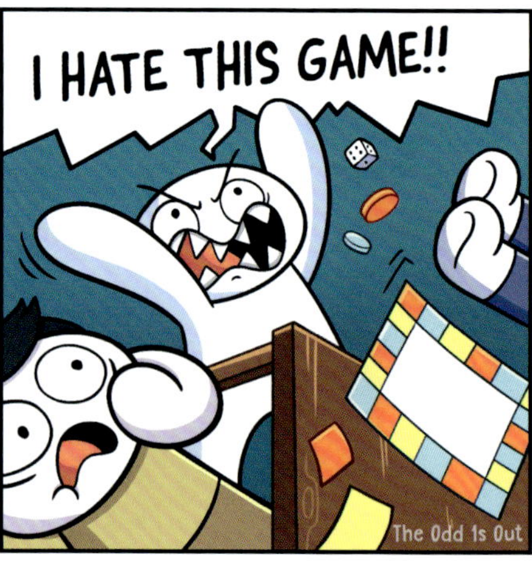

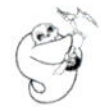

30 MINUTES

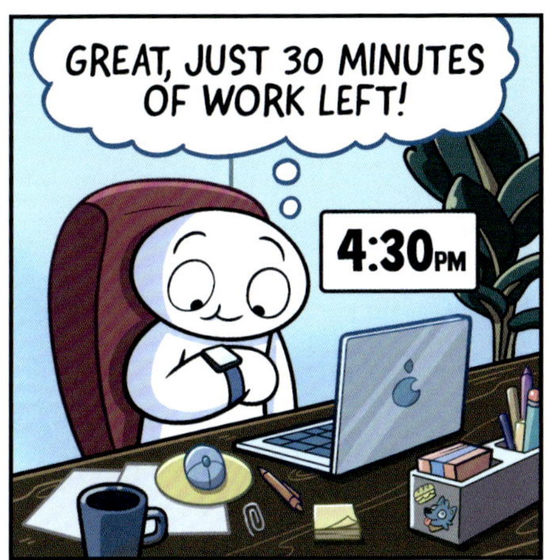
GREAT, JUST 30 MINUTES OF WORK LEFT!
4:30PM

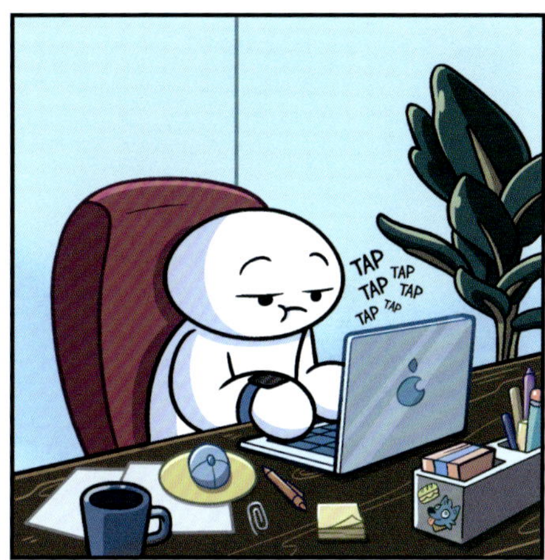
TAP TAP TAP TAP TAP TAP

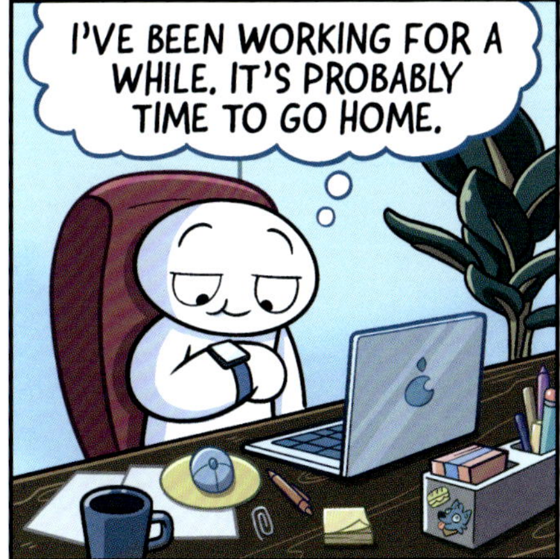
I'VE BEEN WORKING FOR A WHILE. IT'S PROBABLY TIME TO GO HOME.

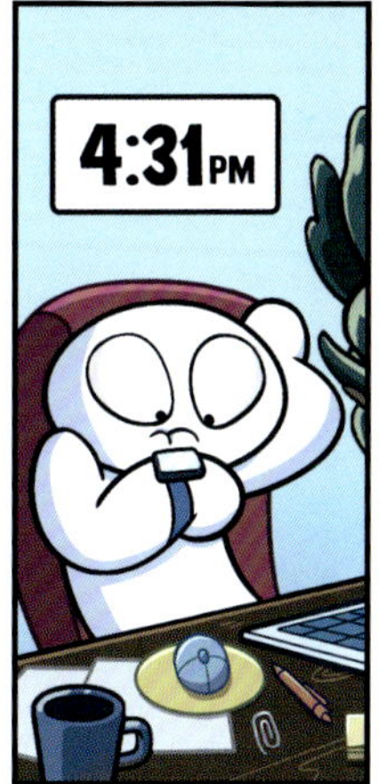
4:31PM

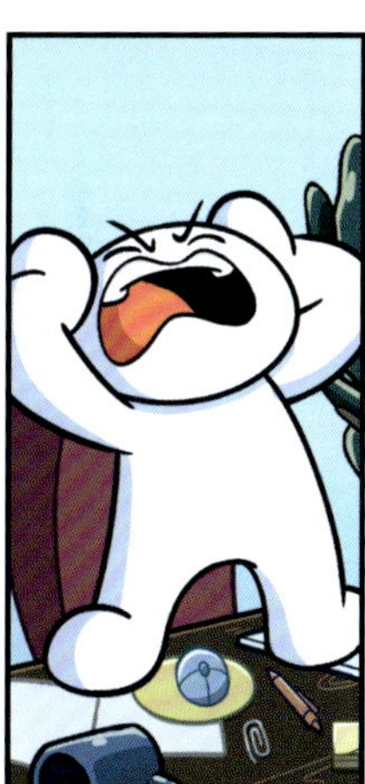

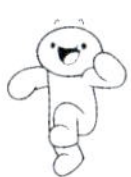

BEST PART

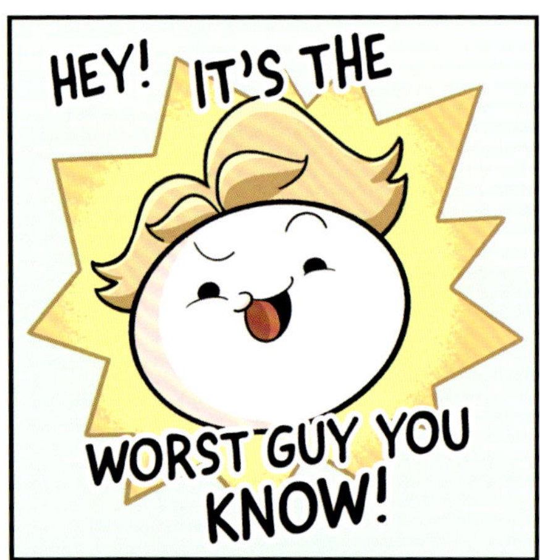
HEY! IT'S THE
WORST GUY YOU KNOW!

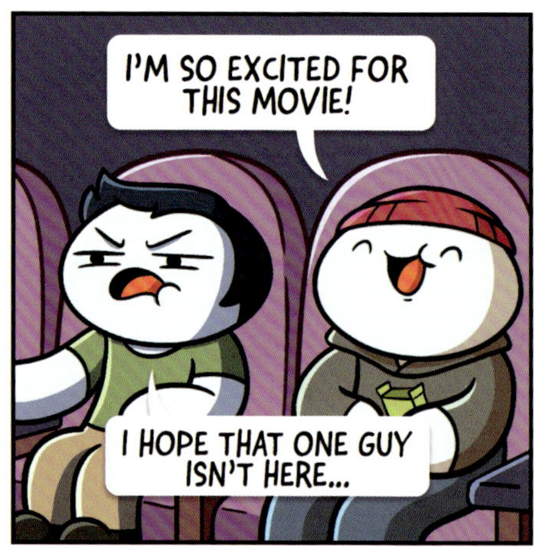
I'M SO EXCITED FOR THIS MOVIE!
I HOPE THAT ONE GUY ISN'T HERE...

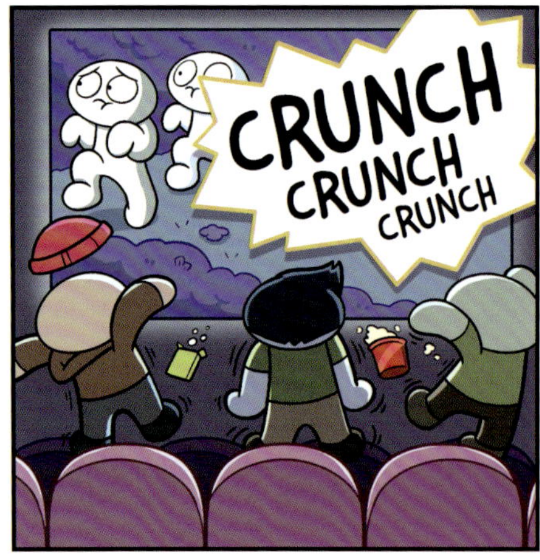
CRUNCH
CRUNCH
CRUNCH

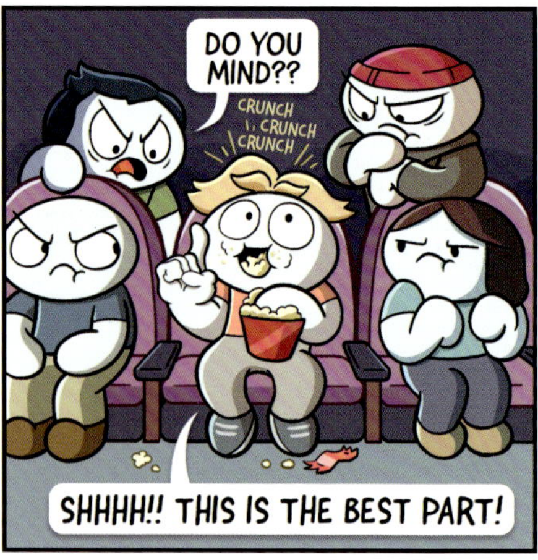
DO YOU MIND??
CRUNCH CRUNCH CRUNCH
SHHHH!! THIS IS THE BEST PART!

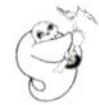

ST. PATRICK'S DAY

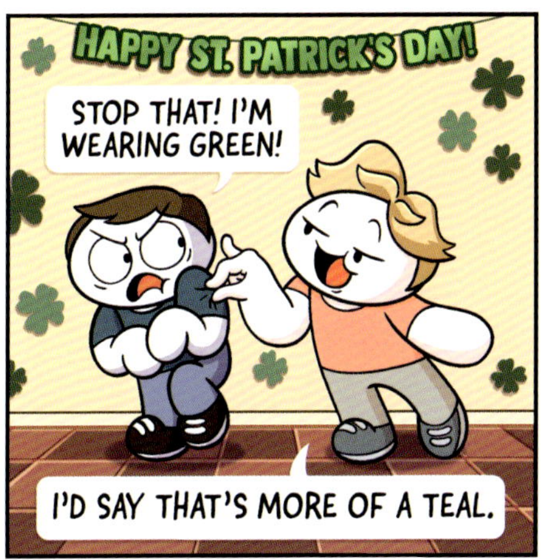

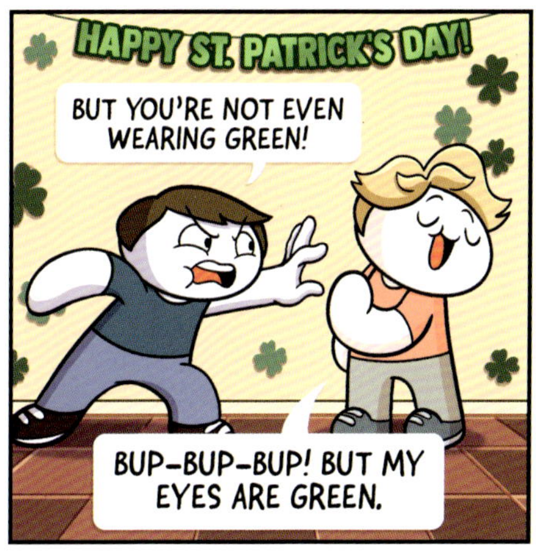

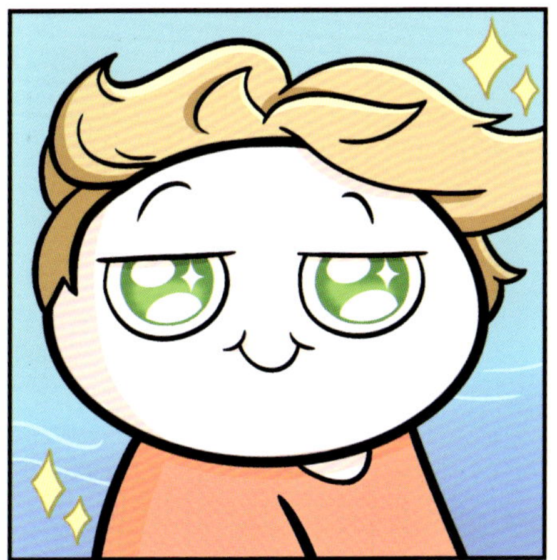

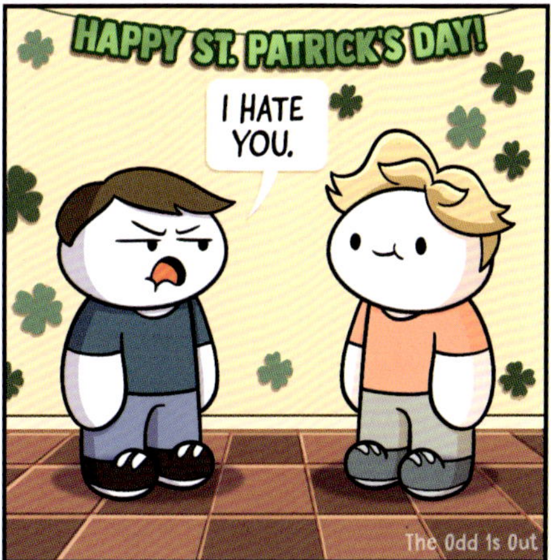

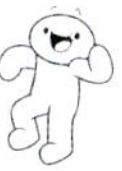

NIGHTMARES THROUGH THE AGES

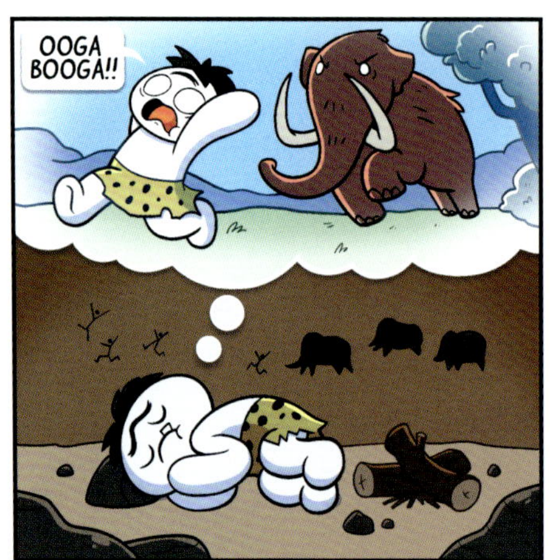

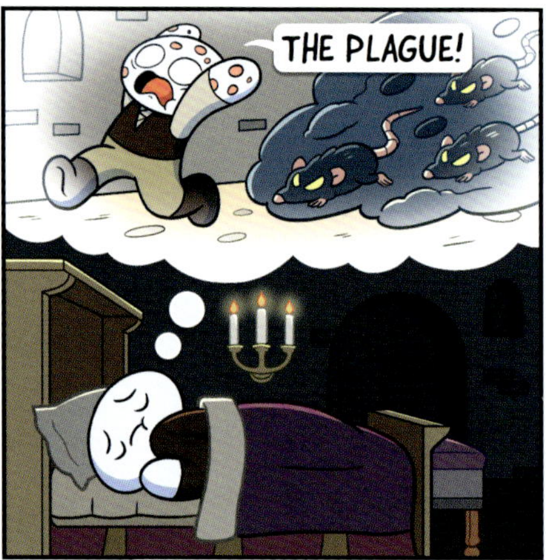

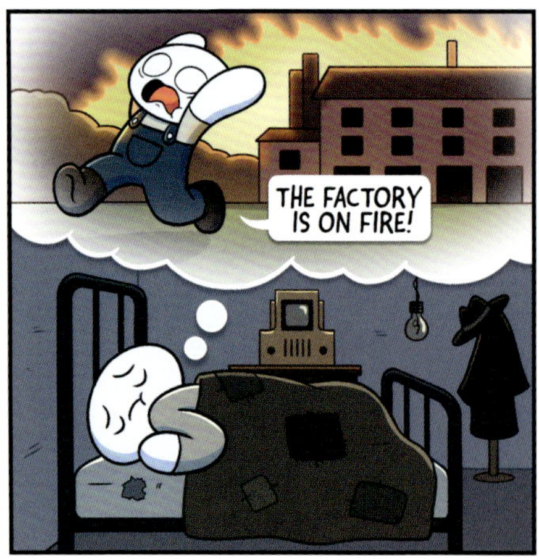

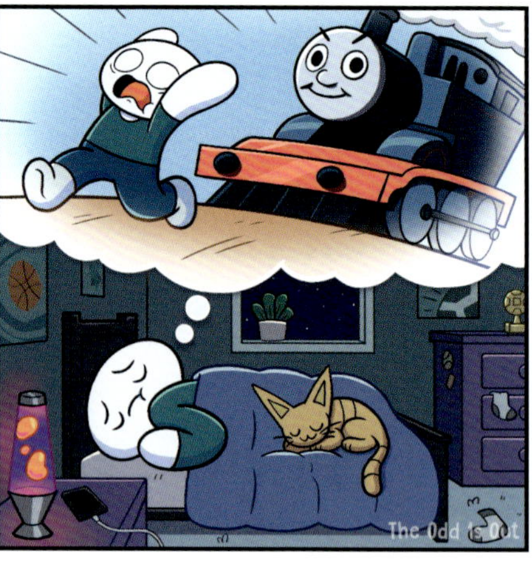

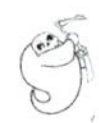

YOGA

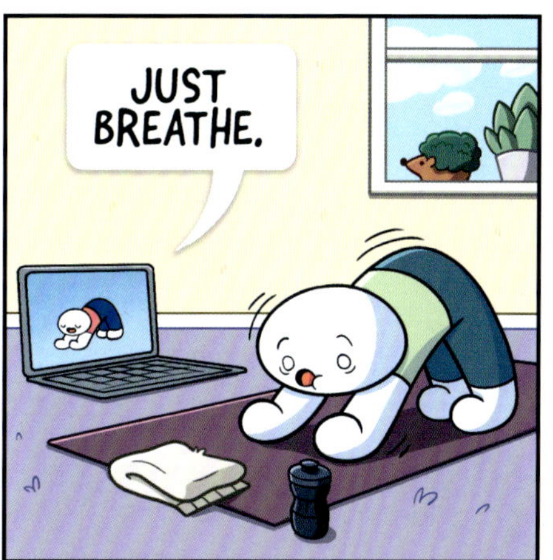
JUST BREATHE.

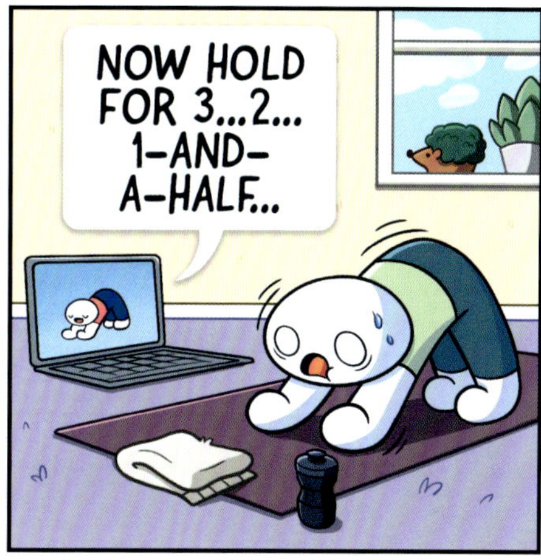
NOW HOLD FOR 3...2... 1-AND-A-HALF...

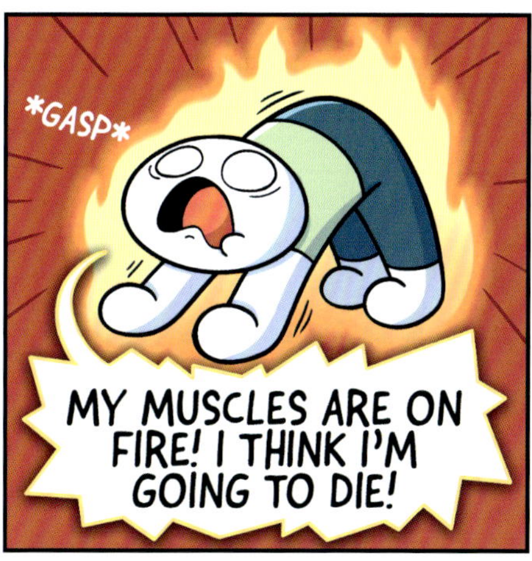
GASP
MY MUSCLES ARE ON FIRE! I THINK I'M GOING TO DIE!

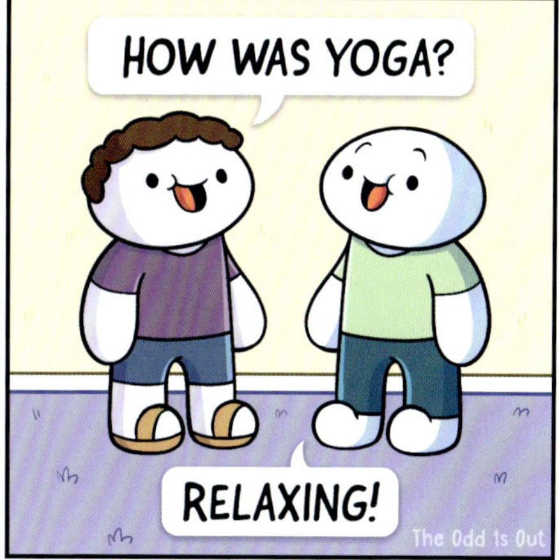
HOW WAS YOGA?
RELAXING!
The Odd 1s Out

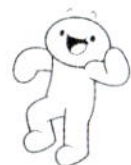

TIKTOK BAN

TikTok is Banned lol
Learn more
Close app

HOUR 1
HOUR 4
Diploma
HOUR 8
HOUR 12

TikTok is back!

The Odd 1s Out

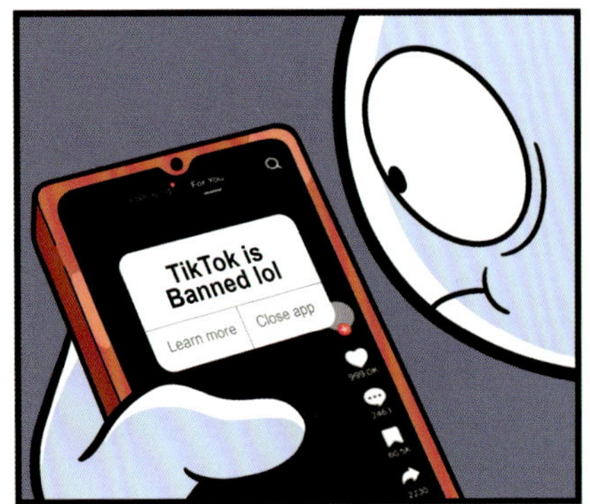

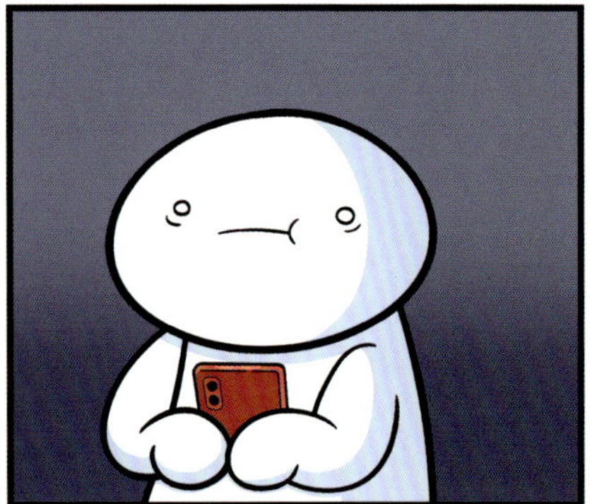

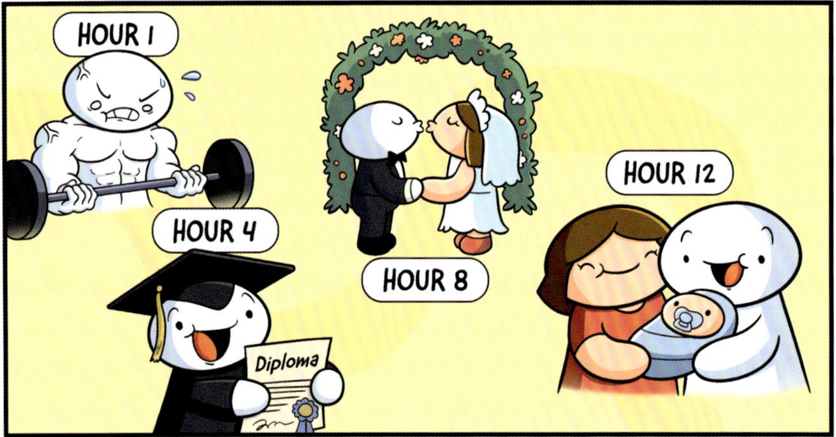

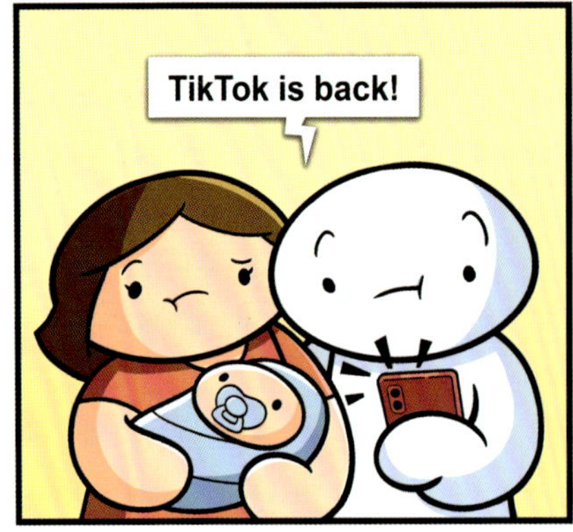

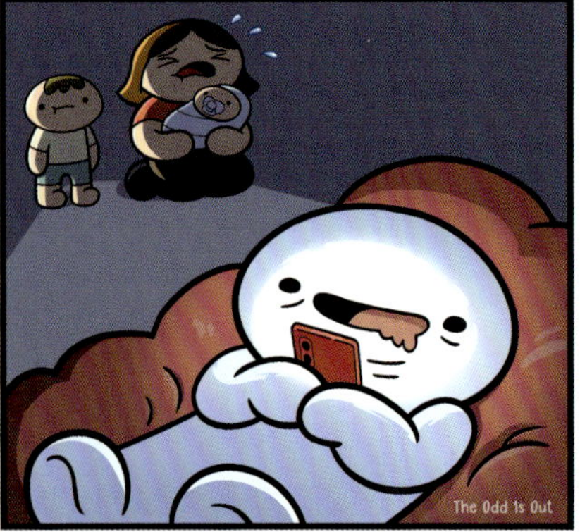

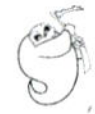

LIFE'S OWL

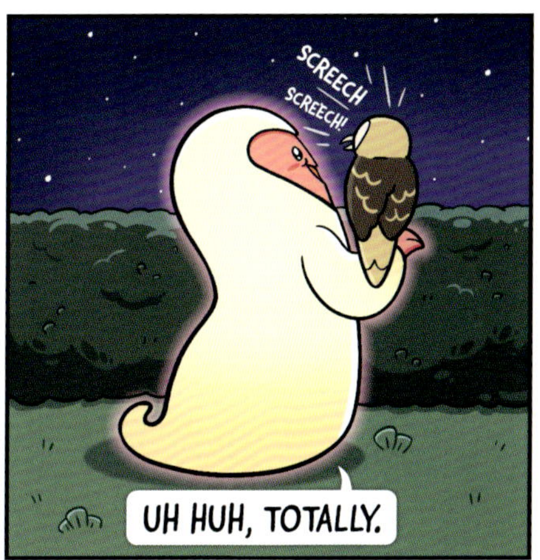
SCREECH
SCREECH!
UH HUH, TOTALLY.

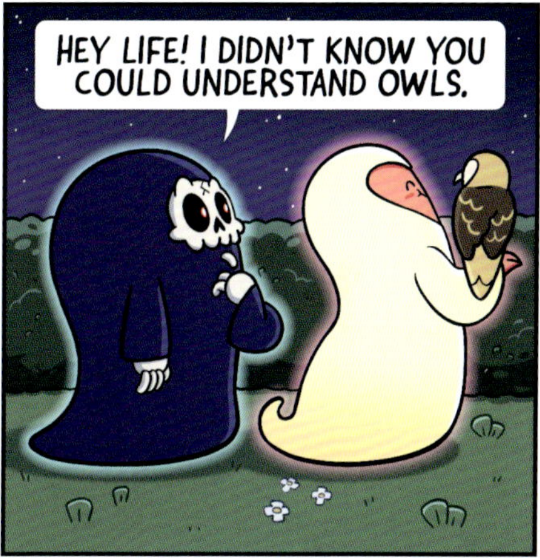
HEY LIFE! I DIDN'T KNOW YOU COULD UNDERSTAND OWLS.

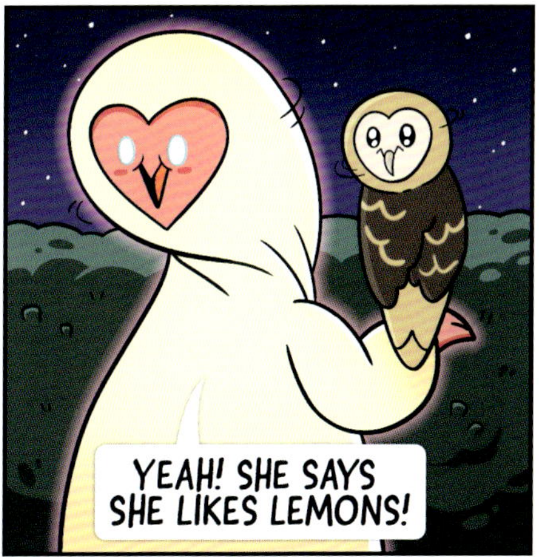
YEAH! SHE SAYS SHE LIKES LEMONS!

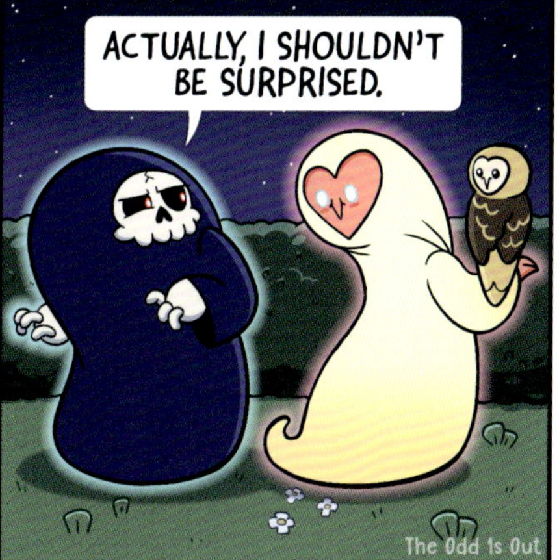
ACTUALLY, I SHOULDN'T BE SURPRISED.
The Odd 1s Out

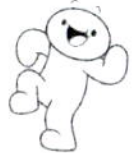

ADDERALL

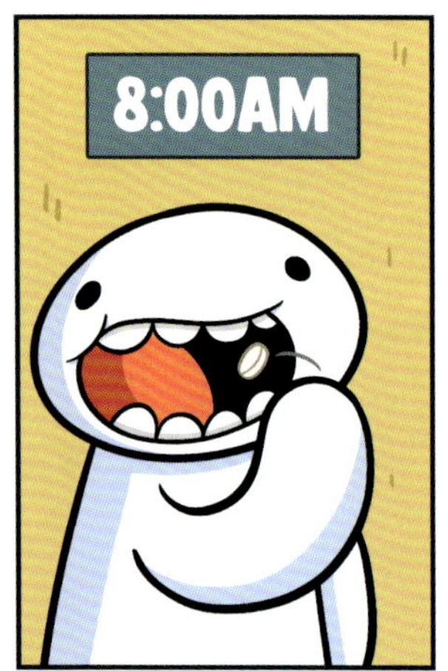

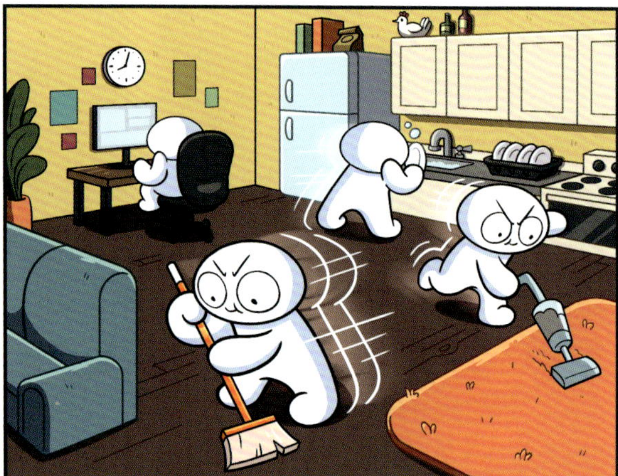

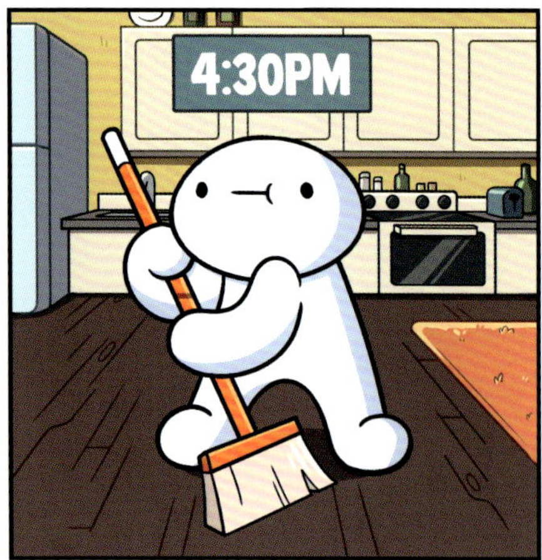

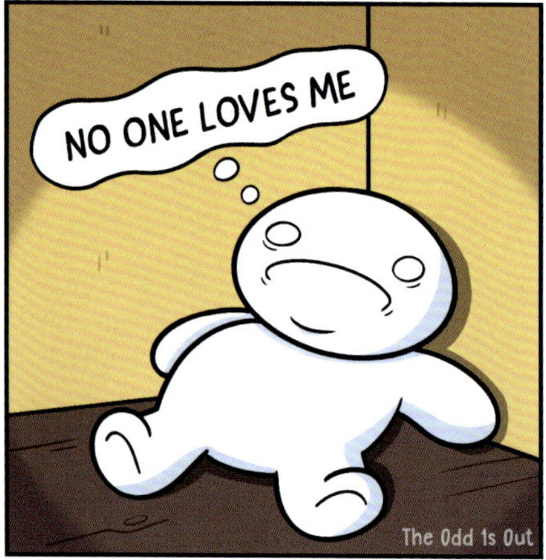

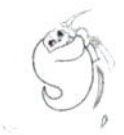

SOCIALIZE

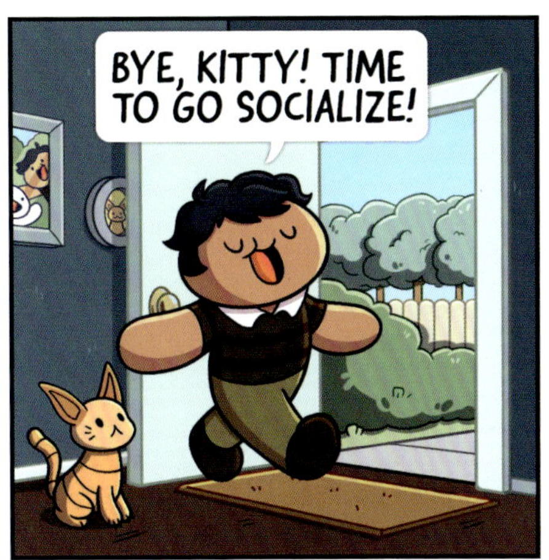

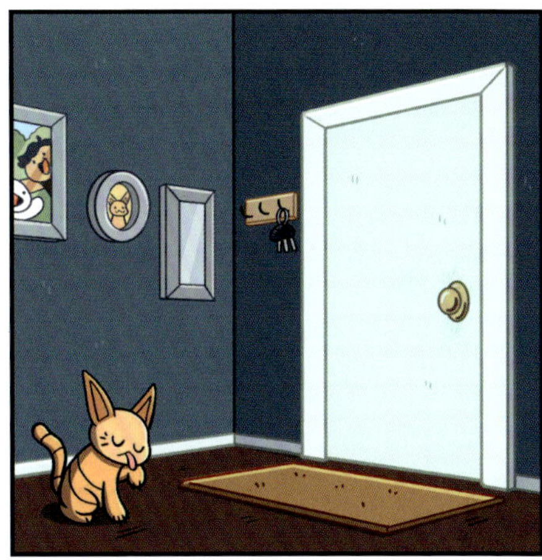

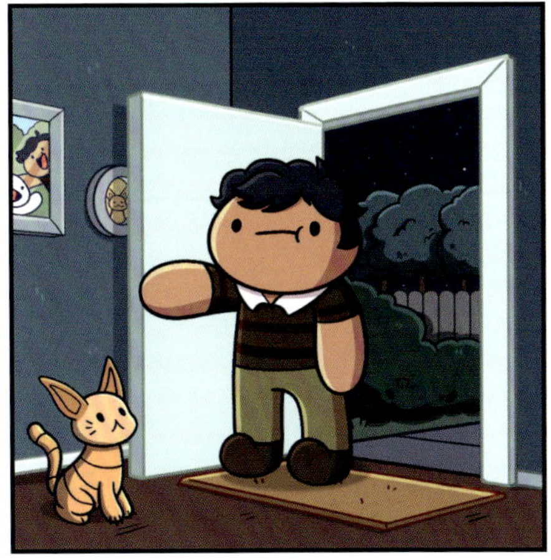

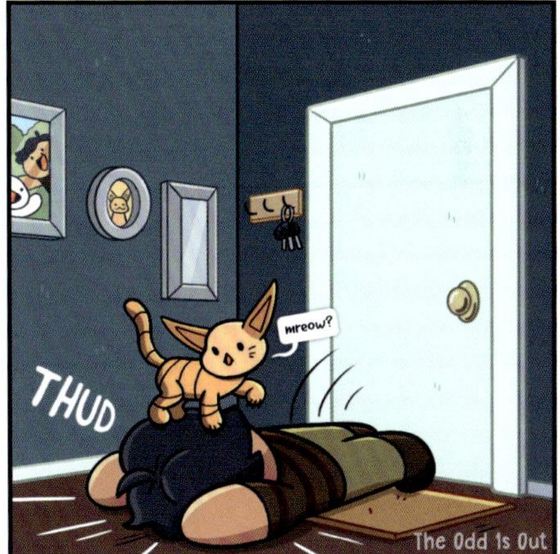

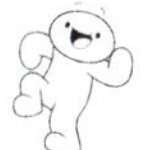

DAD SNEEZE

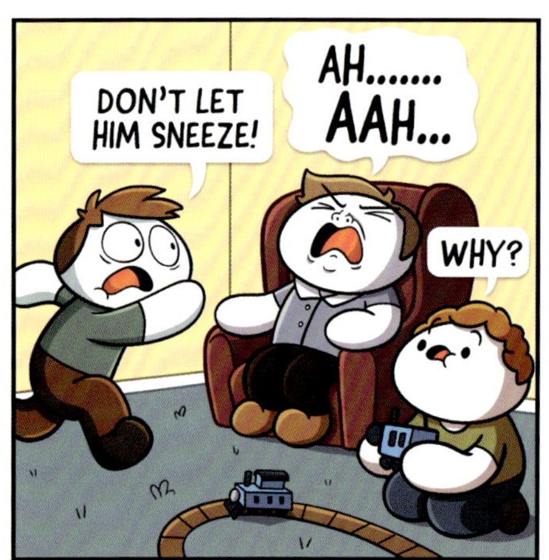
DON'T LET HIM SNEEZE!
AH.......
AAH...
WHY?

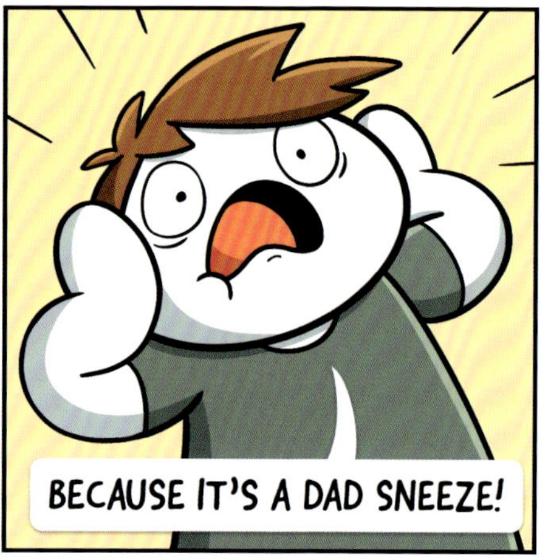
BECAUSE IT'S A DAD SNEEZE!

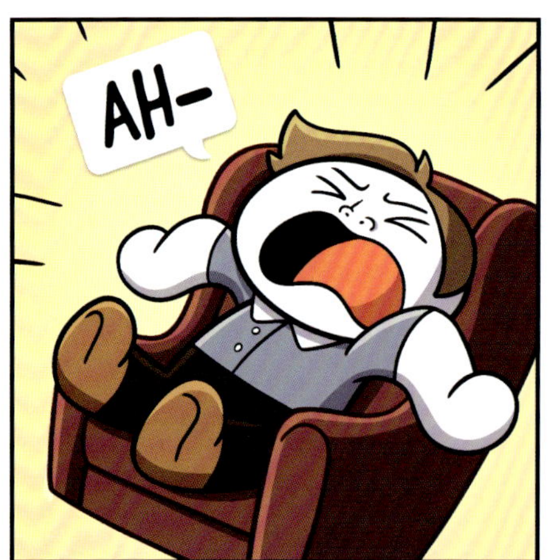
AH-

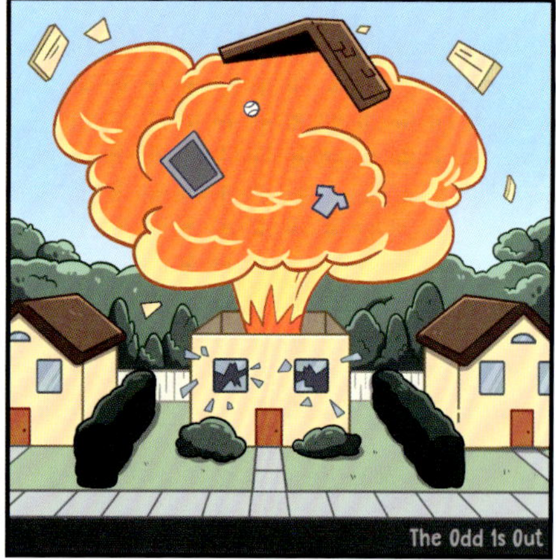
The Odd 1s Out

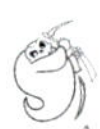

FURRYSAURUS

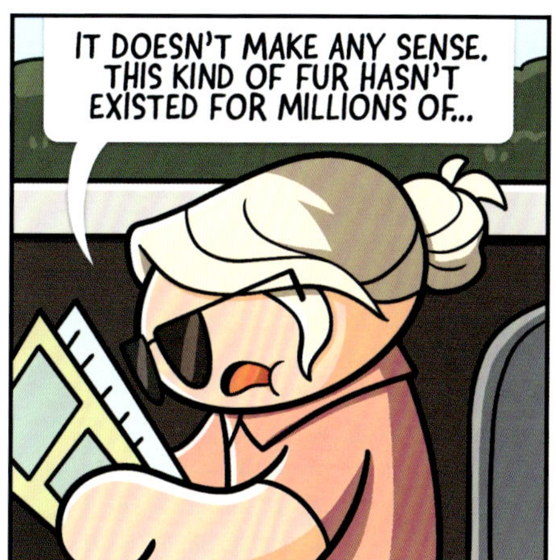

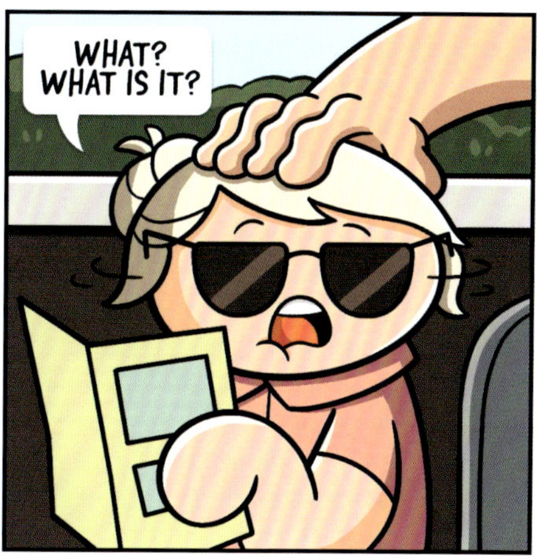

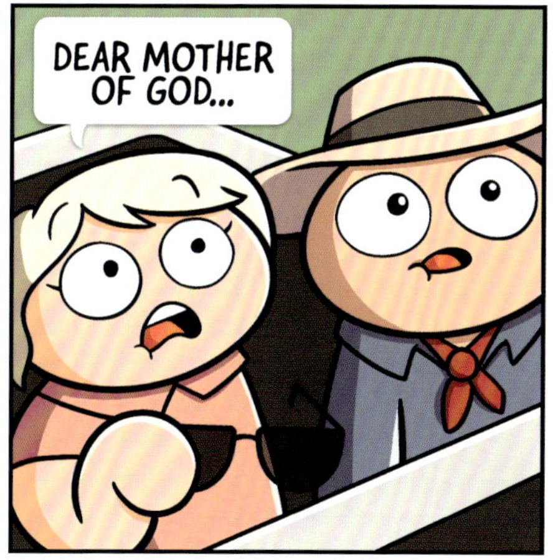

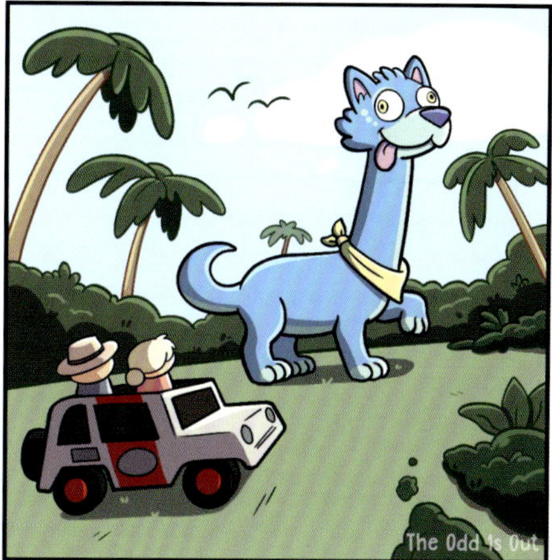

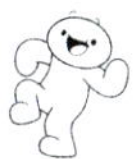

BEDTIME STORY

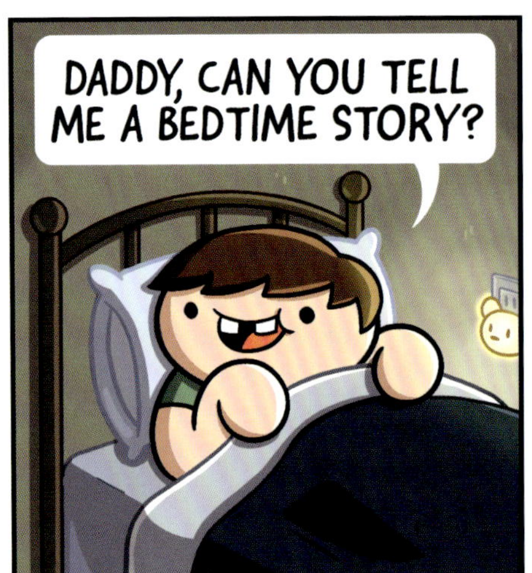

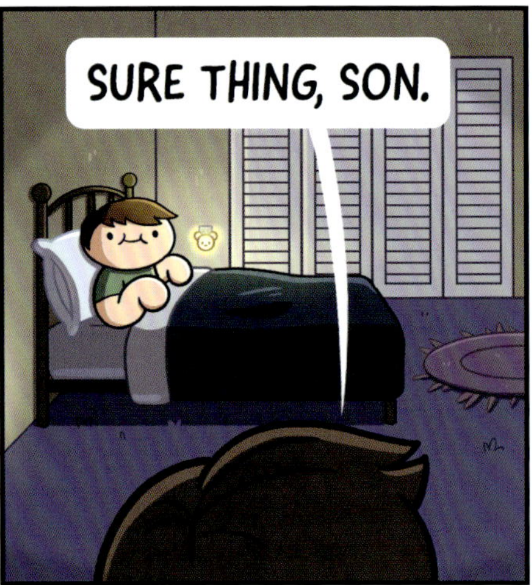

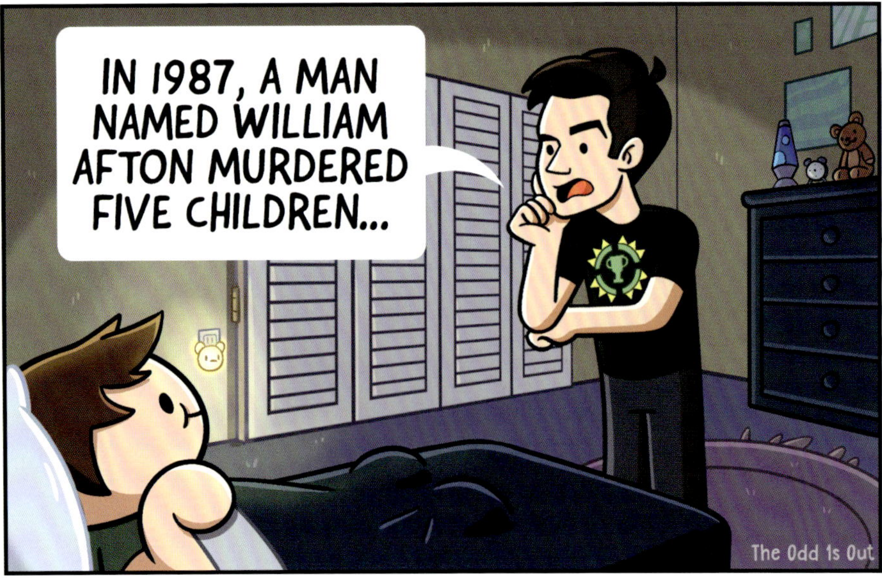

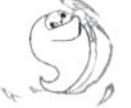

PERFECT DAY

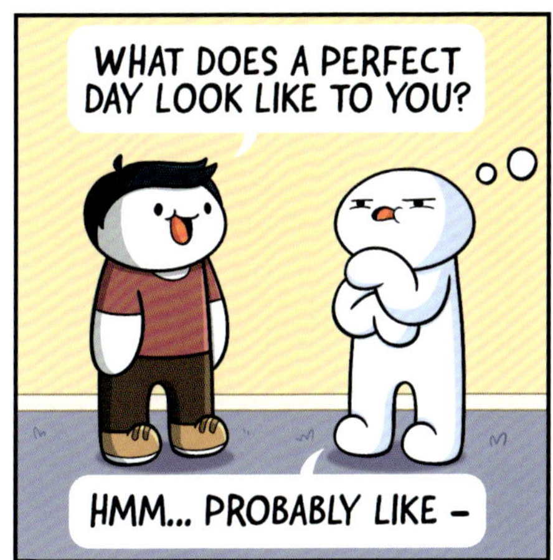
WHAT DOES A PERFECT DAY LOOK LIKE TO YOU?
HMM... PROBABLY LIKE -

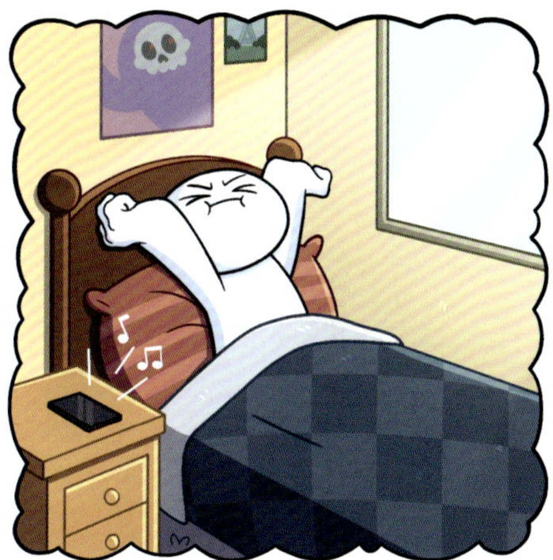

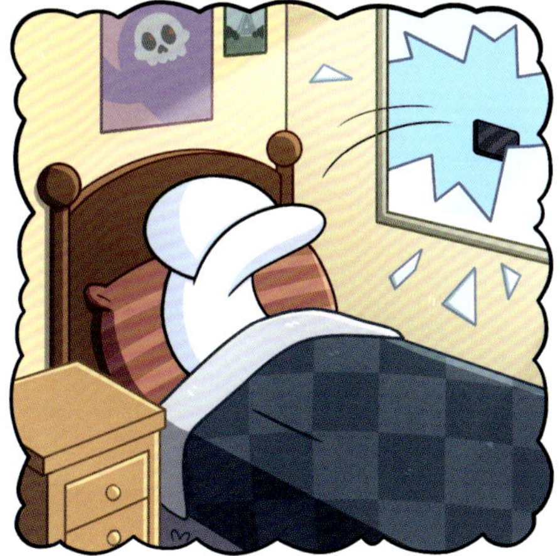

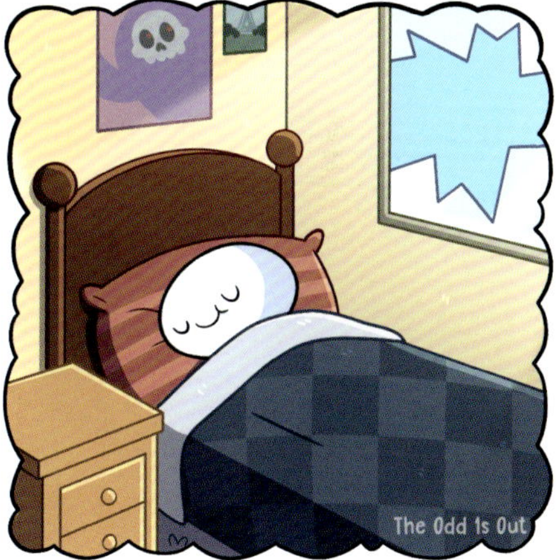
The Odd 1s Out

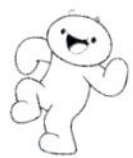

GAINED WEIGHT

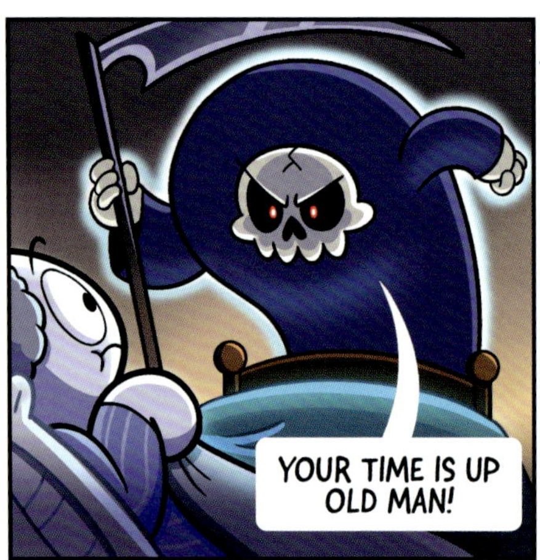

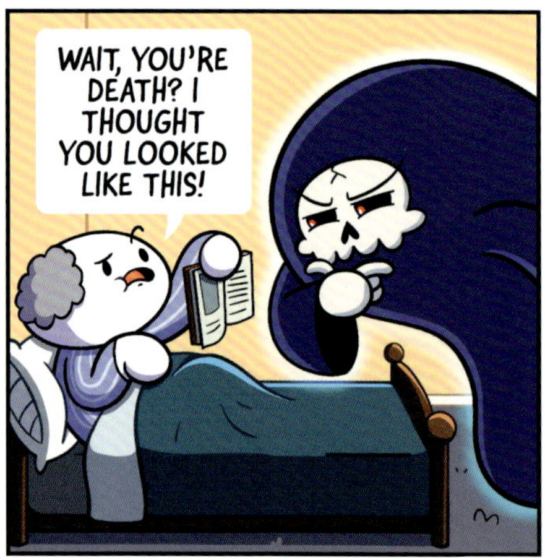

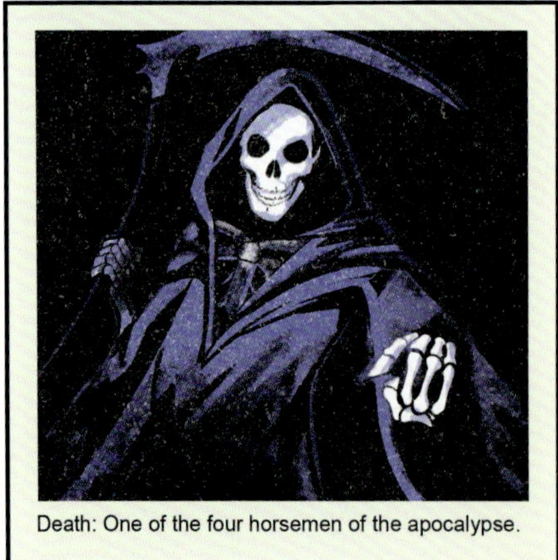
Death: One of the four horsemen of the apocalypse.

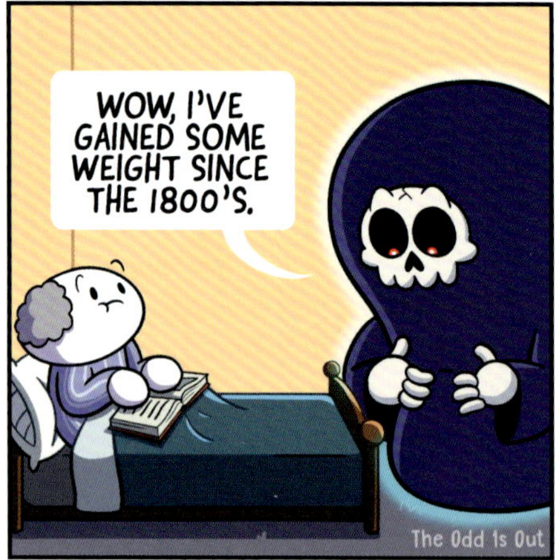

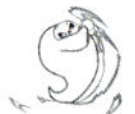

YOU LOSE

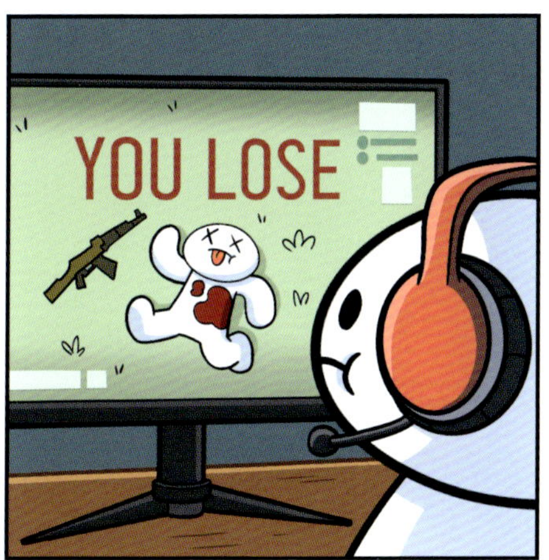
YOU LOSE

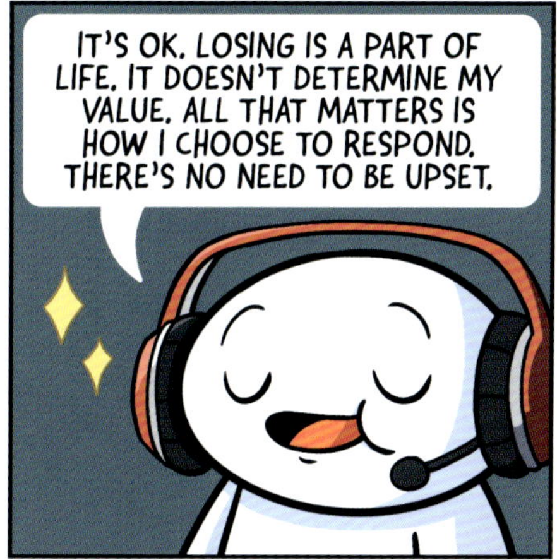
IT'S OK. LOSING IS A PART OF LIFE. IT DOESN'T DETERMINE MY VALUE. ALL THAT MATTERS IS HOW I CHOOSE TO RESPOND. THERE'S NO NEED TO BE UPSET.

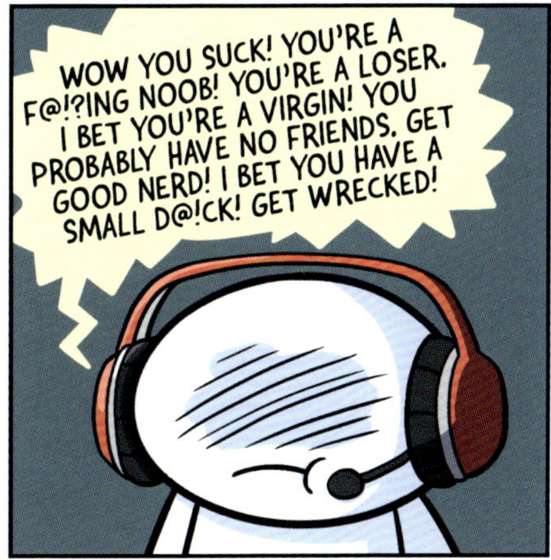
WOW YOU SUCK! YOU'RE A F@!?ING NOOB! YOU'RE A LOSER. I BET YOU'RE A VIRGIN! YOU PROBABLY HAVE NO FRIENDS. GET GOOD NERD! I BET YOU HAVE A SMALL D@!CK! GET WRECKED!

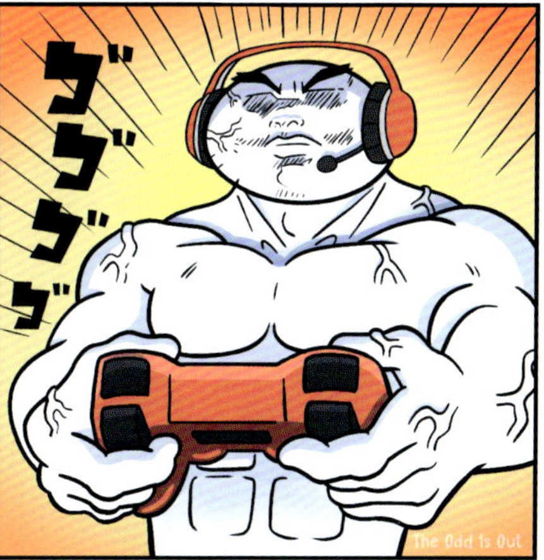
The Odd 1s Out

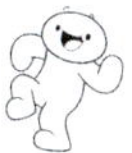

DEVILED EGGS

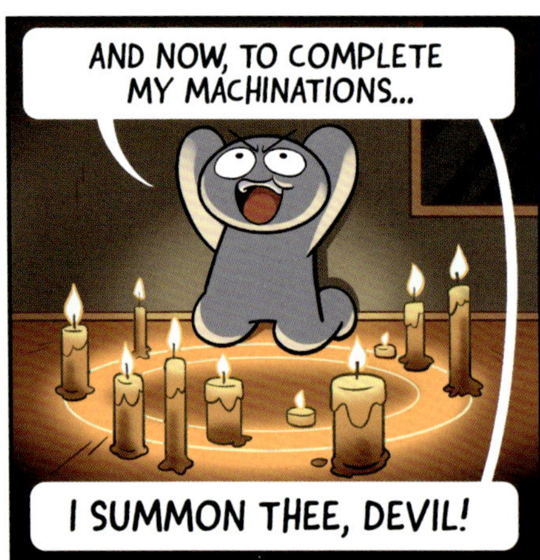

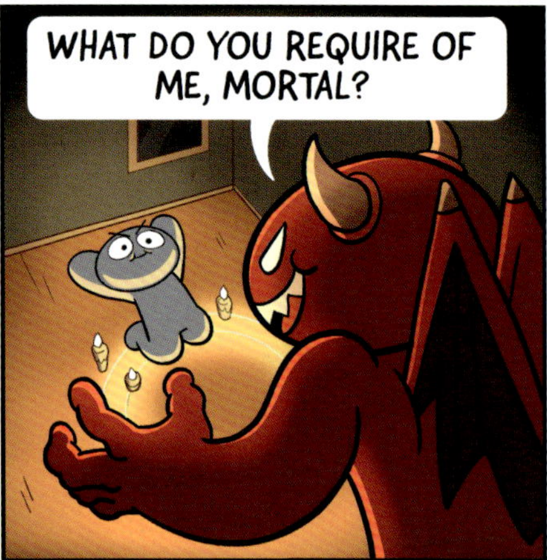

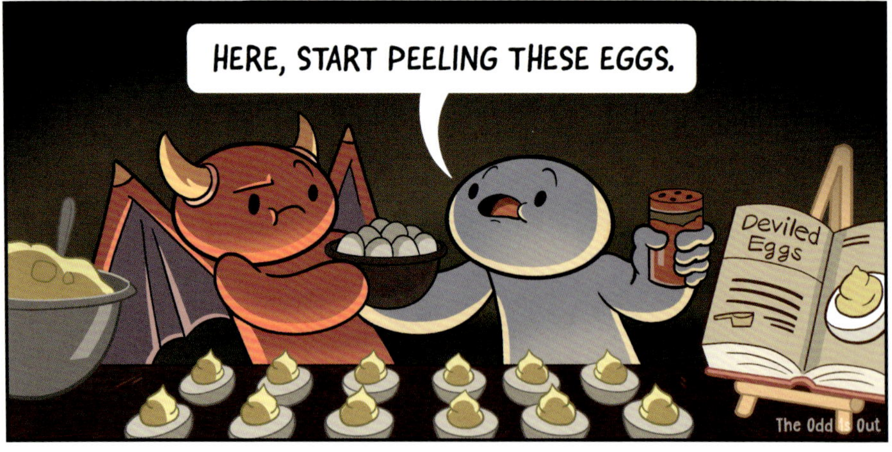

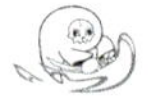

MANLY

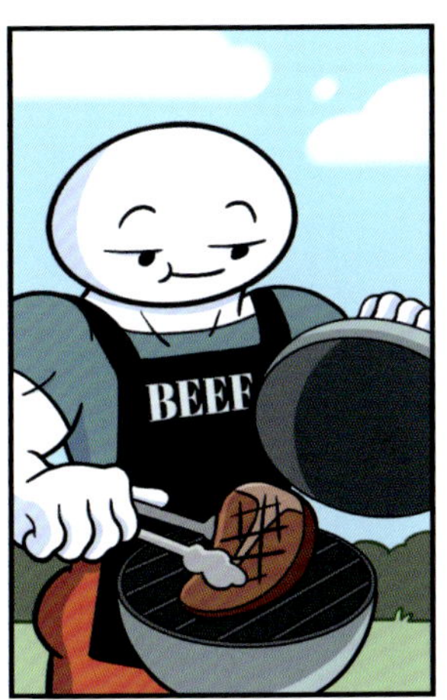
BEEF

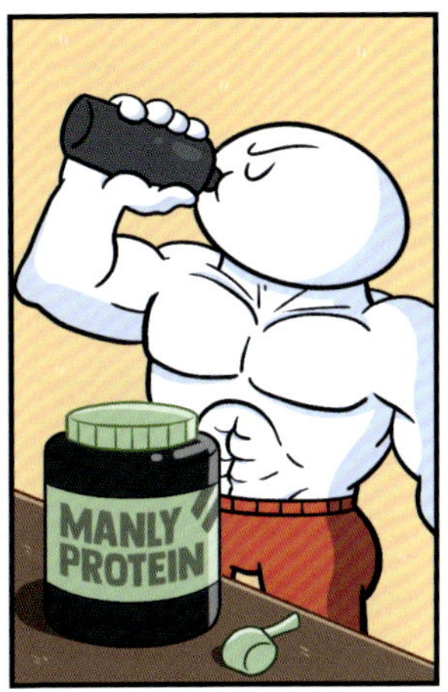
MANLY PROTEIN

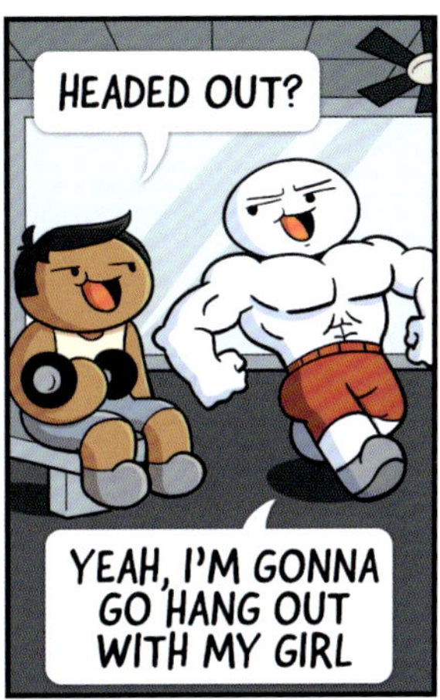
HEADED OUT?
YEAH, I'M GONNA GO HANG OUT WITH MY GIRL

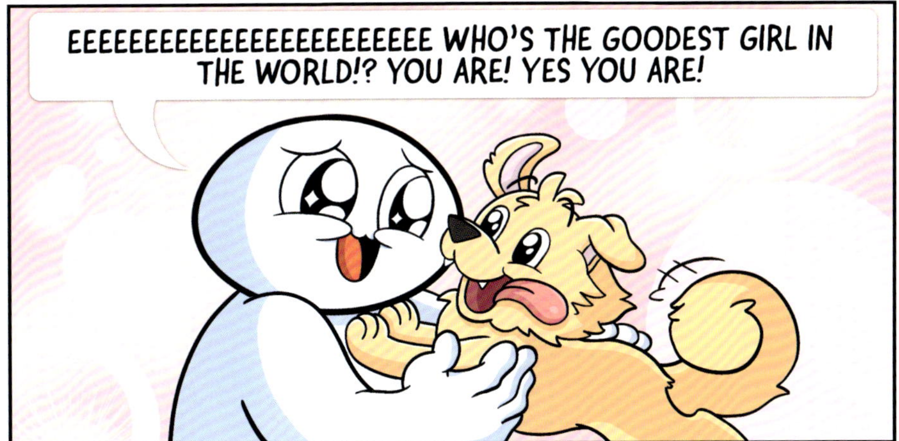
EEEEEEEEEEEEEEEEEEEEEEEE WHO'S THE GOODEST GIRL IN THE WORLD!? YOU ARE! YES YOU ARE!

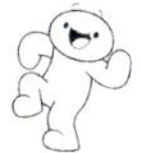

BURRITO

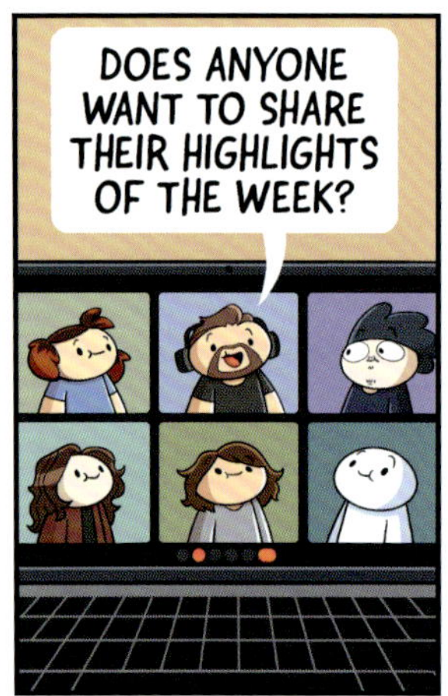
DOES ANYONE WANT TO SHARE THEIR HIGHLIGHTS OF THE WEEK?

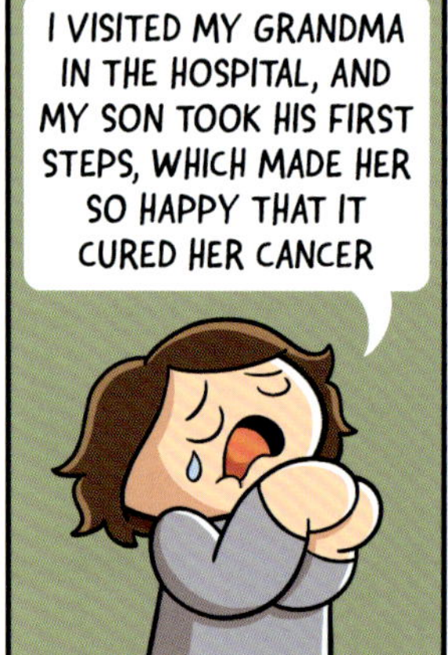
I VISITED MY GRANDMA IN THE HOSPITAL, AND MY SON TOOK HIS FIRST STEPS, WHICH MADE HER SO HAPPY THAT IT CURED HER CANCER

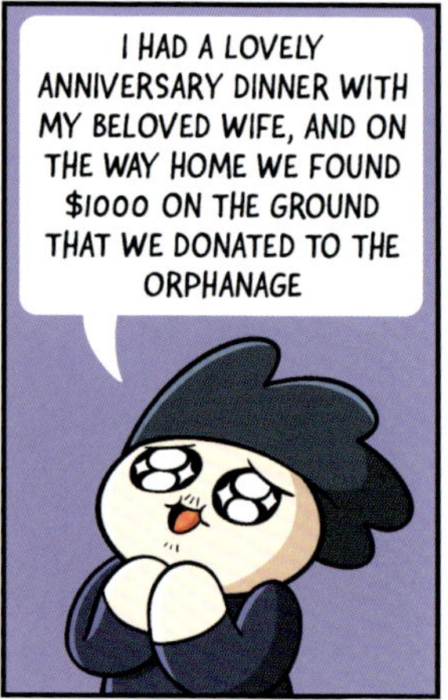
I HAD A LOVELY ANNIVERSARY DINNER WITH MY BELOVED WIFE, AND ON THE WAY HOME WE FOUND $1000 ON THE GROUND THAT WE DONATED TO THE ORPHANAGE

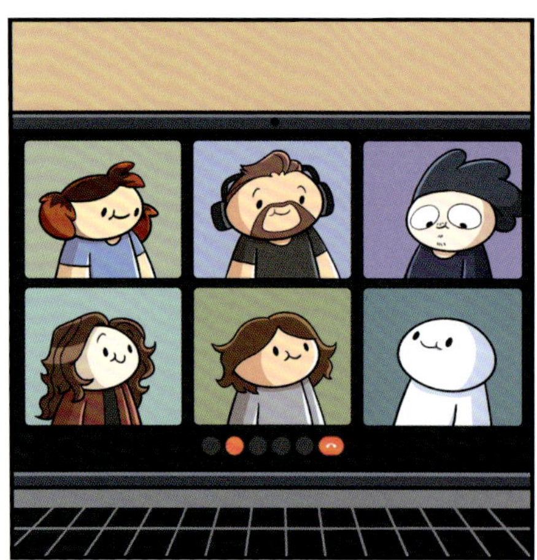

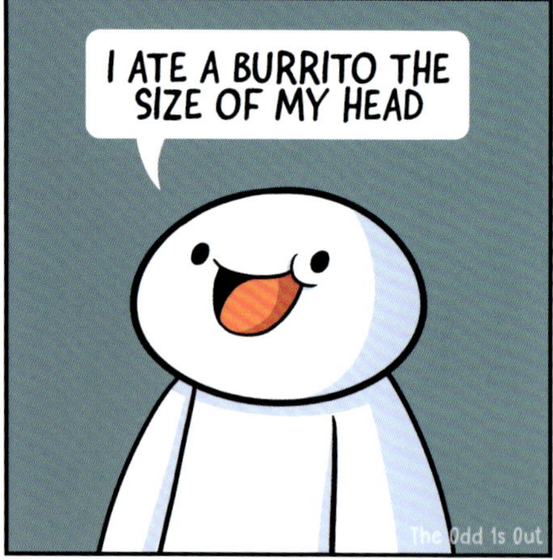
I ATE A BURRITO THE SIZE OF MY HEAD
The Odd 1s Out

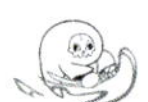

60 DEGREES

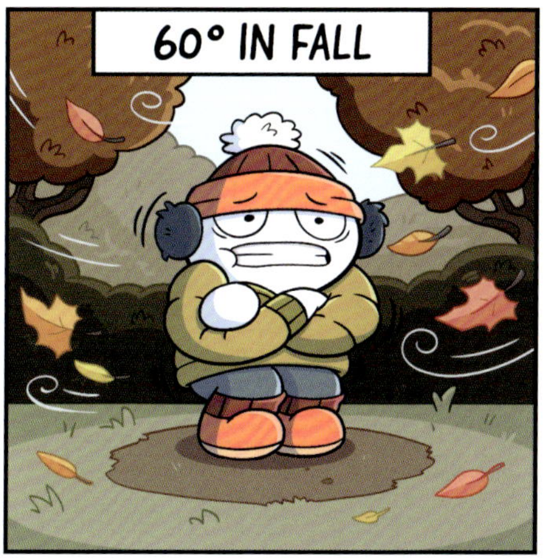

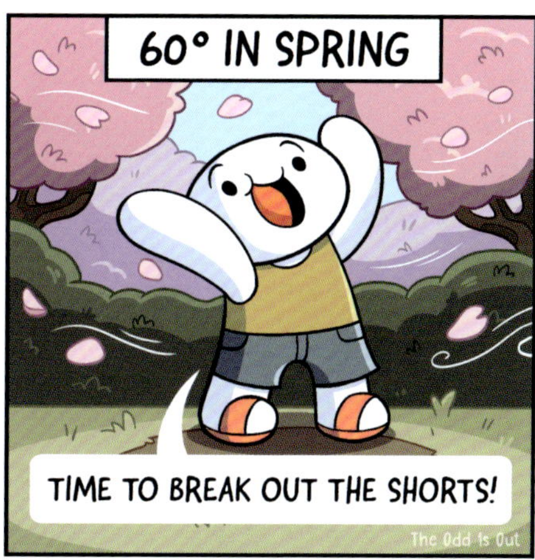

CRACKED SPIDER

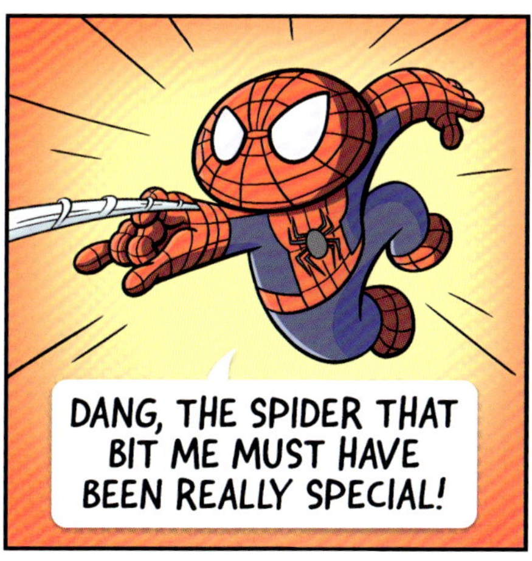

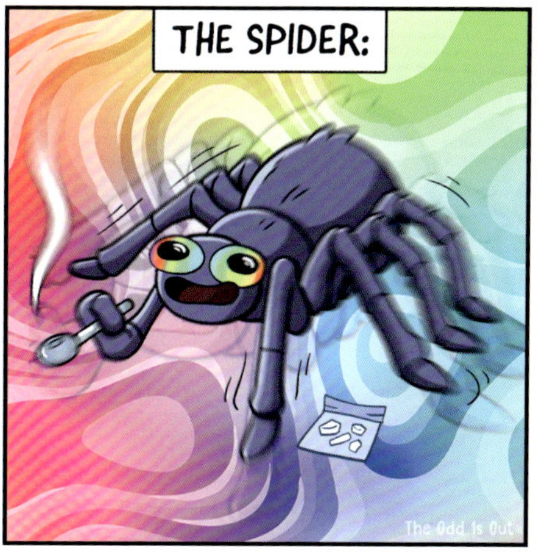

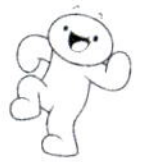

WORK DREAM

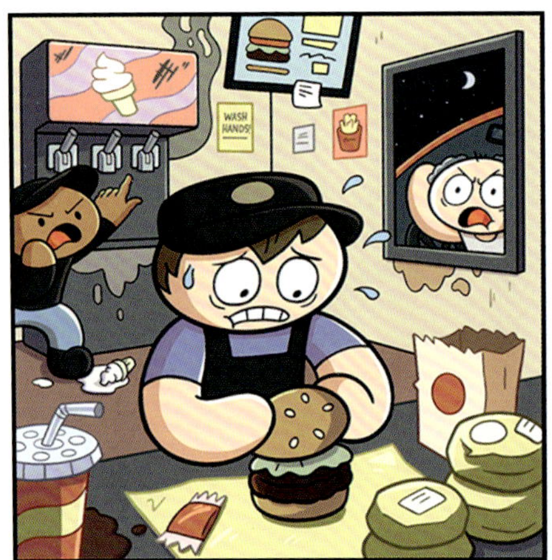
WASH HANDS!

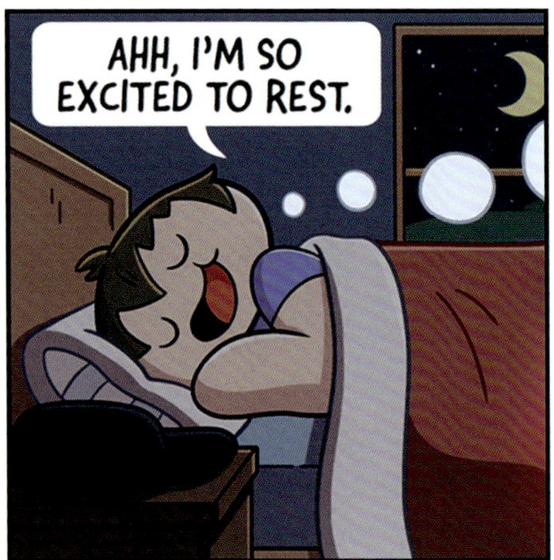
AHH, I'M SO EXCITED TO REST.

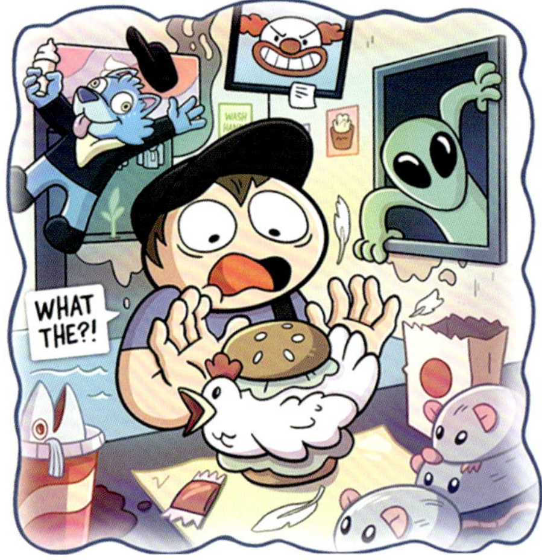
WHAT THE?!
WASH HANDS

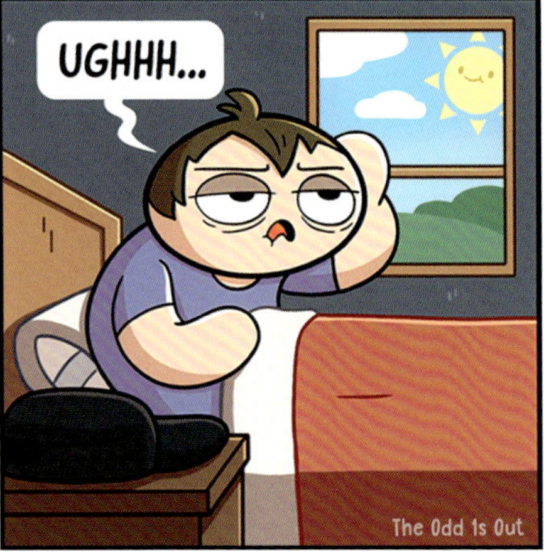
UGHHH...
The Odd 1s Out

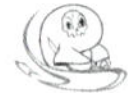

MINECRAFT

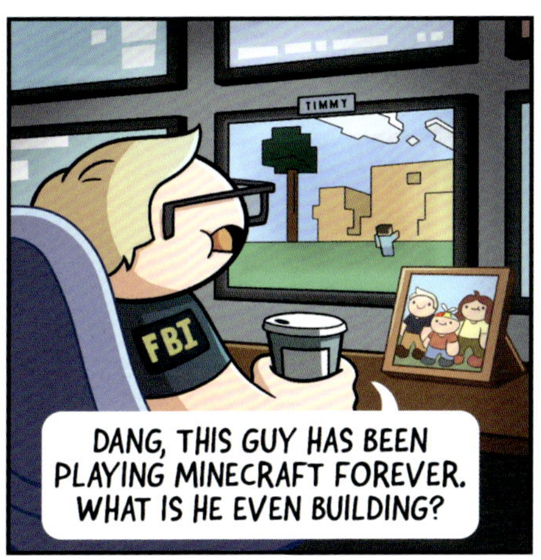
TIMMY
FBI
DANG, THIS GUY HAS BEEN PLAYING MINECRAFT FOREVER. WHAT IS HE EVEN BUILDING?

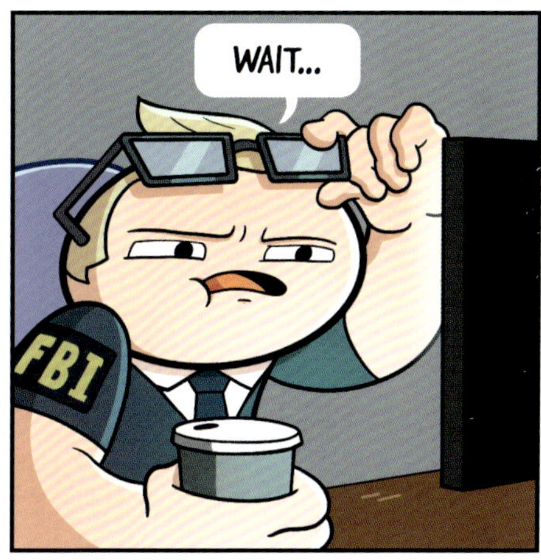
WAIT...
FBI

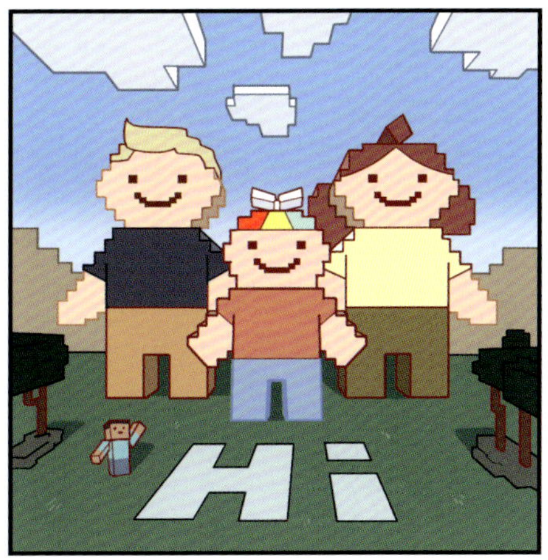
HI

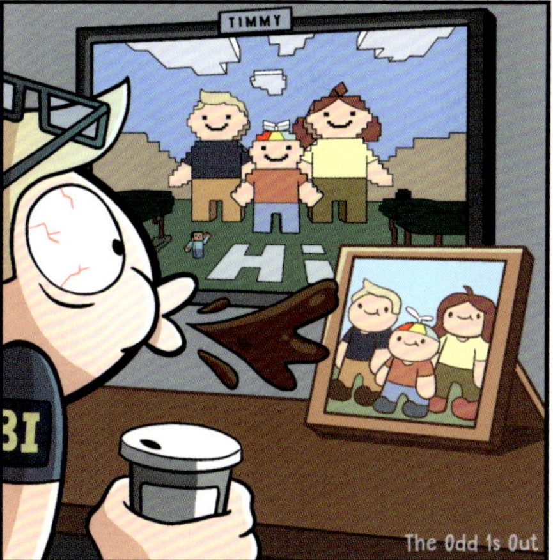
TIMMY
The Odd 1s Out

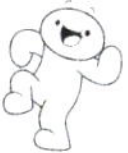

FACTORIAL

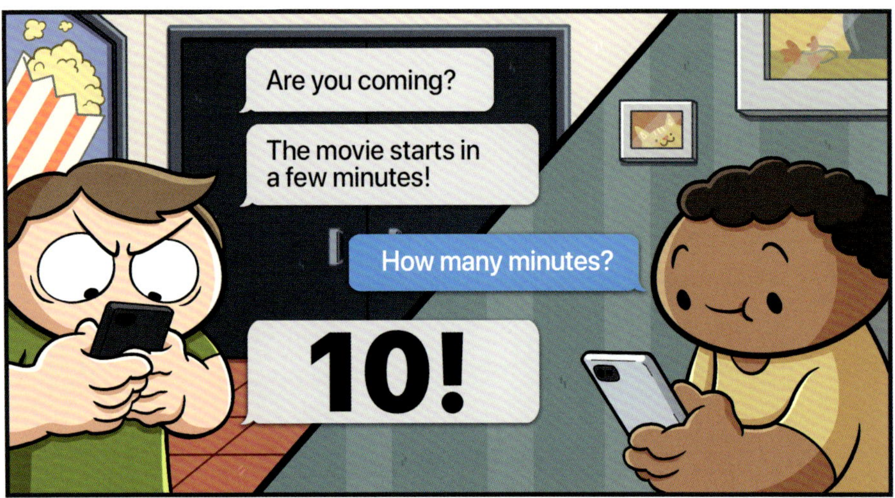

3,628,800 MINUTES LATER
(6.904 YEARS)

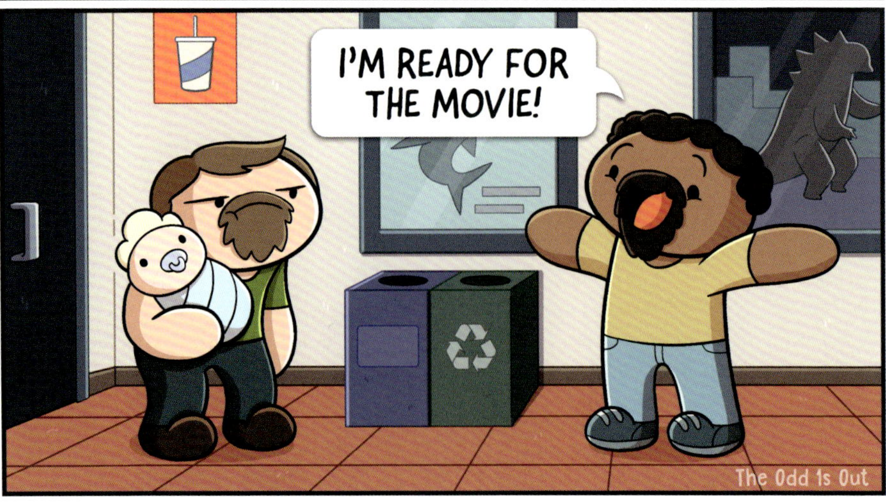

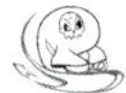

COOKIE DIET

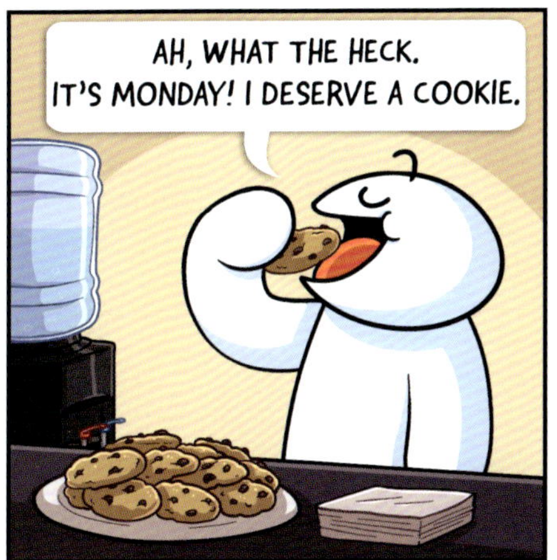
AH, WHAT THE HECK.
IT'S MONDAY! I DESERVE A COOKIE.

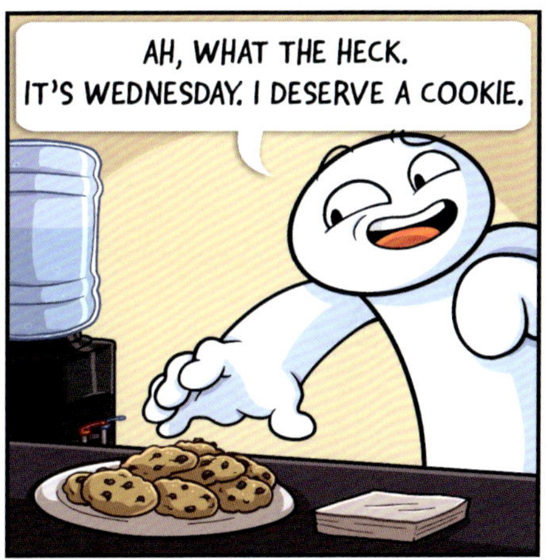
AH, WHAT THE HECK.
IT'S WEDNESDAY. I DESERVE A COOKIE.

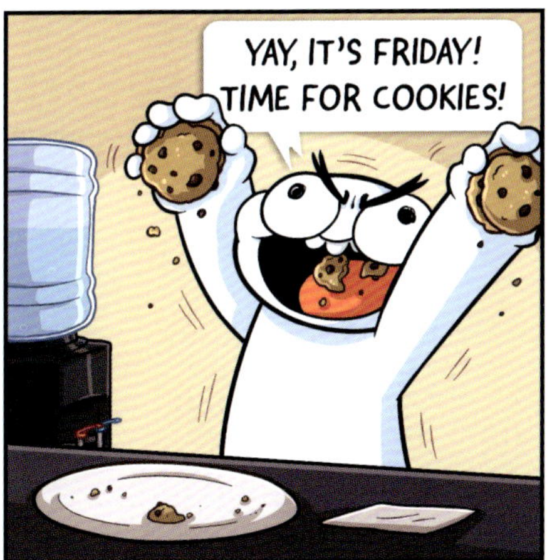
YAY, IT'S FRIDAY!
TIME FOR COOKIES!

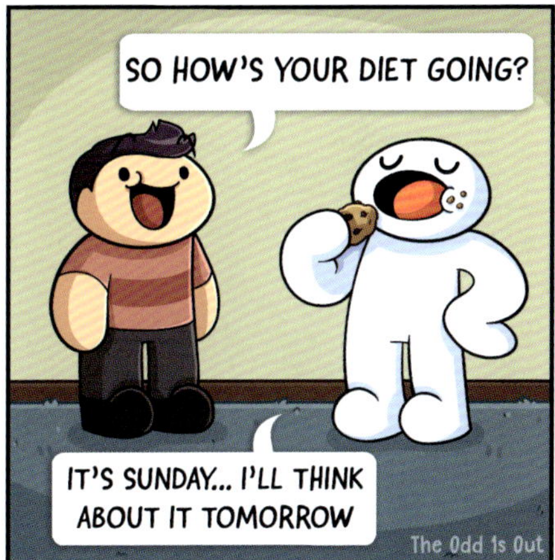
SO HOW'S YOUR DIET GOING?
IT'S SUNDAY... I'LL THINK
ABOUT IT TOMORROW
The Odd 1s Out

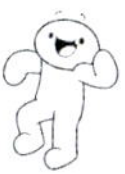

LIGHTBULB

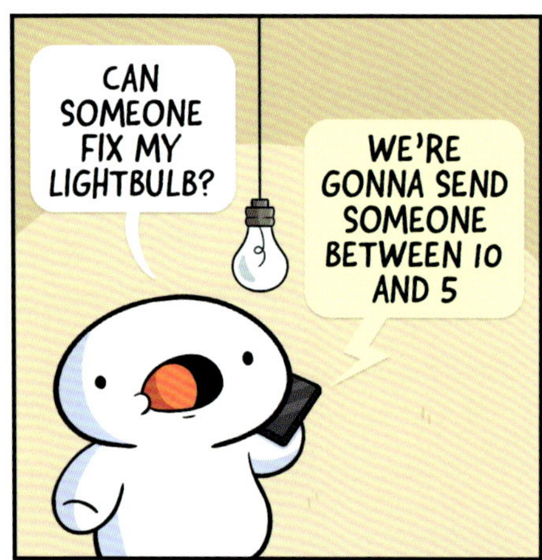
CAN SOMEONE FIX MY LIGHTBULB?
WE'RE GONNA SEND SOMEONE BETWEEN 10 AND 5

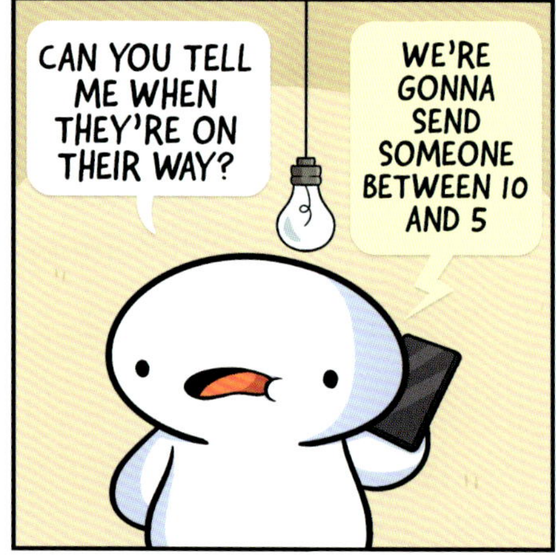
CAN YOU TELL ME WHEN THEY'RE ON THEIR WAY?
WE'RE GONNA SEND SOMEONE BETWEEN 10 AND 5

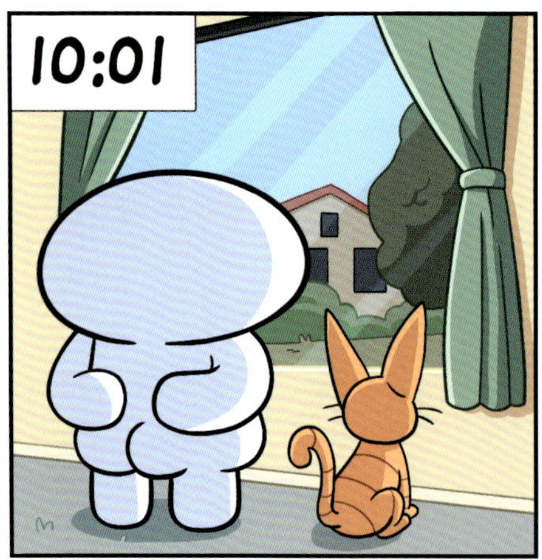
10:01

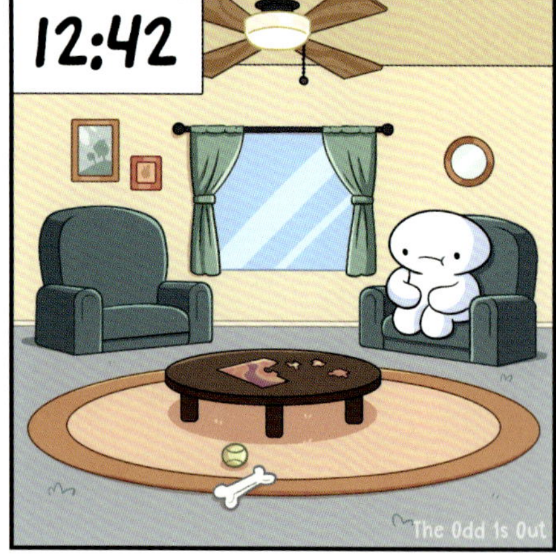
12:42
The Odd 1s Out

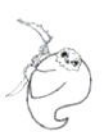

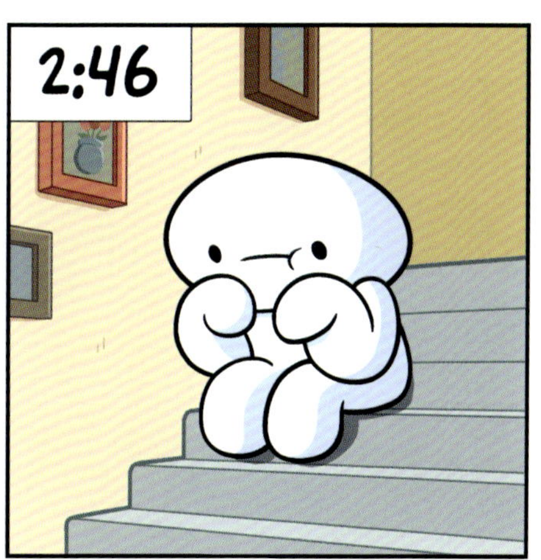
2:46

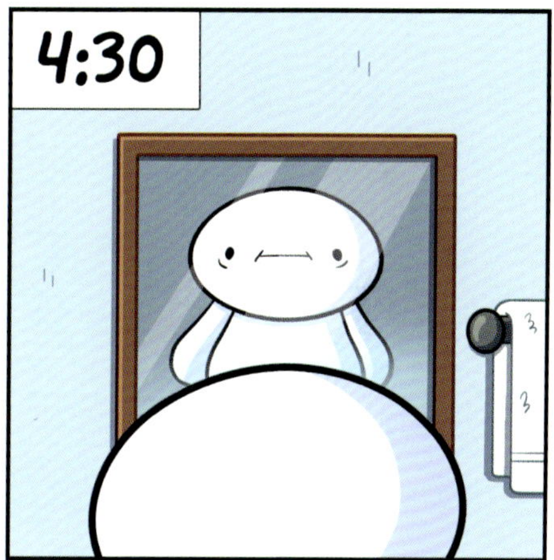
4:30

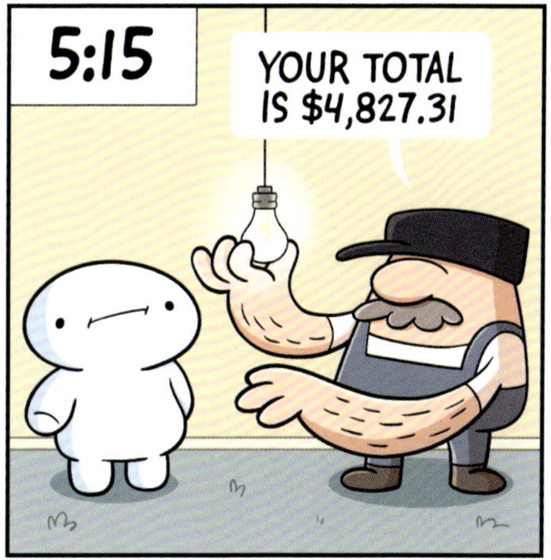
5:15
YOUR TOTAL IS $4,827.31

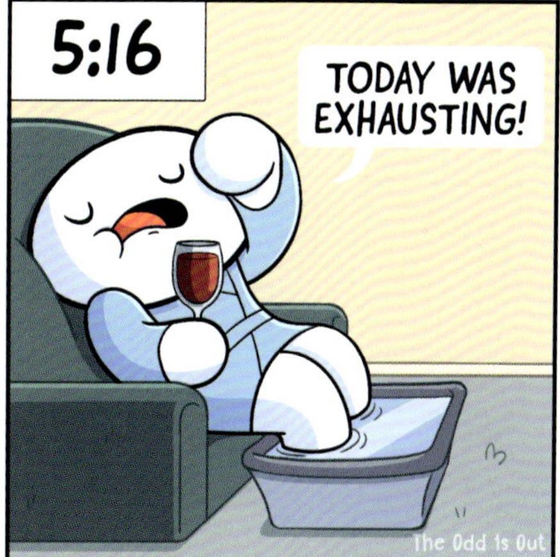
5:16
TODAY WAS EXHAUSTING!
The Odd is Out

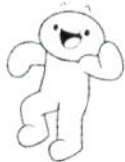

SPOILERS

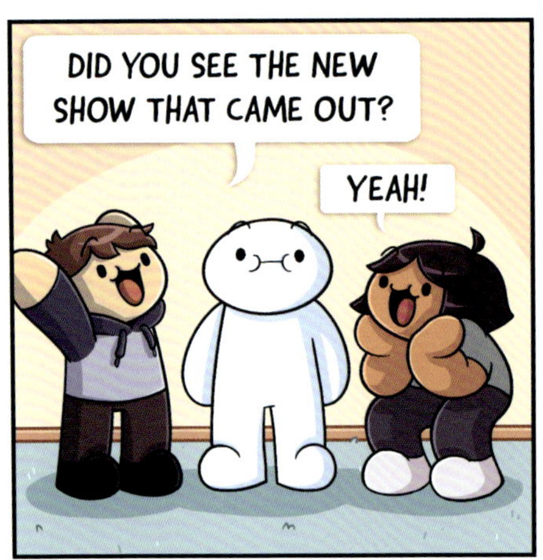
DID YOU SEE THE NEW SHOW THAT CAME OUT?
YEAH!

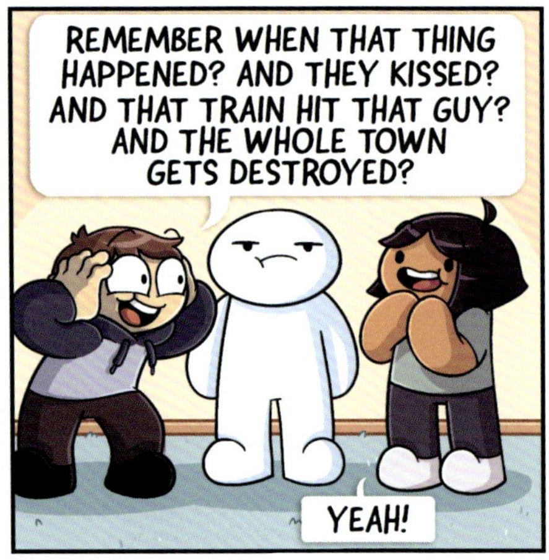
REMEMBER WHEN THAT THING HAPPENED? AND THEY KISSED? AND THAT TRAIN HIT THAT GUY? AND THE WHOLE TOWN GETS DESTROYED?
YEAH!

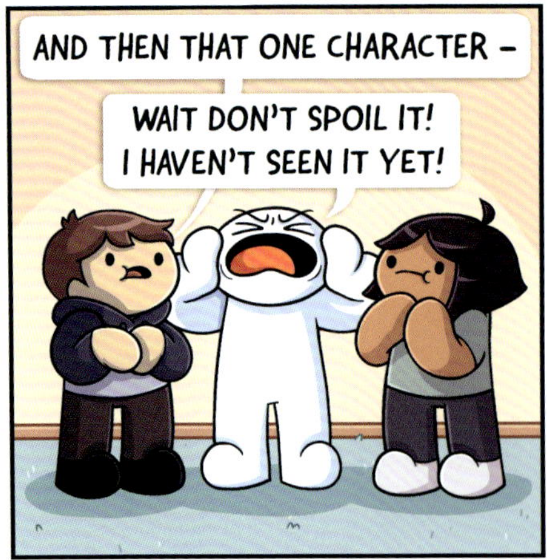
AND THEN THAT ONE CHARACTER –
WAIT DON'T SPOIL IT! I HAVEN'T SEEN IT YET!

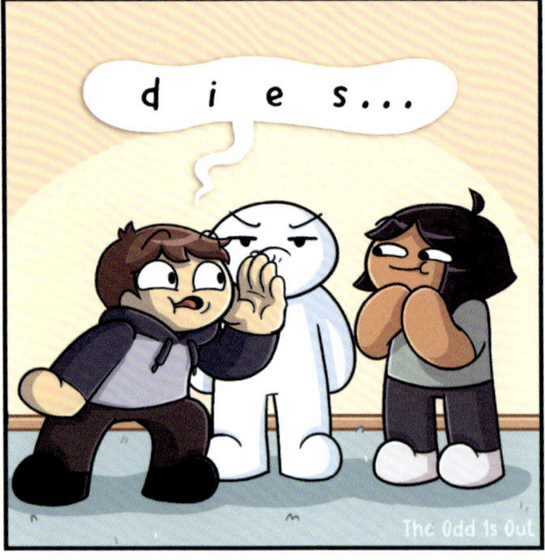
d i e s...
The Odd 1s Out

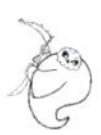

SPOOKED

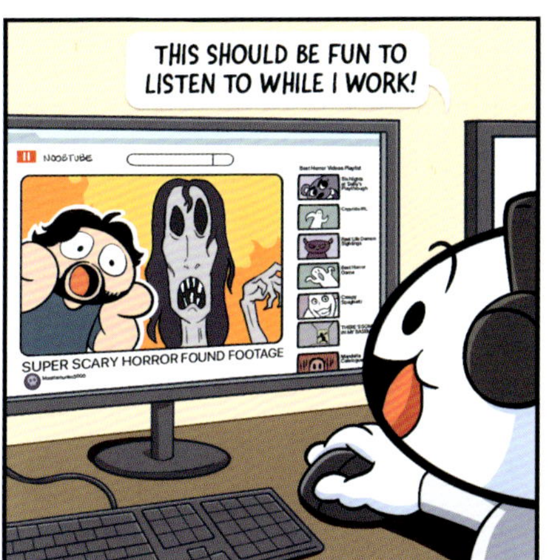
THIS SHOULD BE FUN TO LISTEN TO WHILE I WORK!
NOOBTUBE
SUPER SCARY HORROR FOUND FOOTAGE

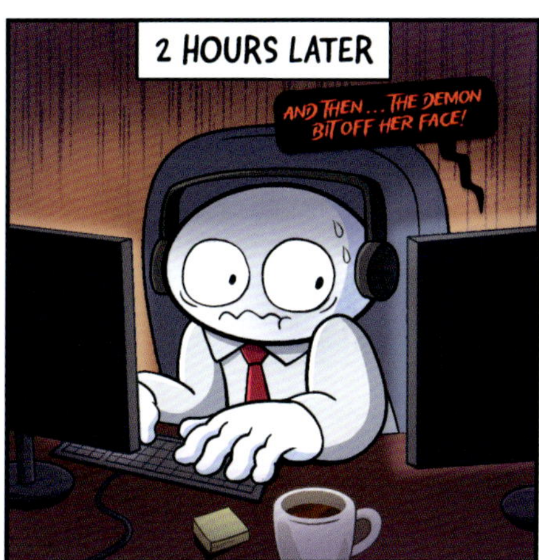
2 HOURS LATER
AND THEN... THE DEMON BIT OFF HER FACE!

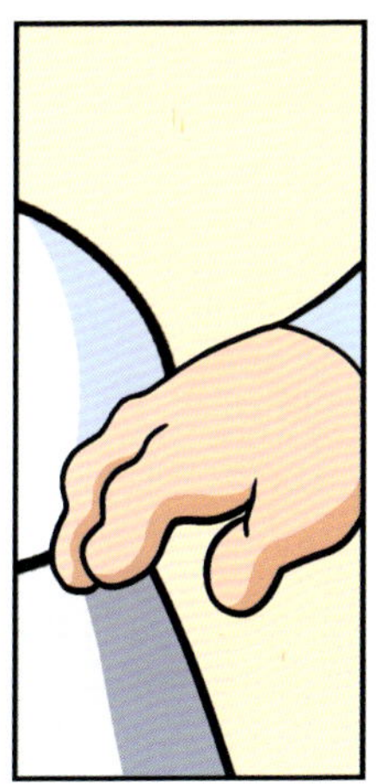

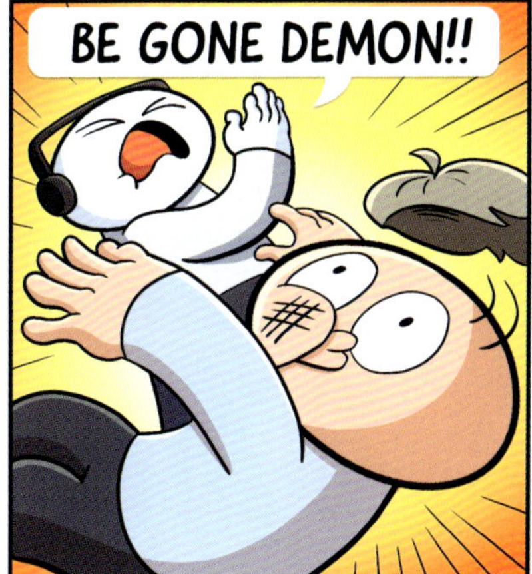
BE GONE DEMON!!

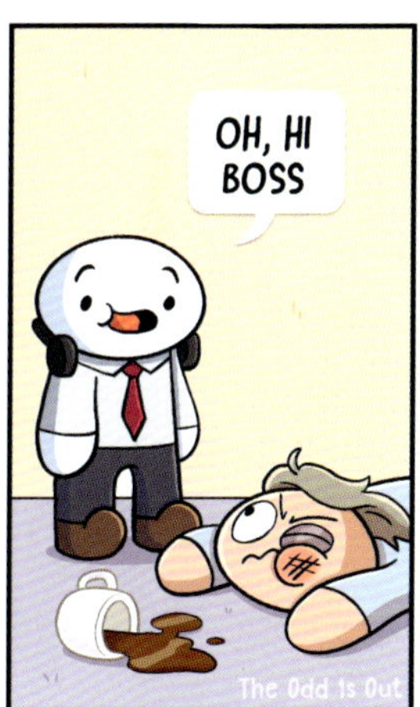
OH, HI BOSS
The Odd 1s Out

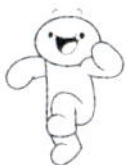

BLUEBERRIES

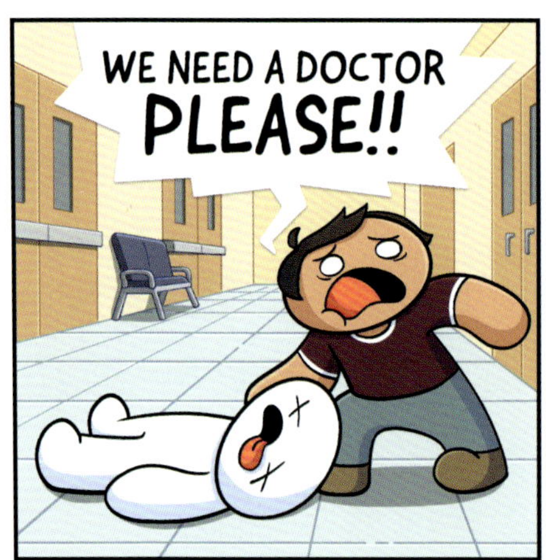

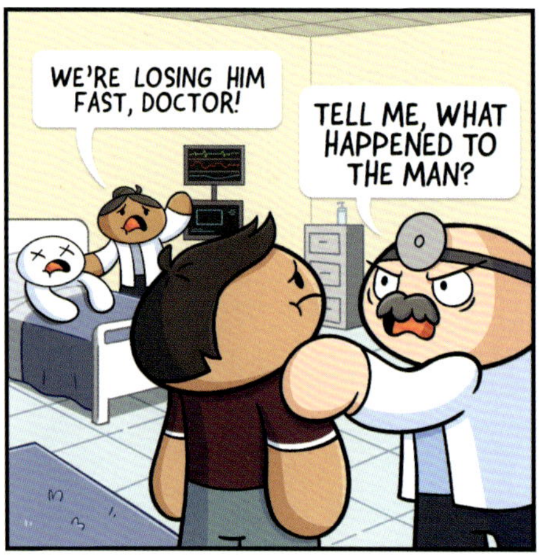

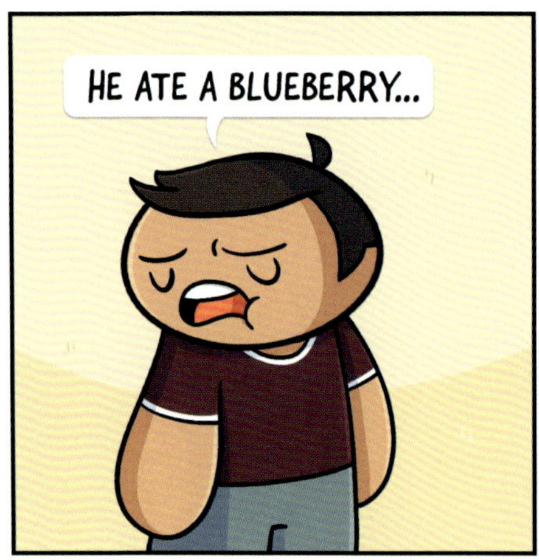

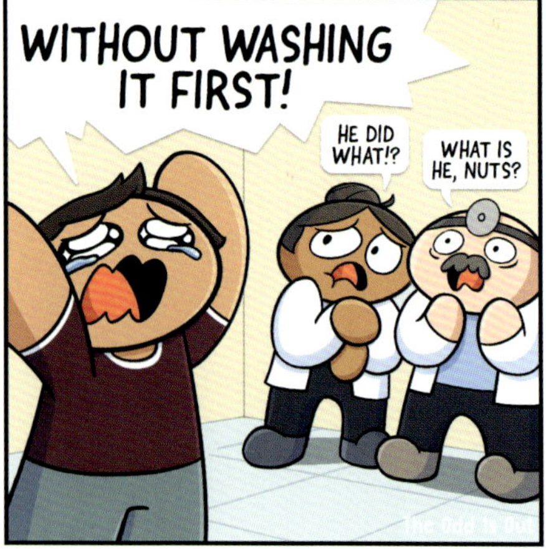

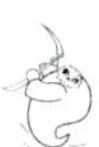

WISH

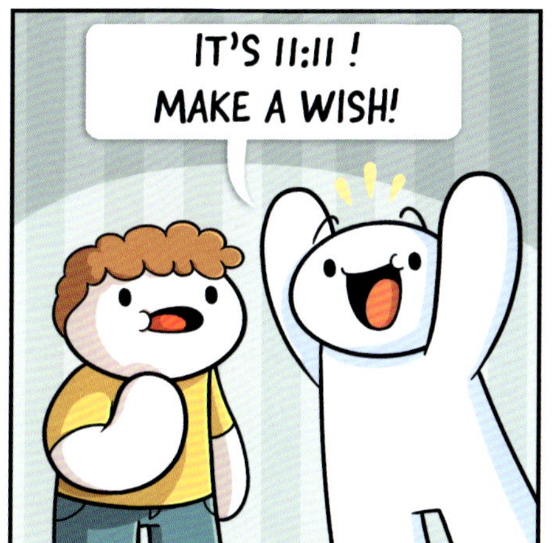
IT'S 11:11 !
MAKE A WISH!

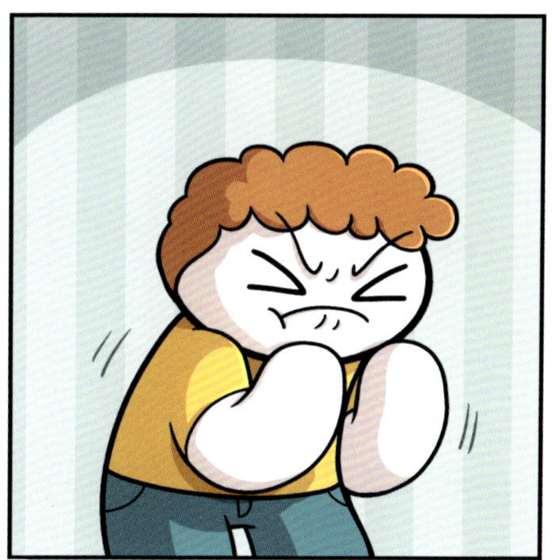

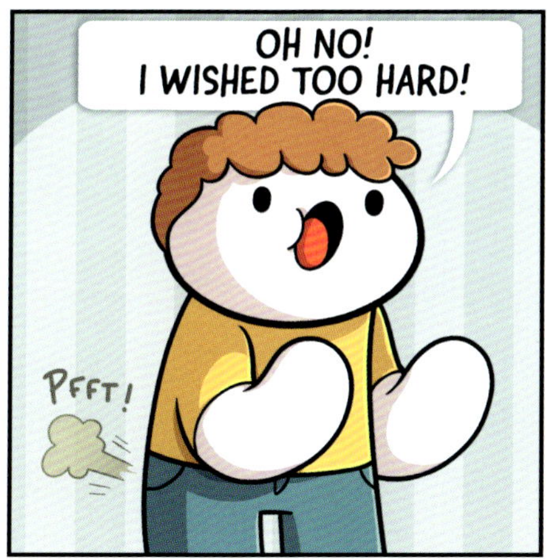
OH NO!
I WISHED TOO HARD!
PFFT!

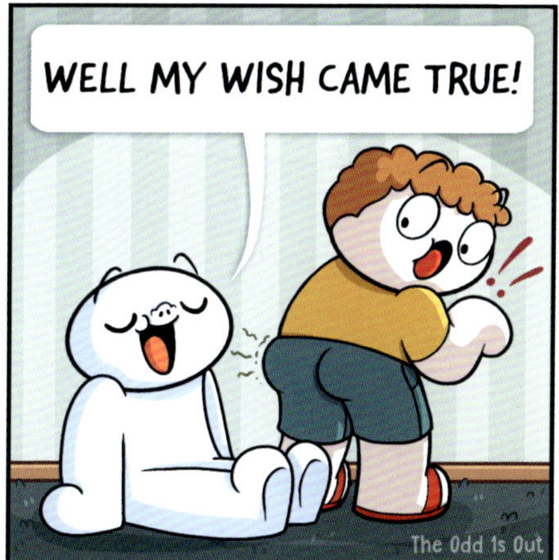
WELL MY WISH CAME TRUE!
The Odd 1s Out

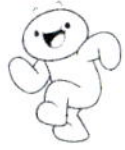

SERIAL KILLER

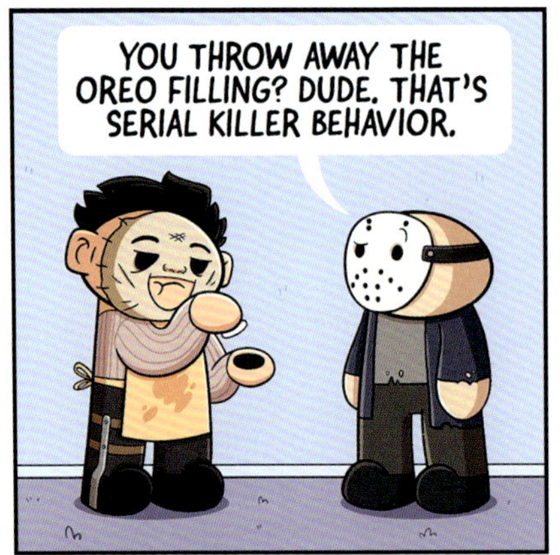

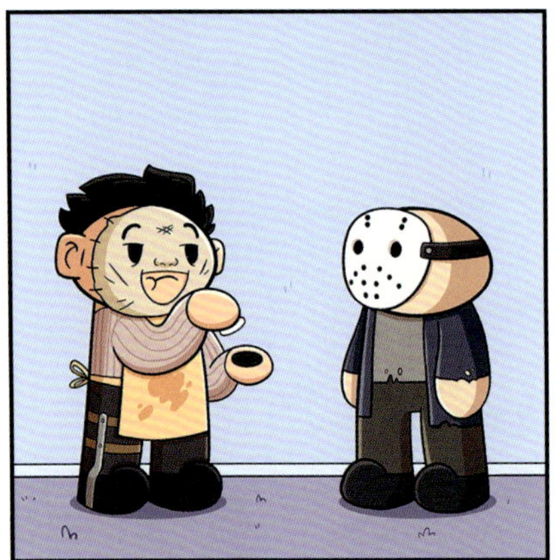

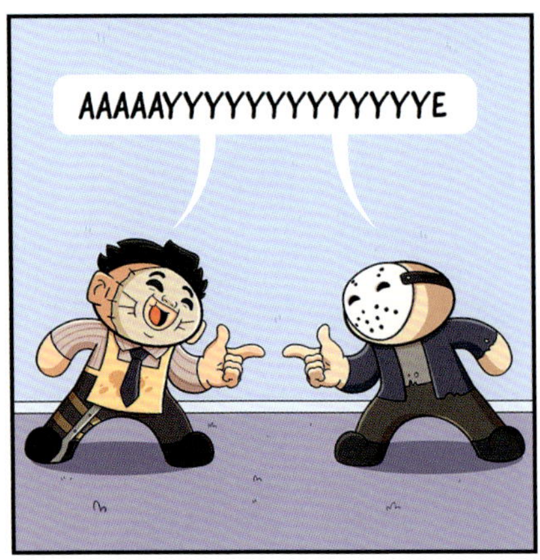

PRAYING MANTIS

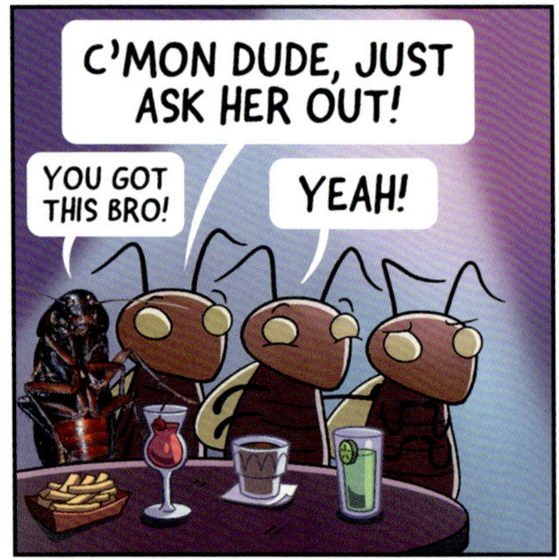

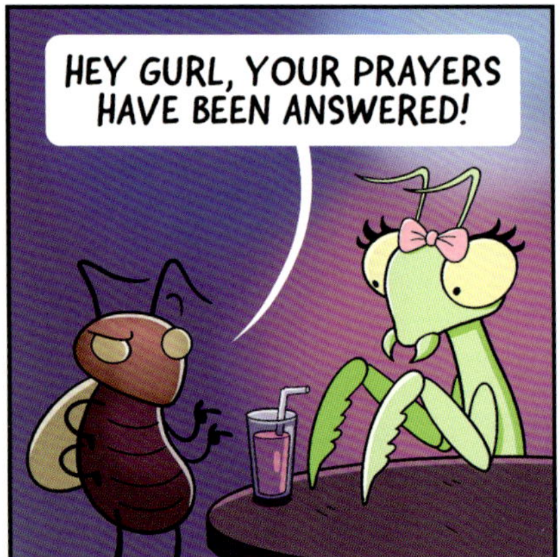

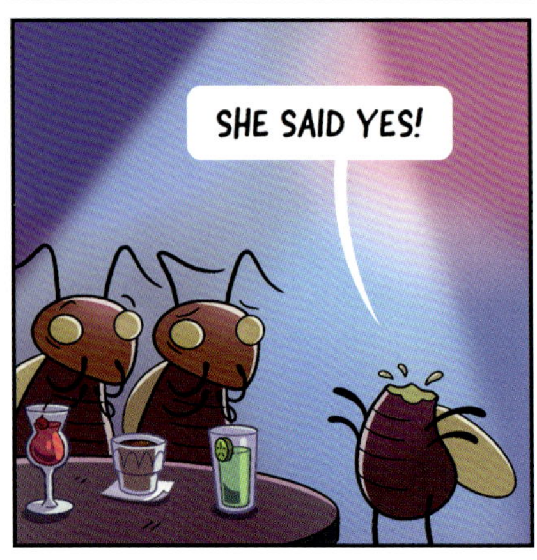

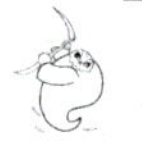

THROW UP

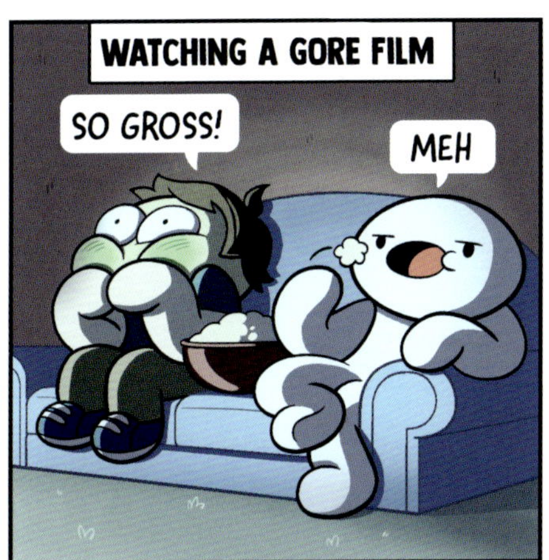
WATCHING A GORE FILM
SO GROSS!
MEH

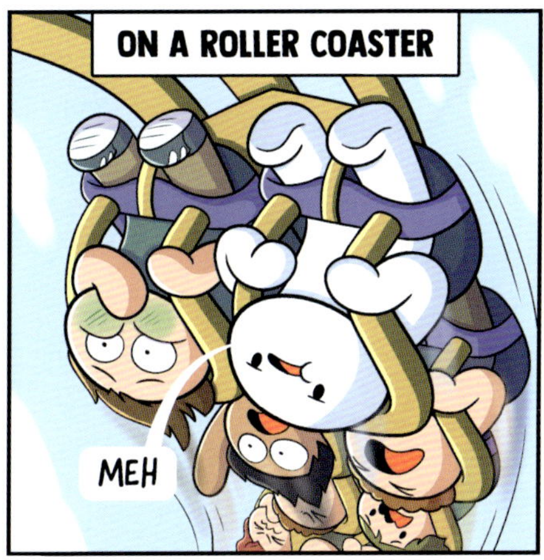
ON A ROLLER COASTER
MEH

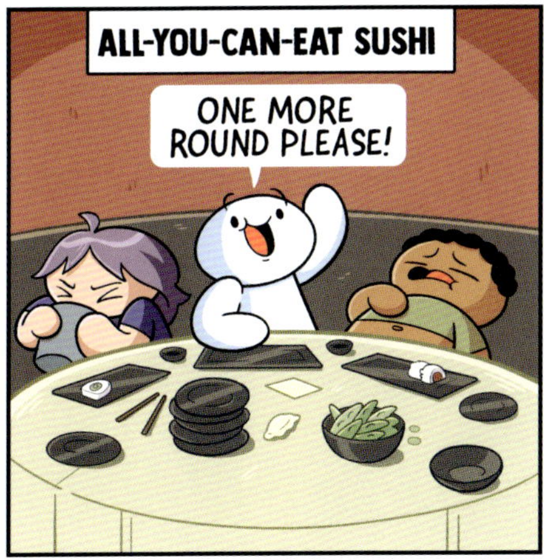
ALL-YOU-CAN-EAT SUSHI
ONE MORE ROUND PLEASE!

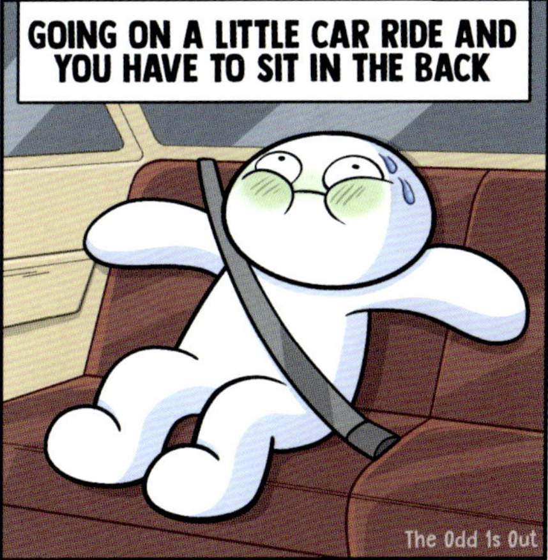
GOING ON A LITTLE CAR RIDE AND YOU HAVE TO SIT IN THE BACK
The Odd 1s Out

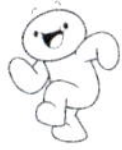

FUNKO POPS

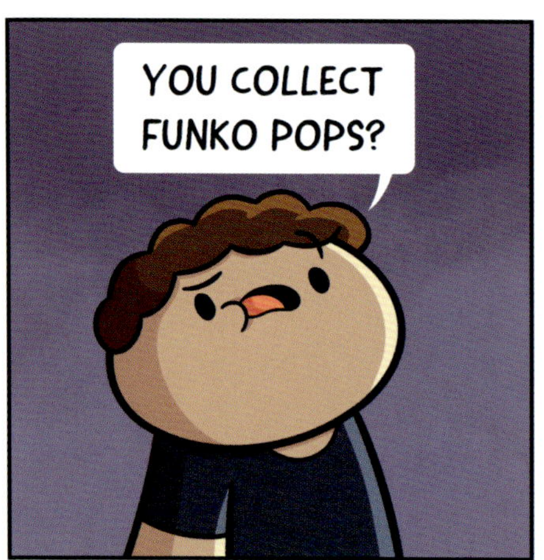
YOU COLLECT FUNKO POPS?

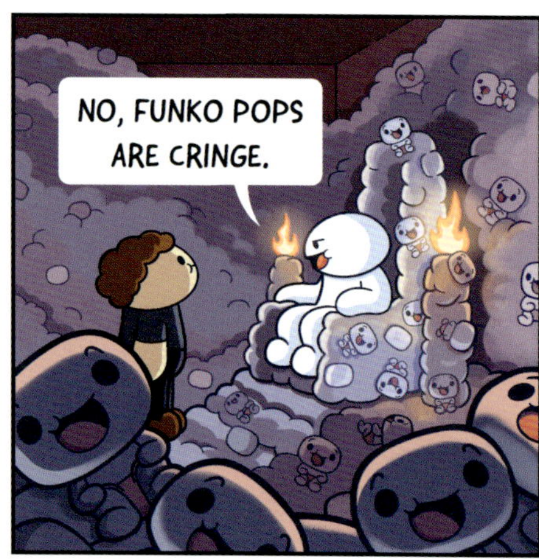
NO, FUNKO POPS ARE CRINGE.

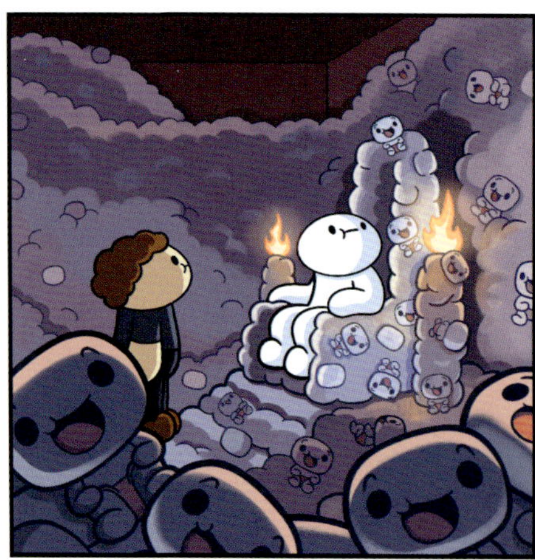

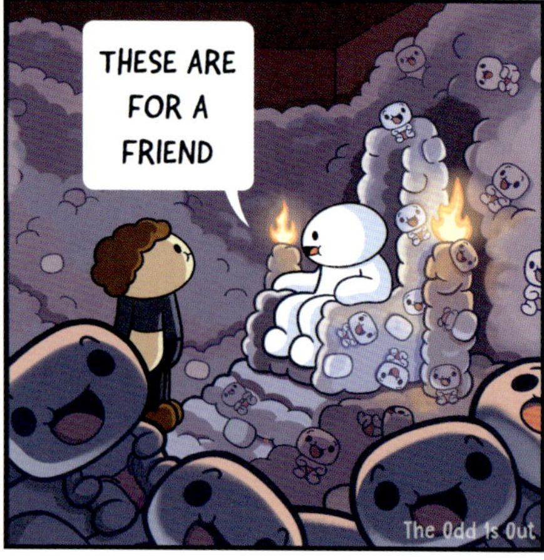
THESE ARE FOR A FRIEND
The Odd 1s Out

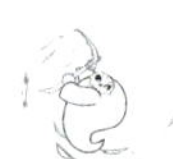

THERMOSTAT

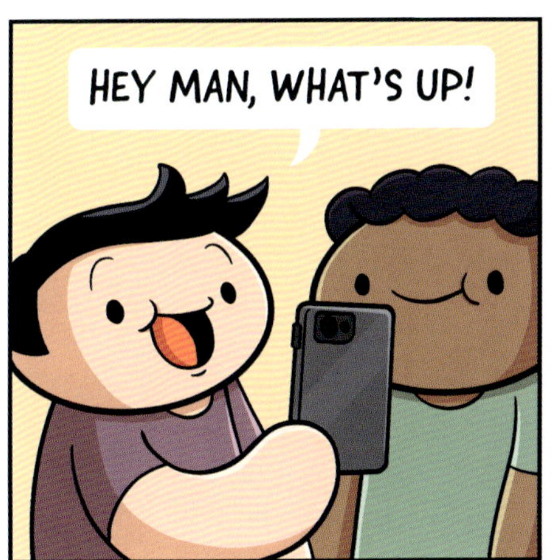
HEY MAN, WHAT'S UP!

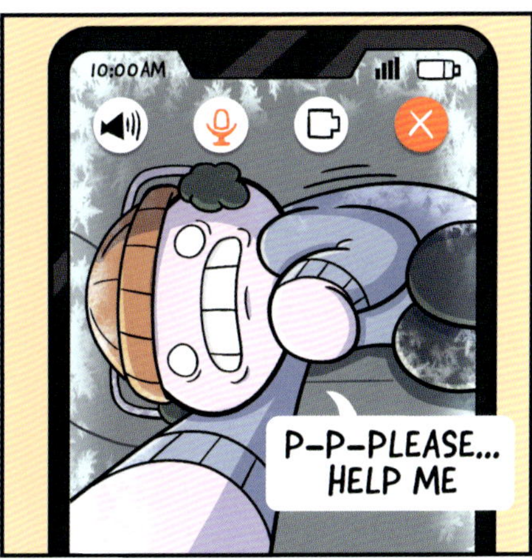
10:00AM
P-P-PLEASE...
HELP ME

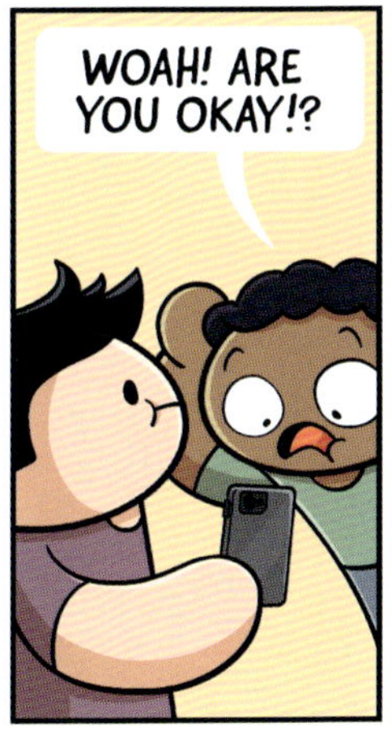
WOAH! ARE
YOU OKAY!?

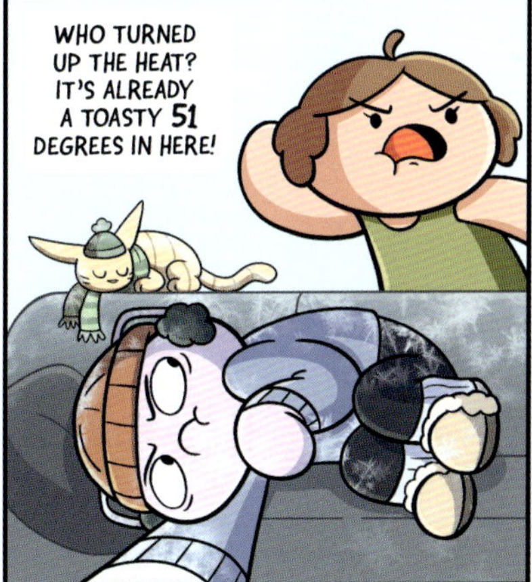
WHO TURNED
UP THE HEAT?
IT'S ALREADY
A TOASTY 51
DEGREES IN HERE!

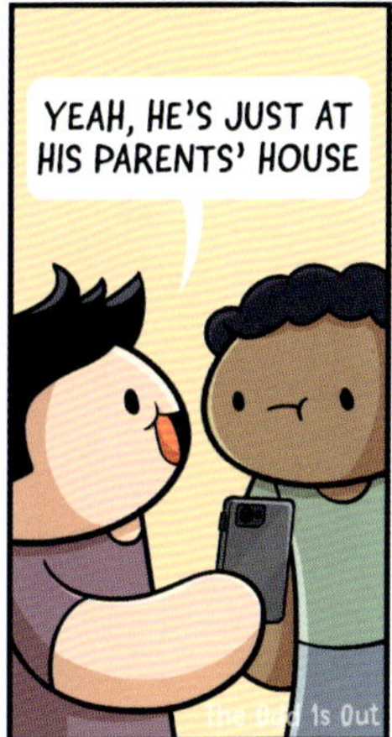
YEAH, HE'S JUST AT
HIS PARENTS' HOUSE

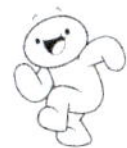

HUMPTY DUMPTY

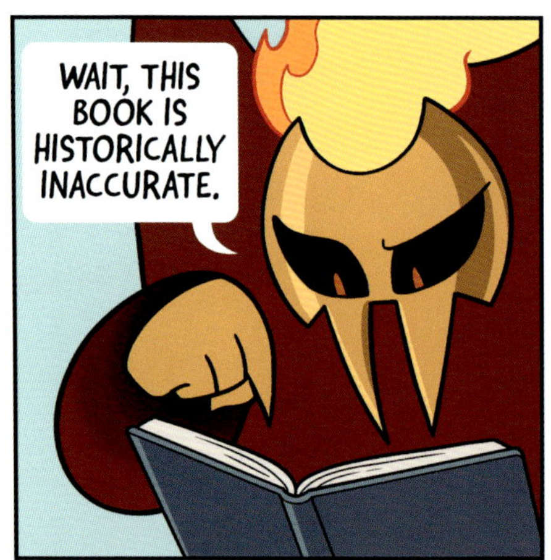

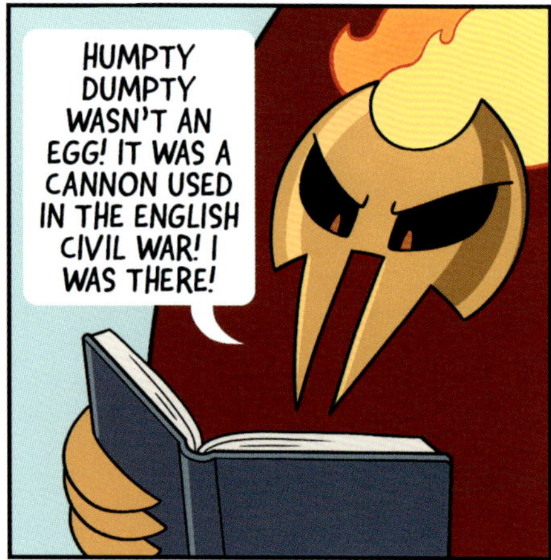

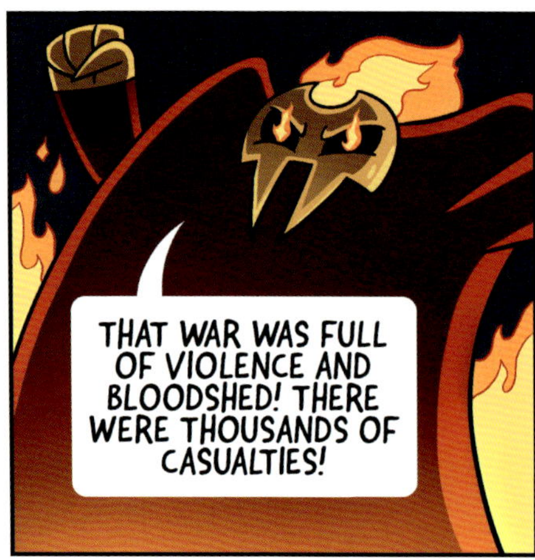

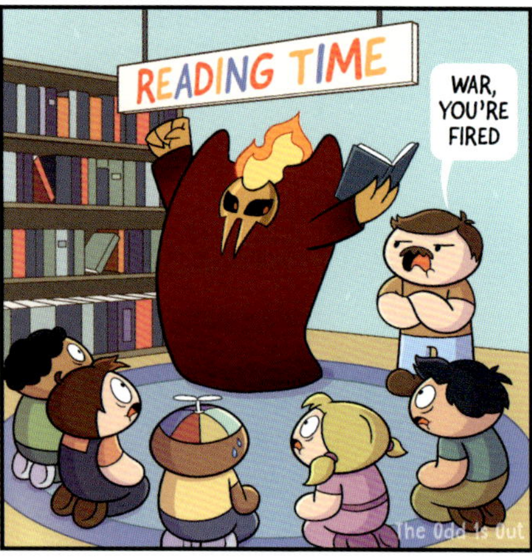

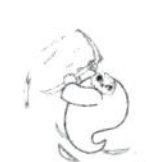

DOG PARK

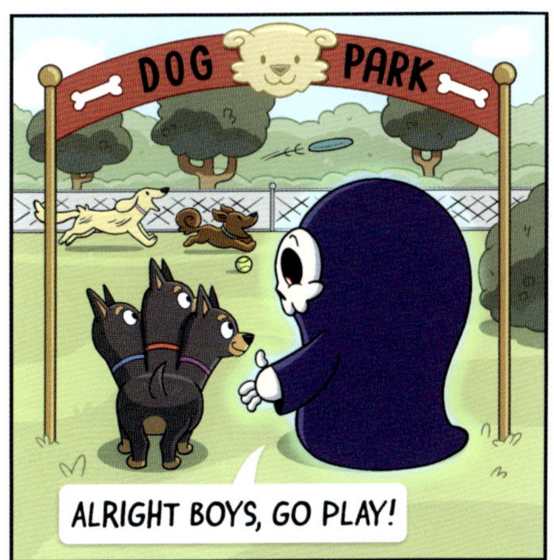
DOG PARK
ALRIGHT BOYS, GO PLAY!

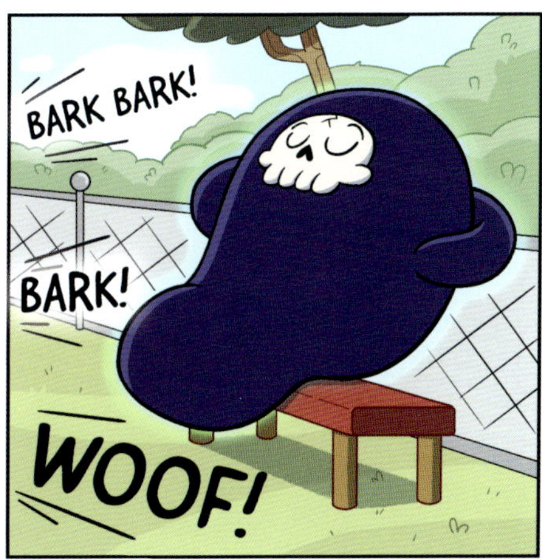
BARK BARK!
BARK!
WOOF!

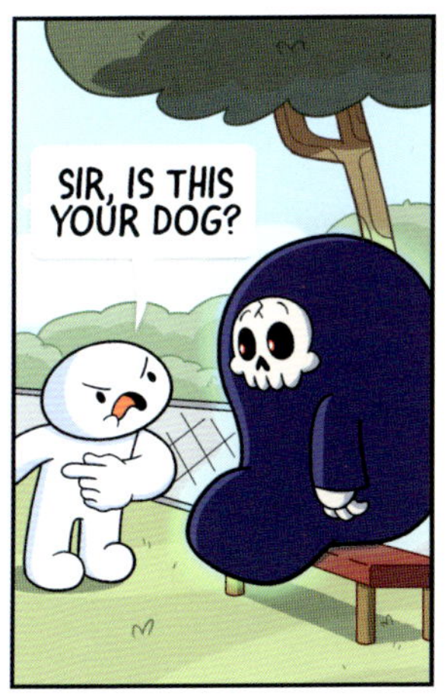
SIR, IS THIS YOUR DOG?

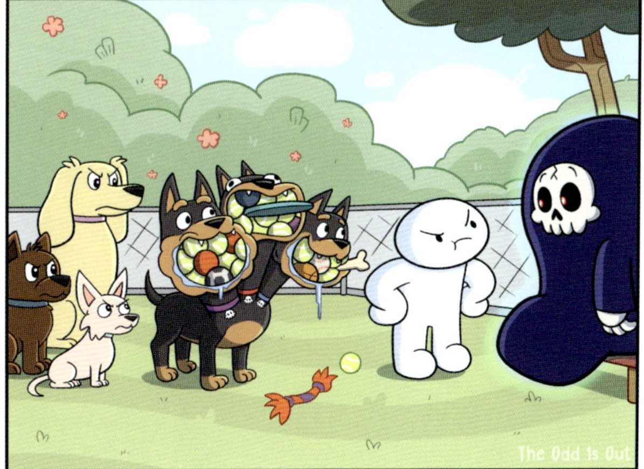
The Odd 1s Out

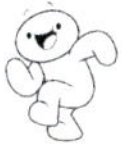

THROWBACK

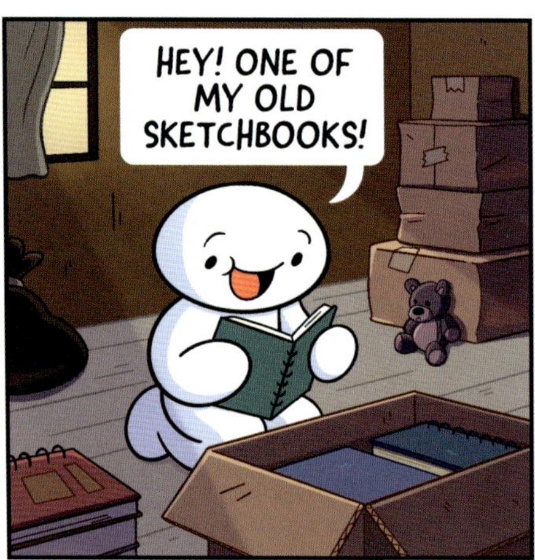
HEY! ONE OF MY OLD SKETCHBOOKS!

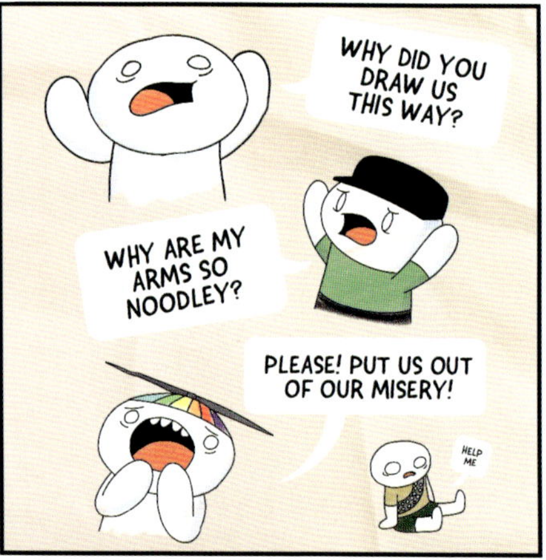
WHY DID YOU DRAW US THIS WAY?
WHY ARE MY ARMS SO NOODLEY?
PLEASE! PUT US OUT OF OUR MISERY!
HELP ME

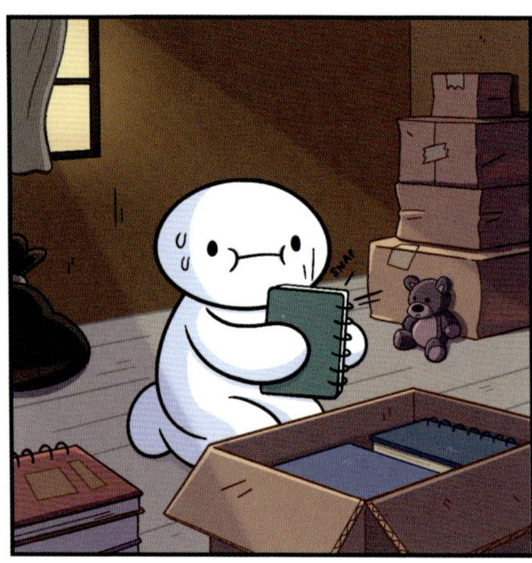
SNAP

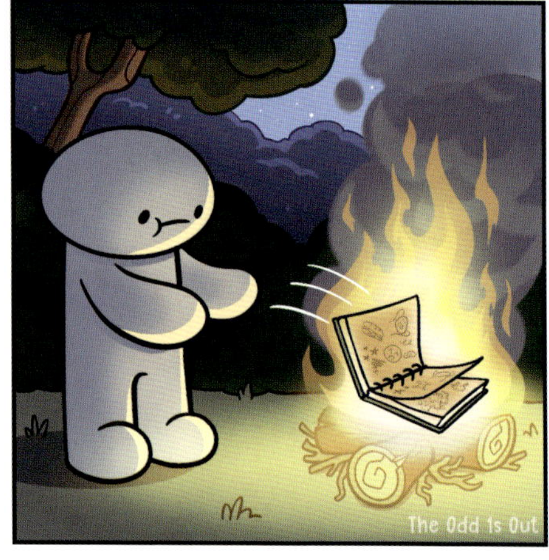
The Odd 1s Out

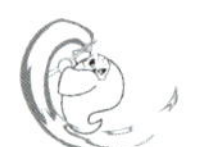

SPACE CRABS

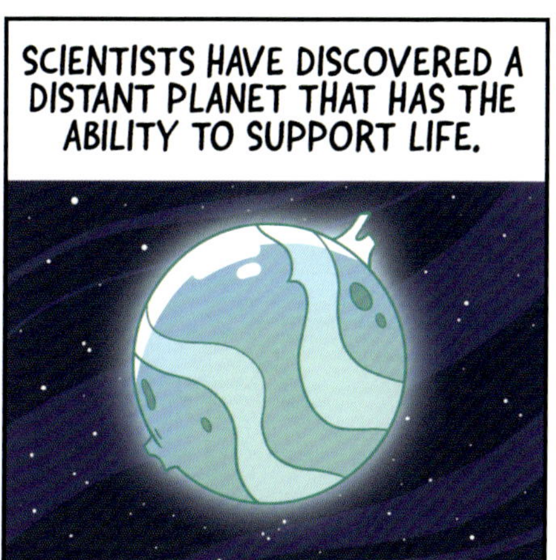
SCIENTISTS HAVE DISCOVERED A DISTANT PLANET THAT HAS THE ABILITY TO SUPPORT LIFE.

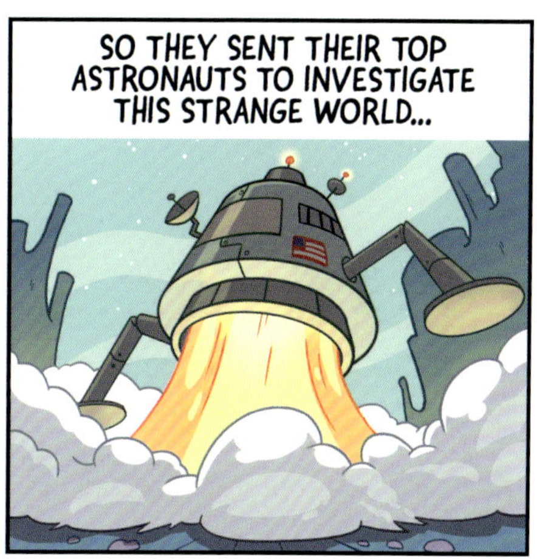
SO THEY SENT THEIR TOP ASTRONAUTS TO INVESTIGATE THIS STRANGE WORLD...

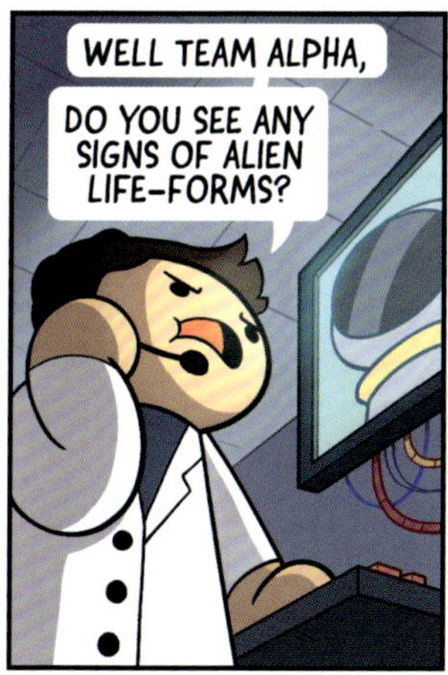
WELL TEAM ALPHA,
DO YOU SEE ANY SIGNS OF ALIEN LIFE-FORMS?

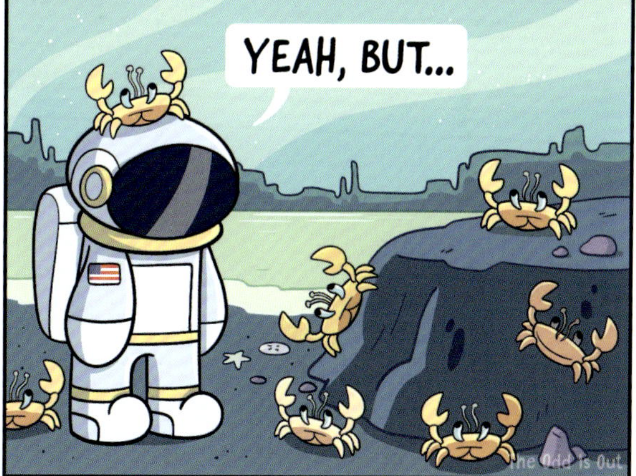
YEAH, BUT...
The Odd 1s Out

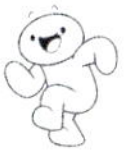

RECIPE

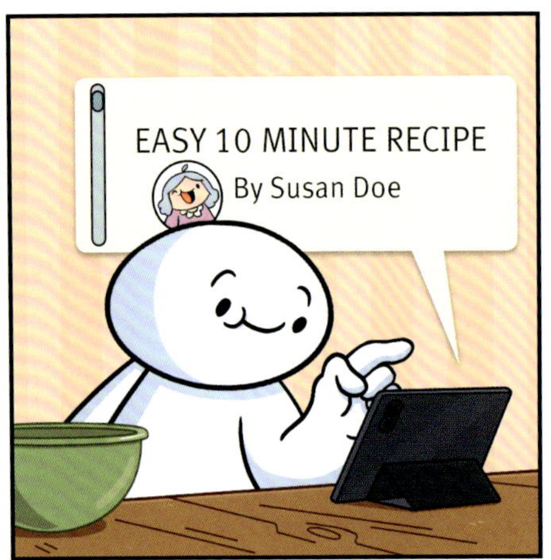

EASY 10 MINUTE RECIPE
By Susan Doe

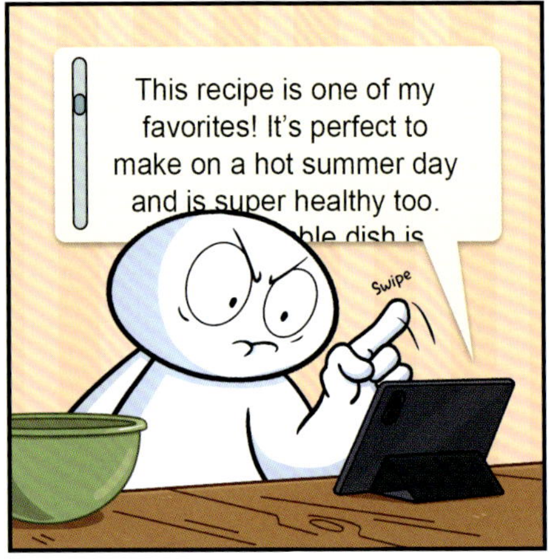

This recipe is one of my favorites! It's perfect to make on a hot summer day and is super healthy too.
Swipe

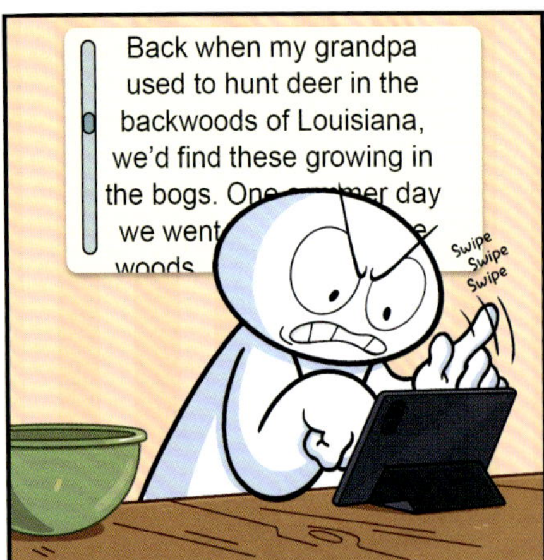

Back when my grandpa used to hunt deer in the backwoods of Louisiana, we'd find these growing in the bogs.
Swipe Swipe Swipe

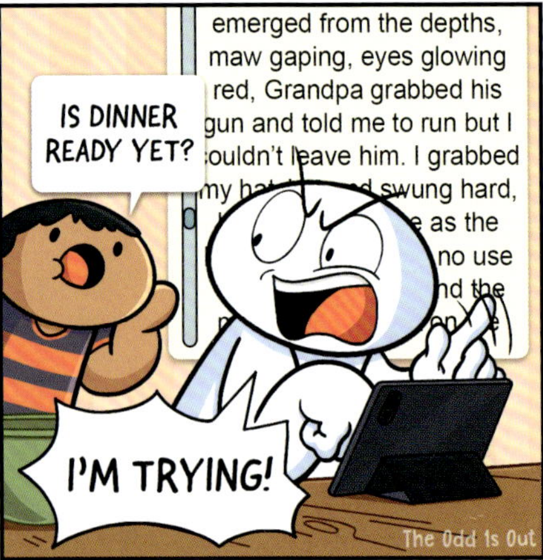

emerged from the depths, maw gaping, eyes glowing red, Grandpa grabbed his gun and told me to run but I
IS DINNER READY YET?
I'M TRYING!
The Odd 1s Out

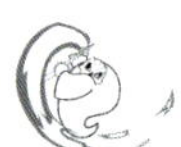

FROLIC

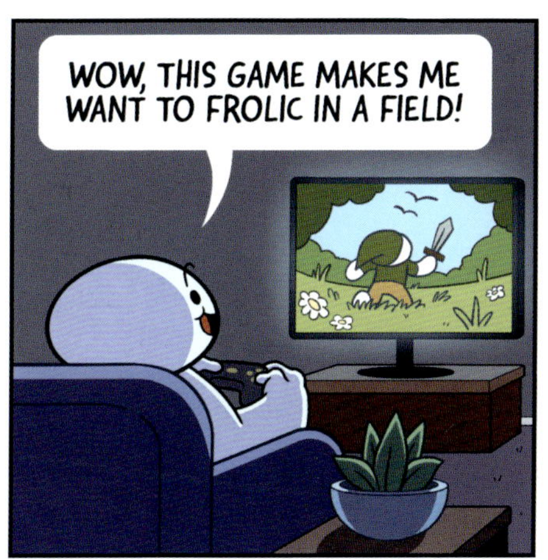
WOW, THIS GAME MAKES ME WANT TO FROLIC IN A FIELD!

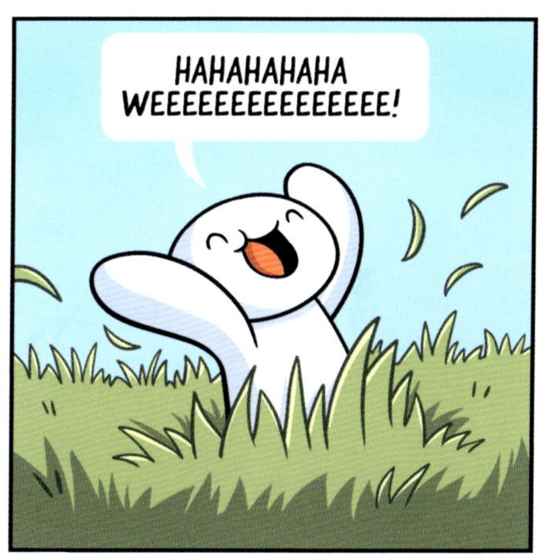
HAHAHAHAHA WEEEEEEEEEEEEEE!

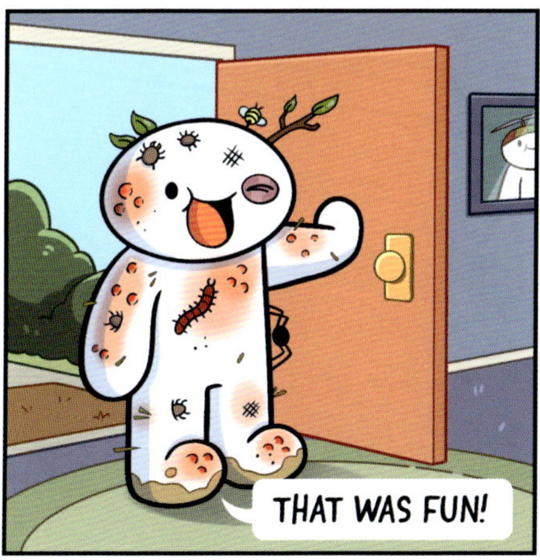
THAT WAS FUN!

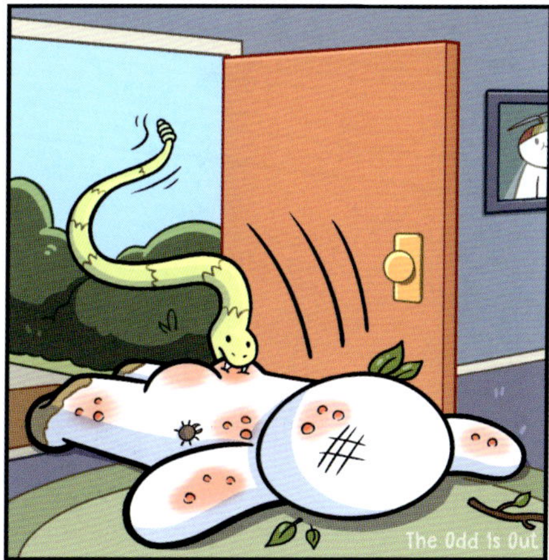
The Odd 1s Out

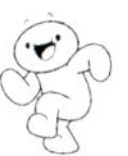

JENGA

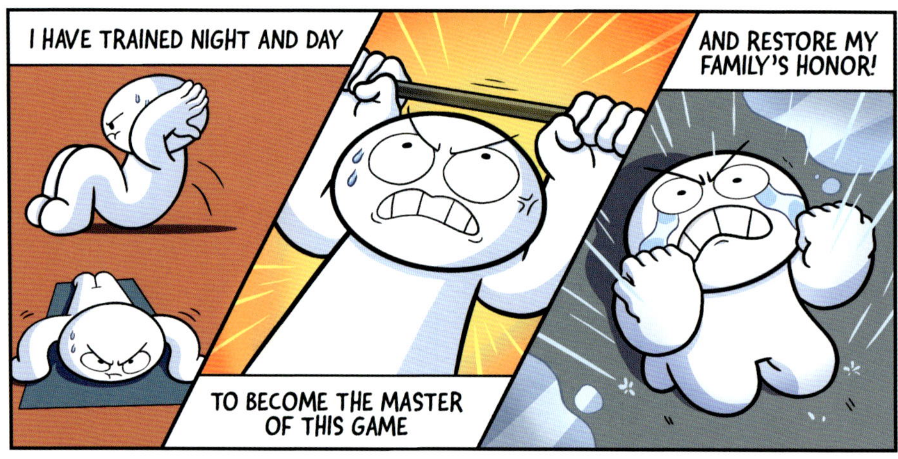
I HAVE TRAINED NIGHT AND DAY
TO BECOME THE MASTER OF THIS GAME
AND RESTORE MY FAMILY'S HONOR!

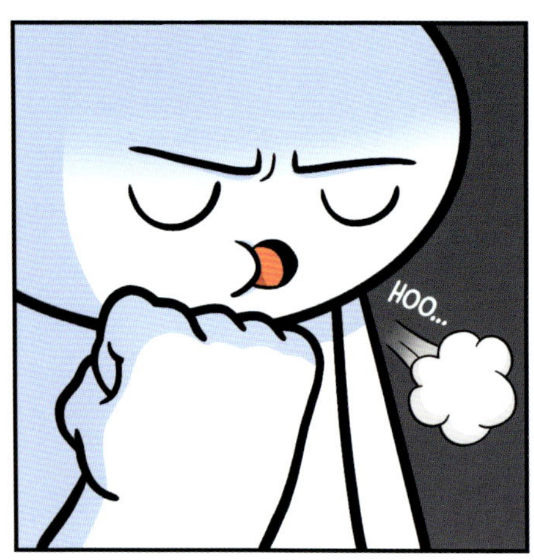
HOO...

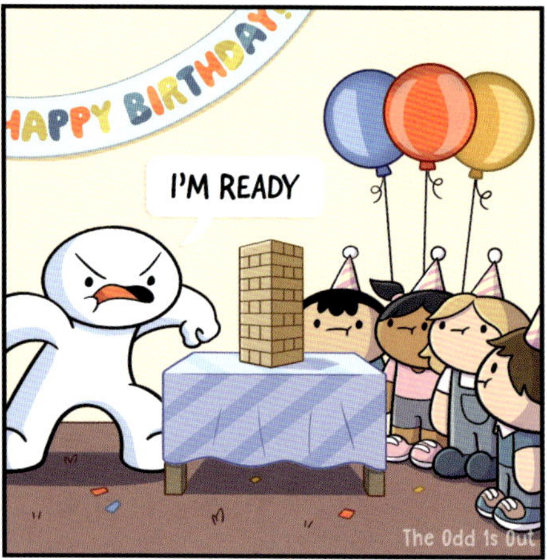
HAPPY BIRTHDAY!
I'M READY
The Odd 1s Out

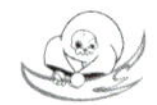

MUSCLES

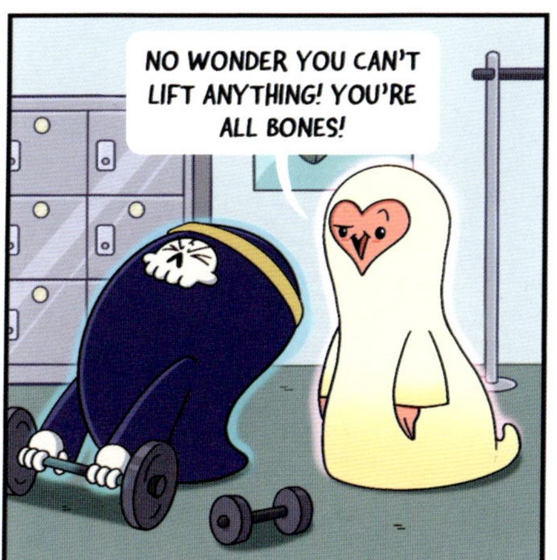
NO WONDER YOU CAN'T LIFT ANYTHING! YOU'RE ALL BONES!

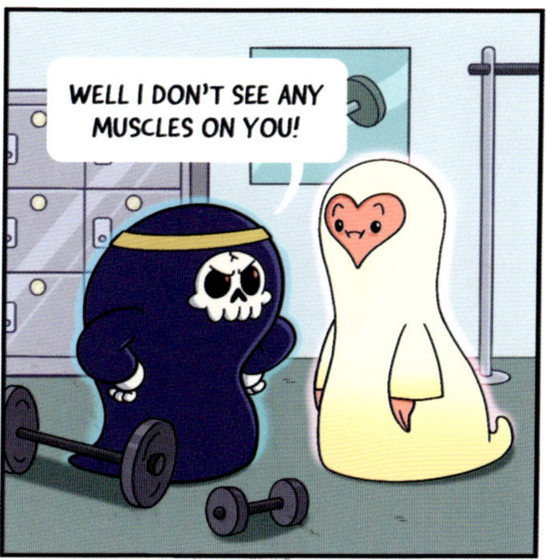
WELL I DON'T SEE ANY MUSCLES ON YOU!

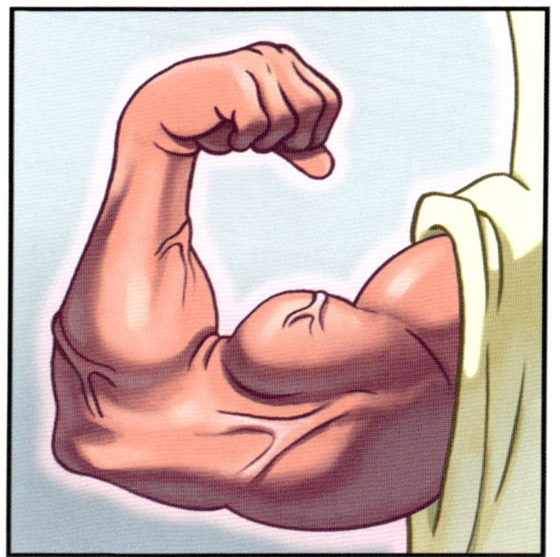

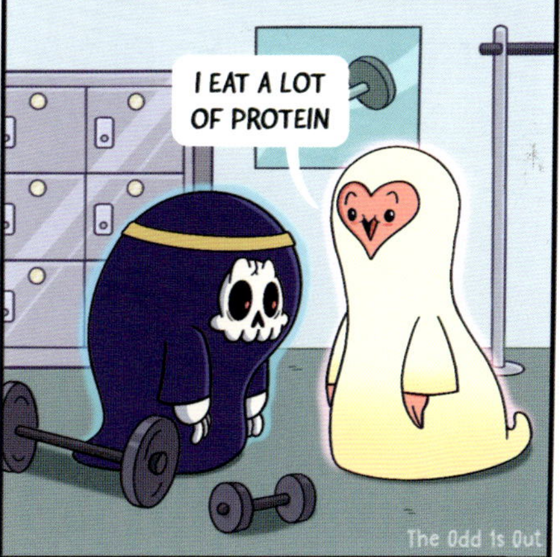
I EAT A LOT OF PROTEIN
The Odd 1s Out

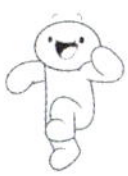

ARIZONIANS

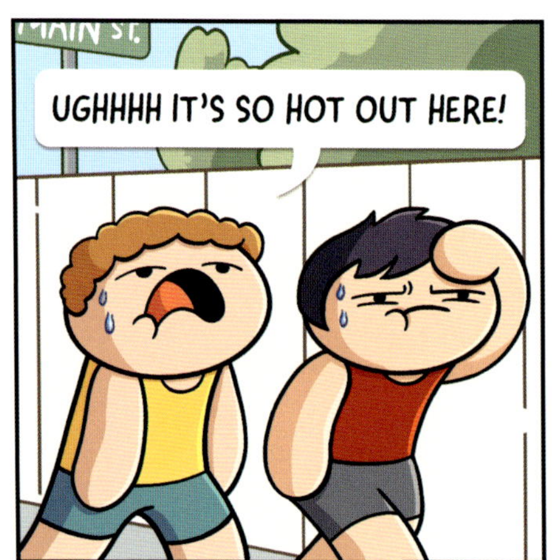
MAIN ST.
UGHHHH IT'S SO HOT OUT HERE!

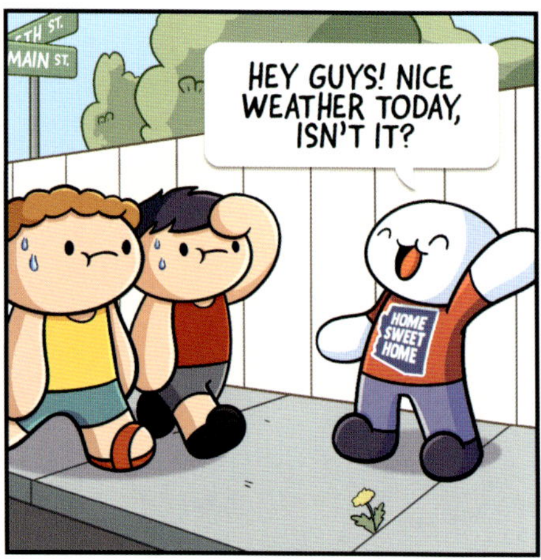
MAIN ST.
HEY GUYS! NICE WEATHER TODAY, ISN'T IT?
HOME SWEET HOME

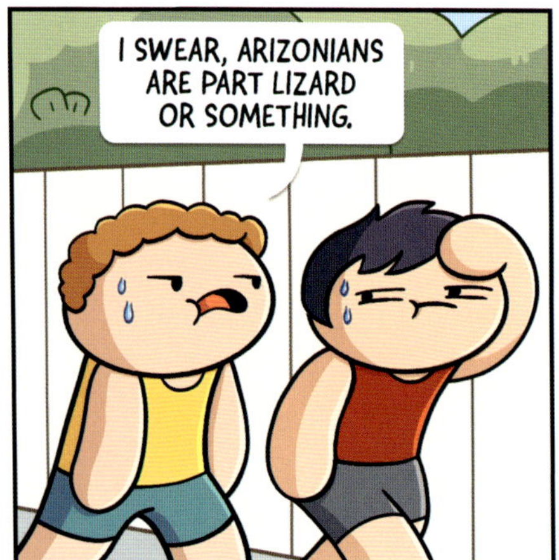
I SWEAR, ARIZONIANS ARE PART LIZARD OR SOMETHING.

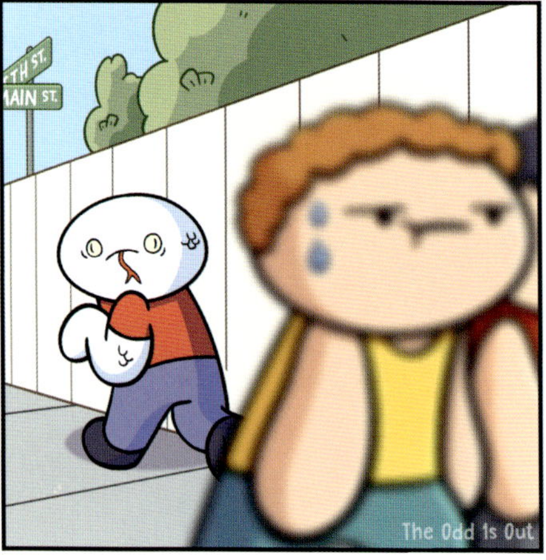
The Odd 1s Out

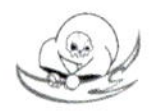

GLASS SPONGE

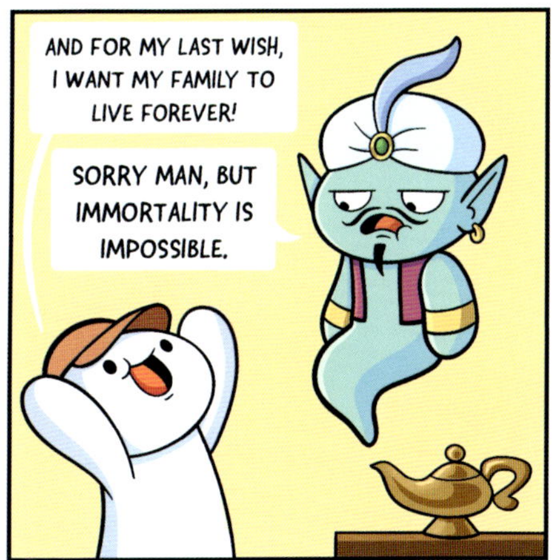

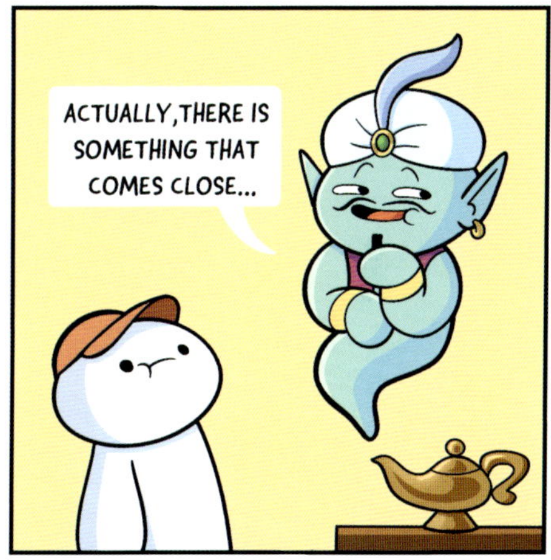

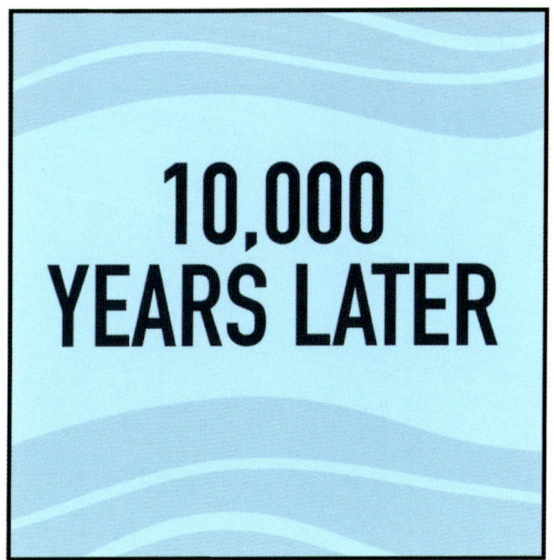

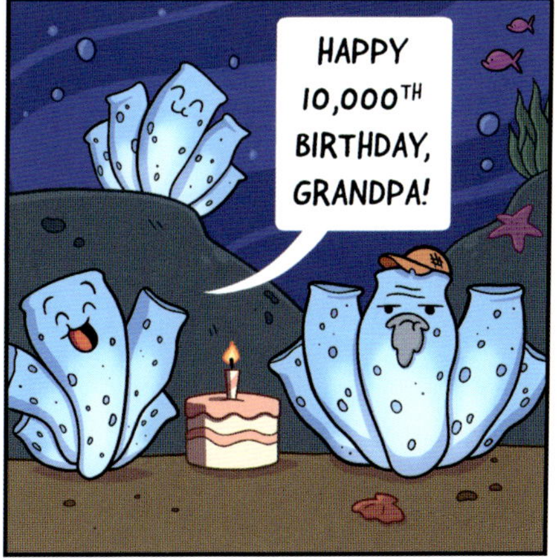

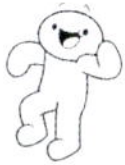

COUNTRY

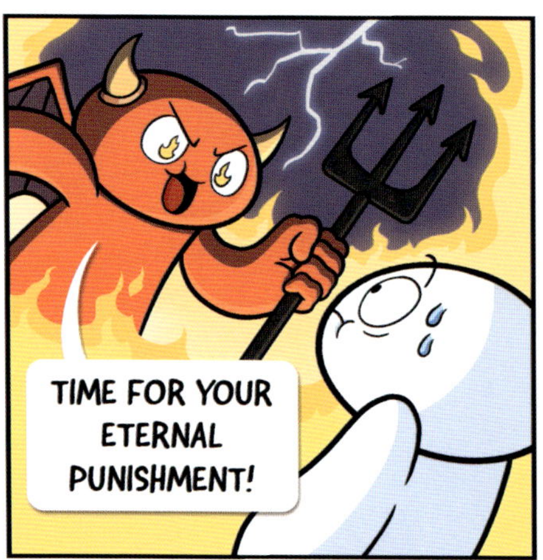
TIME FOR YOUR ETERNAL PUNISHMENT!

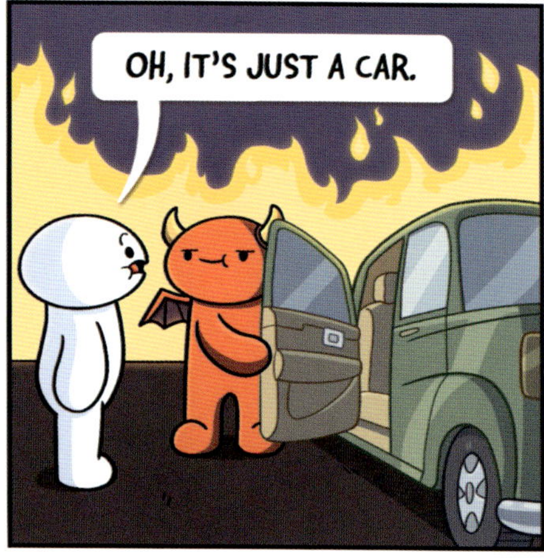
OH, IT'S JUST A CAR.

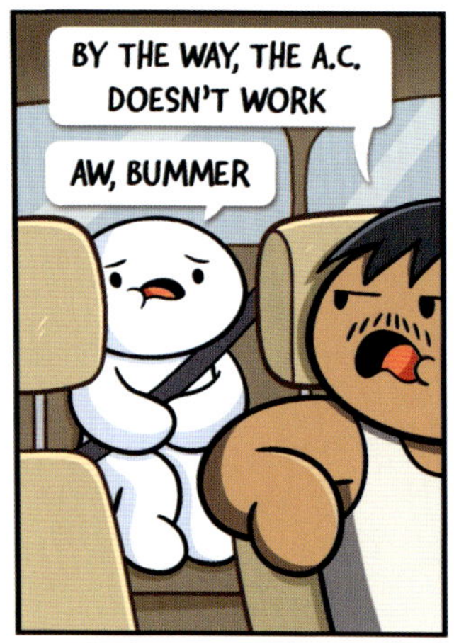
BY THE WAY, THE A.C. DOESN'T WORK
AW, BUMMER

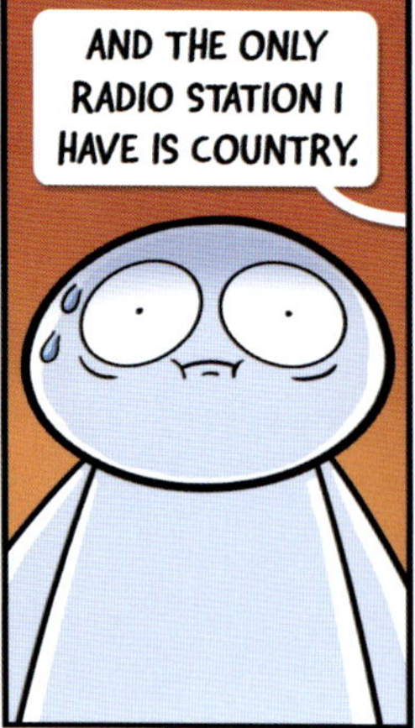
AND THE ONLY RADIO STATION I HAVE IS COUNTRY.

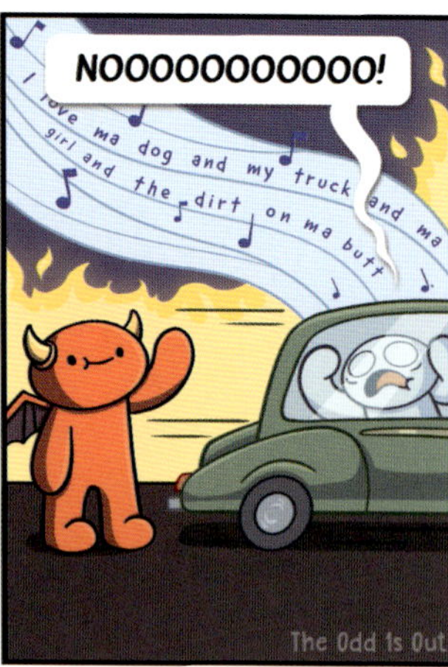
NOOOOOOOOOOO!
I love ma dog and my truck and ma girl and the dirt on ma butt
The Odd 1s Out

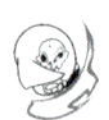

OLYMPICS

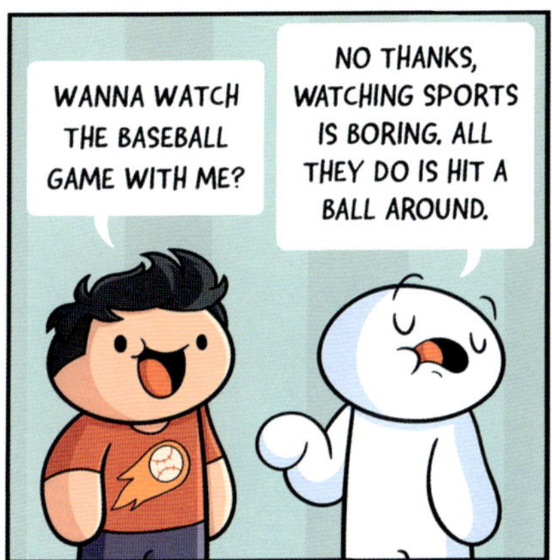

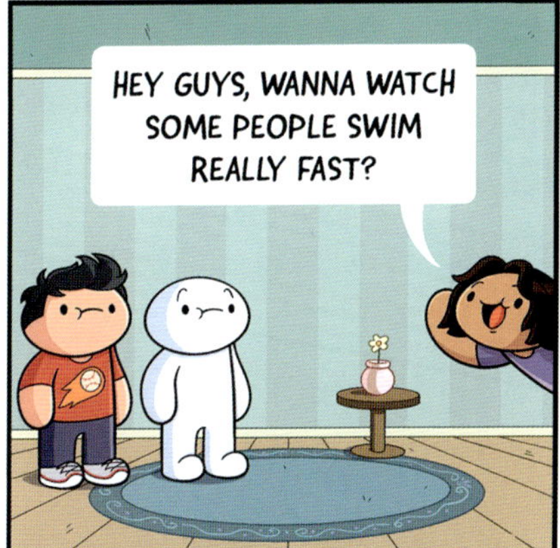

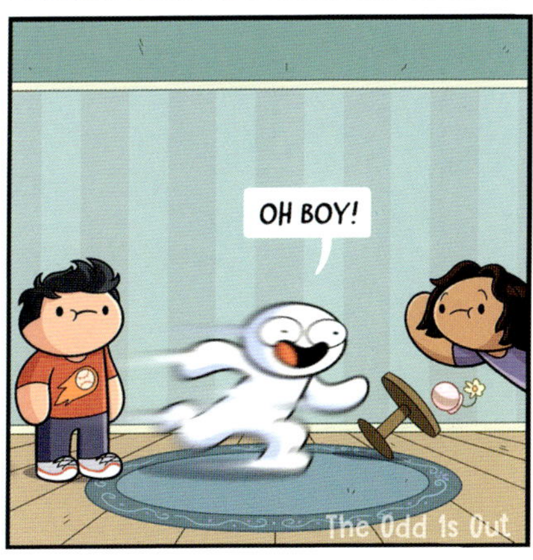

NO GPS

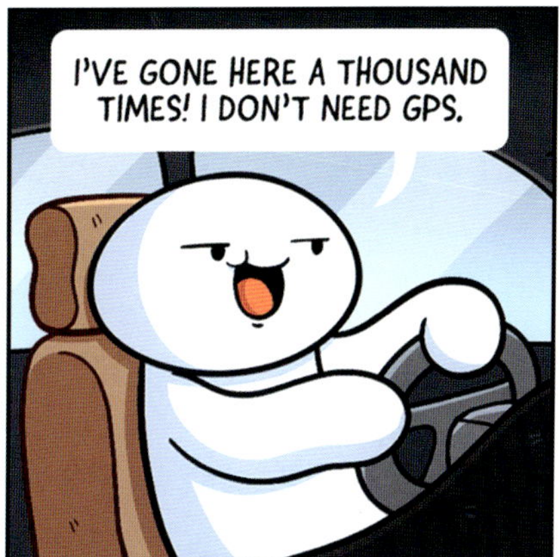

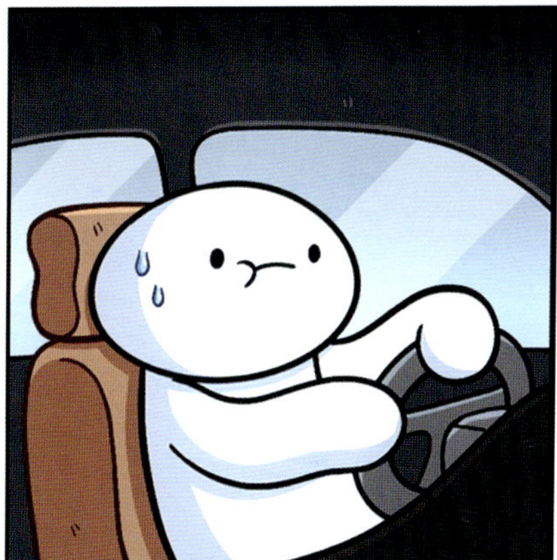

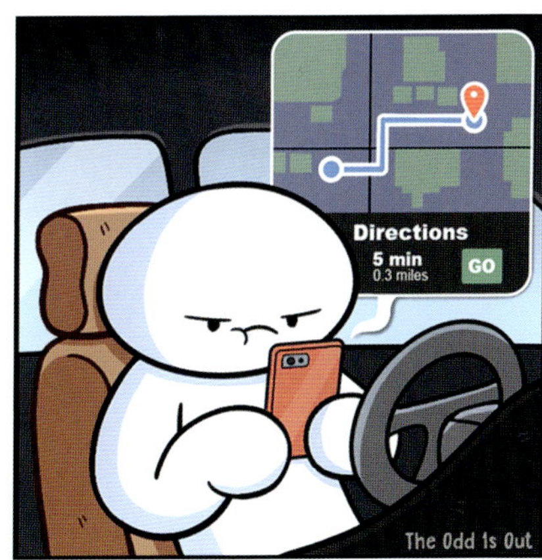

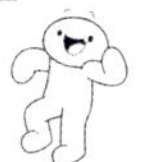

SPLASH

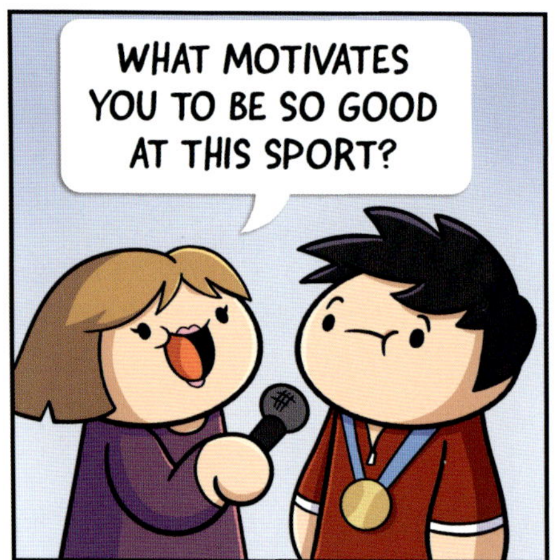
WHAT MOTIVATES YOU TO BE SO GOOD AT THIS SPORT?

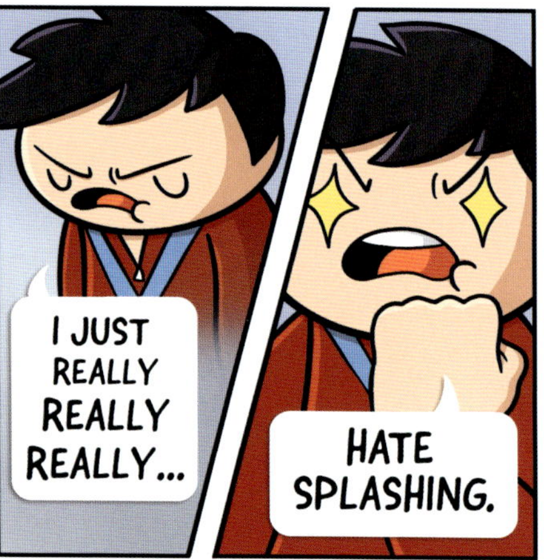
I JUST REALLY REALLY REALLY...
HATE SPLASHING.

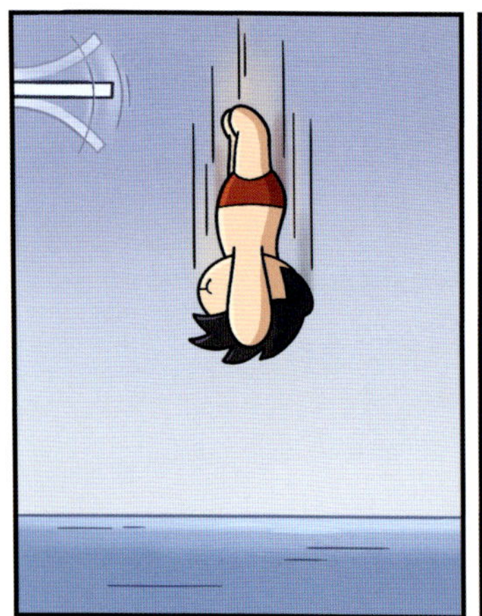

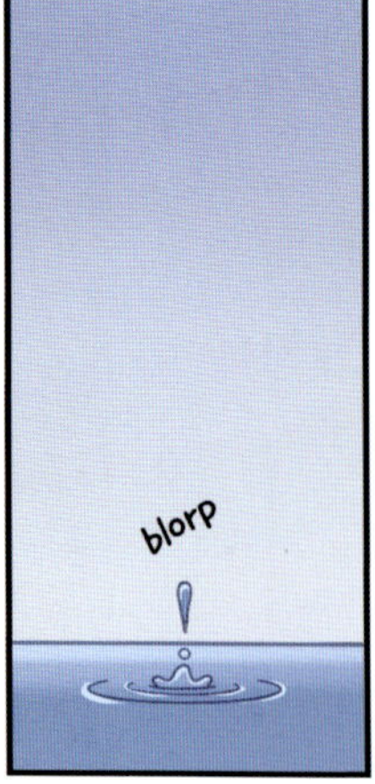
blorp

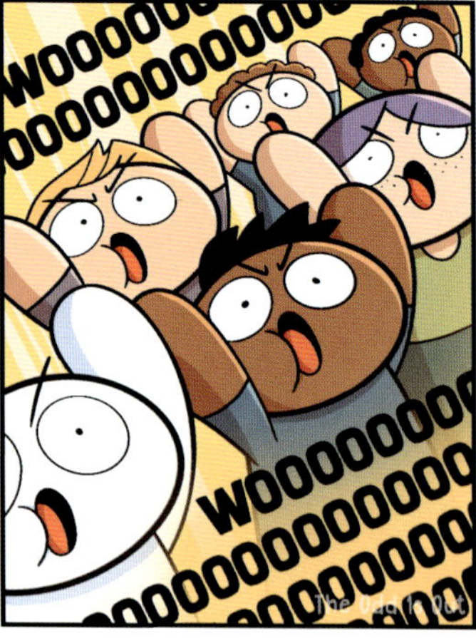
WOOOOOOOOOOOOOOOOOOOOOOOOO
WOOOOOOOOOOOOOOOOOOOOOOOO
The Odd 1s Out

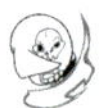

WHERE'S THE BODY

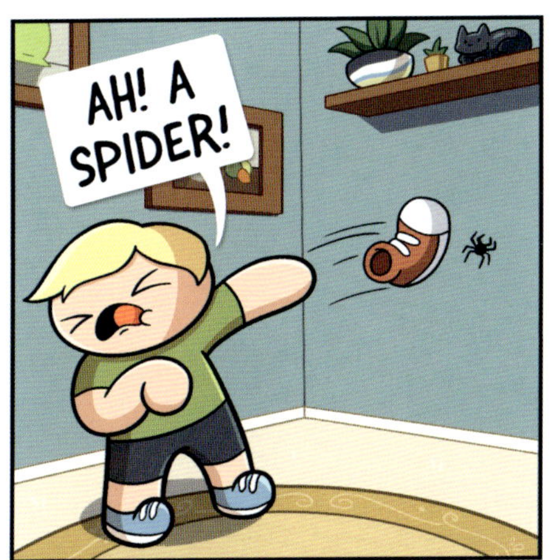

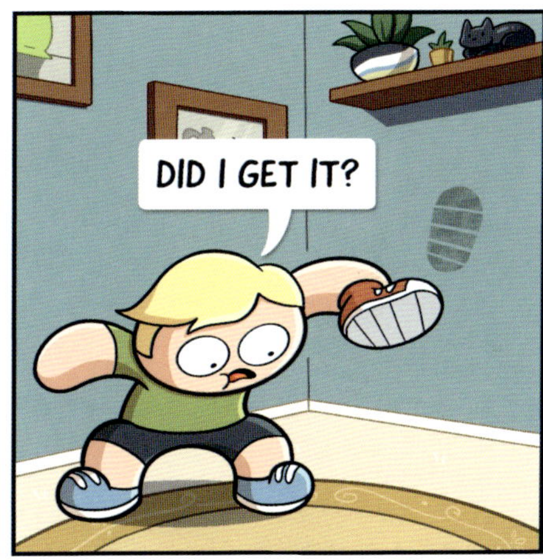

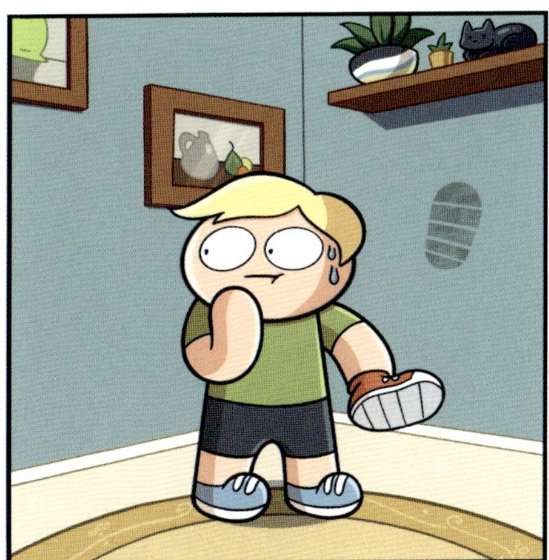

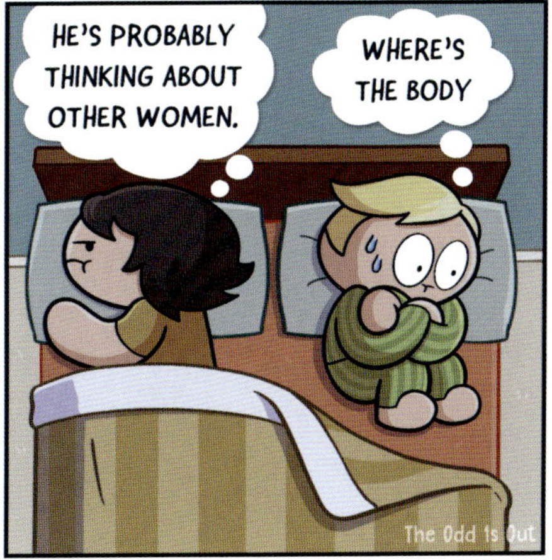

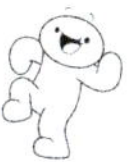

WHITE HAIR

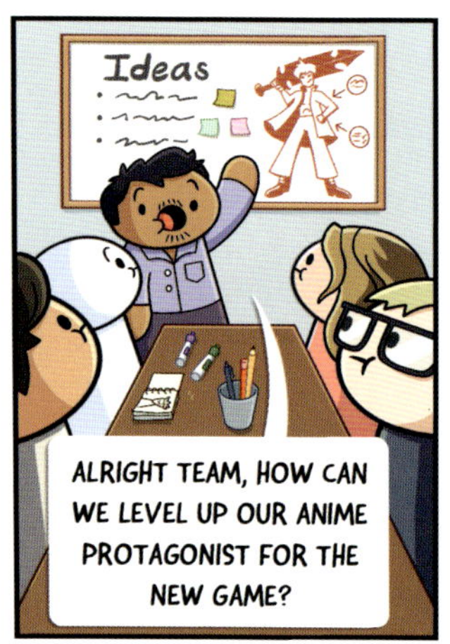
Ideas
ALRIGHT TEAM, HOW CAN WE LEVEL UP OUR ANIME PROTAGONIST FOR THE NEW GAME?

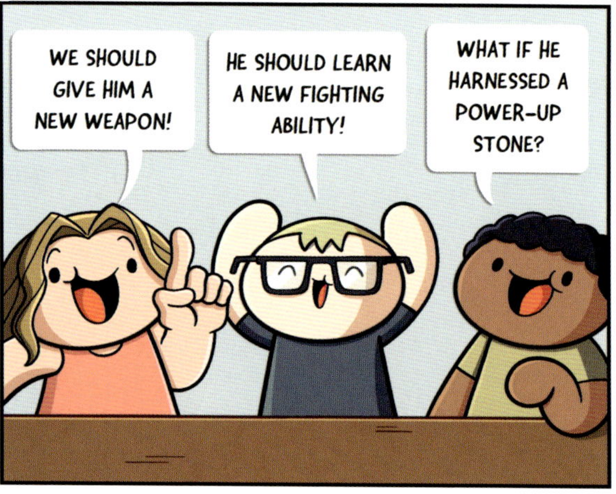
WE SHOULD GIVE HIM A NEW WEAPON!
HE SHOULD LEARN A NEW FIGHTING ABILITY!
WHAT IF HE HARNESSED A POWER-UP STONE?

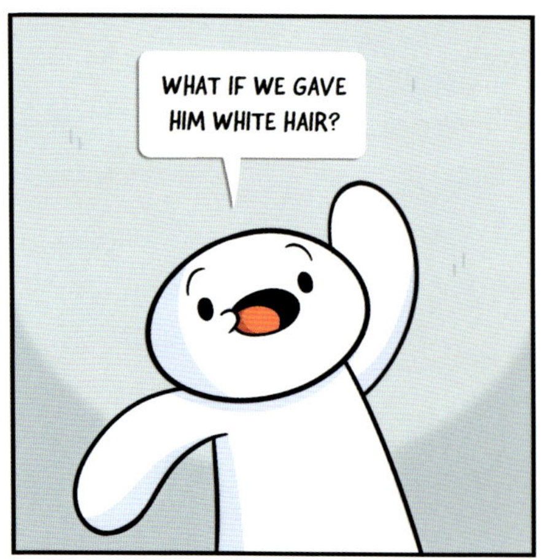
WHAT IF WE GAVE HIM WHITE HAIR?

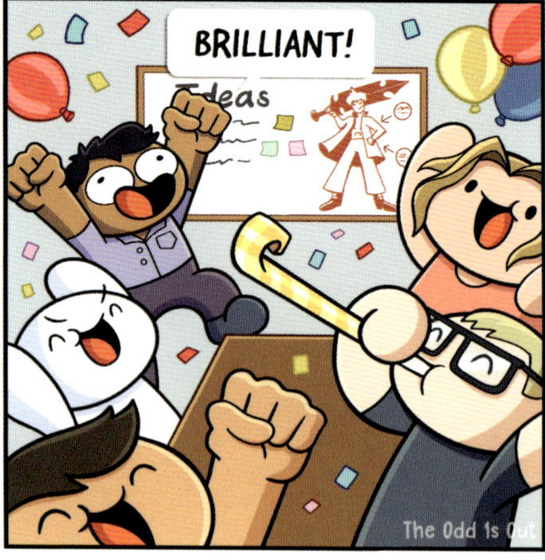
BRILLIANT!
The Odd 1s Out

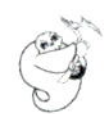

IMPORTANT CALL

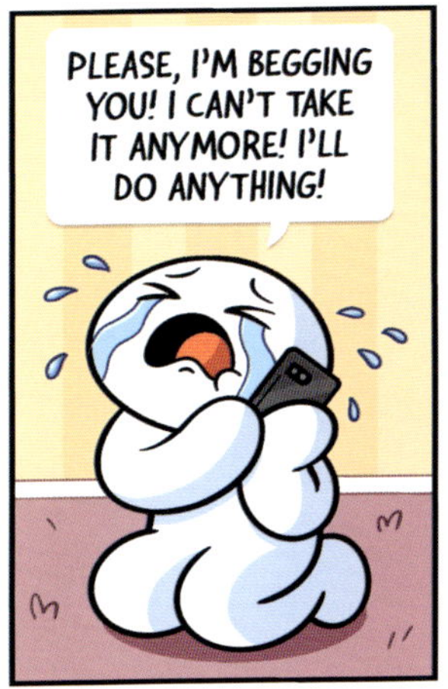

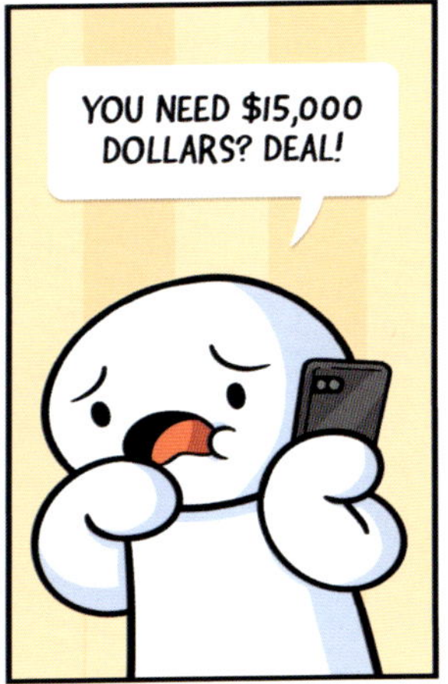

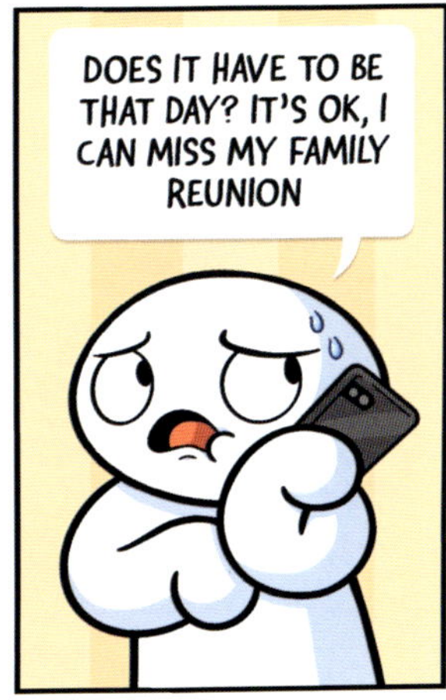

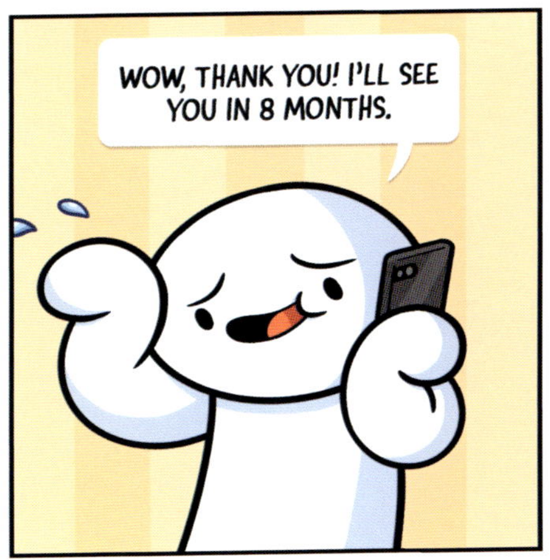

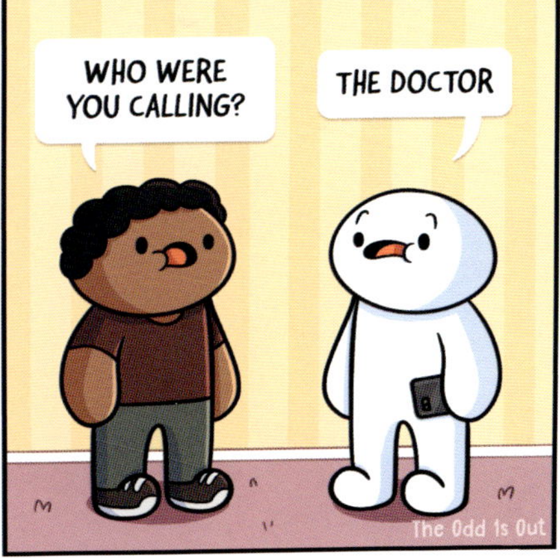

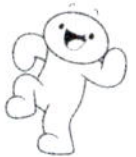

SUPER SONIC

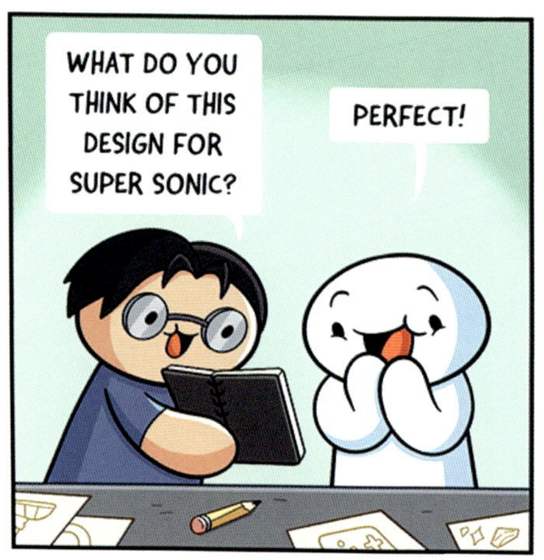

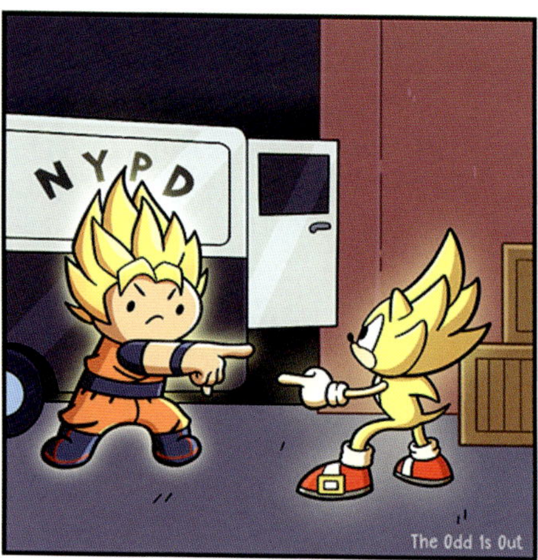

BIRDWATCHERS

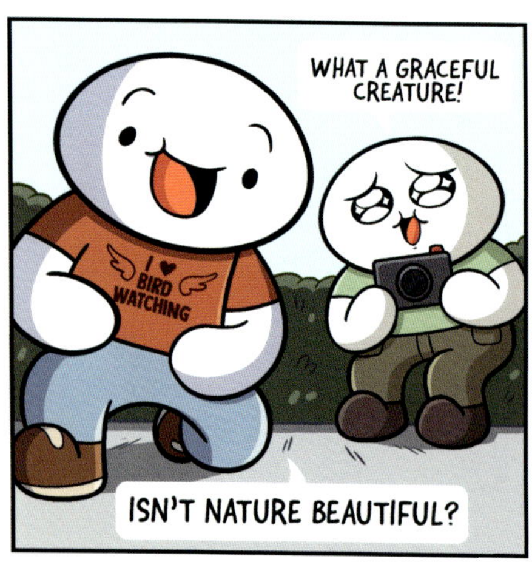

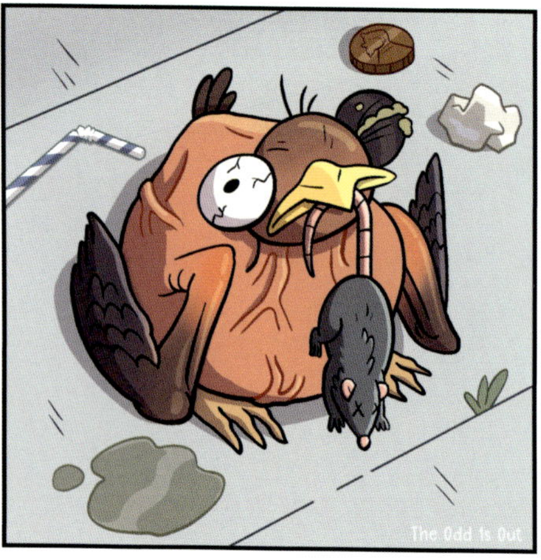

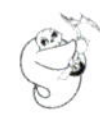

STEAK

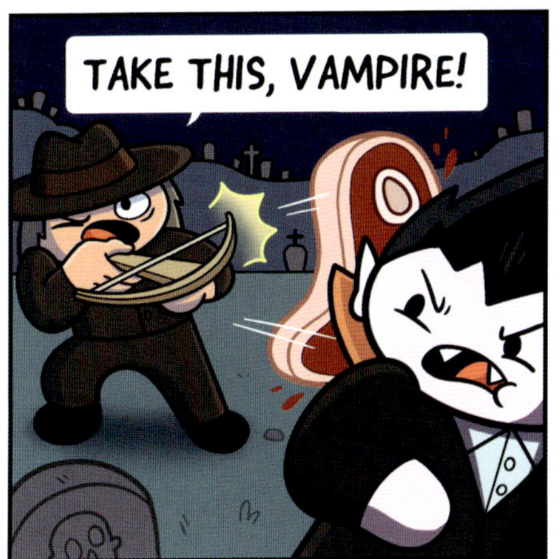
TAKE THIS, VAMPIRE!

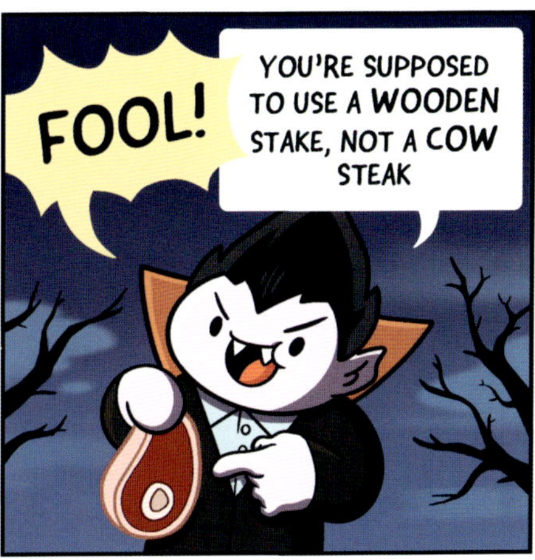
FOOL!
YOU'RE SUPPOSED TO USE A WOODEN STAKE, NOT A COW STEAK

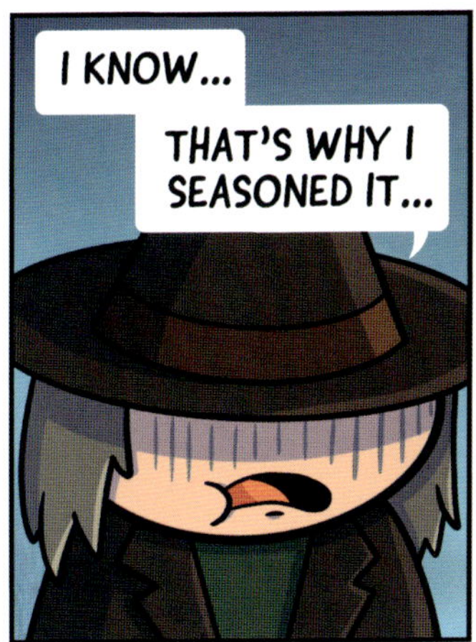
I KNOW...
THAT'S WHY I SEASONED IT...

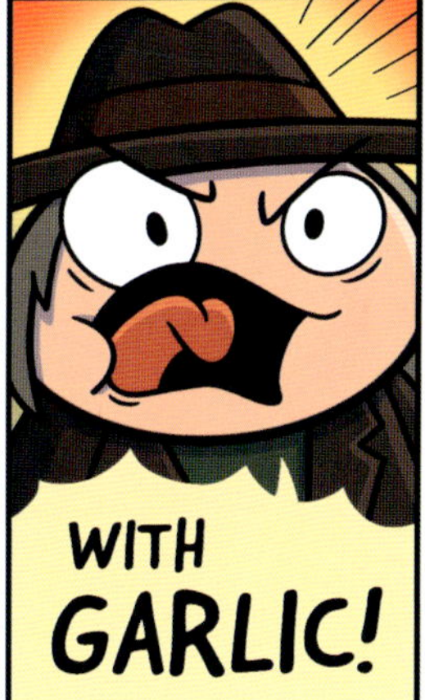
WITH GARLIC!

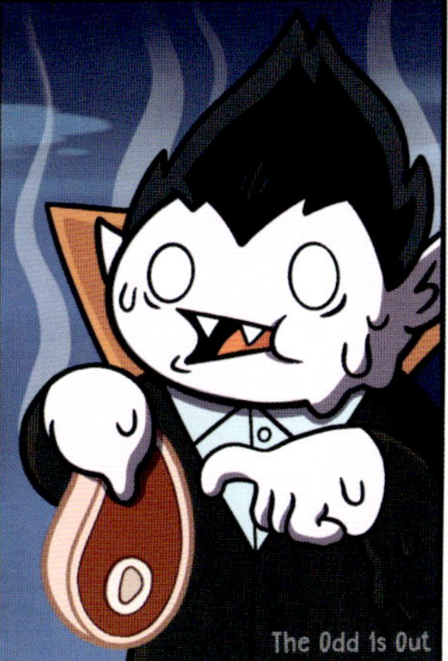
The Odd 1s Out

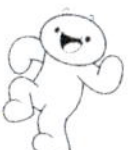

BLACK MARKET

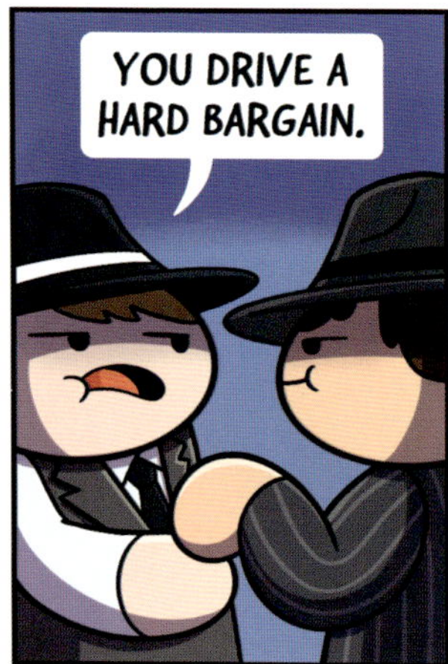

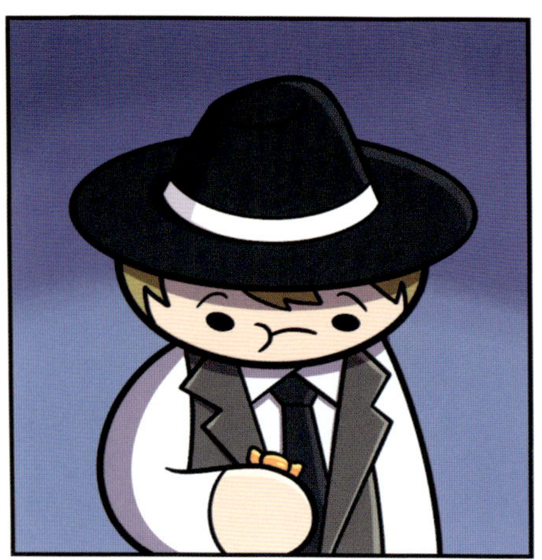

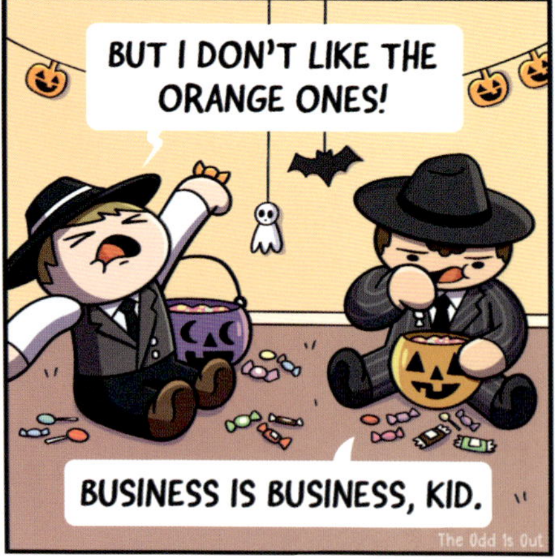

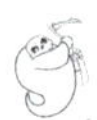

GHOSTLY CRUNCH

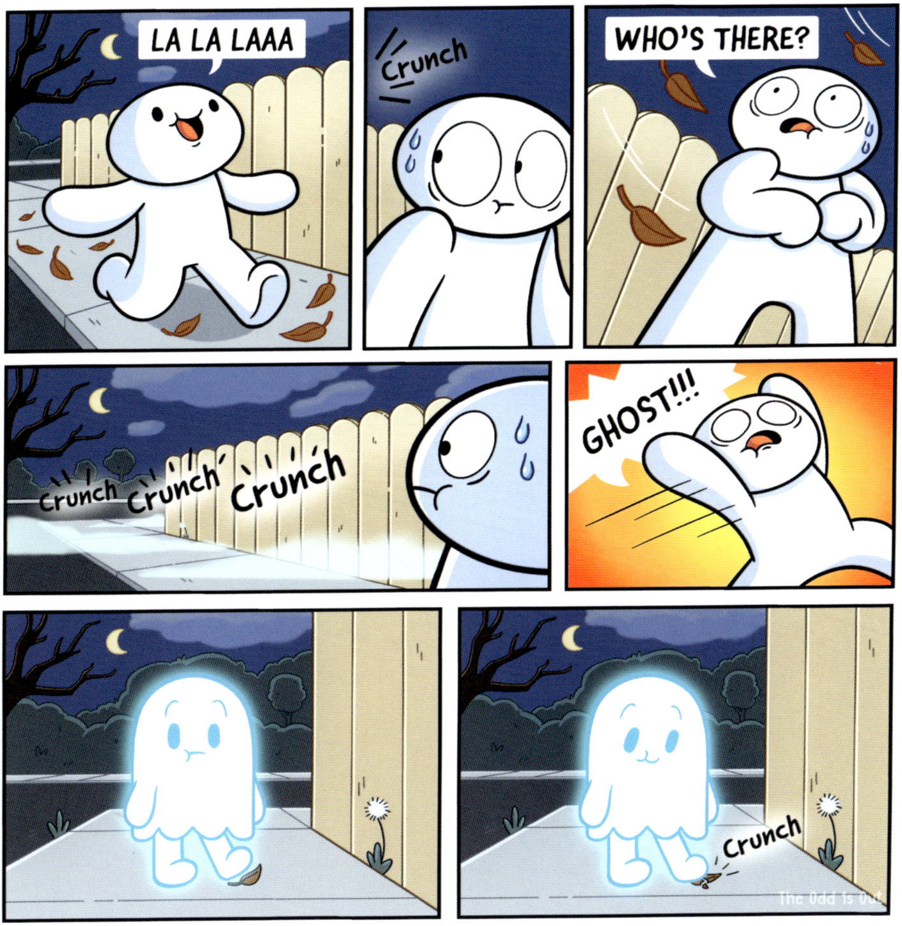

LA LA LAAA

Crunch

WHO'S THERE?

Crunch Crunch Crunch

GHOST!!!

Crunch

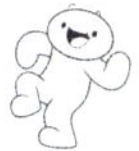

STOCKINGS

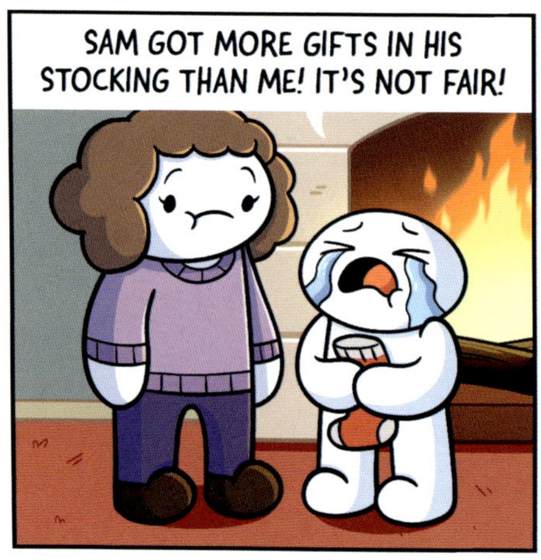

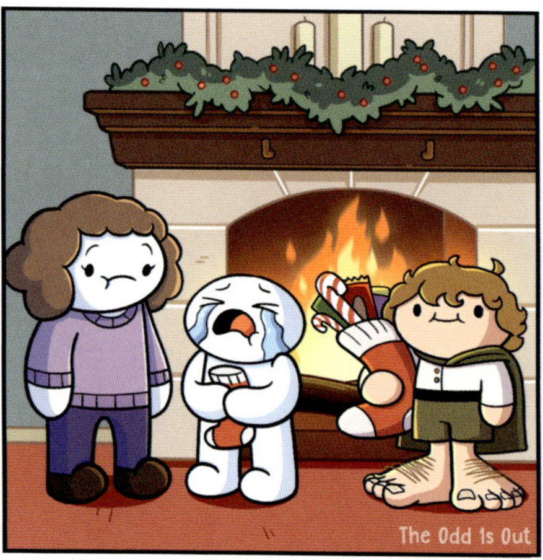

SNOW

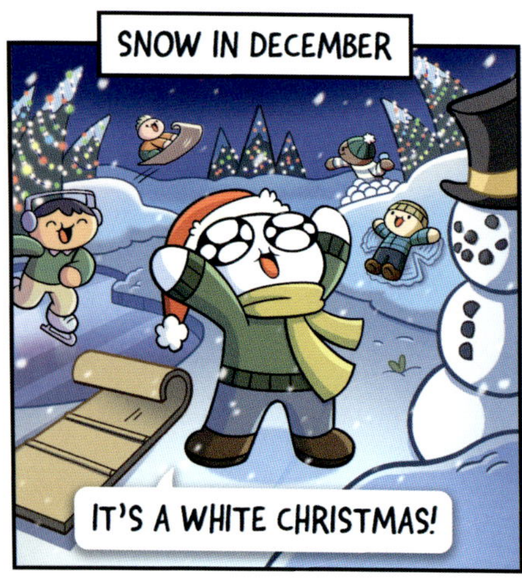

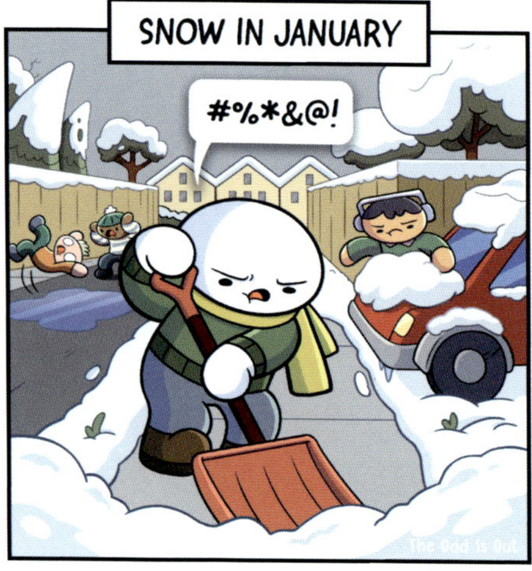

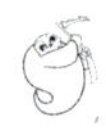

KRAMPUS

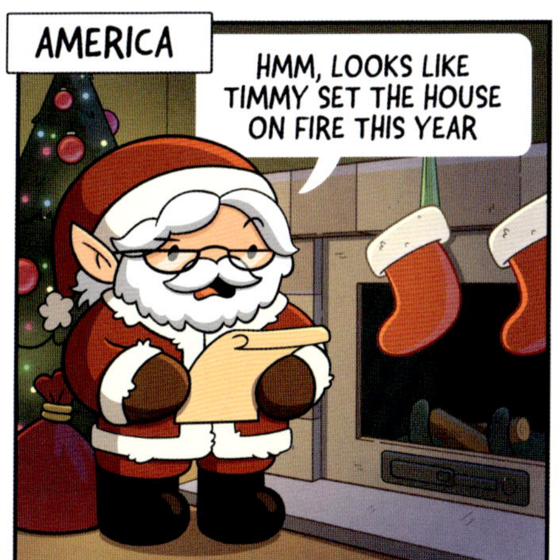
AMERICA
HMM, LOOKS LIKE TIMMY SET THE HOUSE ON FIRE THIS YEAR

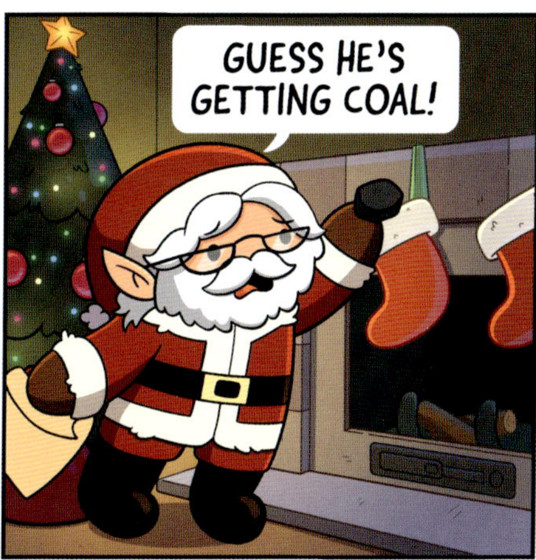
GUESS HE'S GETTING COAL!

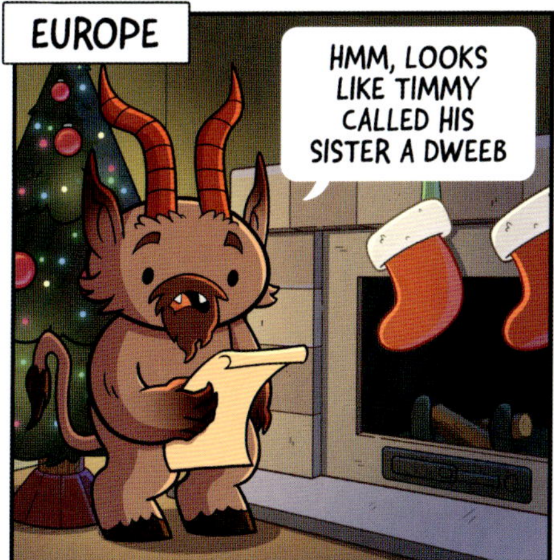
EUROPE
HMM, LOOKS LIKE TIMMY CALLED HIS SISTER A DWEEB

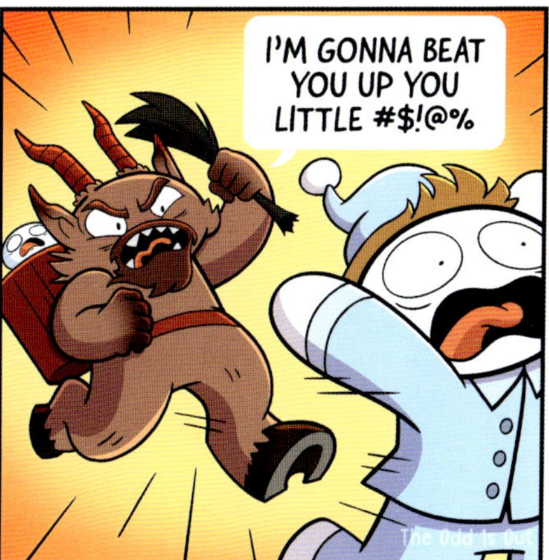
I'M GONNA BEAT YOU UP YOU LITTLE #$!@%
The Odd 1s Out

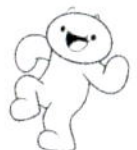

VACATION

I'M SO EXCITED FOR A RELAXING VACATION!

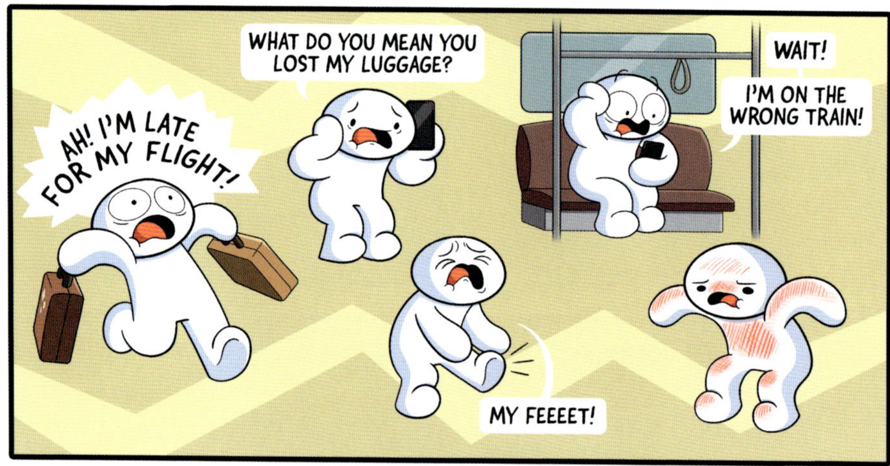

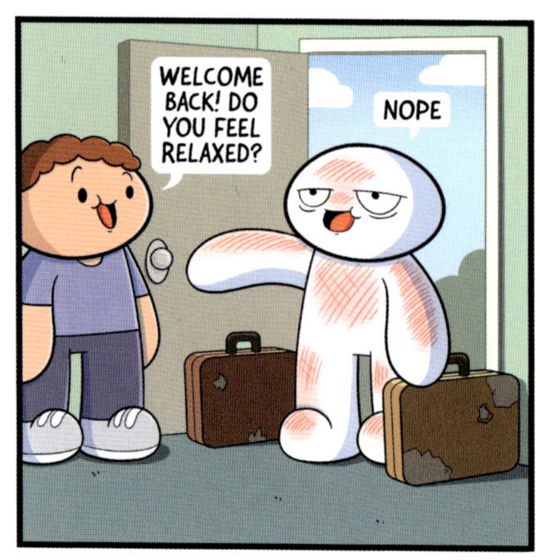

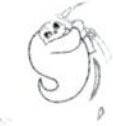

BAGEL BITES

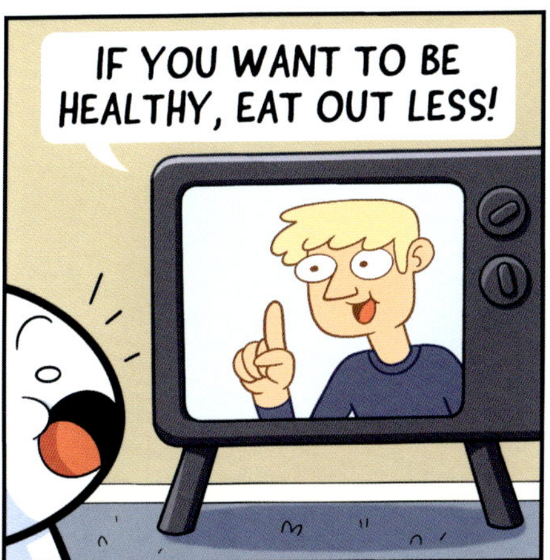
IF YOU WANT TO BE HEALTHY, EAT OUT LESS!

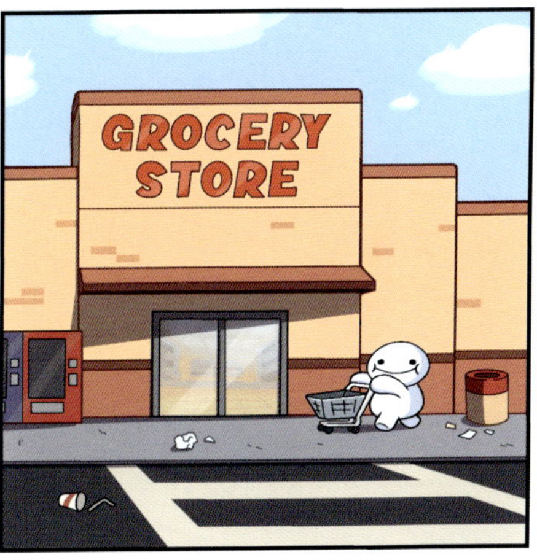
GROCERY STORE

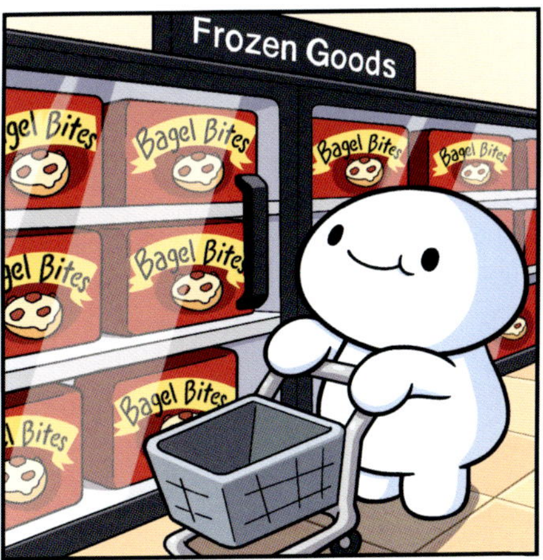
Frozen Goods
Bagel Bites

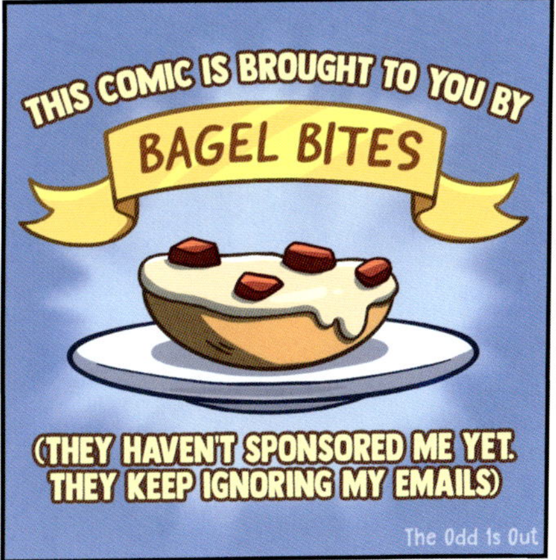
THIS COMIC IS BROUGHT TO YOU BY
BAGEL BITES
(THEY HAVEN'T SPONSORED ME YET. THEY KEEP IGNORING MY EMAILS)
The Odd 1s Out

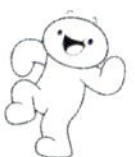

WIENERSCHNITZEL

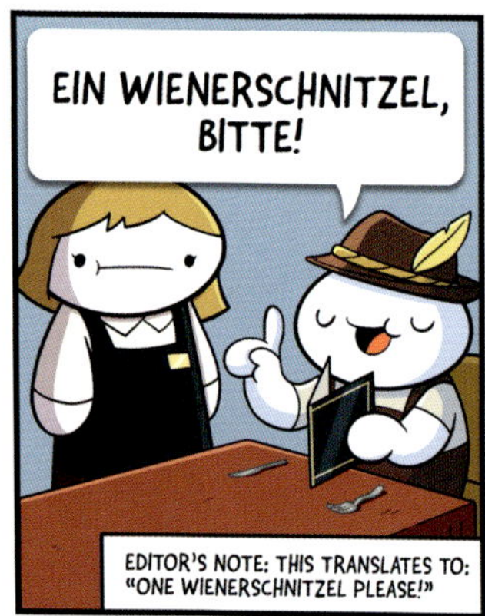

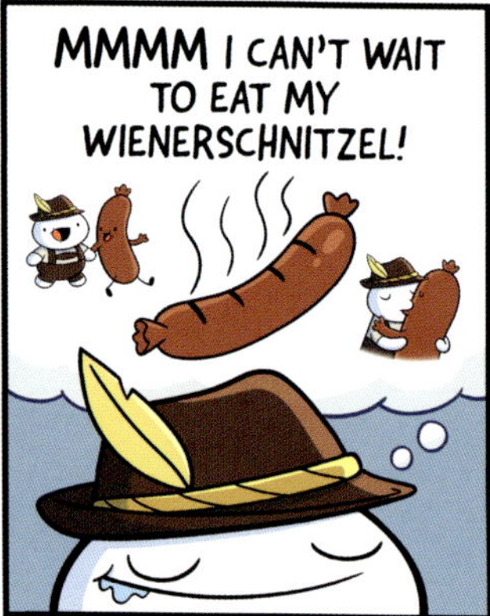

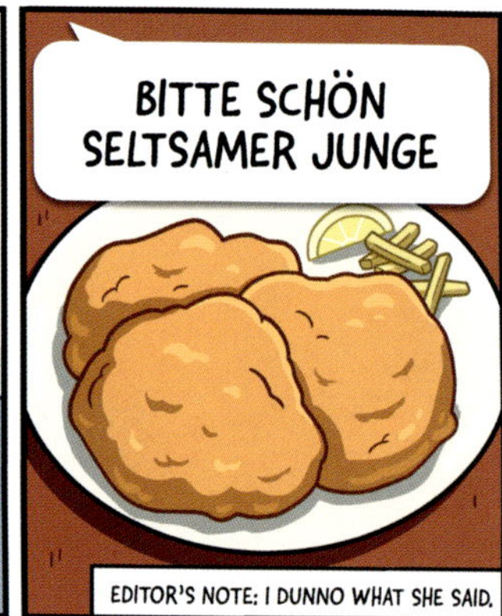

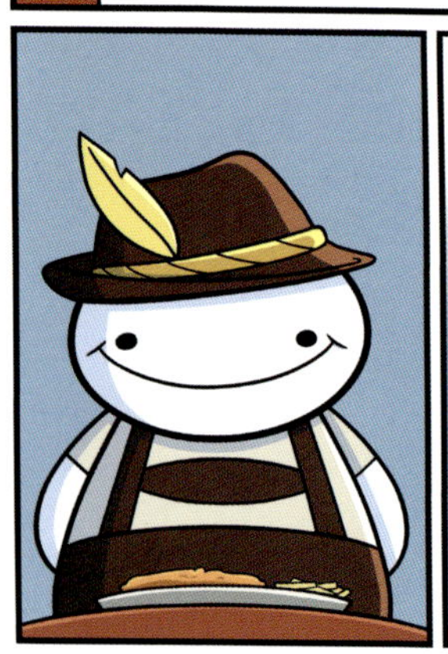

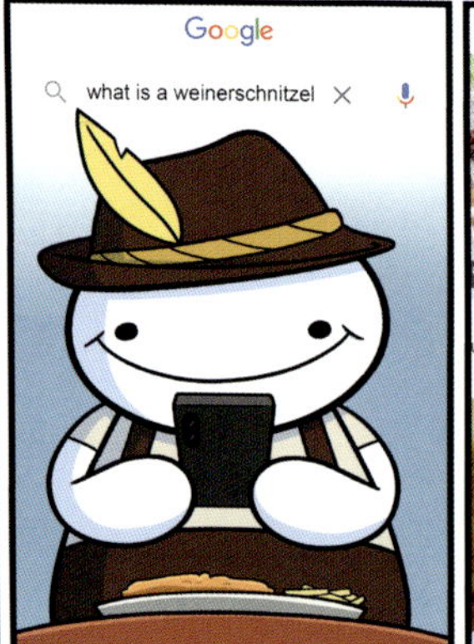

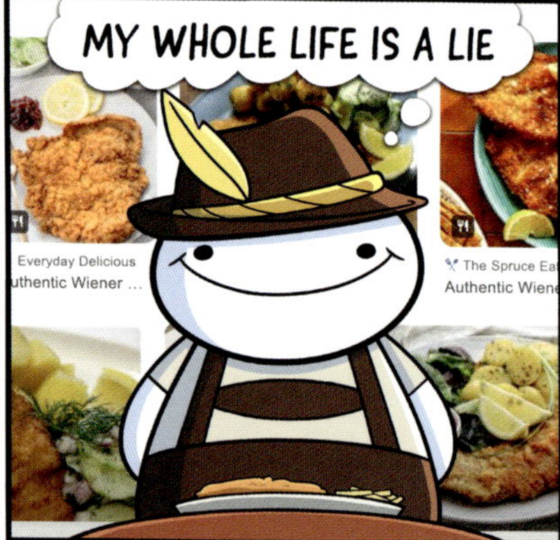

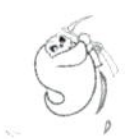

VALENTINES

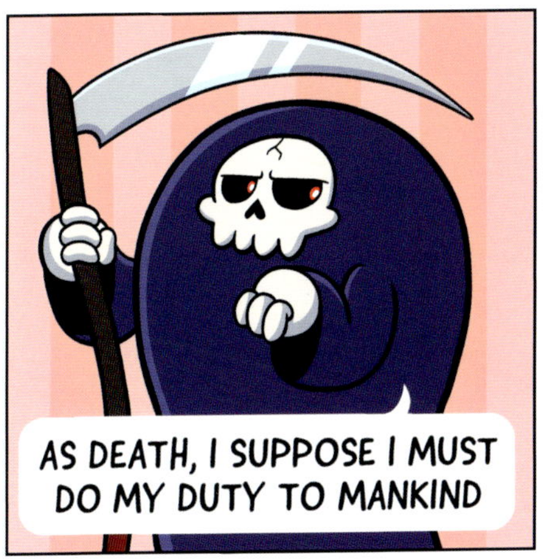
AS DEATH, I SUPPOSE I MUST DO MY DUTY TO MANKIND

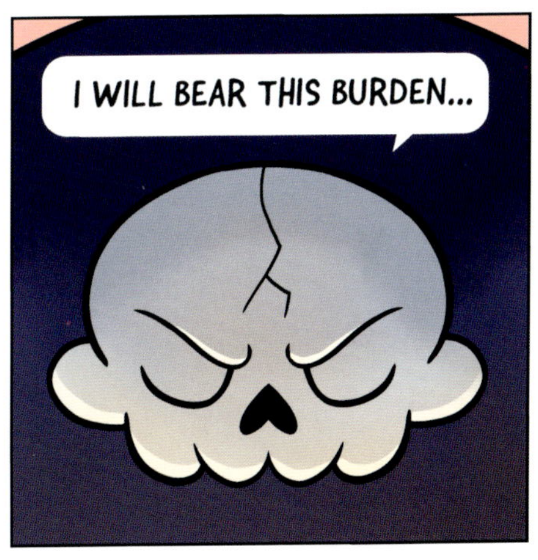
I WILL BEAR THIS BURDEN...

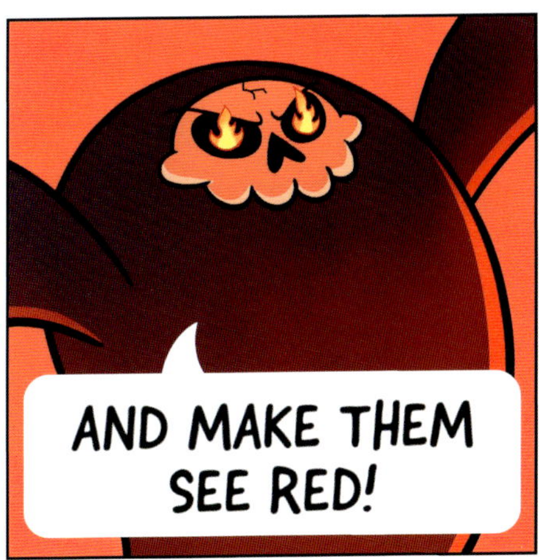
AND MAKE THEM SEE RED!

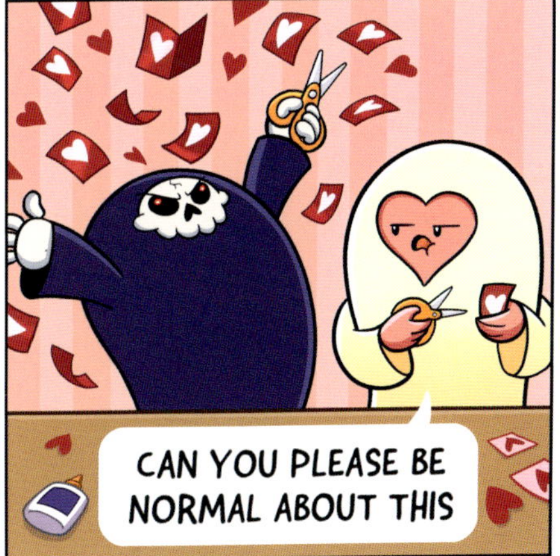
CAN YOU PLEASE BE NORMAL ABOUT THIS

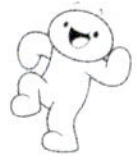

MAYO

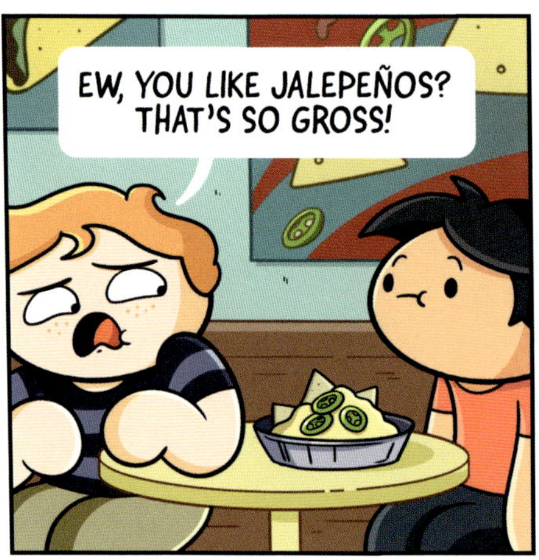

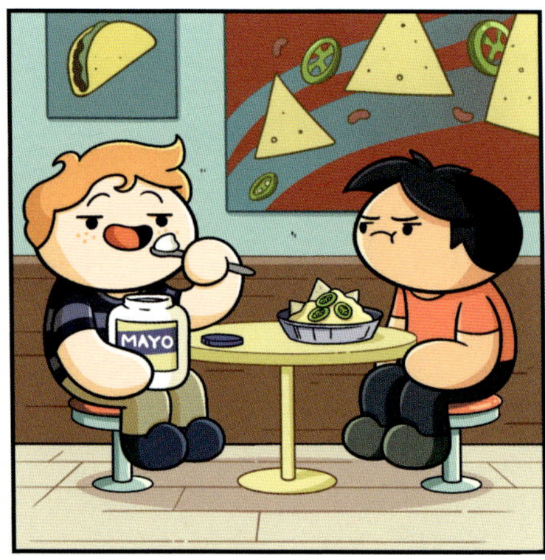

LATE NIGHTS

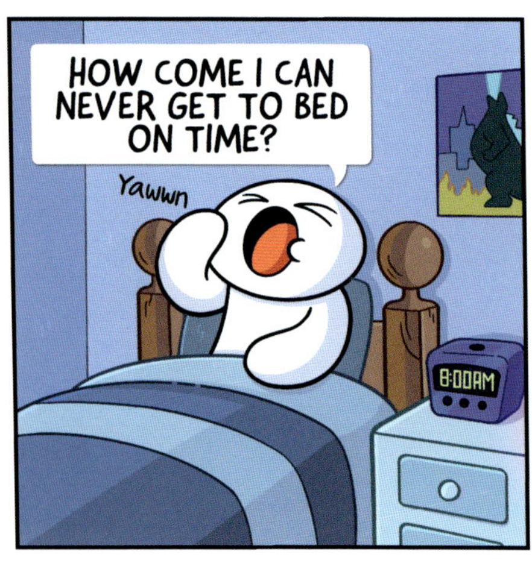

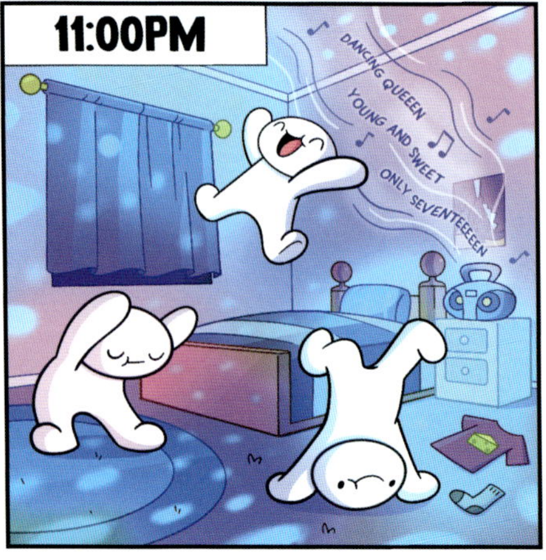

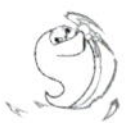

DEATH VALLEY

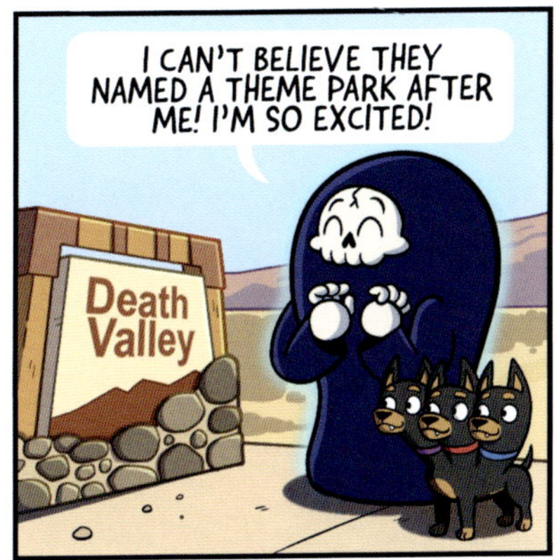

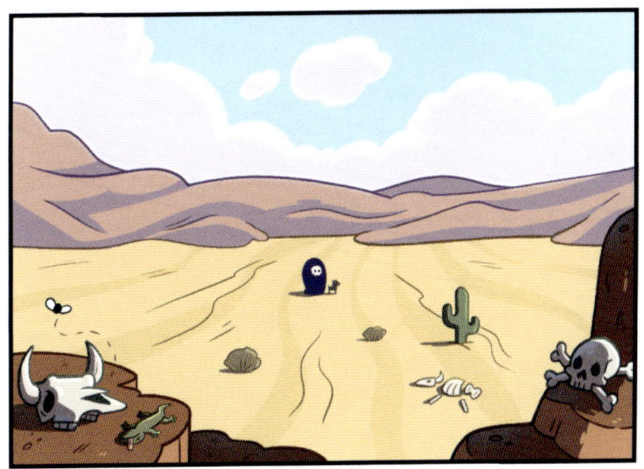

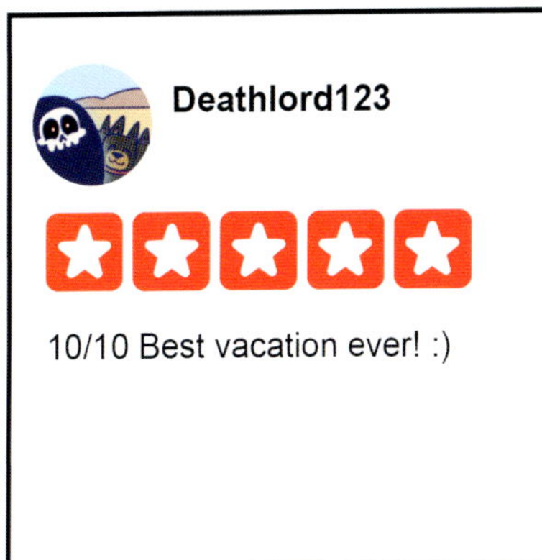

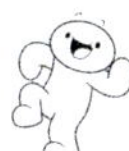

DREAM LAND

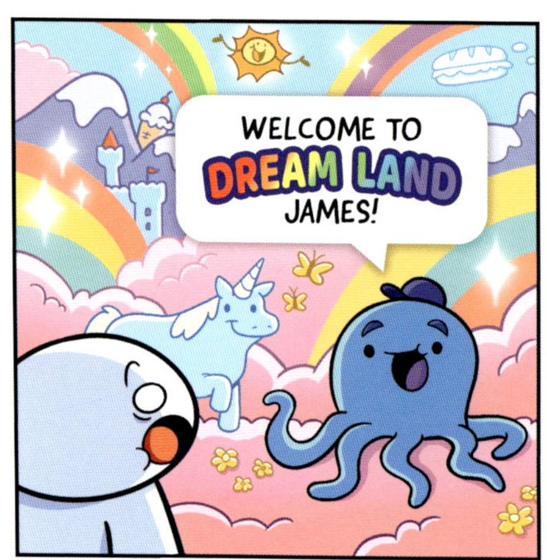
WELCOME TO
DREAM LAND
JAMES!

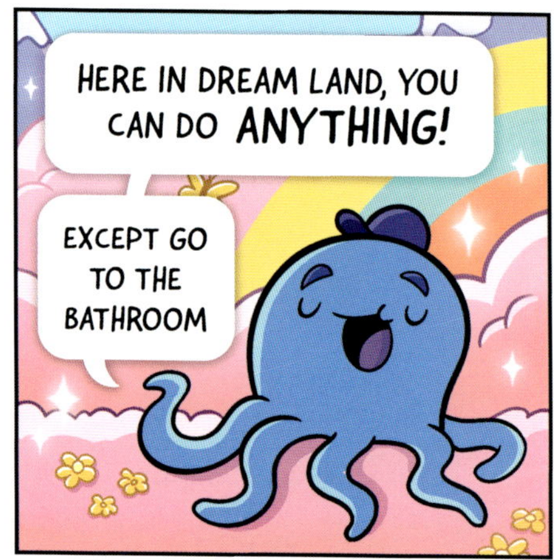
HERE IN DREAM LAND, YOU CAN DO ANYTHING!
EXCEPT GO TO THE BATHROOM

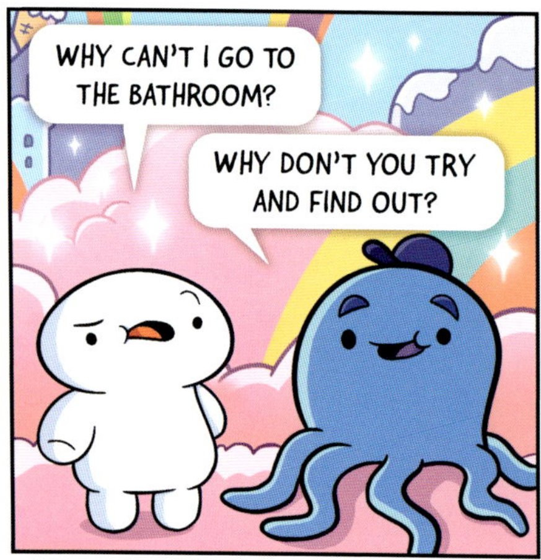
WHY CAN'T I GO TO THE BATHROOM?
WHY DON'T YOU TRY AND FIND OUT?

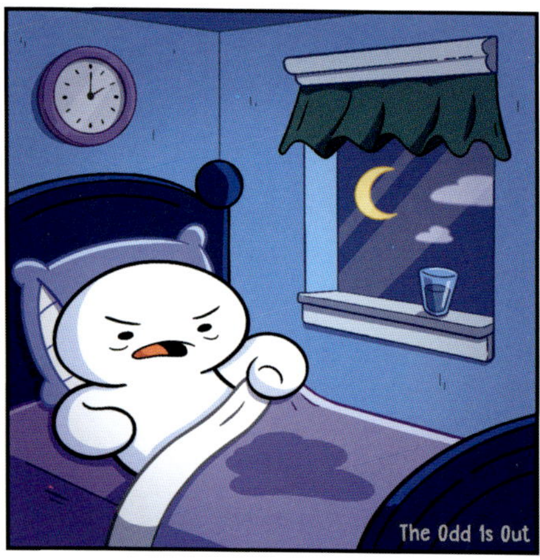
The Odd 1s Out

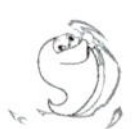

SHOPLIFT

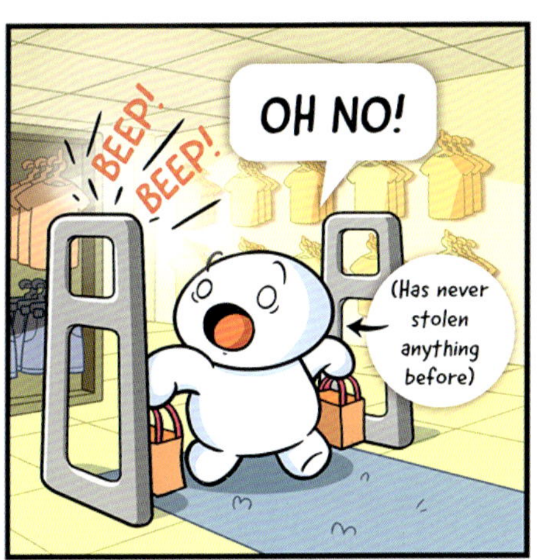
BEEP!
BEEP!
OH NO!
(Has never stolen anything before)

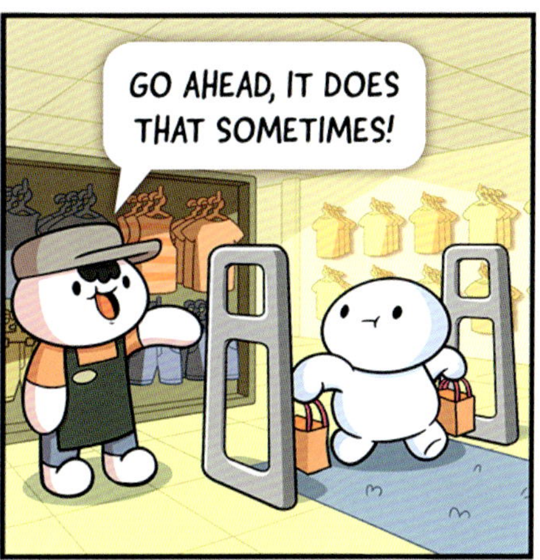
GO AHEAD, IT DOES THAT SOMETIMES!

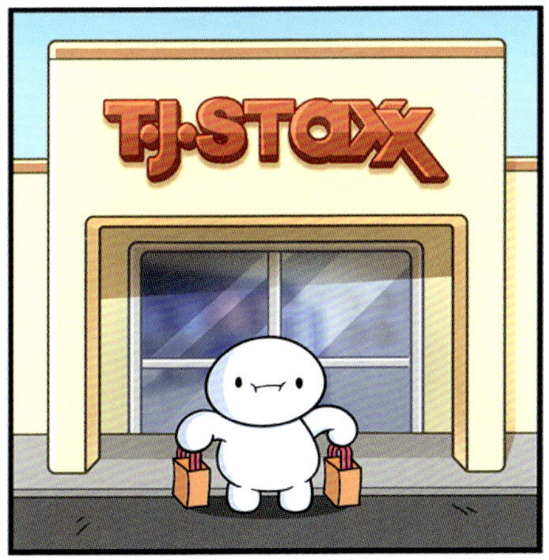
T.J.STAXX

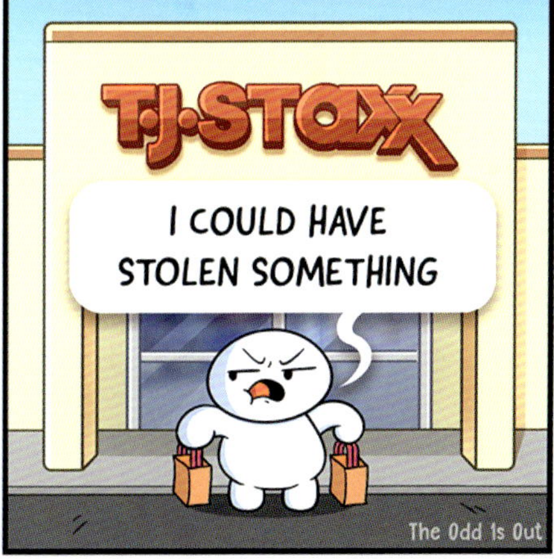
T.J.STAXX
I COULD HAVE STOLEN SOMETHING
The Odd 1s Out

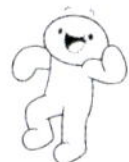

CHARACTERS

JAMES

My bubble boy has evolved a lot over the years (and grown a few appendages). All the other "human" characters are drawn with clothes and accessories, but the bald, naked one? That's me.

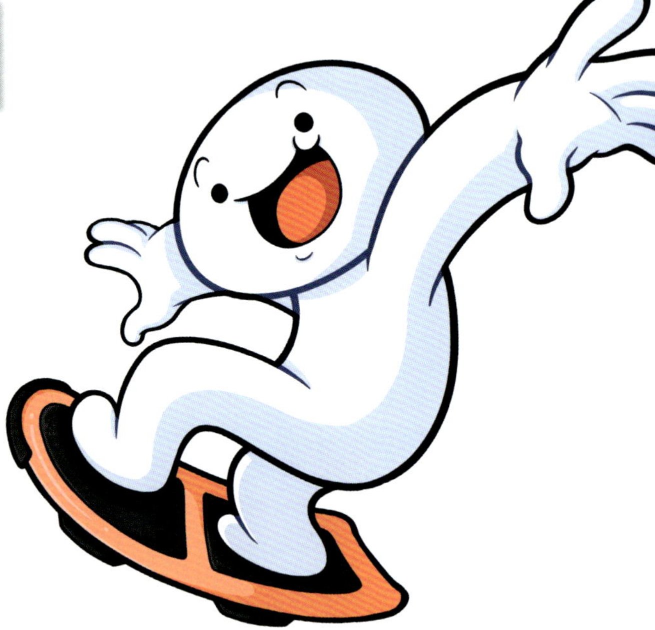

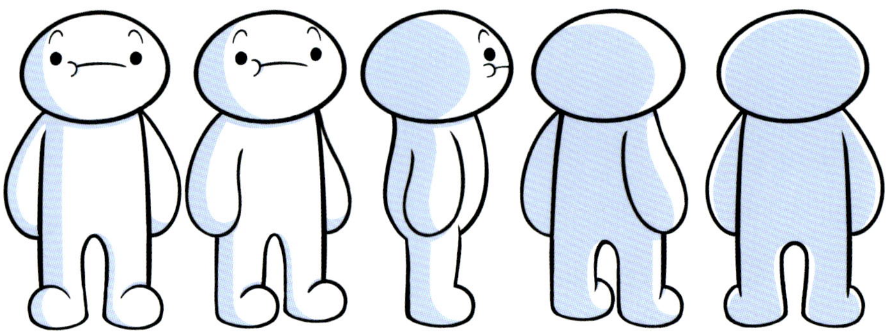

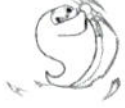

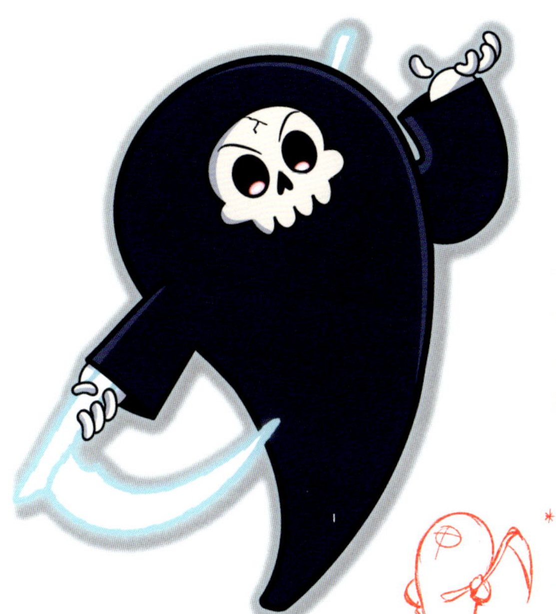

DEATH

Death was another comic character—turned YouTube star! He's intimidating on the outside, but secretly he's a big softie!

LIFE

As we started to make more and more shorts with Death, we decided it would be fun to create his optimistic (and slightly creepy?) counterpart.

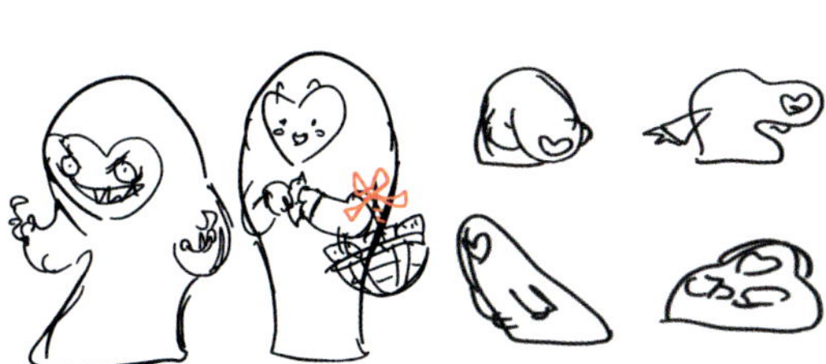

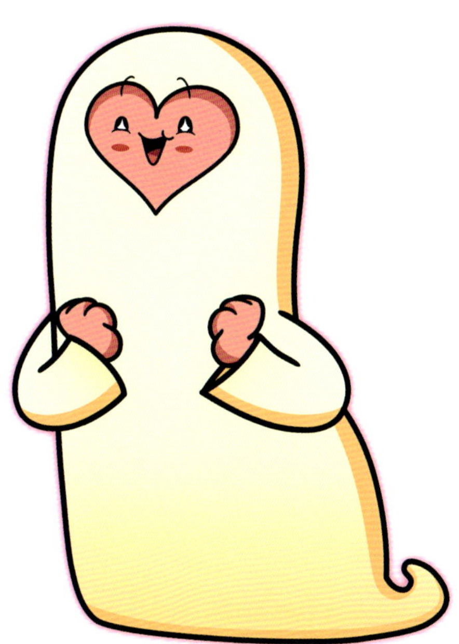

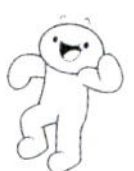

FLOOF

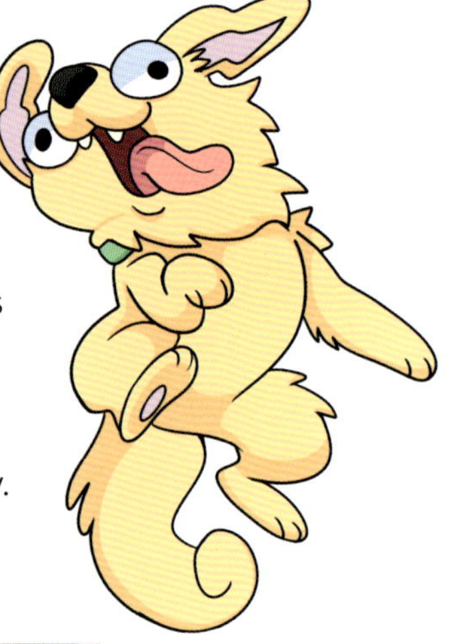

I'd be lying if I said I haven't used animation to immortalize some of my favorite pets. Floof has made star appearances in a handful of videos and across all my social channels. I even gave her a plush-toy version of herself for a chew toy. Does that count as dog cannibalism?

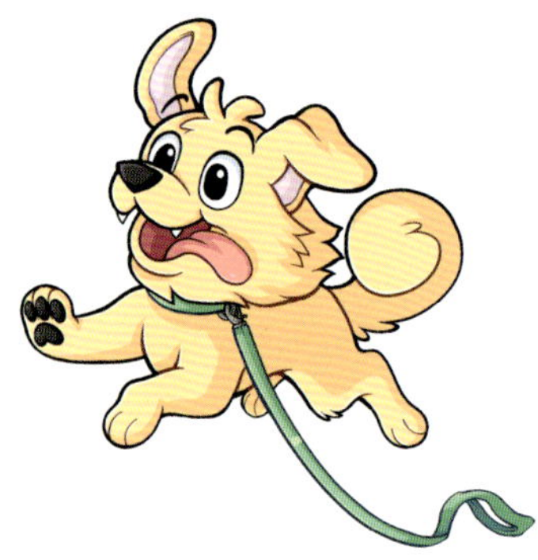

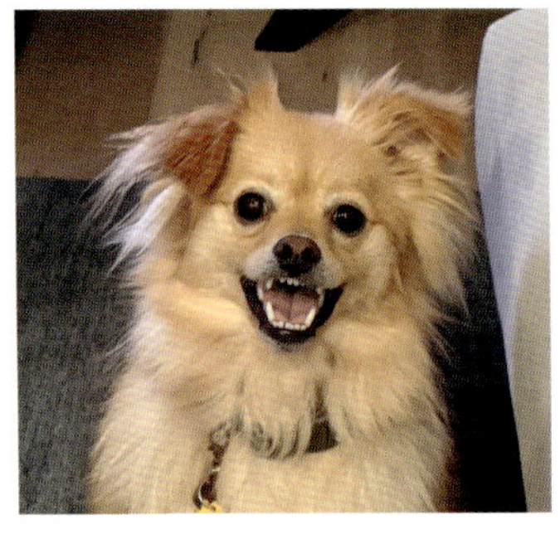

LIZARD CUPID

This is another character who made a debut in comic form and has evolved alongside my art style over the years.

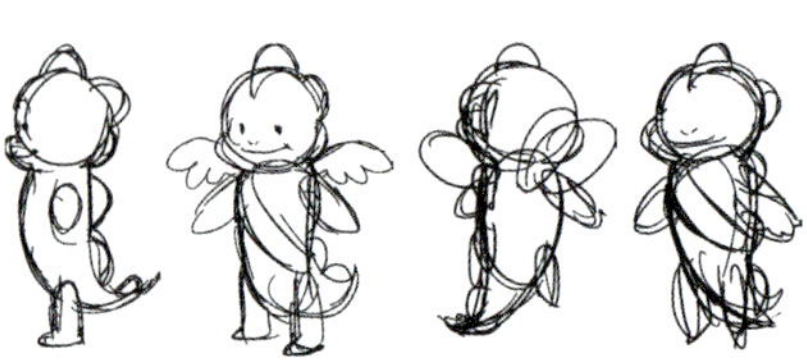

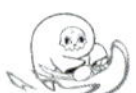

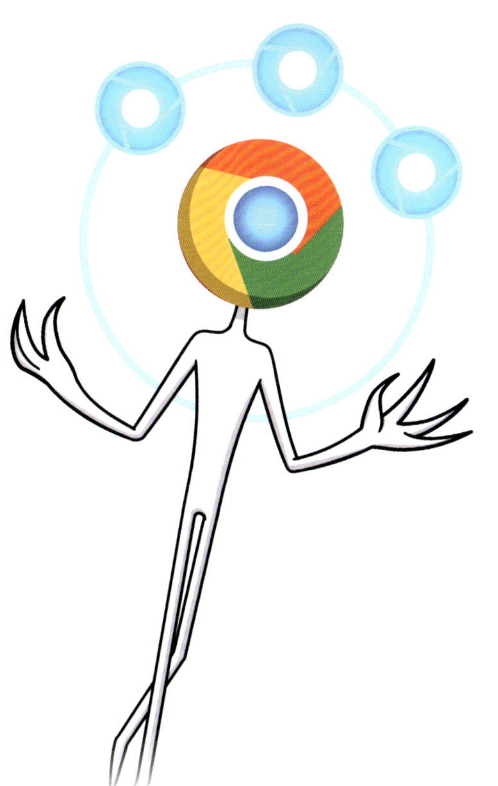

GOOGLE

With the internet being as powerful as it is, we had to give Google a godlike presence. This is the version we ultimately settled on.

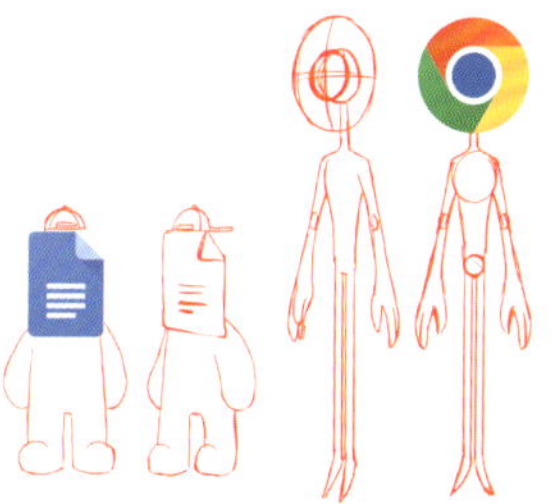

TASK MANAGER

Being the only app who unquestionably follows orders, Task Manager is one of my favorite characters. He fixes unresponsive software by murdering them…I mean, shutting them down.

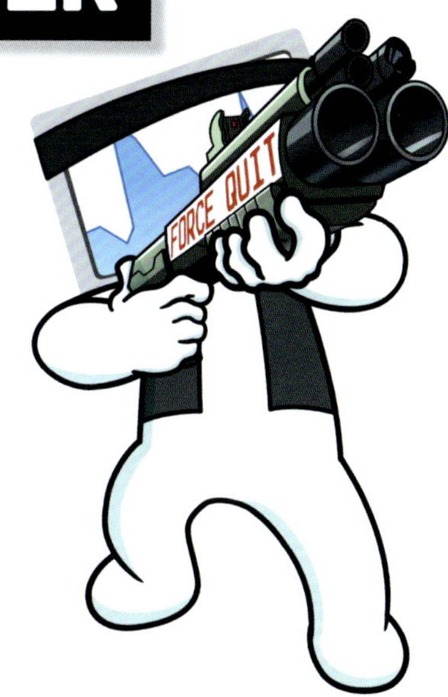

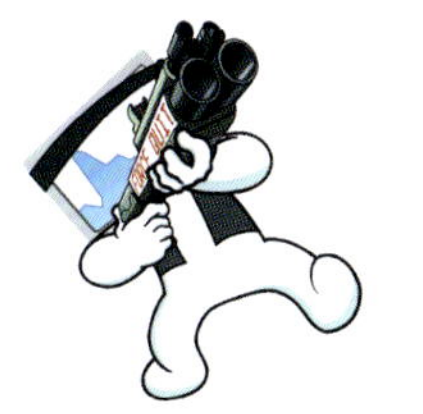

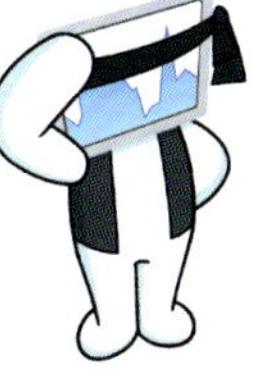

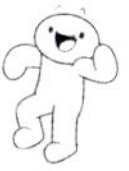

SHORTS

When short-form videos started taking off, we realized some of our comics would make great bite-sized animations. It's been a fun challenge to tell stories in under sixty seconds, but sometimes less really is more!

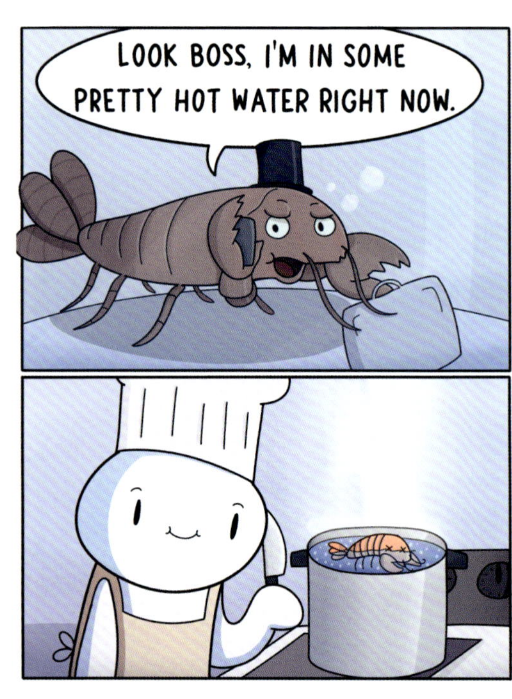

We started by selecting some of our favorite old comics, which served as our initial storyboards, and recorded voice lines for all the characters. To enhance the visuals, we added extra details with new backgrounds and animation, creating a more refined storyboard.

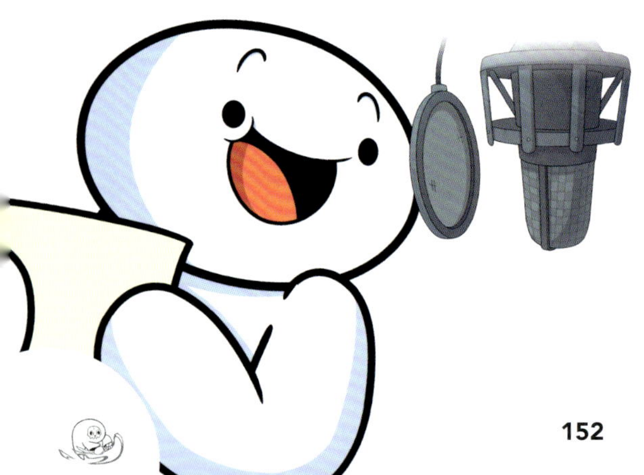

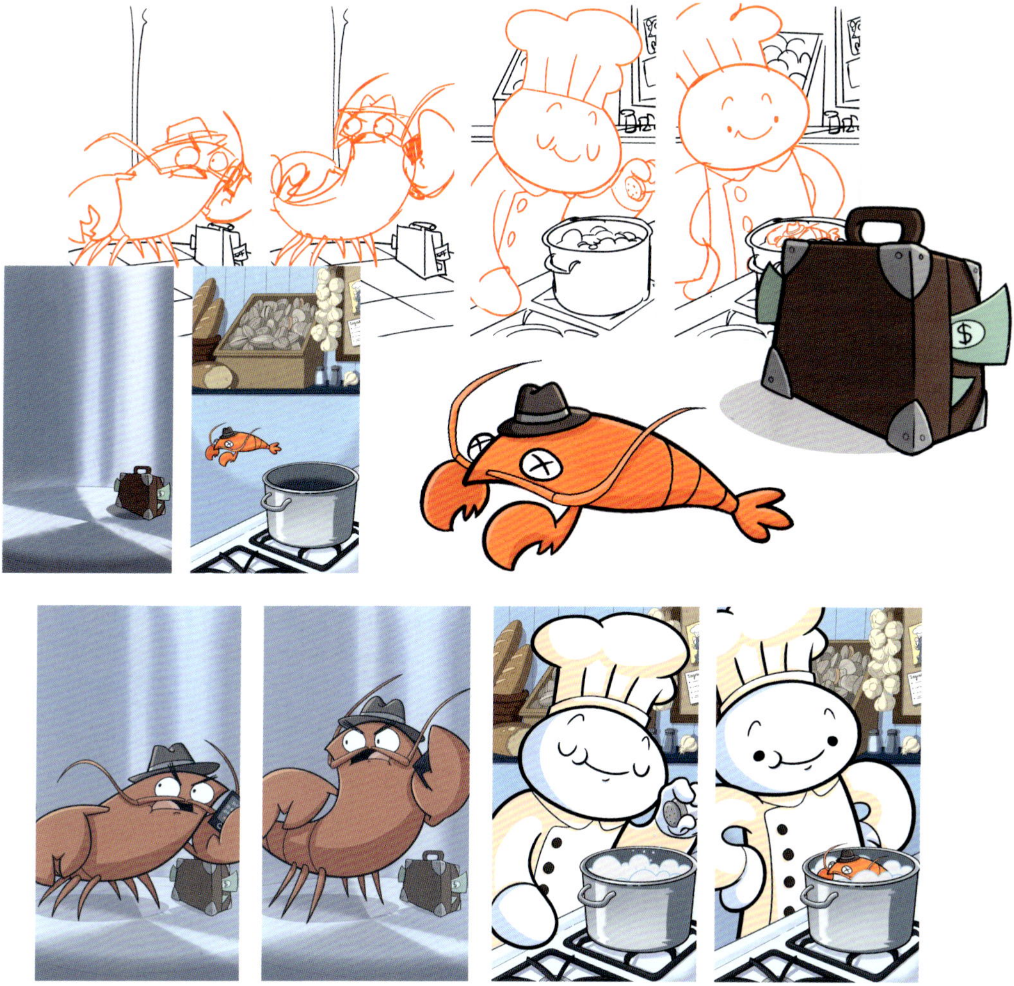

We also assigned a color script to help the artists understand the overall color direction. Once that was set, we finalized the backgrounds, locked in the colors, and got ready to bring everything to life through animation.

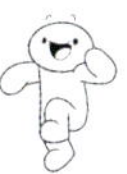

BACKGROUNDS

In these videos, storytelling is everything! And nothing tells a story like color. So before any backgrounds are drawn, we decide the mood of each scene by making a color script, which is a mini painting of each shot. For the "Welcome to the Harvest" video, we took color inspiration from horror movies like *Texas Chainsaw Massacre*. The dull colors make the audience feel like something is off about the Odd 1s Family Farm (spoilers, something definitely is)!

COLOR SCRIPT

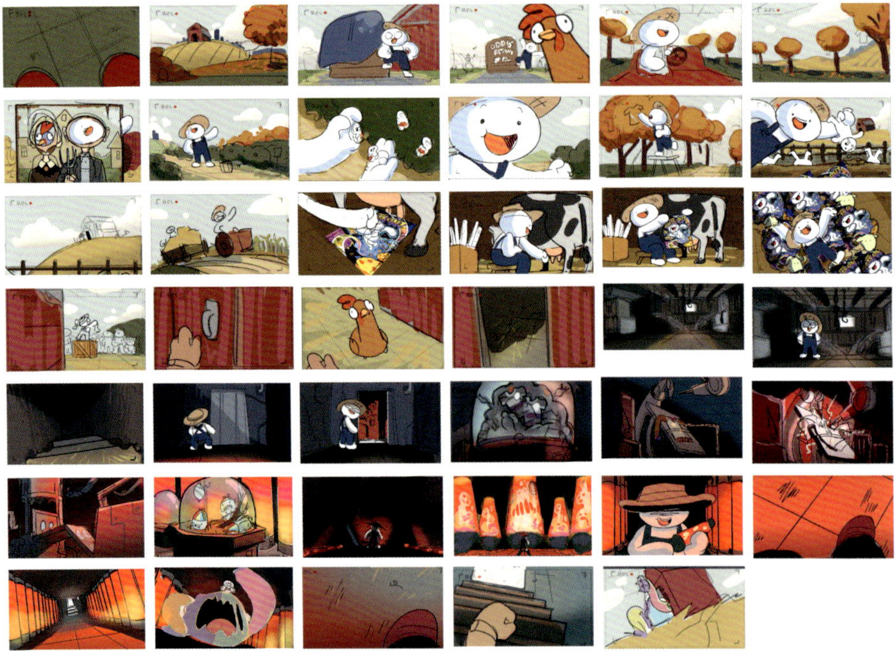

Color Script: Kelly Jensen

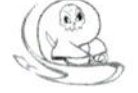

Background artists never go straight into the final painting! We always draw a nice sketch first to decide perspective and composition. This is followed by linework, color, and shading.

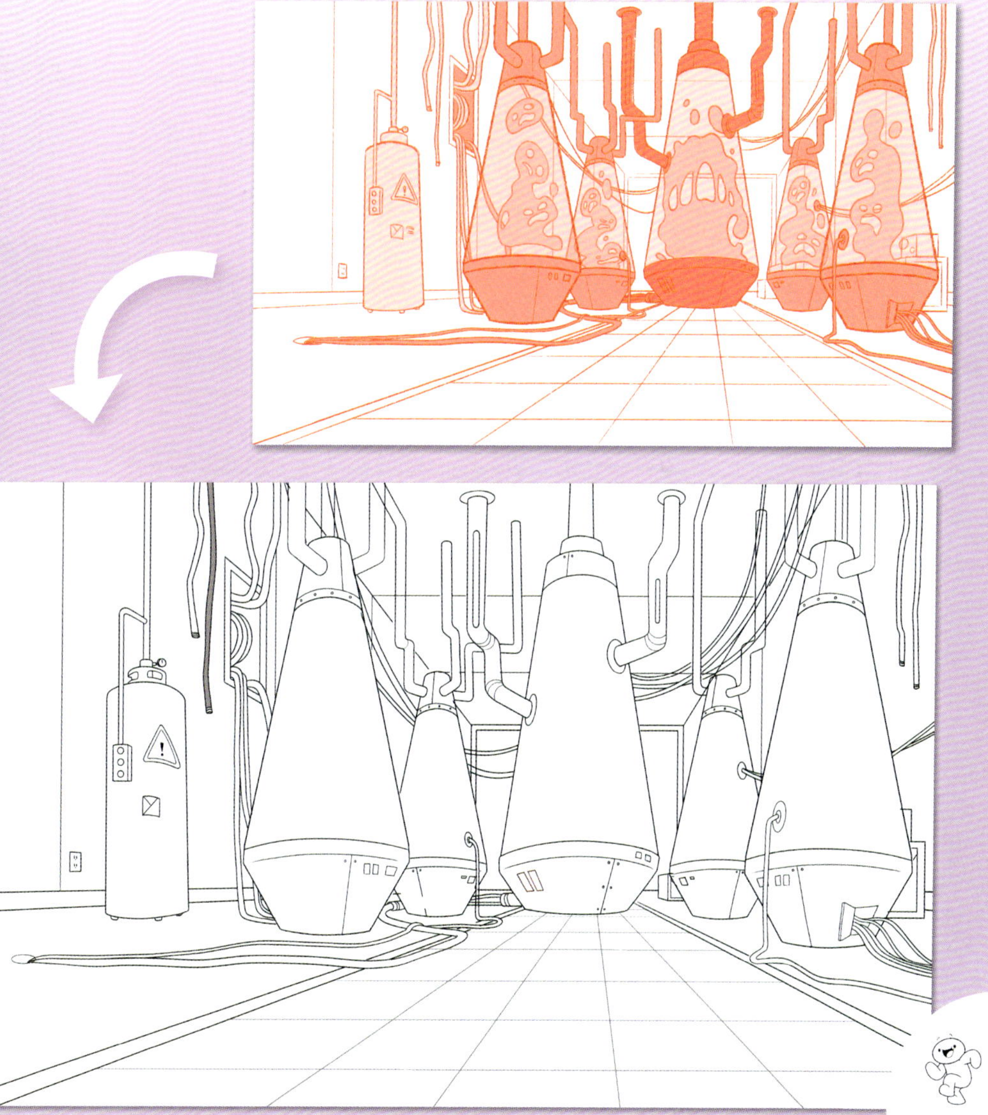

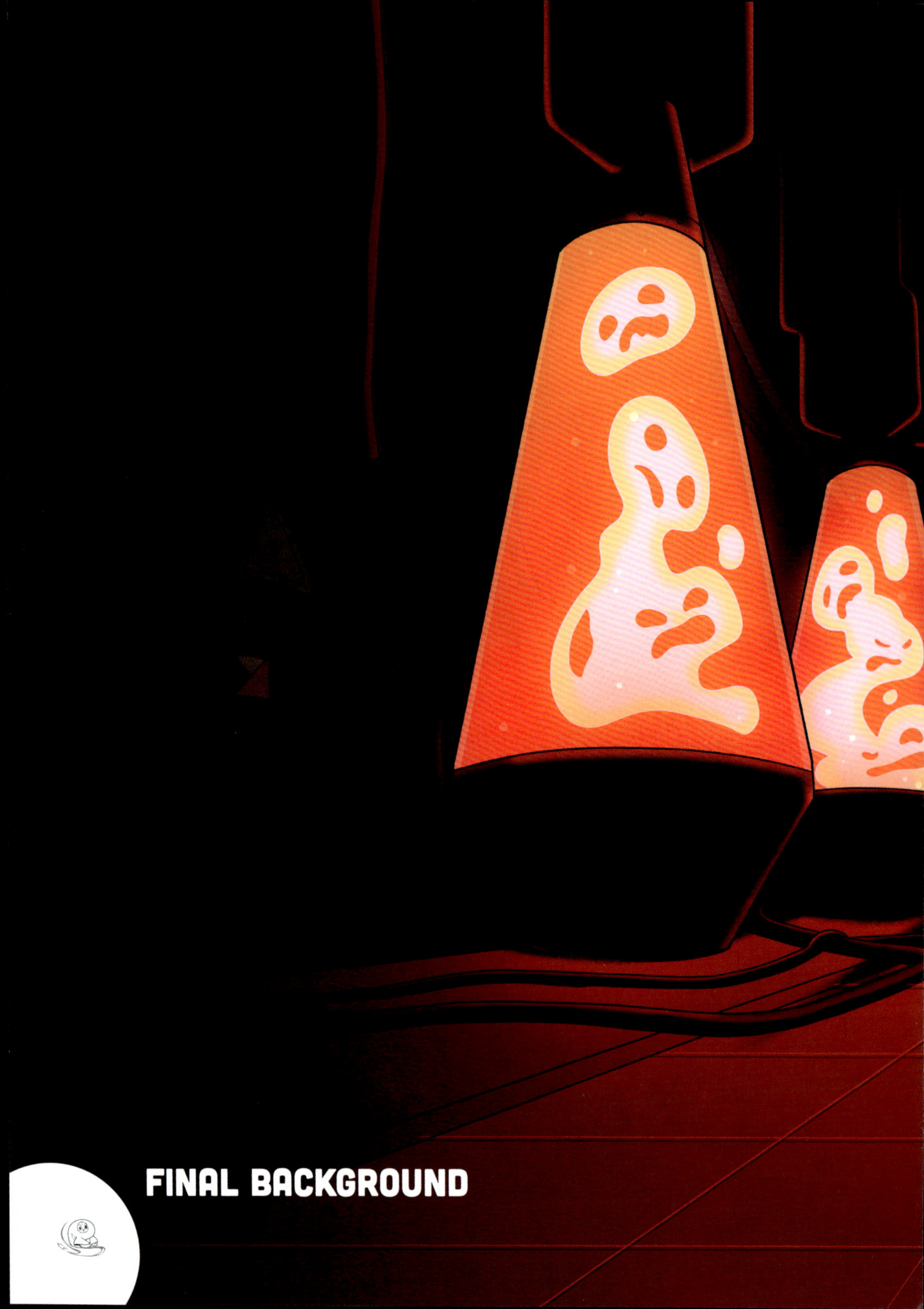
FINAL BACKGROUND

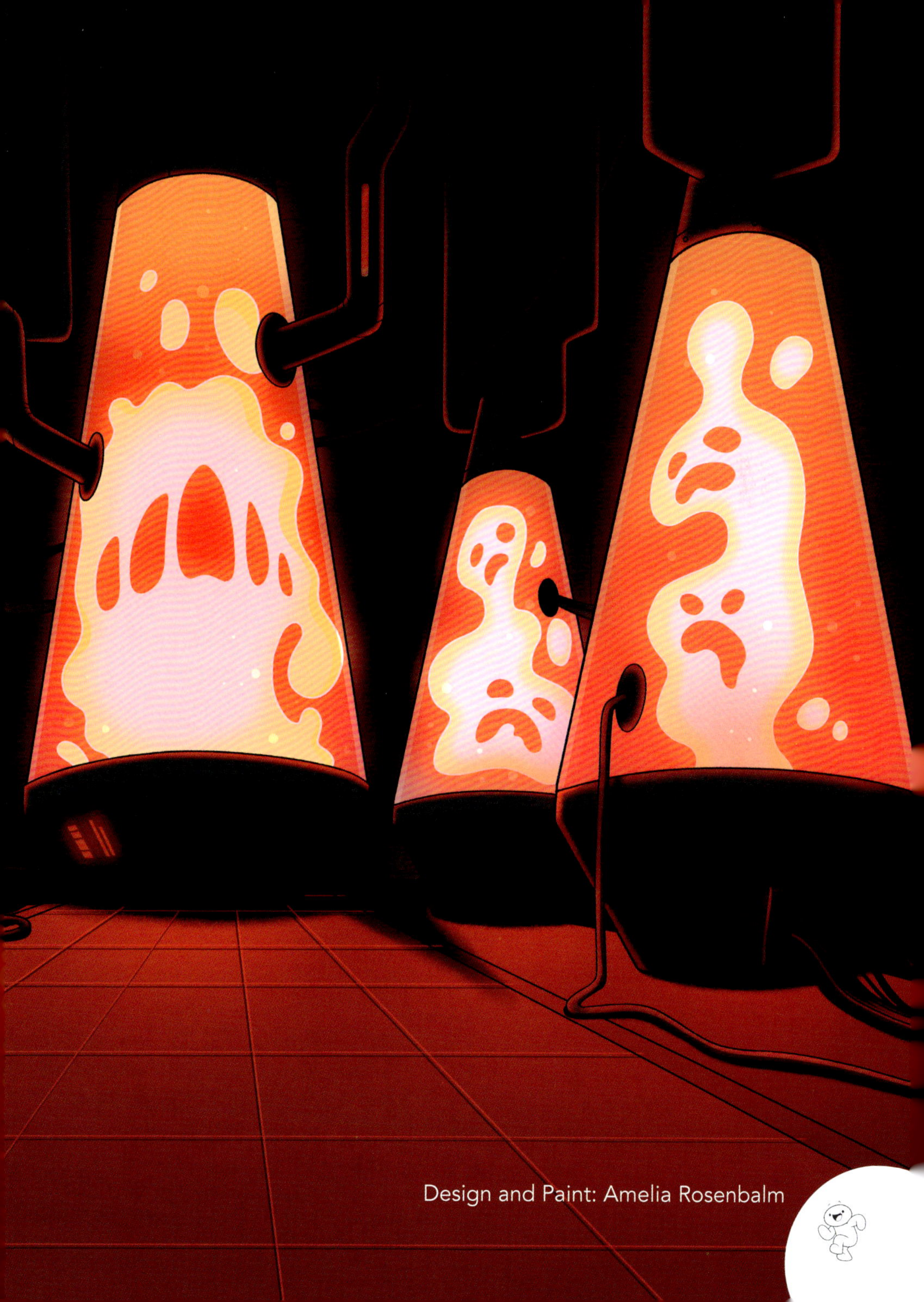
Design and Paint: Amelia Rosenbalm

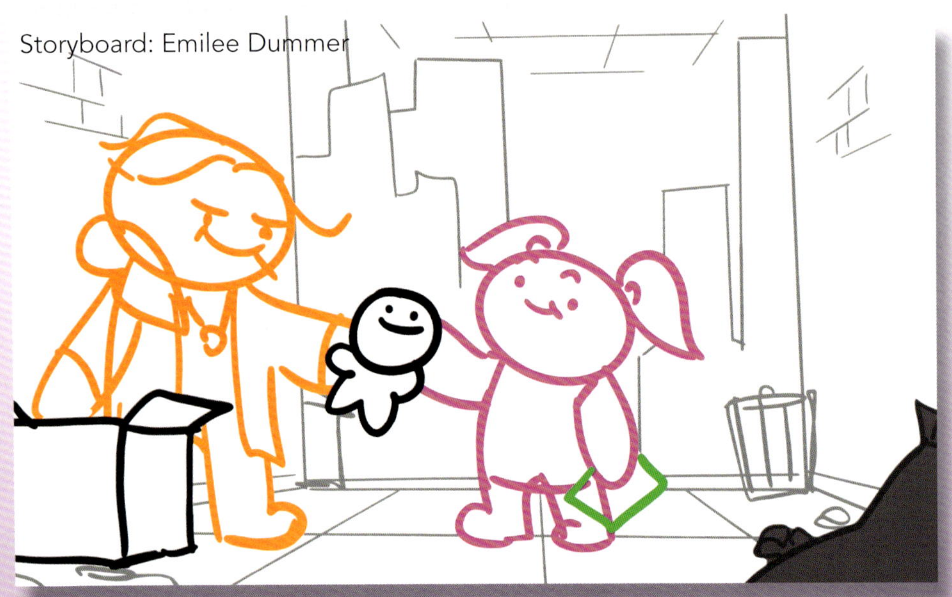
Storyboard: Emilee Dummer

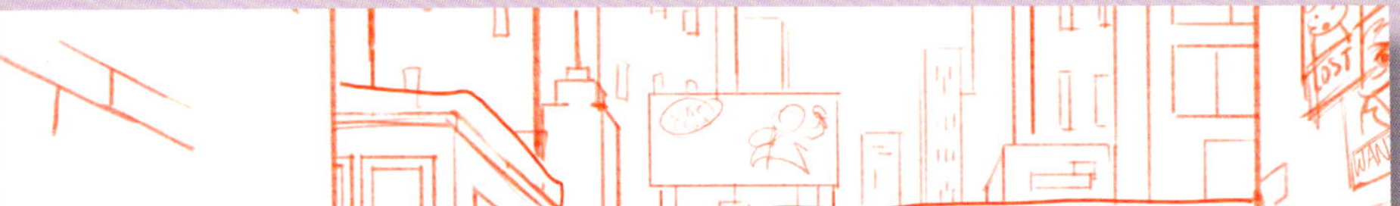

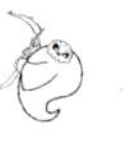

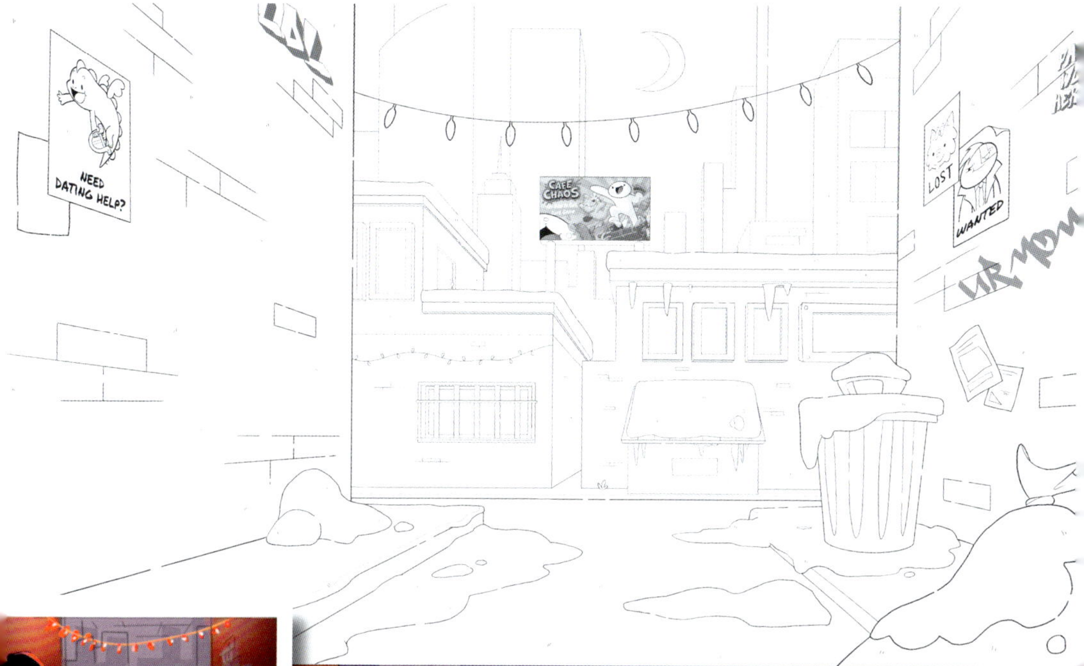

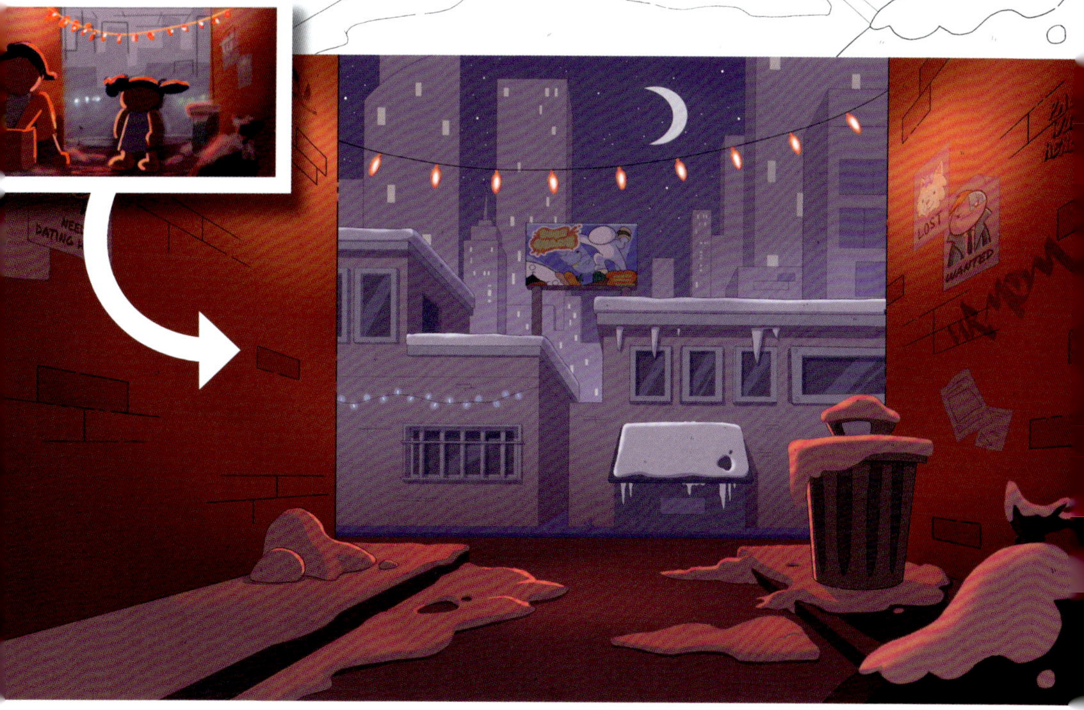

Design and Paint: Kelly Jensen

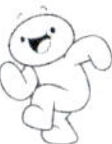

The colors in a background can change how we feel about a scene. Soft greens and blues make this park feel happy and joyful, while deep reds and oranges make it feel like there is danger. Cool pinks and purples give the park a quiet or peaceful feeling, and make it feel like dusk.

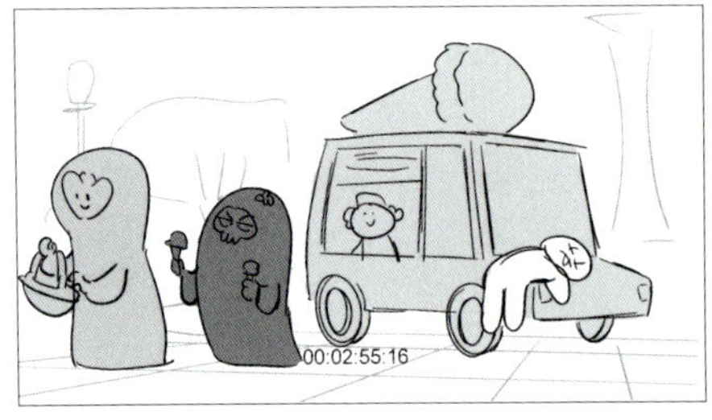

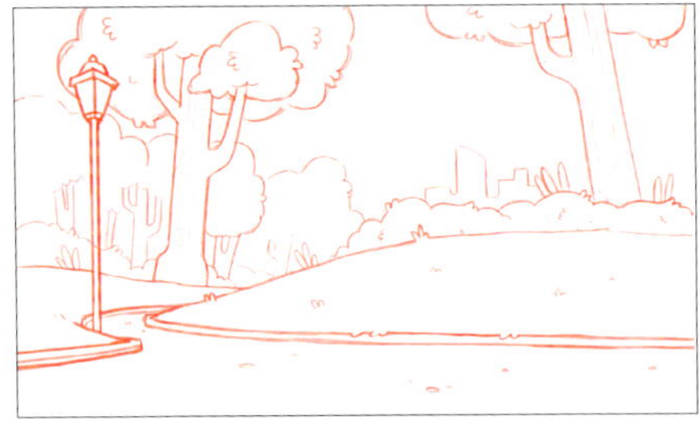

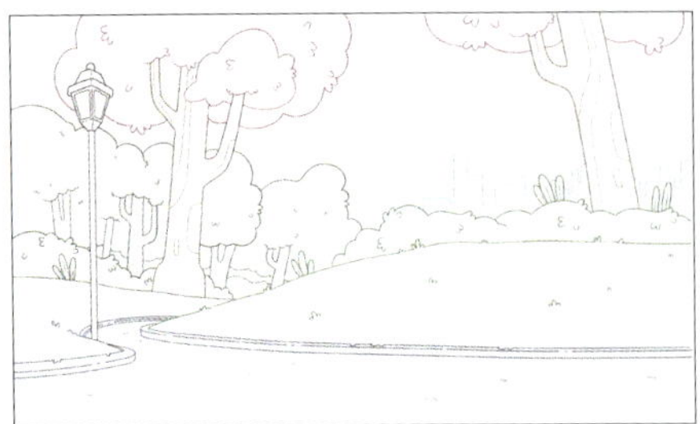

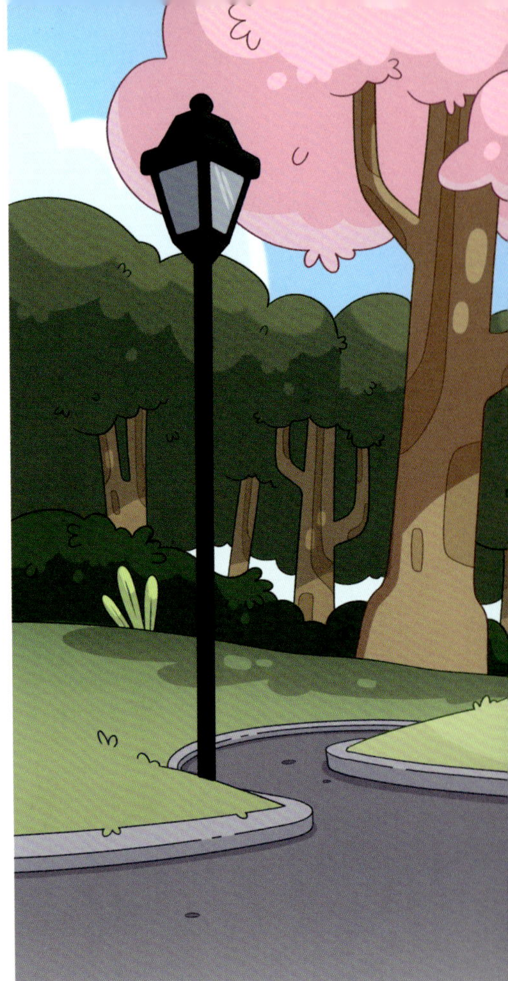

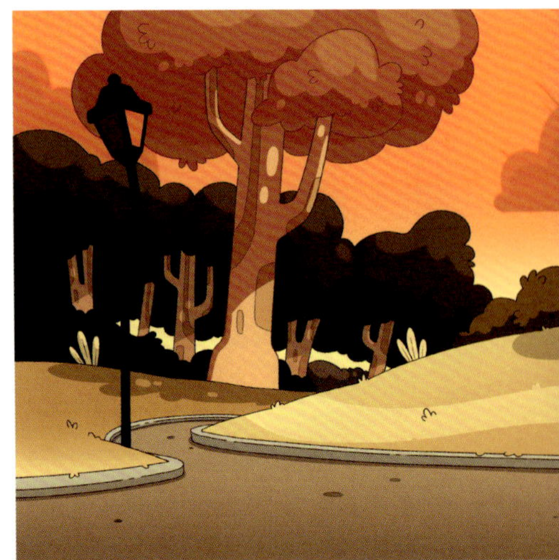

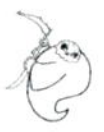

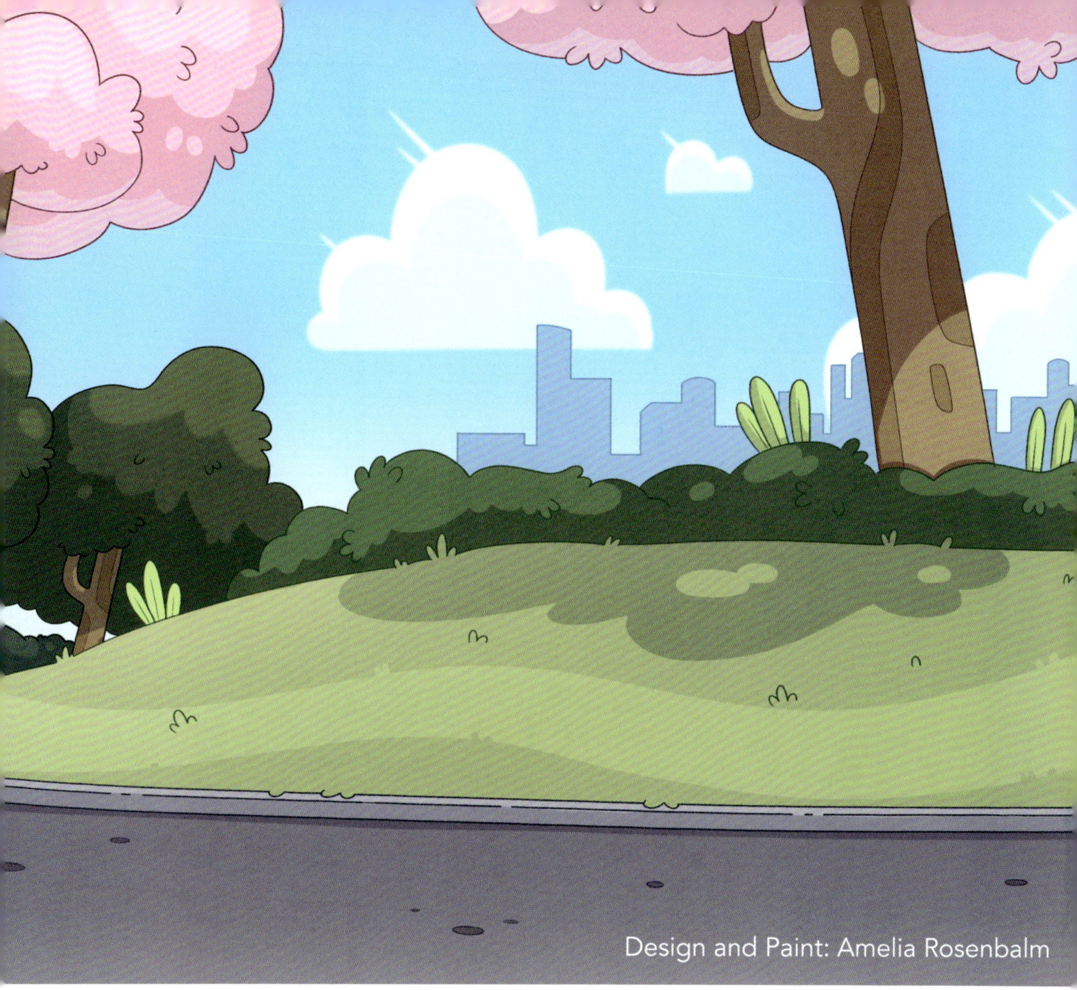

Design and Paint: Amelia Rosenbalm

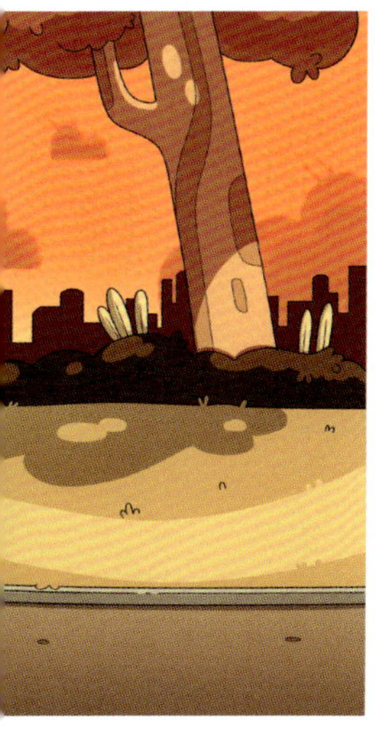

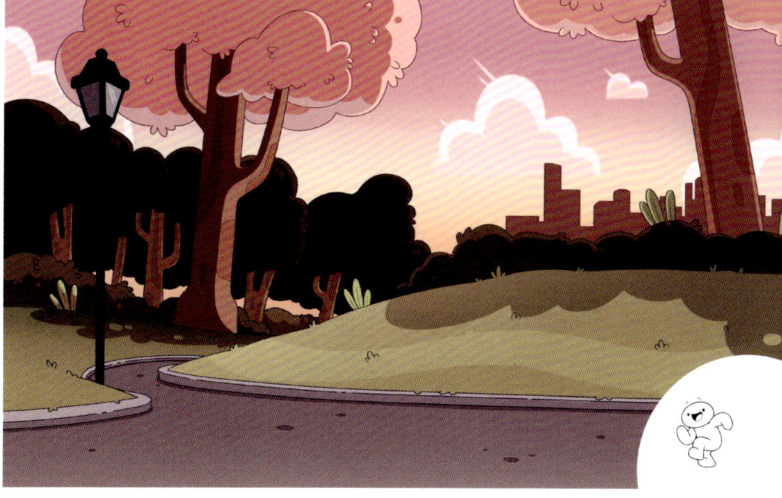

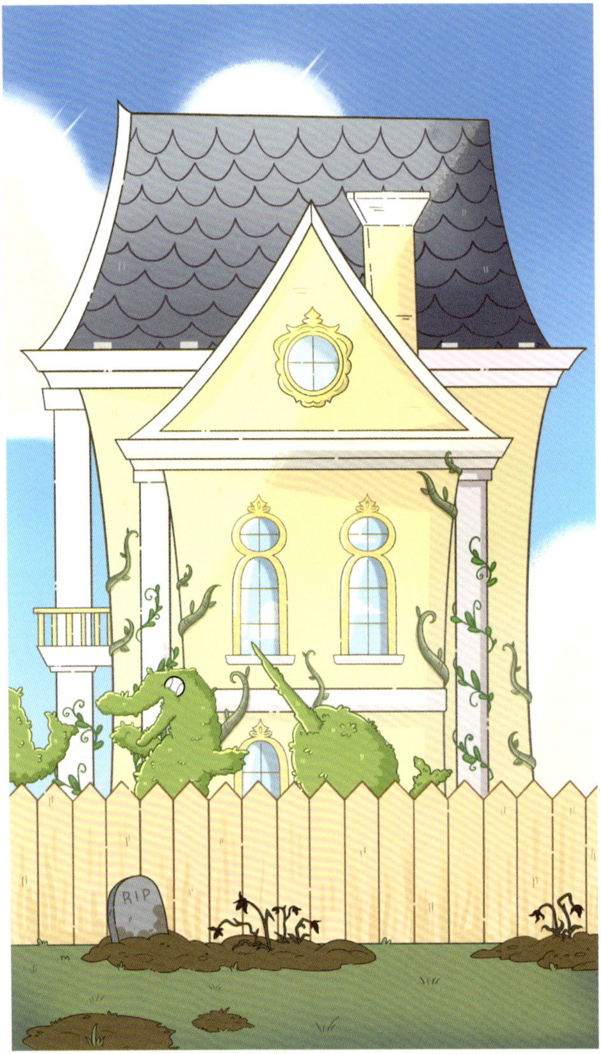

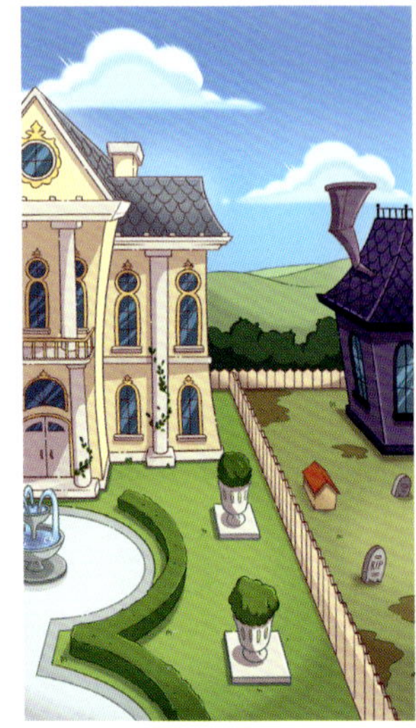

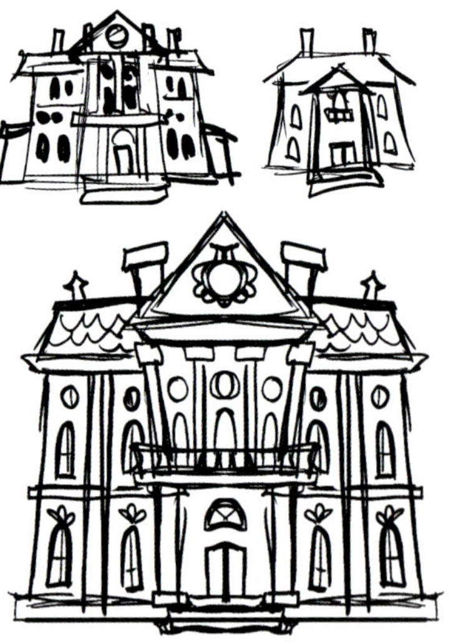

Design and Paint: Amelia Rosenbalm

When designing for the "Life vs. Death" short, we wanted to emphasize the contrast between our characters. Death's yard is unkempt and full of graves and dead flowers. On the other hand, anything Life touches will grow and live, so Life's yard is overgrown and wild.

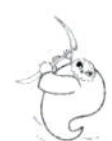

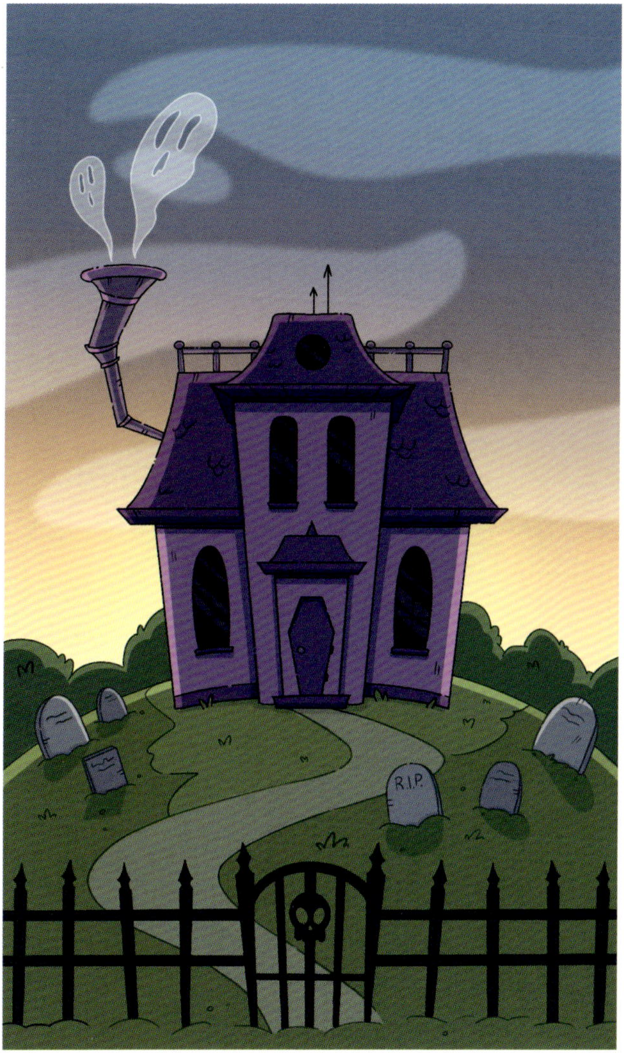

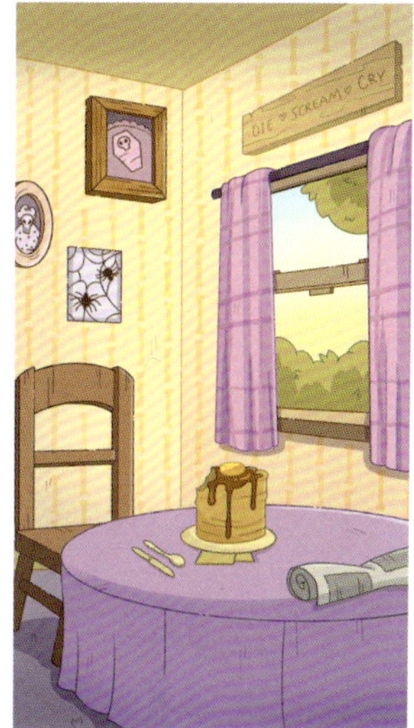

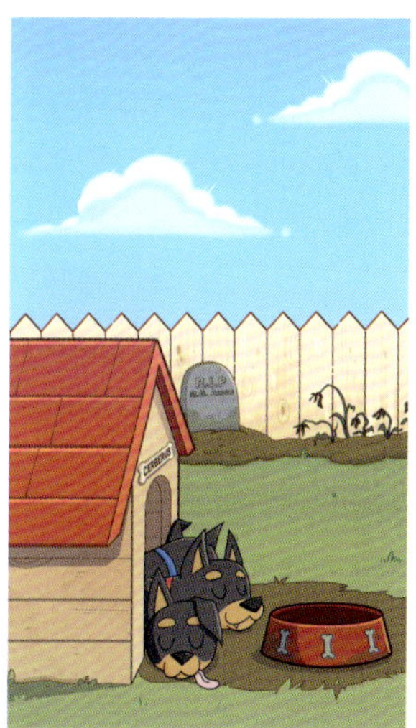

Left: Manon Hale, Top Right: Manon Hale, Bottom Right: Kelly Jensen

Death's house might look spooky on the outside, but the inside is quite cozy. Despite his affinity for destruction, we wanted to show that he enjoys the little things in life.

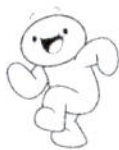

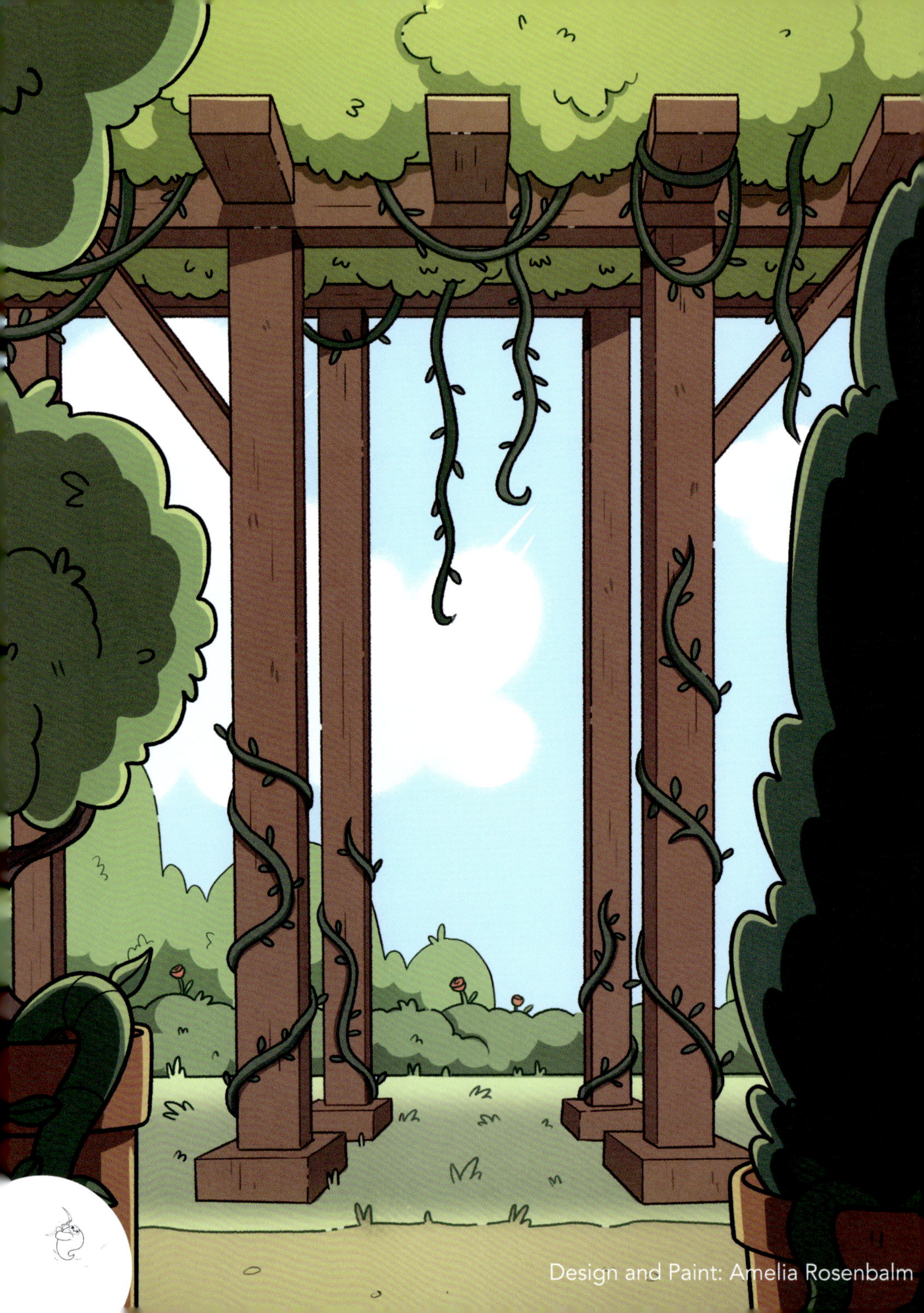
Design and Paint: Amelia Rosenbalm

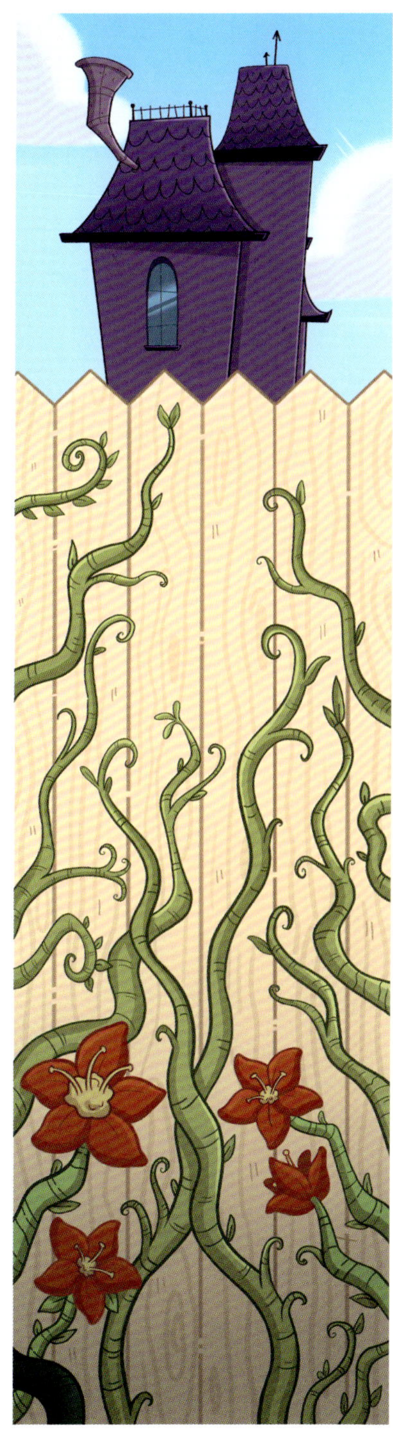

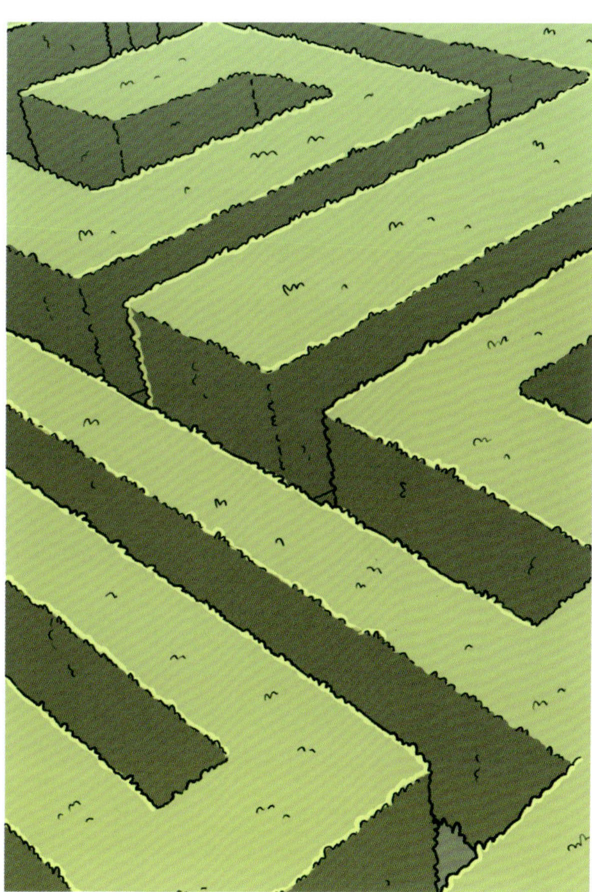

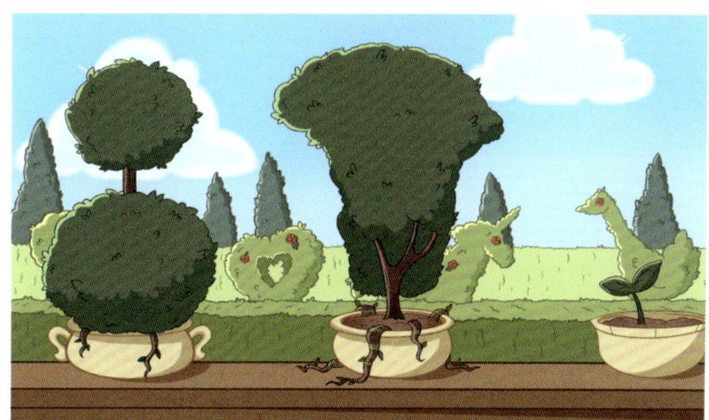

Design and Paint: Manon Hale

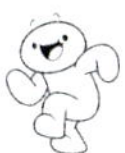

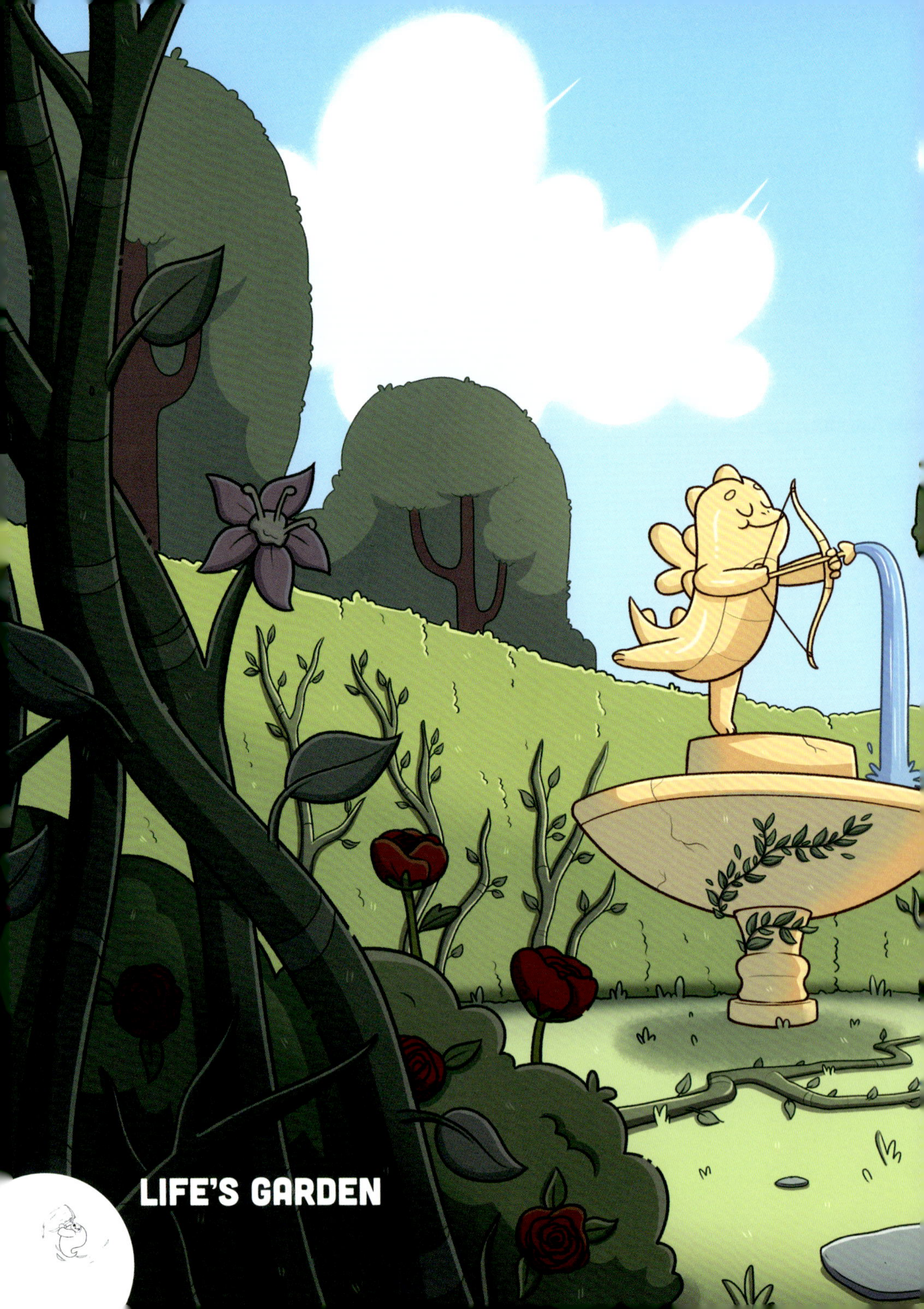
LIFE'S GARDEN

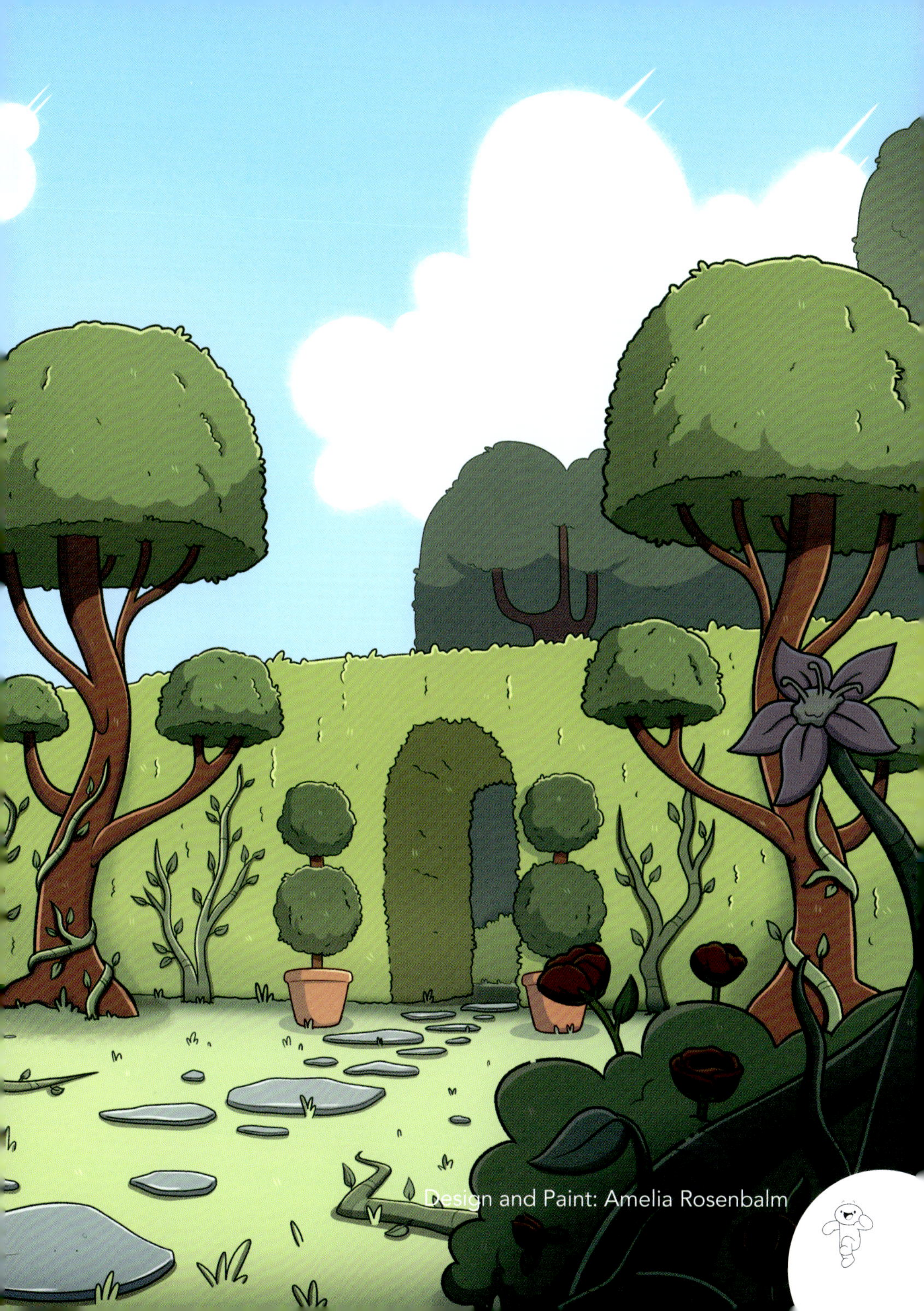
Design and Paint: Amelia Rosenbalm

ACKNOWLEDGMENTS

The TheOdd1sOut universe wouldn't be what it is today without the incredible artists and creatives who have helped bring it to life. From the very first doodles to the fully animated videos, every background, character, and expression has been shaped by a team of talented people who share a passion for storytelling.

A special thanks to the names on the page. Your work on this book helped make it something truly special! Another special thanks goes out to all the artists I've crossed paths with over the years. Whether you've helped animate, design merch, or brainstorm ideas, you've played a part in turning this dream into reality.

And of course, a massive thank you to you (the fans)! Your love for these characters, stories, and ridiculous jokes is what keeps this whole thing going. So from the bottom of my squishy, cartoon heart, thank you!

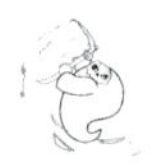

FEATURED TEAM MEMBERS

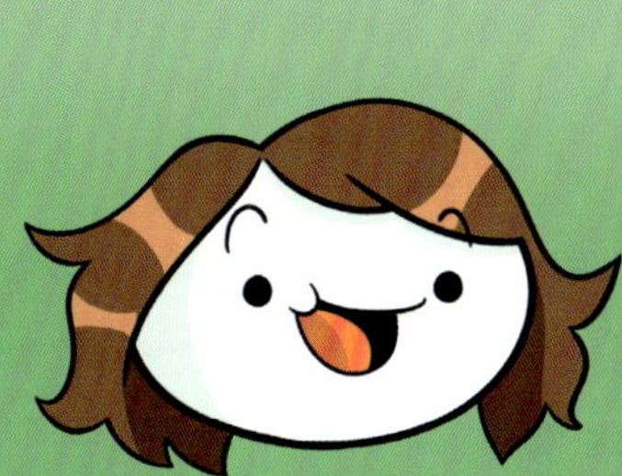

Amelia Rosenbalm

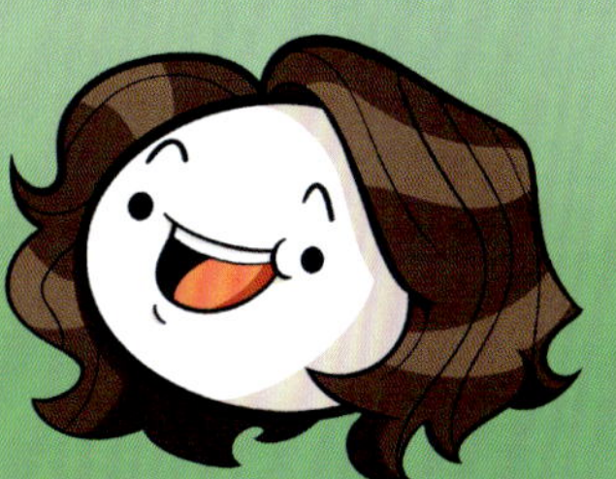

Claire Hardy

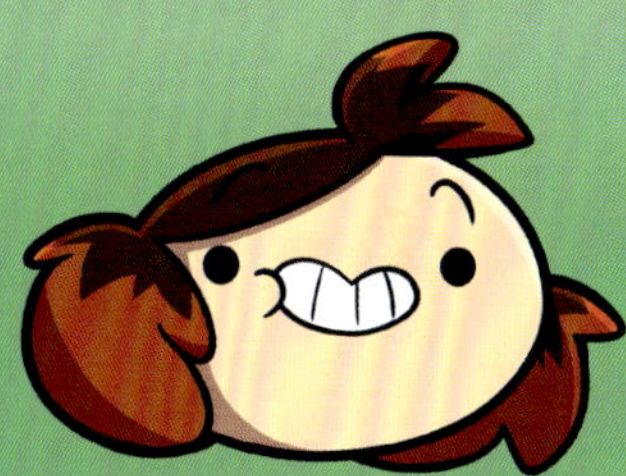

Emilee Dummer

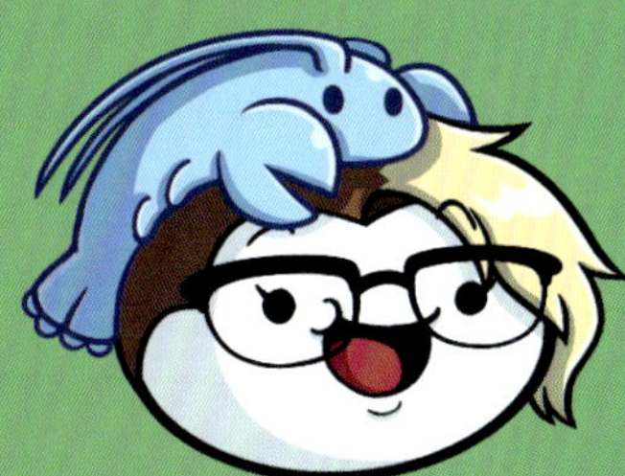

Julia Klimas

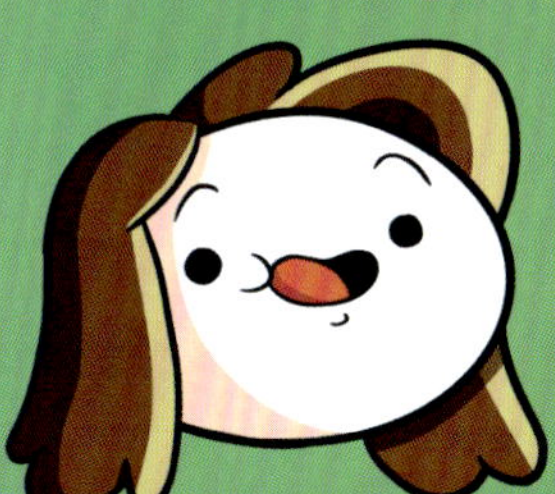

Kelly Jensen

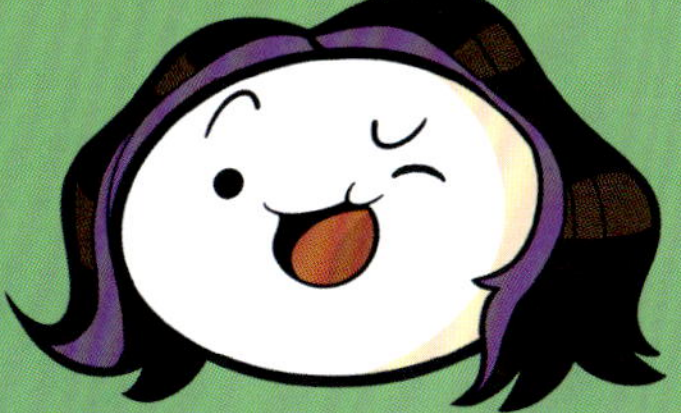

Manon Hale

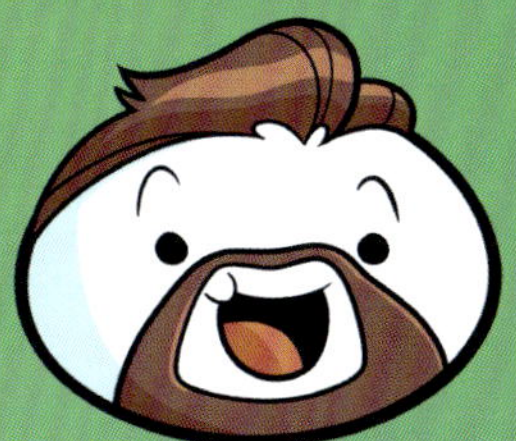

Paul Quinn

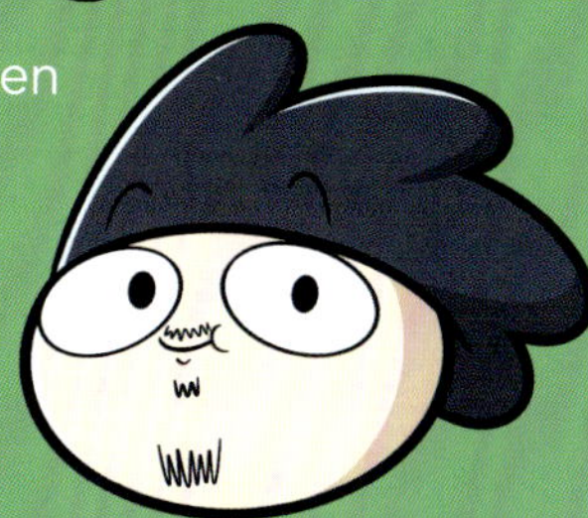

Riki Kuniyuki

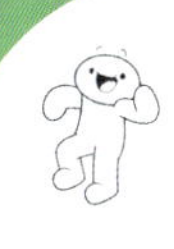

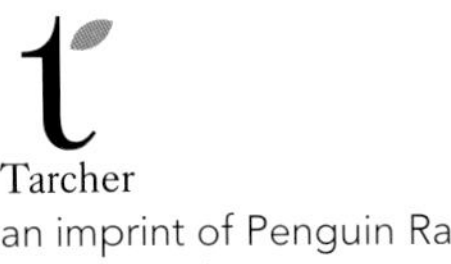

Tarcher
an imprint of Penguin Random House LLC
1745 Broadway, New York, NY 10019
penguinrandomhouse.com

Book design by James Rallison

Library of Congress Cataloging-in-Publication Data

Names: Rallison, James author
Title: The odd 1s out: art and comics collection / James Rallison.
Other titles: Odd ones out
Description: New York: Tarcher, 2026.
Identifiers: LCCN 2025043458 (print) | LCCN 2025043459 (ebook) |
ISBN 9798217177196 hardcover | ISBN 9798217177202 epub
Subjects: LCGFT: Webcomics | Humorous comics
Classification: LCC PN6727.R354 O28 2026 (print) | LCC PN6727.R354 (ebook) |
DDC 741.5/973—dc23/eng/20251202
LC record available at https://lccn.loc.gov/2025043458
LC ebook record available at https://lccn.loc.gov/2025043459

Printed in China
1 3 5 7 9 10 8 6 4 2

The authorized representative in the EU for product safety and compliance is Penguin Random House Ireland, Morrison Chambers, 32 Nassau Street, Dublin D02 YH68, Ireland, https://eu-contact.penguin.ie.

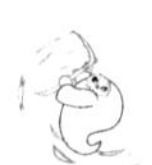

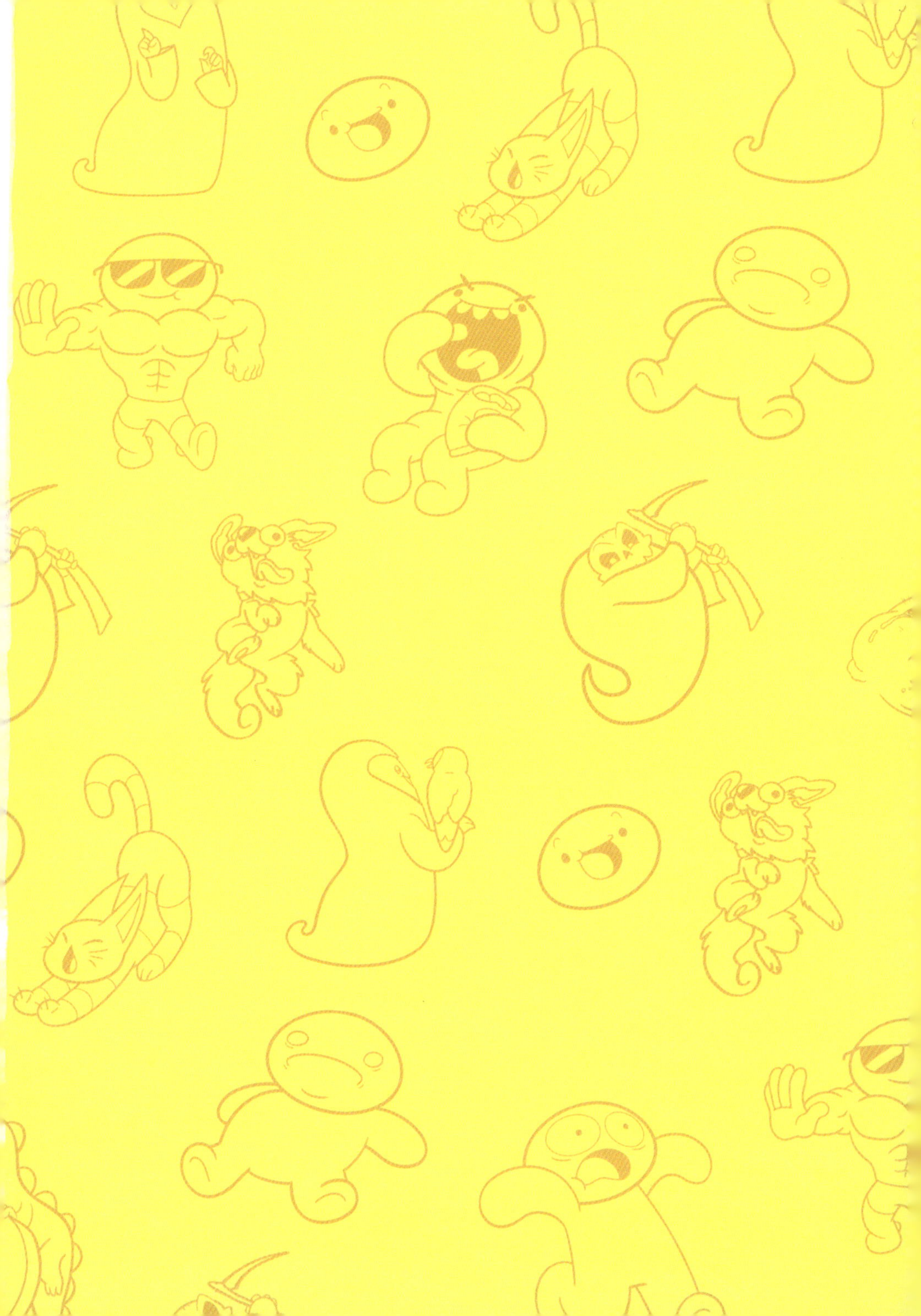

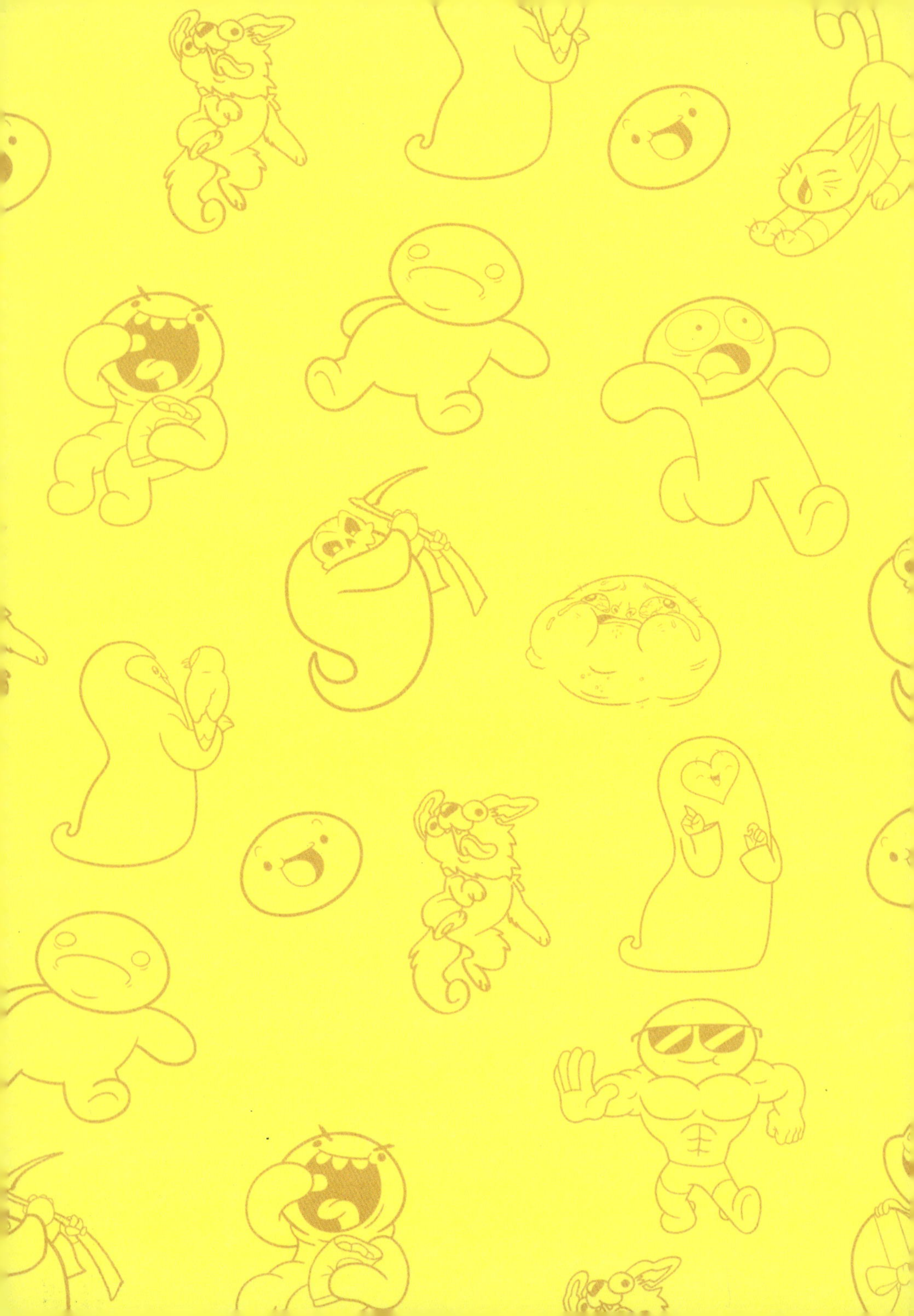